THE HARDEST VICTORY

The endpapers show the 'nose art' on Halifax *Friday the 13th Esq*, DFC, DFM, which completed its 100th operation on 22 January 1945

THE
HARDEST
VICTORY

RAF Bomber Command in
the Second World War

DENIS RICHARDS

W. W. NORTON & COMPANY
New York   London

Printed in the United States of America

Manufacturing by the Maple-Vail Manufacturing Group, Inc.

ISBN 0-393-03763-0

W. W. Norton & Company, Inc.
500 Fifth Avenue, New York, N.Y. 10110
W. W. Norton & Company Ltd.
10 Coptic Street, London WC1A 1PU

1 2 3 4 5 6 7 8 9 0

Contents

Illustrations

Mid-upper Gunner.
Rear-gunner.
Navigator.
Bomb-aimer.

Between pages 172 and 173

GREAT AIRMEN

Air Vice-Marshal D. C. T. Bennett CBE, DSO.
Group Captain Basil Embry DSO and 2 Bars, DFC, AFC.
Squadron Leader H. B. ('Mick') Martin, DSO and Bar, DFC and 2 Bars, AFC.
Group Captain G. L. Cheshire VC, DSO and 2 Bars, DFC
Wing Commander Guy Gibson VC, DSO and Bar, DFC and Bar.

AFTER THE DAMS RAID

Pilot Officer F. M. Spafford DFM, RAAF (centre) and Pilot Officer H. T. Taerum RCAF of 617 Squadron, the bomb-aimer and the navigator of Gibson's aircraft, at debriefing with an Intelligence officer. Looking on, Sir Arthur Harris and A V–M. Ralph Cochrane.

FOUR VCS

Wing Commander Hughie I. Edwards VC, DFC.
Squadron Leader John D. Nettleton VC.
Squadron Leader Ian W. Bazalgette VC, DFC.
Captain Edwin Swales VC, DFC, SAAF.

GERMAN NIGHT-FIGHTERS

Messerschmitt 110, photographed at Farnborough in October 1945.
Dornier 217, 1942: a bomber developed into a not very successful night-fighter. The LICHTENSTEIN radar is visible in front.
A Junkers 88 which landed by mistake at Woodbridge in July 1944. Its Flensburg and SN2 radars yielded useful information.

ON THE GROUND

Getting ready to 'bomb up' a Halifax.
Refuelling a Halifax.

TWO SUCCESSFUL 'DAYLIGHTS'

Halifaxes attacking the *Gneisenau* at Brest by daylight, 18 December 1941.
Philips' works, Eindhoven, under daylight attack, 6 December 1942.

BOMB DAMAGE AT HAMBURG

Bomb damage at Hamburg showing flak tower with four gun positions.
Bomb damage, 1943.

Bomb damage, including to midget submarines, at Blohm and Voss shipyards, 1945.
THE MÖHNE DAM
Breached by 617 Squadron, 16/17 May 1943.

Between pages 268 and 269
'SOUTHDOWN'
Entrance to underground ops room at HQ Bomber Command.
'FIDO'
The petrol flames on either side of the runway have dispersed the fog, and a Lancaster is taking off, 1945.
AFTER THE RAID
Interrogation of Lancaster crews after raid on Berlin, 22/23 November 1943.
Engineer sergeant questioning crew about the performance of their Lancaster on their return from Berlin, 23 November 1943.
WOMEN AT WORK
Factory worker producing WINDOW.
Airwoman cleaning and testing a Lancaster's 96 sparking plugs.
Airwomen inspecting flotation jackets ('Mae Wests'). On left, inspected parachutes hanging up to air.
Airwoman belting up ammunition for a Lancaster.
PRECISION BOMBING
Locomotive shop at Krupps, gutted in 1943 and further damaged in 1945.
The Arnsberg viaduct wrecked by a 'Grand Slam'.
The *Tirpitz* capsized after bombing, 12 November 1944.
PRECISION ATTACKS IN FRANCE
Railway centre at Chambly, France, after attack on 1/2 May 1944.
Gnome et Rhône aero-engine works at Limoges after attack on 8/9 February 1944.
PRECISION BOMBING
Grusonwerk (subsidiary of Krupps) factory at Magdeburg for manufacture of telescopes and torpedoes, 1945.
Railway viaduct at Bielefeld after attack on 14 March 1945.
DAMAGE FROM AREA BOMBING
Bomb damage in Krefeld, 1945.
Bomb damage in central Berlin. Photographed during a reconnaissance flown on 8 March 1945.

LAST GLIMPSES

The Wilhelmstrasse, Berlin, 1945, taken from the bombed Air Ministry.

Ju 88 night-fighters, mostly from NJG3, abandoned at the end of hostilities. Lack of petrol had immobilised many in the last weeks of the war.

ENDPAPERS

The 'nose art' on Halifax Friday the 13th, Esq., DFC, DFM, which completed its 100th operation on 22 January 1945.

All photographs reproduced by permission of the Trustees of the Imperial War Museum. Crown copyright.

Maps

Abbreviations
and
Code-Names

AA	Anti-Aircraft
AASF	Advanced Air Striking Force
AEAF	Allied Expeditionary Air Force
AI	Air Interception: airborne radar
AOC	Air Officer Commanding
AOC-in-C	Air Officer Commanding-in-Chief
ASV	Air to Surface Vessel: airborne radar
BA	Bomb-aimer
BAFF	British Air Forces in France
BEF	British Expeditionary Force
CH	Chain Home: standard radar stations
CHASTISE	Attack on German dams, 16/17 May 1943
CHL	Chain Home Low: low-reading radar stations
CIGAR	Jamming German VHF radio
CIRCUS	Escorted short-range attacks to bring the Luftwaffe to battle
CO	Commanding officer
CORONA	Counterfeit orders to German fighters
COSSAC	Chief of Staff to Supreme Allied Commander
CROSSBOW	Attacks on German V-weapon launching sites
D/F	Direction-Finding
DYNAMO	Code-name for evacuation from Dunkirk
EATS	Empire Air Training Scheme
ENIGMA	German encoding machine
ETA	Estimated Time of Arrival
ETD	Estimated Time of Departure
FREYA	German long-range ground radar
GARDENING	Minelaying

GEE	Radar aid to navigation
GH	Radar aid to navigation and blind-bombing
GOMORRAH	Intensive attacks on Hamburg, July–August 1943
GOODWOOD	Operation in close support of Allied armies 18th July 1944
'Grand Slam'	22,000-lb deep penetration bomb
H2S	Airborne radar aid to navigation and target identification
HCF	Heavy Conversion Flight
HCU	Heavy Conversion Unit
IFF	Identification, Friend or Foe (radar identification system)
INTRUDER	Operations to harass German Air Force and airfields in occupied territory
Ju	Junkers
LICHTENSTEIN	German air interception apparatus in fighters
LMF	Lack of Moral Fibre
LORAN	Radar aid to navigation, long range
MANDREL	Radio Swamping of German early warning radar
Me	Messerschmitt
MILLENNIUM	'Thousand-Bomber' raid on Cologne, 30/31 May 1942
NCO	Non-commissioned officer
OBOE	Radar aid to navigation and blind-bombing
Ops	Operations
ORB	Operations Record Book
OTU	Operational Training Units
OVERLORD	Allied invasion of Normandy, June 1944
PFF	Pathfinder Force
POINTBLANK	Directive for the Combined Bomber Offensive, June 1943
RAAF	Royal Australian Air Force
RAE	Royal Aircraft Establishment, Farnborough
RAFVR	Royal Air Force Volunteer Reserve
RAMROD	Escorted short-range attack to damage installations in occupied territory
RCAF	Royal Canadian Air Force
RCM	Radio countermeasures
RDF	Radio direction-finding (British name until 1943 for radar)
RFC	Royal Flying Corps
R/T	Radio telephony

SBA	Standard Beam Approach
SBC	Small-bomb container
SEALION	Projected German invasion of Britain, 1940
SERRATE	Airborne radar for homing on to enemy airborne radar
SHAEF	Supreme Headquarters Allied Expeditionary Forces
SOUTHDOWN	Bomber Command headquarters
Stuka	Dive-bomber (Ju 87)
'Tallboy'	12,000-lb deep penetration bomb
TORCH	Allied invasion of French North Africa, November 1942
TR	Transmitter-receiver
TRE	Telecommunications Research Establishment
ULTRA	Highest grade of secrecy – decrypts of messages encoded on the ENIGMA machine
UPKEEP	'Bouncing' bomb for destruction of German dams
U/S	Unserviceable
USAAF	United States Army Air Forces
USSAFE	United States Strategical Air Forces in Europe (later USSTAF)
VEGETABLES	Mines
VHF	Very high frequency radio
Vics	V formations
WAAF	Women's Auxiliary Air Force
W/T	Wireless telegraphy
WÜRZBURG	German short-range ground radar for control of fighters, guns and searchlights

Preface

In 1973, lunching one day in Christ Church, Oxford, I found myself sitting near W. H. Auden. He was in expansive mood, holding forth to three of the younger dons about the Allied bombing of Germany. The RAF's area attacks, he explained, had been useless. Only the Americans' daylight precision raids had helped towards victory.

Intrigued by the certainty with which the former Oxford Professor of Poetry delivered these verdicts, I ventured to enquire if he had made a special study of the subject. 'Oh yes,' he replied, 'I was a member of the United States Strategic Bombing Survey team which investigated all this at the end of the war.'

Coming from one who, I seemed to remember, had left England for the United States with a fellow poet early in 1939 to avoid the approaching European storm, this gave me some surprise. But the views which Auden expressed were in themselves not surprising, for in recent years they had appeared, in less crude form, in much historical writing. I rose from the table at Christ Church with the feeling that, if ever I had the time, I should like to write a book about Bomber Command.

A long life and the interest of my publisher, John Curtis, have finally provided the opportunity. The account which follows does not, I regret to say, contain new material concerning the damage inflicted by bombing on the German war economy. No one person, nor any team, could attempt to reinvestigate all the production figures arrived at by the eleven hundred Americans and a few dozen British for the official surveys made at the end of the war. The research resources, the evidence on the ground, the documentation, the key witnesses, for the most part no longer exist. Such originality of material as the following pages possess will be found largely in the comments of the crews.

What I have tried to do is to give a substantial account of Bomber

Command's achievement by telling the story of its operations throughout the war, without disguising faults or failures but also without too much use of hindsight. As the operations took place on nearly 1500 nights and more than 1000 days and involved some 387,000 individual sorties the story is inevitably a long one, and has left little space for dealing with such vital matters behind the operations as, for instance, training or station organisation. Nevertheless the operations are the heart of the matter, and it is my hope that the reader may judge from these the extent of Bomber Command's contribution to victory. I also hope that the story will be recognisable by those who took part in it, and that it may be of interest to their younger contemporaries and descendants with a taste for twentieth-century history.

I owe a considerable debt of gratitude to many who have assisted me with the book. John Curtis has shown much forbearance on finding that it was taking me three years to write instead of the scheduled two. Group Captain Ian Madelin and his staff at the Air Historical Branch of the Ministry of Defence have been unfailing in their encouragement and in making documents available. David Parry of the Imperial War Museum has helped me to select the photographs; Dr Horst Boog, Director of the Military History Centre at Freiburg, has supplied me with a German reading list. And I am especially indebted to Douglas Radcliffe, Secretary of the Bomber Command Association, for arranging that a questionnaire should be circulated to the Association members: about three hundred of them, whose names are listed in the Acknowledgements at the end of the book, sent in replies, and a brief selection of their observations (which varied in length from one to a hundred or more pages) appears in Chapter 25. All these replies will be passed in due course to the Archives Section of the Royal Air Force Museum, for the benefit of future researchers.

I must also thank Air Commodore Maurice Harvey and Robert Nelson, Research Officer of the Bomber Command Association, for kindly reading the typescript and making valuable suggestions; Mrs Elizabeth Hennessy, for research assistance; Mrs Jackie Gumpert, for producing a beautiful-looking typescript from a horrible-looking manuscript; two golfing friends, Sandy Sandford DFM and Tom Taylor DFC, veterans of about 130 bombing operations between them, for much informative converse between, and sometimes over, the rounds; and my wife for dealing with the questionnaire and putting up for so long with husbandly abstraction. I should also say how useful I have found *The Bomber Command War Diaries* by Martin Middlebrook and Chris Everitt as a handy reference book and a source of information about German civilian casualties. The list of those to whom I am indebted seems endless, but I cannot omit a final name, that of Mr Alan Wilson MSc, MD, FRCS, consultant surgeon at the Whittington Hospital, whose skills preserved me at an awkward moment a year ago and got me back on track.

DENIS RICHARDS
March 1994

I

Small Beginnings

D
ay One of the West's new Armageddon ran contrary to
expectations. At 11.31 on 3 September 1939, a few minutes
after Neville Chamberlain's broken-hearted tones had faded
from the air, the London sirens wailed forth – but only for a
friendly Frenchman, flight plan unfiled. The day passed, and no
cascade of bombs descended on the hapless British populace. The
60,000 hospital beds set aside for the first weeks' casualties remained
spectacularly empty.

Almost but not quite as forbearing as the Luftwaffe was the Royal
Air Force. While the Prime Minister was informing the nation that
it was at war with Germany, a Blenheim of No. 139 Squadron
Bomber Command, pilot Flying Officer A. McPherson, naval observer
Commander Thompson and wireless operator/air-gunner Corporal V.
Arrowsmith, stood waiting at Wyton. The aircraft took off just after
midday, successfully reconnoitred the German North Sea naval bases,
and photographed a strong force of German warships in the Schillig
Roads outside Wilhelmshaven. Corporal Arrowsmith at once tried to
wireless this eagerly awaited information back to England, where a
striking force was standing by: but his set had 'gone U/S'* in the
extreme cold at 24,000 feet, and further action had to await the
Blenheim's return to base.[1] In the early evening 15 Hampdens and
nine Wellingtons then took off to attack. Amid thunderstorms and
gathering gloom they saw no sign of the enemy.

* Become unserviceable.

I

The Hampdens and Wellingtons were still on their way back when ten Whitleys of Nos. 51 and 58 Squadrons headed out for north Germany and the Ruhr. Their task, successfully accomplished, was to drop thirteen-and-a-half tons of leaflets. Composed within the Foreign Office, these informed the German people that their Führer's promises were worthless, that their country was near to bankruptcy and in no position to resist Allied strength, and that they could, if they would, insist on peace at any time.[2]

Such restrained behaviour on both sides immediately raised a question, much debated by American journalists who were soon to coin the phrase 'a phoney war'. Why had hostilities not opened with mass slaughter, as confidently predicted by writers of science fiction and as dreaded, until that moment, by the French authorities and, until recently, by the British?

The answer was deceptively simple, though not widely appreciated. The Germans, observing good military precepts, preferred to deal with one enemy at a time – just now, the Poles. The British and French, from considerations of humanity, were firmly resolved not to initiate bombing of a kind which might kill civilians. They had therefore endorsed President Roosevelt's appeal to belligerents, on 1 September, that there should be no 'bombardment from the air of civilian populations or unfortified cities'. The two Allies, however, also had another reason for circumspection. Their bombing capacity as yet, in September 1939, was less than that of the Luftwaffe – but within perhaps a year it would be greater. It was in their interest, they considered, to defer unrestricted bombing until their strength in the air exceeded that of Germany. For the moment – and the moment was to last eight months – discretion was for the Allies the better part of valour.[*3]

To understand why the Royal Air Force in 1939 was reckoned to be inferior in strength to a Luftwaffe which had officially been in existence only since 1935, it is necessary to glance back at the inter-war years.

At the end of the First World War the RAF had 188 operational and 194 training squadrons, and Britain was the strongest air power in the world. But revulsion from the horrors of the Western Front, the lack of any obviously hostile major power, the hopes pinned on

---

* Hitler's reply to Roosevelt, despatched some days later, referred to 'fearful atrocities against German soldiers' perpetrated by Polish civilians, and to the war against German women and children waged by the British in the form of the blockade. It nevertheless undertook that the Germans would conduct the war 'in a chivalrous and humane manner'.

the League of Nations, and a passionate governmental concern for economy had almost at once led to wholesale disarmament. Within two years nine-tenths of Britain's air strength of 1919 had been swept away. The fervent efforts of admirals and generals to dismember the newly created 'independent' RAF in the interests of their own Services assisted the process, and by 1923 rock bottom had been reached.[4] In March of that year the Secretary of State for Air informed the Commons that there were 'only sixteen first line machines equipped and ready for Home Defence', and that 'all the squadrons in India were grounded for lack of spares'. He could have added, he wrote later, 'that the squadrons in India had received no new engines for seven years, and that they were buying bits and pieces in the bazaars for patching up their obsolete equipment'.[5]

A month before this statement the French, in response to Germany's default on the payment of reparations, had occupied the Ruhr. Britain and France were suddenly on divergent paths, and disarmament lost its allure. During the summer of 1923 Parliament accordingly sanctioned a 'Home Defence Air Force' of 52 squadrons, roughly two-thirds bombers and one-third fighters, which was to be built up over the next five years. As the number of such squadrons in the country had fallen to three, this was certainly a substantial reversal of policy.

But then the international climate changed again. The rift with France was healed, the Locarno Treaties of 1925 seemed to usher in a new era of Franco-German *rapprochement*, preparations were in train for a great international Disarmament Conference. Completion of the 52-squadron scheme was postponed – three times. The Cabinet's 'Ten Year Rule' – the assumption for defence estimates purposes that there would be no major war for ten years – held continuing sway. And on top of all came the Great Depression, spreading from the USA until by 1931 it had all Europe in its grip. More than ever, the British Government – now the new National Government under Ramsay MacDonald – clung to the doctrine of economy.

When Hitler came to power in January 1933 and set about recreating the Luftwaffe and outstripping the air forces of Britain and France, his task was thus not as formidable as it might have seemed. As a basis he had a very strong civil aviation, an active Flying Club movement, a promising aircraft industry, and secret air cadres built up by the Defence Ministry during the Weimar Republic. As possible opponents, he had the neglected, fast-deteriorating Armée de l'Air and the RAF Home Defence Force of only 42 squadrons – still ten less than approved in 1923. Moreover, Hitler could benefit from his timing: he could take advantage of recent revolutionary developments in aviation. His officers, headed by Goering at his new Air Ministry, could place orders for the new fast metal monoplanes with retractable undercarriages, while the RAF and the French Air Force were stocked up with slower, fixed-undercarriage, obsolescent wooden biplanes. And he could perhaps count on two years before Britain and France woke up to the full scope of his ambitions.

However, there was an important factor on the other side. Though the RAF in 1933 was small and equipped mainly with aircraft strongly reminiscent of those of 1914–18, it had its own special strength. Basically still 'Trenchard's Air Force' – the air force which Sir Hugh Trenchard, Chief of the Air Staff from 1919 to 1929, had saved from the assaults of his fellow Chiefs of Staff and built up during the 1920s – it was exceptionally well organised and trained. Lacking the money for any large number of aeroplanes or their frequent replacement by more modern types – the annual Air Estimates from 1921 to 1929 averaged only about £16,000,000 – Trenchard had concentrated on building what he called a 'sound framework' for the future. His great creations – the Cadet College for officer pilots at Cranwell, the Staff College for senior officers at Andover, the research establishments, and very notably the Apprentices' Schools at Halton and Cranwell – gave a Service training unsurpassed anywhere in the world. Other innovations, too, including the Auxiliary Air Force, the University Air Squadrons, and the revolutionary introduction of short-service commissions (five years, followed by four years in the reserve) ensured that in emergency the RAF could call on many qualified pilots beyond the limited numbers on its permanent strength. At the outbreak of war, for instance, over 700 pilots were available from past members of the Oxford University Air Squadron alone.

In another way, too, Trenchard served the RAF exceptionally well during the years before Hitler. By such prominent achievements as the Hendon Air Displays, the long-distance record flights, the Empire Air Mail, and the Schneider Trophy successes, he captured the popular imagination and won general affection for his Service. This was to prove no mean asset when things grew difficult, as they did in 1940. Above all, perhaps, Trenchard made the RAF highly attractive to young men eager to fly. His creation of the inter-war years appealed to, and embodied, the spirit of adventurous youth – a spirit which infected and inspired the newcomers in the sterner years ahead.

*   *   *

4

It was more than a year before the British Government took serious notice of Hitler by starting a modest rearmament. In 1934, in response to his withdrawal the previous autumn from the Disarmament Conference and the League of Nations, but still more in response to Japan's aggressions in China,* Parliament agreed to 'repair deficiencies' in the British forces. For the RAF this came to mean a new target of 75 Home Defence squadrons by March 1939. But Goering's announcement in March 1935 of the existence of a reborn German Air Force, and Hitler's declaration (however misleading) only a fortnight later to the astonished Sir John Simon and Anthony Eden that the Luftwaffe was already as strong as the RAF, quickly showed the need for swifter action. In May 1935 the target for the Home Defence Force became 112 squadrons instead of 75, the date for completion March 1937 instead of March 1939. This, Stanley Baldwin informed Parliament, would ensure parity with Germany in 1937. Undoubtedly it would have done, had Hitler stood still – which he had no intention of doing.

Within a matter of months, however, Britain had another potential enemy. When Italy invaded Abyssinia in October 1935, and Britain joined in the League's sanctions, the continuing weakness of the RAF became manifest: squadrons had to be withdrawn from Home Defence and sent to Egypt and Aden to guard against possible Italian attacks. Waiting until the November 1935 elections were safely over, and the still widely-shared anti-armament sentiment could be disregarded, Baldwin's government accordingly approved yet further RAF expansion. This was Scheme F – a scheme in depth which for the first time made little alteration to the number of squadrons but provided for reasonable reserves, new heavy bombers with a much greater bomb-load, and fresh manufacturing capacity. Previous schemes had concentrated almost entirely on numbers in the first line: a 'shop-window' policy intended, vainly, to impress Hitler.

Thus far the German dictator had made one big, but unsuccessful, external move – the Nazi *putsch* in Vienna in 1934, intended to bring about the '*Anschluss*' ('union') with Austria forbidden by the Treaty of Versailles. Now, however, came the series of aggressions that marked the rest of Hitler's career and cast ever-deeper shadows over Europe. In March 1936 there was the remilitarisation of the Rhineland in contravention of Versailles, and in November the despatch of the *Legion Kondor* to support Franco in the Spanish Civil War. In March

---

* Japan had wrested Manchuria from China in 1931 and invaded Jehol province in 1932. Condemned internationally, she left the League of Nations in March 1933.

1938 came the entry into Austria, to be followed a few months later by the strident demands on Czechoslovakia that brought Europe to the brink of war and led to the Anglo-French humiliation at Munich.

This 'devil's progress' prompted at each stage another RAF expansion scheme. None was completed before the next began, and their details are not as important as the fact that for the first four years of rearmament the pace was very moderate. Tight financial limits prevailed throughout, but beyond this there was also the sacred principle of 'no interference with the normal course of trade', or, to put it more crudely, 'business as usual'. Traditional trade union practices and demarcations, the Government felt, must be fully respected: there must be no direction or dilution of labour, no controls over strategic materials. No one could know, of course, if and when war would actually come; and the Cabinet felt it more important that Britain should maintain a strong economy for future needs than that the expansion of the RAF should be hurried forward irrespective of the danger to financial and industrial stability.

The Air Staff, too, had no desire for a hothouse growth. They would have welcomed larger sums, but they were anxious not to fill the new squadrons with the existing obsolescent aircraft and with indifferently trained crews. They wanted a measured expansion covering the infrastructure and allowing time to specify and bring in new aircraft types – as was brilliantly done with the Hurricane and Spitfire specifications in 1934 and the new heavy bomber specifications in 1936. The Air Staff feared that Trenchard's framework, though sound, might not sustain a massive burden very rapidly imposed. Those well-trained young airmen, the operational trainers of the future, and those admirably organised stations and establishments, could deal with only limited numbers of recruits if quality was to be maintained. Time must pass before the fresh seeds could come into full growth: before the new recruits could take their place in the expanded front line and train further recruits up to operational standard.

These factors help to explain why, after nearly four years of rearmament, Baldwin's promised 'parity' with the parvenu Luftwaffe had not been achieved, at least in numbers of first-line bombers; for Hitler had meanwhile been proceeding at a fast totalitarian pace, with lavish orders to the German aircraft industry. Not 'business as usual' but 'guns before butter' was the Nazi watchword. After the *Anschluss* in 1938, however, the British Cabinet swiftly took off the brakes. 'No interference with the normal course of trade' went by the board, and the RAF received authority to order aircraft up to the limit of the industry's manufacturing capacity. Very importantly, the 'Shadow

Factory' scheme, originally intended for implementation only after the outbreak of hostilities, was brought into operation in 1938. Ardently advocated by Lord Swinton, an outstanding Secretary of State for Air from 1935 to 1938, and approved in 1936, it involved building new aircraft factories at government expense, to be run by the big motor manufacturers – Austin, Morris, Rootes – under the guidance of the established aircraft firms. This was a key innovation of vital importance for the future. By 1939 the output of Britain's aircraft factories had nearly caught up with that of Germany. By 1940 it had established a clear lead.

The expansion of 1934–9, for all its deficiencies, nearly trebled the size and strength of the RAF. One of its earliest consequences was a new Command structure at home. With a large influx of additional squadrons the old overall Command, consisting of bombers, fighters and coastal aircraft, and known as the Air Defence of Great Britain, would, it seemed, become too big for one man to control. In 1936 it was broken up into its component functions, to produce the three great Commands so familiar during the war – Bomber, Fighter and Coastal.* Within these Commands were their subordinate formations, the Groups, and within the Groups the stations and squadrons. Above them all, but not in any sense of day-to-day control, was the Chief of the Air Staff in Whitehall, who from time to time issued broad policy directives.

Merely to list some of the major developments in the five years before the war will indicate that the RAF, if it did not keep pace with Germany in front-line aircraft, was far from standing still. Revolutionary new, clean-lined, metal monoplanes were specified, designed and put into production. Huge tracts of land were acquired and airfields and stations built, often against strong local opposition. The bomber squadrons, previously located in the south-central regions of the country for security and ease of intervention over France, were given newly built stations in the east in East Anglia, Lincolnshire and Yorkshire – more convenient for attacking Germany. The repair and maintenance organisation was greatly strengthened. The RAF Volunteer Reserve (RAFVR), instituted in 1937 and aiming to recruit largely from the products of the grammar schools, provided

* With these came also Training Command and a Maintenance Group, soon to become Maintenance Command. Balloon Command was added in 1938, and Reserve Command in 1939. In 1940 Training Command and Reserve Command merged to form Flying Training Command and Technical Training Command.

weekend flying and other training for young men of limited means –
a reserve for the whole Air Force, unlike the Auxiliaries, who formed
units of their own. The Women's Auxiliary Air Force (WAAF),
separated from the Auxiliary Territorial Service (ATS) in 1939,
tapped the reservoir of female labour for the ground services, and
by 1940 provided an indispensable, as well as a civilising, element
on almost every station. Fundamentally important, too, negotiations
were in progress which soon after the outbreak of war would lead to
the great Empire Air Training Scheme (EATS). By arrangements
with the Dominions concerned, in the vast and enemy-free spaces
of Canada, Rhodesia and South Africa, the scheme was to provide a
ceaseless flow of aircrews without whom the ever-increasing output of
aircraft could never have been manned.

These were great achievements, but there was another greater still
– the revolution in Britain's air defence brought about by radar.* At
the beginning of 1935 radar – the detection and tracking of objects,
in this case aircraft, by measuring in time and strength the return or
'echo' of radio pulses directed against them – was an idea, as far as
Britain was concerned, largely in the minds of Robert Watson Watt
and his assistants at the National Physical Laboratory. By September
1939 a chain of effective radar stations guarded Britain's eastern and
south-eastern coasts, so that defending fighters could take off on the
actual approach of an enemy instead of wastefully patrolling the skies
in search of one that might never come, or taking off after he had
already arrived.

This revolution in Britain's air defence, involving not only radar
and the new fast eight-gun fighters but also close control of the latter
from the ground, was of course a direct help to Bomber Command
by ensuring better protection of the bomber bases and the aircraft
factories. But it also hampered Bomber Command's expansion in the
last year before the war. Until radar, Baldwin's famous dictum of 1932,
'the bomber will always get through', though an exaggeration, had been
broadly true. If close defence was so fallible, the counteroffensive as
a means of defence was all the more important. The early expansion
schemes accordingly preserved what had become the fairly standard
RAF ratio of about two bombers to every fighter. But when new
possibilities of effective fighter interception suddenly opened up, and
at the same time the menace of Hitler grew ever greater, it was natural

---

* Until 1943 radar was known in the Services as RDF – radio direction-finding, a deliberately
misleading term. When its existence was acknowledged in 1941, it was given the public name
'radiolocation'. The word 'radar' (radio direction-finding and ranging) was an American one,
adopted in 1943 in the interests of uniform Anglo-American terminology.

that priority should shift from offensive defence to close defence. In addition there was the compelling consideration, to the politicians, that fighters were much cheaper to produce than bombers.

Faced with an Air Ministry programme in 1938 which it considered too costly, the Cabinet, on the suggestion of Sir Thomas Inskip, Minister for Coordination of Defence, accordingly approved the proposals for more fighters but heavily reduced those for more bombers.[6] This was one among the many factors which left Bomber Command far weaker in the early stages of the war than had been hoped.

In August 1939, when the idea still persisted of deterring Hitler by a show of strength, Bomber Command's front line consisted of 53 squadrons. If the full complement of 16 aircraft per squadron is (wrongly) assumed to have been in place, this meant 848 aircraft. It had been recognised for some time, however, that much of this was window-dressing. The Command had no effective second line, and as the training organisation was as yet so small there would be virtually no reserve with which to support a sustained offensive. If one was launched, the whole force might easily be obliterated within three or four weeks. To obviate this, it had been decided not only to conserve the force as much as possible, but also to relegate 20 of the squadrons, on the outbreak of war, to non-operational status. This meant that some would concentrate on training both themselves and newcomers, others only themselves – thus also acting as a reserve. In addition the least modern, lightest and shortest in range of the bombers, the Battles of No. 1 Group, had been earmarked to form the RAF Advanced Air Striking Force in France, primarily to collaborate with the Allied armies in resisting a German invasion of France or the Low Countries. On 2 September 1939 the ten Battle squadrons sped across the Channel in readiness for the big moment, and took up their allotted stations around Reims. With their departure, and the classification of 20 squadrons as non-operational, Bomber Command's front-line strength suddenly shrank from 53 squadrons to 23 – not much over 350 aircraft.

Bearing in mind the need to avoid civilian casualties and retaliation by the Luftwaffe, which at that time was reckoned to possess about 1200 first-line long-range bombers, what could usefully be done with so small a force? The question had come under urgent discussion in the months before the war, both in the Air Ministry and at Bomber Command. The Plans Directorate of the Air Staff, with the energetic and fertile brain of Group Captain J. C. Slessor at its head, had spent much of 1938–9 devising plans for bombing offensives of various kinds. These made up by far the major part of the series known as the W.A. (Western Air) Plans. By September 1939 there were plans ready, or well in train, to attack the German Air Force, the German Navy, and the German Army in any invasion of France and the Low Countries. These were considered purely 'military' objectives, fully legitimate by the strictest of standards. In the wider realms which might inadvertently kill substantial numbers of civilians, there were plans to attack German military communications, forests, war industry (especially the aviation industry, and the great industrial complex of the Ruhr) and oil installations. There was also a plan to undermine German morale by dropping leaflets.

Considering all these plans, and deciding that attacks on the widely scattered airfields of the Luftwaffe would probably be ineffective, the Air Staff and HQ Bomber Command in the dying days of peace came to a similar conclusion. If civilian casualties were to be avoided, and Germany not to be provoked into a bloody retaliation, there were only two of these thirteen or so bombing plans which could be put into effect at the beginning of the war. One was to attack the German fleet, preferably at sea to avoid civilian casualties. The other was to drop leaflets. Hence Bomber Command's operations on Day One of the West's new Armageddon.

2

Order of Battle

The 23 squadrons of Bomber Command's effective striking force in September 1939 were all on twin-engined aircraft. The Blenheims, much smaller and lighter than the rest, were classed at the time as 'medium' bombers, as were the still lighter single-engined Battles in France. All the others – the Wellingtons, Hampdens and Whitleys – were deemed 'heavies'. Later, in 1941, when four-engined bombers came into service, the Blenheims and Battles were termed 'light' bombers, the Wellingtons, Hampdens and Whitleys 'medium'. It is best to think of them that way from the start.

This force was in four operational Groups – Nos. 2, 3, 4 and 5 (No. 1, most of whose Battles had gone to France, was non-operational). The light bombers – the six squadrons of Bristol Blenheims – were in No. 2 Group with headquarters at Wyton, near Huntingdon. The Group commander, the New Zealander Air Vice-Marshal C. T. Maclean, had served with distinction in the First World War and had later commanded the RAF in Aden and in the Middle East; but he was nearing retirement and in January 1940 was succeeded by Air Vice-Marshal J. M. Robb, a greatly liked and respected airman who was later commander of the RAF in North-West Africa, Chief of Staff (Air) to General Eisenhower, AOC-in-C Fighter Command, and Vice-Chief of the Air Staff. If No. 2 Group were to suffer heavy casualties in 1940, as it did, it would not be for want of skill or sympathy in its commander.

As their range was comparatively short, the six Blenheim squadrons

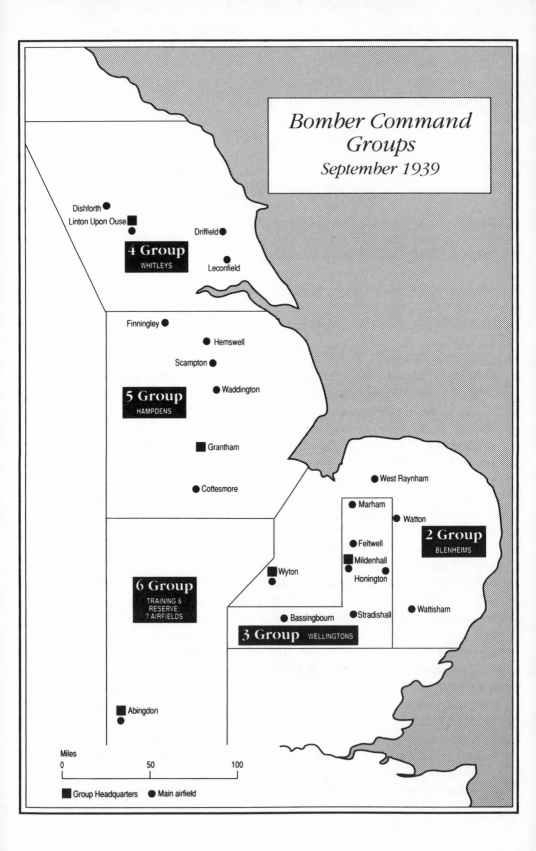

Bomber Command
Groups
September 1939

Dishforth

Linton Upon Ouse

Driffield

4 Group
WHITLEYS

Leconfield

Finningley

Hemswell

Scampton

Waddington

5 Group
HAMPDENS

Grantham

Cottesmore

West Raynham

Marham

Watton

Feltwell

2 Group
BLENHEIMS

Mildenhall

Wyton

Honington

6 Group
TRAINING &
RESERVE:
7 AIRFIELDS

Wattisham

Bassingbourn

Stradishall

3 Group WELLINGTONS

Abingdon

Miles

0   50   100

■ Group Headquarters   ● Main airfield

were stationed at Wyton, at Wattisham in Suffolk, and at Watton in Norfolk, with satellite airfields nearer the coast. From these bases they were expected to attack fringe targets in north-west Germany, warships at sea, and the communications of the German Army if it invaded France or the Low Countries. The Blenheim IVs – the 'long-nosed' Blenheims – with which these squadrons had recently been re-equipped were an elongated version of the Blenheim I, the first batch of which had been ordered 'straight from the drawing board' in 1935, to obviate the long delays attendant on trials with prototypes. This had been possible because the Blenheim I was a military version of an already proved aeroplane, a small civil aircraft built by the Bristol Aeroplane Company for Lord Rothermere, who had generously presented it to the nation. Named *Britain First*, it had been the first stressed-skin metal monoplane with a retractable undercarriage to be built in Britain.

As compared with the Blenheim I, the Blenheim IV which came into service in 1939 had an extended range (about 1460 miles with full bomb-load of 1000 lb) and better armament (five .303 guns instead of two), while still carrying a crew of three. Its maximum speed, bombed-up, of 266 mph was only six miles an hour greater than that of the Mark I. At this speed, however, it was still the fastest aircraft in Bomber Command.

Also in East Anglia were the six Vickers Wellington squadrons of No. 3 Group, with headquarters at Mildenhall in Suffolk. The Group commander was Air Vice-Marshal J. E. A. Baldwin, another popular officer, of cavalry provenance, who was later to command the Third Tactical Air Force. Unusually for one of his rank, he was to fly now and again with his crews on operations – a practice discouraged by the Command headquarters from a desire to preserve experienced commanders and a fear that, if they fell into enemy hands, they would be maltreated to extract secret information.

Almost twice the weight of the Blenheim, the Wellington differed from the other aircraft of Bomber Command in that it was not of stressed-skin metal construction. It was built instead on the 'geodetic'* principle of metal lattices, fabric-covered – a principle already used successfully by the designer, Barnes Wallis, in the Wellington's single-engine predecessor, the Wellesley. Designed to carry what for the time was heavy armament and a big bomb-load,

* 'A geodetic line: the shortest possible line that can be drawn from one point of a surface to another, the plane of curvature of which will be everywhere perpendicular to the surface' (*Oxford English Dictionary*).

together with a crew of six (including a second pilot), the Wellington Mark I had been a long time in gestation – the specification was written in 1932 and the first aircraft reached the squadrons only in October 1938. When they did so, the Vickers turrets soon gave trouble, and early modifications included their replacement by Nash and Thompson turrets, front and rear, and the abandonment of the ventral turret in favour of two beam guns. All of the six squadrons held some of this more satisfactory version, the Mark Ic, by September 1939. Its ceiling at maximum weight was only 15,500 feet, and its top speed no more than 235 mph. It could, however, travel nearly twice as far as a Blenheim IV with the same bomb-load, or, over the Blenheim's maximum range, carry four times the weight of bombs.

North of No. 3 Group's Wellingtons were the six Handley Page Hampden squadrons of No. 5 Group, in Lincolnshire, with head-quarters at Grantham. The Group commander from 20 September 1939 was the friendly but formidable Air Vice-Marshal A. T. Harris, fighter pilot in the First World War, a former head of Plans at the Air Ministry, and until recently AOC Palestine and Transjordan. Dating, like the Wellingtons, from a specification of 1932, the Hampdens were faster than the Wellingtons and almost as fast as the Blenheims, which they greatly exceeded in range and bomb-carrying capacity. They had a better ceiling at maximum weight – 20,000 feet – than the Wellingtons but without power turrets they were much inferior in armament, with guns of only a limited traverse. For the crew of four in the extremely narrow fuselage conditions were at best cramped, and at worst, in an emergency, dangerous.

Lastly, north of No. 5 Group, was No. 4 Group, in Yorkshire. It was commanded by the Australian-born, New Zealand-reared Air Vice-Marshal A. ('Maori' or 'Mary') Coningham, a brilliant fighter pilot in the First World War and later to become famous as the commander of the Desert Air Force, the First Tactical Air Force in North-West Africa, and the Second Tactical Air Force in Europe. From headquarters at Dishforth No. 4 Group controlled five squadrons of Armstrong-Whitworth Whitleys, the first version of which had entered service in March 1937. By September 1939 four of the Whitley squadrons had the Mark III or IV, and one had the Mark V. In this, the most developed form at that time, the Whitley had a maximum speed of 222 mph, slower than all the other bombers, and (at maximum load) an indifferent ceiling of 17,600 feet. It had, however, a good range and could carry a big bomb-load – as much as 8000 lb over a short distance or 3500 lb over nearly 2000 miles. It was manned by a crew of five, with one gun forward and four aft, and despite its lack of speed and – for long – any cockpit heating, it was popular with its crews for its spaciousness, sturdiness and reliability. In flight it was immediately recognisable, even to the layman, by the fact that it flew 'nose-down'.[1]

All these aeroplanes had their merits and served the RAF well. The Blenheim in particular bore the brunt of nearly all the most dangerous daylight bombing raids in the early years of the war, and the Wellington became one of the RAF's most enduring and honoured workhorses. So far as immediate operations against Germany were concerned, however, they all had the same weakness – lack of speed. The essence of the matter can be seen in the history of the fastest of them, the Blenheim IV. When the Mark I had appeared in 1937 – to thrill the spectators at the Hendon Air Display – its top speed of 260 mph had surpassed that of contemporary biplane fighters. But by the time the Mark IV came into service in 1939, with a speed only six miles an hour greater, biplanes had virtually disappeared and the fighter world had been transformed. The new Blenheim was slower by around 90 mph than Britain's Spitfire and, more to the point, than Germany's Messerschmitt 109 and 110.

How, then, were the British bombers with their 222–266 mph going to live against German fighters capable of over 350 mph? The answer might have been sought – as it was finally by the Americans – in fighter escort. But it was not, and for a number of reasons.

The first was the time scale of the developments. By 1939 the British bombers in service had mostly been initiated six or seven years previously; but fighter defence had been revolutionised only in the last two years. In 1932 Baldwin had proclaimed 'The bomber will always get through' and gone more or less uncontradicted. In 1939 this was clearly no longer true; with radar and ground control and new fast fighters – assuming he could get enough of them – Sir Hugh Dowding at Fighter Command was very confident that he could knock plenty of enemy bombers from the sky if they tried to attack by day from Germany. But because this transformation was so recent, its implications had not yet been fully absorbed – on either side of the North Sea.

The second reason why fighter escort had not been contemplated was theoretical, and related to Trenchard's dictum that 'the aeroplane is an offensive weapon'. Basically true enough, this becomes untrue if it is taken to mean that the aeroplane has no useful role in defence.

But in Trenchard's mind it meant, among other things, that the aeroplane had offensive capabilities denied to other weapons. Since wars are usually won in the end by offensives, effort should therefore be concentrated – not entirely, but mainly – on the aeroplane in its most offensive form, the bomber.

The third reason was at once logistical, financial and political. It was already difficult enough in Britain to build up a bomber force which – it was hoped – would deter Hitler from aggression, and at the same time a fighter force strong enough to hold off any German attack. If, in addition, enough fighters – and of a more elaborate and expensive kind – had to be provided to accompany all the raids of Bomber Command, the task might be beyond prudent financial limits, or manufacturing capacity, or the RAF's facilities for accommodation and training.

The final reason, as important as any, was technological. Escorted raids into Germany would need a fighter of very long range, and whenever efforts had been made to produce such an aircraft they had turned out unsuccessfully. By the time provision had been made for the extra fuel and usually extra navigational facilities and a second crew member, the long-range fighter on account of its greater weight and lesser manoeuvrability was no match for a good short-range fighter. A classic example, late in the day, was the very fast German long-range fighter introduced in 1939, Goering's vaunted *Zerstoerer* or destroyer, the twin-engined, twin-crew, Me 110. Though it later had a useful life as a night-fighter, it was soon to reveal its limitations as a bomber escort in the Battle of Britain, when the Germans had to supply it with Me 109 protection – an escort for an escort.

To this long-standing technological problem an answer was to be found, in 1943–4 at a time of Allied need, in a superb aircraft, the 'stretched' Mustang, fitted with auxiliary drop tanks. No such answer was available on the British side in 1939–40; and on the German side the Me 110 was to prove inadequate.

As Bomber Command's aircraft were 90 mph slower than the German fighters, yet were to have no escort, how could they hope to penetrate Germany? The Air Ministry knew little about the enemy's radar – though there were stations in north-west Germany – so it was still possible to think of achieving surprise, at least against fringe targets. At night, too, there would be very little fighter opposition. Night-bombing, however, would have nothing like the accuracy of daylight-bombing, so only the slowest and most vulnerable of the British bombers, the Whitleys, were given this as their main role. All the rest had had some training in night-flying, but not much –

in 1938 about a tenth of the time devoted to daylight-flying. Their task was to attack by day.

This would be possible, it was hoped – but not universally believed – through the virtues of collective fire power. If the bombers with their five or six guns, preferably in rotating power turrets, held together in close formation, their mutually supporting fire might see off the attacking fighters. In the nature of things, this was a theory which in peacetime could be demonstrated only on paper, or by models, or by exercises involving bombers, fighters and cine-guns. But often there weren't enough cine-guns, or they didn't work, or the exercise didn't take place because of the weather, or the bomber and fighter crews held contradictory opinions on the success of their efforts. Truth, as opposed to theory or belief, had to await the start of the shooting war.

The Group commanders were all able men whose job was to run an efficient Group and to pass on experience and make representations to HQ Bomber Command. They had nothing to do officially with the formulation of policy except by tendering advice – sought or unsought – to their commander-in-chief at High Wycombe. To a lesser extent, this also applied to that officer himself. His task, too, was basically the implementation, though by ways and means and times of his own devising, of policy directives which came from above, from the Chief of the Air Staff at the Air Ministry. And these directives in turn, in their broadest aspects, such as the priority to be given at any time to attacking different classes of objectives, usually stemmed from still higher authority – the War Cabinet (or later, under Churchill, the Defence Committee) as advised by the Chiefs of Staff of the three Services.

Just as the Chief of the Air Staff conferred with his fellow Chiefs of Staff and the War Cabinet, so in a more informal way did the AOC-in-C Bomber Command confer with the Chief of the Air Staff and his subordinates at the Air Ministry. Bombing policy accordingly tended to be less something handed down arbitrarily from Whitehall than something which emerged from consultation between Whitehall and Bomber Command. And there can be no doubt that in the two years before the war and in its opening phase the views of the AOC-in-C Bomber Command, Air Chief Marshal Sir Edgar Ludlow-Hewitt, had, if not inspired, at least reinforced the decision to restrict offensive operations and conserve the bomber force.

'Ludlow', as he was commonly known, had taken over Bomber

Command from its first head, Air Chief Marshal Sir John Steel, in September 1937. The son of a vicar, he was a tall, not readily approachable man, who had joined the Royal Flying Corps (RFC) from the regular army and done brilliantly as a pilot in 1914–18 – MC, DSO, Legion of Honour, six mentions in despatches, and a brigadier by the age of 21. In the inter-war years he had been Commandant of the RAF Staff College, AOC Iraq Command, Director of Operations and Intelligence at the Air Ministry, and AOC RAF India. As a Christian Scientist he sat a little strangely in RAF company, but he was immensely respected for his unsurpassed knowledge of the Service. Sir Arthur Harris, who was not given to handing out praise lightly, was to write of him later: 'He was far and away the most brilliant officer I have ever met in any of the three Services. If he had a fault, it was that he had such immense knowledge of every technical and operational detail of his subject, of every aspect of air warfare, that he sometimes appeared to think too much about details.'

It was this extremely knowledgeable commander who, surveying his force in 1938 at the time of the Czechoslovakia crisis, was painfully struck by its many deficiencies – of which he informed the Air Ministry. The official historians of the air offensive against Germany later wrote of that time: 'There was hardly a ten per cent reserve of aircraft, and of the planned 2500 reserve of pilots only 200 were ready for immediate operations. Many of the aircraft available lacked essential equipment, such as turrets. The only way to obtain a sufficiency of spare parts was to break up squadrons. Many of the squadrons had only had their aircraft for a short period. It was calculated that, if peace-time standards were applied, not fifty per cent of the force was fit to fight.'[2]

Despite many improvements in equipment and organisation, Ludlow-Hewitt grew no more optimistic in the months which followed Munich. Rather, he became increasingly concerned about the unreadiness of his Command for war, and in particular the likelihood that his squadrons would suffer crippling losses if they tried to attack targets in Germany by day. In July 1939 he wrote to the Air Ministry: '. . . the gunners have no real confidence in their ability to use this equipment effectively in war, and the captains and the crews have, I fear, little confidence in the ability of the gunners to defend themselves against enemy fighters.' He even suggested, as the RAF had no long-range fighters, that it might be best to base the greater part of his force in France, so that fighter escort might be possible – if the fighters could be spared.

As for the alternative of bombing by night, the outlook to Ludlow-Hewitt seemed just as bleak. There would be safety in the dark, but in the absence of sophisticated navigational aids could the crews find and hit precise targets? A report from one of his Group commanders in 1938 had indicated that, above cloud, aircraft navigating by dead reckoning alone could not rely on arriving any nearer than about fifty miles away from their target. There was also the chilling statistic that in a period of two years, in peacetime, Bomber Command aircraft had made 487 forced landings through losing their way at night *over the British Isles*.

So it was not simply the Government, or the Air Ministry, which favoured a policy of leaflet-dropping and restricted bombing. All Ludlow-Hewitt's advice was in the same direction. In particular, he wanted time for more intensive night-training, more navigational aids, more bombing and firing practice, more facilities for photographic reconnaissance. And had he dwelt, at that stage, on his squadrons' lack of armour and self-sealing petrol tanks, he would have been more apprehensive still.

Most of Bomber Command's problems in September 1939 did not stem, as many critics have averred, from elementary lack of foresight and preoccupation with the theory, instead of the practicalities, of strategic bombing. They stemmed instead from the haste and extent of the pre-war expansion. So much had been done; but so much remained still to do.

Fortunately Ludlow-Hewitt's doubts and fears, though not unshared by his Group commanders, had not become so well-known that the morale of his force was in any way affected. The crews of the Blenheims and the Wellingtons, the Hampdens and the Whitleys, may have been aware of deficiencies in their equipment and training – though for the most part they felt well-trained, and thought highly of their aircraft. But reflections of this kind were not uppermost in their minds. They had a job to do. If they possibly could, they would do it.

3

Experience Teaches

The German fleet had escaped damage on 3 September. The next day Bomber Command tried again.

At 08.35 Flying Officer McPherson was airborne from Wyton in his Blenheim, intent on repeating his brilliant reconnaissance of the previous afternoon. This time there was persistent rain, with cloud solid up to 17,000 feet. But he pressed on, hugging the deck, and at 250 feet swept unchallenged over the German bases. With satisfaction his naval observer recorded two large warships off Brunsbüttel, another near Wilhelmshaven, and four destroyers in the Jade Roads nearby.[1]

Once again, however, wireless communication failed. The coded message reached base in corrupt and largely unintelligible form. As on the previous day, nothing could be done until McPherson returned.

Because of the weather, Command headquarters ordered part of the waiting bomber force to stand down. The final plans were for 15 Blenheims – from Squadrons 107, 110 and 139 – to attack the large warship near Wilhelmshaven (or, failing that, the destroyers) and 14 Wellingtons, of 9 and 149 Squadrons, to attack the two warships off Brunsbüttel. The dense cloud dictated low-level attack with bombs fused for 11 seconds' delay – to allow the second and third aircraft of each section to drop their bombs before those of the first exploded.

The Blenheims took off between 15.30 and 16.00. In the foul weather the five from 139 Squadron probably searched the wrong estuary. They found nothing, but got back safely. The five from 107 became split up: in the course of their attacks one blew up from its own bombs and the others went down to fierce anti-aircraft fire.[2] But the five from 110 Squadron, led by Flight Lieutenant K. C. Doran, fared better. Ken Doran later told the story:

> After a bit of feverish map-reading we decided we were in the approach to the Schillig Roads. By an incredible combination of luck and judgement we were bang on our track.
>
> Within a few minutes cloud base lifted to 500 ft and we saw a large merchant ship: just beyond it was the Admiral Scheer* . . . anchored in shallow water near the bank and protected on the landward side by a pincushion balloon-barrage . . .
>
> We climbed as high as we could, which was about 500 ft, and made our attack in a shallow dive. As we approached we saw the matelots' washing hanging out around the stern, and the crew idly standing about on deck. It seemed as though we had literally caught them with their pants down.
>
> However, when they realized that our intention was hostile they started running like mad, and as aircraft No. 1 came over at mast-head height and dropped its bombs bang amidships, their AA got into action, and this together with shore-based AA kept us pretty busy carrying out evasive measures. The bombs from the second aircraft undershot by about ten yards and exploded in shallow water directly under the ship. No. 3 found he could not get over within the 11 seconds and dropped his bombs on another target . . .[3]

For their gallantry and success, McPherson and Doran received the first DFCs of the war. But the balance sheet of the Blenheim raids was far from satisfactory. The bombs which hit the *Scheer* failed to explode and bounced off her armoured decks: she was in service again within five weeks. The cruiser *Emden*, struck by a Blenheim which crashed on her fo'c's'le, was out of action for only twelve days.[4] On the other side of the reckoning, Bomber Command lost five Blenheims and 16 aircrew. This was 33 per cent of the force despatched and 50 per cent of those who actually attacked – a proportion to strike dismay into the heart of the stoutest commander.

Meanwhile the 14 Wellingtons were seeking out the two warships off Brunsbüttel. In the appalling weather most of them eventually turned back, but six reached the target area. One attacked, unsuccessfully; three retreated before intense anti-aircraft fire; and two succumbed to German fighters. At some stage it seems that one of the Wellingtons

---

* The *Admiral von Scheer* was a pocket battleship.

dropped, or jettisoned, a bomb which killed two civilians in the Danish town of Esbjerg, 110 miles away.[5]

For this operation the balance sheet showed nothing on the credit side for Bomber Command except gallantry. On the debit side the loss was two aircraft and 12 aircrew – 14 per cent of those despatched and 66 per cent of those attacking. Again the rate of wastage was one which no air force could long sustain.

The operations of 3 and 4 September thus showed very clearly how far as yet Ludlow-Hewitt's bombers were from being the 'all weather' force of his desires. How much had still to be learned – and how a young bomber pilot felt on his first operation – may be seen from the account of the abortive raid of 3 September in *Enemy Coast Ahead*, that splendid wartime book by Guy Gibson, of later 'Dambusters' fame. Gibson was on Hampdens with 83 Squadron at Scampton at the time:

He [the Station Intelligence Officer] again repeated that on no account were we to bomb Germany.

After that another man got up and told us how to take off with a bomb-load on. None of us had ever done it before and we did not even know if a Hampden would unstick with 2000 pounds of bombs . . .

About forty miles from Wilhelmshaven the cloud suddenly descended to about three hundred feet in rain and we closed formation . . . To my mind this was fine for bombing warships because we would have been able to attack in bad visibility and climb up into the cloud to avoid the flak. But to my astonishment Willie Snaith [the flight leader] suddenly began to turn to the left. Not quite knowing what he was doing, I followed. I saw poor old Rosy on the other side looking left and right, watching his wing tip which seemed to be about to go into the drink at any minute. Then the leader straightened up, and I suddenly realized that he had turned back. Of course, he was dead right, there was no doubt about that. For all we knew we were miles off our course, the gun flashes ahead might have been the Dutch islands or they might have been Heligoland, and he was not going to risk three aircraft in order to make an abortive attack . . .

. . . When we recrossed the coast at Boston it was dark. All the beacons had been moved to code positions and Willie's navigator got hopelessly lost. We floated around Lincolnshire for about two hours finding our position. It was only when the moon came up that we were able to follow the canal right up to Lincoln and

turned north to our base. And so at last we landed. It was my
first landing in a Hampden at night, and I think that went for all.
What an abortive show, what a complete mess-up! In fact, for all
the danger we went through it couldn't be called a raid . . .[6]

Fortunately for Bomber Command, dropping leaflets over Germany
in the early months of the war was a good deal safer than attacking
the German fleet. For the first seven nights NICKEL operations – to
give them their code-name – proceeded unchecked. From about 50
sorties, nearly all by Whitleys direct from England or refuelling in
France, only one aircraft failed to return. Several, however, made
forced landings, including one which became interned in Belgium.
Another, challenged by a Belgian fighter, is reputed to have shot it
down. The impromptu element in the proceedings was evident on 5
September when 51 Squadron, after refuelling at Reims, had to take
off by the light of car headlamps for lack of a proper flarepath.[7]

The techniques of delivery, too, at first bore signs of the impromptu.
The leaflets were done up in bundles of 1500, each about the size of
a hefty brick, held together by a rubber band. These bundles were in
turn tied up with string in packages of twelve. Inside the confined
space of the aircraft one of the crew had to cut the string, and feed
the bundles one by one down the flare chute.[8] In the slipstream of
the aircraft the leaflets, if all went well, broke loose from the rubber
band and then floated down over the target area. Some of the chutes,
however, proved retentive; and in any case it was a laborious and
draughty business stuffing the bundles down them. On one occasion
rubber bands became detached too early and the leaflets blew about
madly in the aircraft, perilously papering the inside of the windscreen
at the moment of take-off.

Only a week had gone by when a surge of public criticism,
complaining that while Germany dropped bombs on Poland, Britain
dropped only paper on Germany, brought 'Nickelling' to a standstill.
The War Cabinet took thought, but decided it should continue.[9] When
operations resumed on 24 September publicity wisely emphasised
not so much the dropping of leaflets – the texts of which were
for long mysteriously denied to the press – as another function
of the flights: night reconnaissance. With this as their main purpose, three Whitleys of 10 Squadron managed on the night of
1/2 October to scatter leaflets for the first time over Berlin –
leaflets enlightening the inhabitants about the private fortunes of
their Nazi leaders. But soon there was another halt: too many

aircraft had been violating the airspace of Belgium, Holland and Denmark.[10]

After 16 October, when the leaflet raids began again, came a fortnight of atrocious weather. Only some two dozen NICKEL aircraft set out for Germany, and half failed to reach their target areas. Incidents which took place on 27/28 October illustrate the conditions against which the crews not infrequently had to struggle.

On that night five Whitleys of 51 Squadron had been standing by at Villeneuve after refuelling. The met. forecast was unfavourable, but good weather was expected over base on return. The crews took off in the early evening having had no food since midday, and been given none of the usual coffee and sandwiches for the trip. One aircraft, defeated by the weather, turned back early. The other four soon found their wings and controls icing up, and their instrument panels being obscured by frost. In two cases an engine, overheating from the weight of ice, caught fire. Some crew members lost consciousness from lack of oxygen as they struggled to lower their 'dustbin' under-turret for the leaflet-dropping. Others beat their heads on the floor or the navigation table to distract them from the oxygen shortage and the pains of frostbite.

Back over France one of the Whitleys, with six inches of ice on its wings and an engine on fire, hit some treetops and pancaked in a forest clearing. Another, forced down by the weight of ice, landed by itself after the captain had trimmed it to a gentle glide and baled out with the crew. The rear-gunner's intercom point, however, was faulty: he didn't hear the order. He clambered out of the tail, rushed forward to help the others, and found himself alone – one of the most astonished men in World War Two.[11]

Group Captain Tom Sawyer, a regular who served throughout the war, at first on Hampdens, later described the discomforts of this time:

The Hampdens, Wellingtons, and Whitleys . . . had got only rather basic de-icing equipment installed, and very inefficient cabin heating systems. The crews had to stuff themselves into their Sidcot Suits with their separate thick woolly 'Teddy Bear' linings, over their own personal choice of poloneck sweater, which again was beneath a uniform tunic. Sheepskin flying boots and silk inner liners to their flying gauntlets completed the attire apart from the flying helmet with its various attachments and long cord to the earphones. Only the air gunners had the new electrically-heated Irvine Suits and boots, and God knows they needed them. We then waddled – fat and uncomfortable – into our aeroplanes and settled down at our flying stations. Once there we were comfortable enough, however, until the cold started to bite in at altitude. What exaggerated the cold was that on top of everything else, the Whitley and Hampden (probably the Wellington also) were more than somewhat draughty inside. With temperatures as low as −30°C logged regularly during that bitter winter of 1939–40, it was almost impossible at times for crews to feel their own hands and feet, let alone to handle their equipment.[12]

From 27 October to 10 November bad weather stopped all NICKEL operations. On 13 November the Air Ministry, having established, after some interdepartmental wrangling, a power of veto over the text of the leaflets, issued instructions for the following months. Bomber Command was to drop one million leaflets each week over specified areas, together with half a million copies of a miniature news-sheet, the *Wolkiger Beobachter* ('Cloud-Observer' – a play on the title of the well-known Nazi paper, the *Volkischer Beobachter*). By March 1940 occasional leaflet-reconnaissance sorties were reaching as far afield as Austria, Czechoslovakia and Poland.

It was after a flight to Warsaw on 15/16 March that one Whitley of 77 Squadron, piloted by Flight Lieutenant Tomalin, earned a special place in RAF lore. Short of fuel on the return journey the crew landed, as they thought, on a field in France, only to discover, after a few words with the nearest inhabitants, that they were in Germany. Quick thinking and sprinting took them back to their aircraft, and a safe take-off, under the eyes of approaching troops.[13]

From mid-January Hampdens of No. 5 Group joined Whitleys and Wellingtons in this work, in which the Battles of the AASF were also active. The accent was now firmly on reconnaissance, especially of railways, canals, rivers, searchlights, anti-aircraft batteries, airfields and industrial targets. During March repeated reconnaissances prepared the way for the possible mining of Germany's inland waterways (Plan WA16).

On 9 April 1940 Hitler invaded Denmark and Norway, and leaflet-dropping over Germany came to an abrupt halt. Resumed after the fall of France, it was then done incidentally to the dropping of bombs. It continued so during the rest of the war, as did leaflet-dropping to inform and encourage Resistance movements in German-occupied territory.

If the question is asked whether the early leaflet operations in any way sapped German morale, the answer is clearly 'no'. They certainly gave the lie to Goering's claim that British bombers would not be able to operate over Germany. But any scintilla of discontent they may have aroused could only be swept away in the roaring tide of German success in mid-1940. Dropping leaflets to defeated troops, as in Austria-Hungary in 1918, or to recalcitrant tribes in Iraq or the Yemen, had worked well enough. Dropping them to an utterly unsubdued major European people in the grip of nationalist fervour and a highly efficient secret police was, to say the least, over-optimistic.

Air Vice-Marshal A. T. Harris of No. 5 Group, whose Hampdens had shared in the work, and who was later, as AOC-in-C Bomber Command, to organise leaflet-dropping on a mammoth scale, was characteristically uncompromising about the subject: 'My personal view is that the only thing achieved was largely to supply the Continent's requirements of toilet paper for the five long years of war. You have only to think what any man of sense would do with an obviously enemy pamphlet when he picked it up, how he would regard it, and how he would react to the statements in it. Our reaction to enemy pamphleteering had always been to jeer, and at the most to keep some of their leaflets as souvenirs. News to occupied territories was another matter . . .'[14]

Harris's remarks, however, cannot be accepted as the whole verdict on the early leaflet operations. During the so-called 'phoney war' of 3 September 1939–8 April 1940, Bomber Command flew some 366 NICKEL sorties and lost around six per cent of the aircraft employed – about half to enemy action, half to weather and other hazards. This was not an unduly high rate in view of the reconnaissance information obtained, the experience of long-distance night-flying gained by the crews, the boost to morale of operational employment, and the lessons that were learned, fairly cheaply, about equipment. In this last respect, the leaflet operations highlighted the need for, among other things, more advanced aids to navigation, better cockpit-heating and more (and more reliable) electrically heated clothing, better safety and escape devices, and better oxygen supplies, particularly for crews making emergency movements within the aircraft. All these needs were marked, and acted upon.

Inevitably, however, it took time to effect much improvement. In the matter of cockpit-heating, for instance, the essential was to supply more heat, and safely, from the engines, and seal off all unnecessary draughts – not easy with bomb-doors or rotating turrets. Installation of an initial or redesigned heating system was work for the factory rather than the hangar, and was often impractical with existing aircraft. Meanwhile, until better-heated and frost-protected aircraft came along, Ludlow-Hewitt approved a bewildering number of palliatives. These included putting Aladdin heaters overnight into the Battles and Blenheims, wrapping hessian round the wings of the Wellingtons between flights, supplying crystal-heated thigh-pads and electrically heated gloves and boots for the rear-gunners, and inducing all aircrew to swallow vitamin pills and whale oil.[15]

However useful leaflet-dropping and reconnaissance might be, they were not all that the War Cabinet expected of Bomber Command, even in a period of restricted bombing. Among other things, there was still the task of striking a sharp blow against the German fleet.

The first new plan was for 'reconnaissance in force'. Since too much time had elapsed on 3 and 4 September between the reconnaissance and the arrival of the striking force, why not send the striking force itself on the reconnaissance? Twelve Hampdens tried this out on 26 September, but saw nothing they were permitted to attack. Three days later another group of Hampdens found, and unsuccessfully attacked, two destroyers near Heligoland. Unfortunately, however, in the course of their search the British bombers became split into two formations, and radar-warned Me 109s had ample time to intercept the second. At the cost of two of their own number, the German fighters shot down this entire formation of five aircraft, all from 144 Squadron. Only six of the 24 aircrew survived.[16]

Despite this discouraging start, Bomber Command for some time persisted with 'reconnaissance in force'. Several times during October and November 12 to 18 Wellingtons set out on such missions, which were usually prompted by reports from intelligence or from earlier daylight reconnaissance by individual Blenheims – a dangerous business which cost about one aircraft in every five sent out. All these efforts met with no success. Pressure from the War Cabinet, inspired mainly by the Admiralty in the person of Winston Churchill, then led to larger-scale operations.[17] On 3 December 24 Wellingtons from 38, 115 and 149 Squadrons found and attacked two cruisers and attendant merchant ships off Heligoland, taking care not to drop bombs near residential areas. They sank a minesweeper, did some damage to military installations onshore, and shot down an intervening German fighter, all without loss to themselves. The Me

109s and 110s, attacking mainly from the rear, showed a healthy respect for the Wellingtons' two-gun rear turrets, and failed to close in to lethal range.[18]

This success momentarily reinforced confidence in the self-defending powers of Wellingtons in formation. Events, however, soon undermined this. On 14 December 12 aircraft of 99 Squadron, acting on a submarine report, came across a warship heading for the mouth of the Elbe. Too low to bomb, the Wellingtons suffered repeated attacks from Me 109s and 110s. Five of the British aircraft went down into the sea, and another crashed on return.[19]

Worse was to follow. On 18 December 22 Wellingtons of 9, 37 and 149 Squadrons, searching over Wilhelmshaven in completely clear skies, found several warships. But under the instructions then current they could not attack – the vessels were in dock, or lying alongside, and could not be bombed without risk to civilians. The German ships remained unscathed, but trouble had meanwhile engulfed the Wellingtons. Picked up almost at take-off by the German radio interception service and tracked in by radar, they found themselves set upon, well out to sea, by about 25 Me 109s and 110s. Taking care, after their earlier encounters, to keep clear of the Wellingtons' rear turrets, the German fighters repeatedly attacked from the beam and above – a direction quite inadequately covered by the Wellingtons' dustbin under-turret, which could not fire above the level of the fuselage.*

In a notable hour's work the Luftwaffe pilots, who had the advantage of 20-mm cannon which far outclassed the .3-inch machine guns of the British bombers, shot down 12 of the 22 Wellingtons – and claimed 38. Especially grievous was the loss suffered by 37 Squadron – five of its six aircraft.[20]

Another depressing feature of this massacre, suddenly plain to all on both sides, was the extreme vulnerability of the Wellingtons to fire. In the interests of greater speed and bomb-load, they carried no armour, and their petrol tanks were not self-sealing. Many went down with petrol pouring out and their wings fiercely ablaze.

Three days later a hazard of another kind was revealed. Alan Nicoll,† of 44 Squadron, was a 19-year-old sergeant observer in a force of Hampdens and Wellingtons on a fruitless search for the

---

* At that date it was not expected that fighters would attack from the beam owing to the high speed of aircraft and the deflection-shooting required for beam attack.
† Later a pilot and squadron leader.

battleship *Deutschland* off the Norwegian coast. He later recalled:

> The weather deteriorated to rain showers and a cloud base about
> 500', and we were probably fortunate not to encounter the enemy
> under such adverse conditions. At the limit of our endurance we
> turned back for home (the Scottish coast), where tragedy befell.
> On arrival near the Forth estuary we were attacked by Spitfires
> and two Hampdens were shot down into the sea . . .

After the disaster of 18 December 'reconnaissances in force' still
continued, but from then on pilots were under orders not to approach
the German coast until the fire hazard had been reduced. Some
armour was soon added, and by the end of March 1940 almost
the entire bombing force had self-sealing tanks. Efforts were also
being made to produce a non-flammable spray for the fabric-covered
Wellingtons. On 8 January 1940 the Bomber Command Operations
Record Book recorded: 'the only satisfactory medium so far found
was a fireproof dope of German manufacture, which ICI and RAE
[the Royal Aircraft Establishment, Farnborough] were now trying to
reproduce'.[21]

Throughout the early months of 1940 the British bombers, and
particularly the Blenheims, maintained their North Sea sweeps in the
hope of finding and attacking German ships. Bad weather repeatedly
frustrated their efforts. Hampdens and Wellingtons did, however,
succeed in hampering the minelaying activity of German seaplanes
by bombing their marine flarepaths in the East Frisians. They also
struck, on 19/20 March 1940, what was intended to be a major blow
against the menace of the magnetic mine. Two nights earlier the
Luftwaffe had attacked Scapa Flow, and incidentally injured a few
civilians. As a reprisal, Bomber Command was permitted for the first
time to bomb objectives on land – military installations at the isolated
seaplane base of Hoernum, on the island of Sylt. In the biggest raid
of the war thus far, 43 Whitleys and Hampdens managed to attack.
The crews returned with enthusiastic reports of the damage done –
unconfirmed, unfortunately, by subsequent reconnaissance or German
admissions.[22]

In all, from the outbreak of the war to the beginning of the
Norwegian campaign, Bomber Command aircraft flew 861 sorties
against German naval vessels. In the course of these they dropped
only 61 tons of bombs.[23] Apart from the damage to the *Scheer* and
Emden on 4 September, the only significant harm done to the German
fleet was the sinking of one minesweeper and one U-boat – the latter
by Squadron Leader M. V. Dulap's Blenheim, of 82 Squadron, on 11

March. Clearly in April 1940 Bomber Command still had much to learn about finding and attacking warships at sea.

One major lesson, however, it had tacitly absorbed. It was now clear that the Wellingtons and the Hampdens, which had been cast for the later role of destroying German industry, had no hope of fighting their way through to inland targets in daylight against the Me 109s and 110s. The concept of the self-defending bomber formation, so attractive in theory, had not worked out in practice: those aircraft which had remained in tight formation had suffered fewer losses – but flak, fighters or bad weather could readily break up the formations. All Bomber Command's aircraft, however, had ranged the skies of Germany at night more or less with impunity. The implication was clear. Bombing by night would not be as accurate as bombing by day; but if Bomber Command was going to attack Germany at all in the immediate future, by night it would have to be.

So much had become plain both to Ludlow-Hewitt and the Air Staff after the disasters of 14 and 18 December. The Command acknowledged no abandonment of principle but simply changed its expectations and practice. The Wellingtons and the Hampdens took a greater part in the leaflet/reconnaissance operations, to intensify their night-training. The Blenheims, scheduled to operate not only against shipping but also against any German invasion of France or the Low Countries, had to remain primarily a daylight force; but all the 'heavies' of the time would become night-bombers. So the pattern was set for the inevitable moment when one or other of the combatants decided, in the Air Staff phrase of the time, to 'take off the gloves'.

During March 1940 Bomber Command headquarters, originally at Uxbridge, moved from its temporary wartime location at Langley, in Buckinghamshire, to a new, purpose-built centre, complete with underground operations room, at Walter's Ash, some twenty miles distant. Carefully concealed in wooded country, the new headquarters was also protected by above-average secrecy. Orders went forth that the name Walter's Ash should never be mentioned, that the headquarters should be referred to by its code-name, SOUTHDOWN, and that the postal address should be High Wycombe, five miles away.[24] The secrecy, or Luftwaffe ineffectiveness, worked. During the whole course of the war no German bomb disturbed, or even threatened, SOUTHDOWN.

Less than a month after this move, Ludlow-Hewitt found himself relieved of his Command. It is not easy to document the reasons for this. Appointment to, and dismissal from, the most senior military posts is usually a matter for discussion between, among others, the Prime Minister, the Secretary of State, and the Chief of Staff of the Service concerned. Since the discussion often goes unrecorded, explanations of the decision tend to come mainly from hearsay and intelligent guesswork. In the case of Ludlow-Hewitt it may reasonably be surmised that his age (nearly 54) was one factor against him; that his well-founded but depressing pessimism about the current capabilities of his bomber force was another; and that his reluctance to form new squadrons, as the Air Ministry wished, instead of more Operational Training Units (OTUs) as he himself desired, was a third factor.* When to these are added the facts that he had been visibly shaken by the casualties on 4 and 29 September and 14 and 18 December 1939 and that he had aquired a reputation for indecisiveness, the grounds on which a change was made become fairly clear. At all events, 'Ludlow' departed on 2 April 1940 to assume the post of RAF Inspector-General, in which his percipience and extensive Service knowledge were to be utilised to the great benefit of the RAF throughout the rest of the war.

As for Ludlow-Hewitt's successor, there is no mystery why the choice fell on Air Marshal Charles Frederick Algernon Portal DSO and bar, MC – known to his friends as 'Peter'. Portal, then aged 46, had long impressed by his clarity of thought, his complete devotion to duty, his courage and steely resolve, and his quiet but attractive personality. A dashing motor-cyclist despatch rider in the early months of the First World War – he had volunteered on 6 August 1914 while an undergraduate at Oxford – he had later transferred to the RFC and attracted notice as an outstandingly able artillery-observation pilot and squadron commander. Required then to turn his unstable and ill-equipped RE8 reconnaissance planes into night-bombers, he had demonstrated to his doubting and apprehensive crews that this could indeed be done: with a 112-lb bomb slung under each wing he took off three times one night, circled around, and landed back three times – with the bombs on. A few months later, such was his enthusiasm for the newest form of air warfare that he made no fewer than five solo bombing raids over the German lines in a single night.[25]

Between the wars, Portal's talents took him inevitably towards the top. In 1927, as CO of 7 Squadron at Worthy Down, he wrested the RAF 'bombing championship' – in the form of the Laurence Minot Trophy for accurate bombing – away from Arthur Harris's

* For the formation of Operational Training Units, see pages 71–4.

squadron, Portal personally acting as the bomb-aimer. As commander of British forces in Aden from 1934 to 1936 he suppressed a tribal rebellion almost bloodlessly and prepared the colony for defence against Mussolini. As Director of Organisation in the Air Ministry in 1937–8, and later as Air Member for Personnel, he contributed outstandingly to the RAF's growing capability for war, notably in connection with the acquisition and construction of more airfields, the creation of Maintenance Command, Balloon Command, the RAFVR and the WAAF, the inception of Operational Training Units, and the launching of the Empire Air Training Scheme. Such was only part of the achievement of the man whom Churchill dubbed 'the accepted star of the Royal Air Force'.[26]

All his star qualities would be needed at Bomber Command in the months that lay ahead.

4

Against the Tide: Norway

I n the early hours of 7 April 1940 Bomber Command Whitleys of 51 Squadron returned from night reconnaissance with more than routine information. The crews had seen intense activity in four north German ports and convoys of motor transports, lights full on, heading towards Lübeck.[1]

This was not the only indication that the Germans were on the move. On 4 April reconnaissance had spotted some 60 merchant ships in the mouth of the Elbe sailing north, and two days later had photographed a big naval force, including the battle cruisers *Scharnhorst* and *Gneisenau*, at anchor off Wilhelmshaven. The following morning, 7 April, these warships were no longer there. Coastal Command Hudsons then picked them up as they steered north, so enabling 107 Squadron, under their exceptionally fearless and dynamic leader, Wing Commander Basil Embry,* to follow on with a strike. Despite fierce flak which damaged every aircraft in the formation, the Blenheims got in their attack.[2] But their bombs all missed, and the German flotilla, carrying – as it proved – the forces for the seizure of Trondheim and Narvik, continued on its way unscathed.

Taken together with the facts that Britain and France, after months of confused counsels, were about to mine Norwegian waters to disrupt the flow of high-grade iron ore to Germany, and that Hitler would doubtless be aware of this and contemplating some pre-emptive move,

---

* Later Air Chief Marshal Sir Basil Embry, AOC-in-C Fighter Command, 1949–53.

these events might reasonably have suggested that the Germans were about to invade Norway. The Admiralty, however, did not make this deduction. Reports from agents and the embassy in Copenhagen pointed in the same direction as the reconnaissance information, but the First Lord, Winston Churchill, held the firm belief that an invasion of Norway was beyond Germany's powers.[3] Many of his senior advisers felt likewise. As late as 25 March the head of the Northern Department at the Foreign Office, commenting on a warning of Hitler's intentions sent in by the Air Attaché at Stockholm, minuted: 'I wish I could believe his story. German intervention in Scandinavia is just what we want.'[4]

So it came about that when, on 8 April, a Sunderland of Coastal Command in vile weather spotted part of the German force off Norway and reported it as heading west, not north, preconceived ideas in the Admiralty took precedence over the weight of the evidence. The signs were read as an attempt, led by the *Scharnhorst* and *Gneisenau*, to break out into the Atlantic for a foray against Britain's sea lifelines.[5] Lying in the Forth were cruisers containing Allied troops ready to occupy strategic points in Norway if the Germans, in response to the minelaying, showed any signs of moving into Scandinavia. On the First Sea Lord's orders these troops were now turned out of their vessels, which then set out to join the main Home Fleet in heading for the wrong part of the North Sea.[6]

Meanwhile the Germans, by a masterly combination of great surprise (including airborne landings) and a little treachery, began from first light on 9 April to take possession of Norway's major ports and airfields. At the same time, to safeguard their communications and gain convenient bases for the Luftwaffe, they occupied Denmark.

The Allies at once determined to send help to the Norwegians, but inevitably some days elapsed before it could arrive. Meanwhile the first task given to Bomber Command was to harry the German naval forces and supply vessels. But the difficulty of finding and hitting ships at sea four hundred miles or so from the British air bases had become all too plain from earlier operations and was not lessened now by persistent low cloud which created heavy icing on aircraft surfaces. Already, in the days preceding the invasion, Bomber Command had tried three times, unsuccessfully, to bomb German warships. Now, on 9, 10 and 11 April, it tried again – but still in vain. The total reward was one ammunition ship sunk – by 102 Squadron – during a night search on 11/12 April by 23 Whitleys.[7]

This meagre result was certainly not the fault of the aircrews involved. At this stage in the war they were almost all 'regulars', burningly eager for the most part to get down to serious operations. Guy Gibson, on 83 Squadron Hampdens, expressed the mood:

> Then [in September 1939] we were not ready; now, in a limited way we were. We could fly at night; we could navigate fairly accurately; we could drop a bomb within half a mile from 12,000 ft; we could even land on the beam . . . To say that we were keen would be a masterpiece of understatement. For months we had hung around: for months we had waited for this. We had waited so long we were all completely brassed off. It was not unnatural, therefore, that the chance to fly on operations seemed, that day, to be the sweetest thing in the world.[8]

The crews' keenness was there, but advanced navigational aids were not. The targets were distant and fleeting, the weather usually hostile. Above all, the British bombers were too lightly armed, and too slow, to achieve results in the face of German fighters. On 12 April the sharp lessons of the early-daylight operations against the German fleet were again driven home. In the biggest raid of the war thus far, 23 Blenheims, 36 Wellingtons and 24 Hampdens took off to find and attack warships off Kristiansand. Only one of the Hampdens saw – and unsuccessfully bombed – a target. All the rest were foiled by the weather or by German fighters, who shot down six Hampdens and three Wellingtons at a cost of five of their own number.[9] No. 50 Hampden squadron, packed in tight formation near the deck, suffered grievously. Gibson later recorded:

> The Germans were flying in Messerschmitt 110 fighters, which have one gun which can fire sideways. Their mode of attack was to fly in formation with the Hampdens perhaps fifty yards out and slightly to the front, and pick off the outside man with their one gun, aiming with a no-deflection shot at the pilot. The bomber boys could do nothing about it: they just had to sit there and wait to be shot down. If they broke away they were immediately pounced on by three Messerschmitt 109s waiting in the background. If they stayed, the pilot received a machine-gun serenade in his face. One by one they were hacked down from the wing man inwards. Watts [the CO] said it was a terrible sight to see them bursting into flames at about twenty feet, then cartwheeling one wing into the cold sea.[10]

For Portal at Bomber Command, this operation was decisive. Thereafter he used the Hampdens and Wellingtons, like the Whitleys, only at night.

By the close of 12 April all the major enemy warships – except the cruisers *Blücher* and *Königsberg*, sunk respectively by the Norwegians and Fleet Air Arm Skuas – were back in German ports. Bomber Command's effort had failed. At least, however, there was soon one gleam of success on the horizon. Harris, the AOC of 5 Group, when serving in the Air Ministry before the war had sponsored the production of a magnetic sea-mine for dropping from aircraft. He subsequently wrote: '. . . it was discovered that my particular aircraft, the Hampden, was the only aircraft that could carry the mine; this was exactly what might have been expected of it, since in general it would do little and carry little that our specification had demanded of it, but it could do a great deal else, including the minelaying.'[11] On the night of 13/14 April Harris's Hampdens began minelaying in Danish and German waters to initiate an offensive which even in the short space of the Norwegian campaign sank 12 German ships,[12] and which continued with increasing effect throughout the war. It went under the pleasant code-name GARDENING, the mines themselves being 'vegetables', and the areas to be sown named after various plants and fishes. It was not easy work. The flights were long; and the 1500-lb mines, attached to a parachute, had to be dropped from only 600 feet or so above the water from an aircraft travelling at no more than 200 mph – otherwise they broke up. In bad weather the Hampdens often had to return with their mines still on.

With the Germans firmly established in southern Norway but as yet occupying only isolated outposts at Trondheim in the centre and Narvik in the north, the Allies aimed to recover these two ports and then assist the hard-pressed Norwegian Army in the south. Their landings, on either side of Trondheim and near Narvik, began on 14 April. The troops involved were to receive only the scantiest of fighter support – occasionally from carrier aircraft, very briefly from 263 Squadron of Gladiator biplanes, which tried to operate from a frozen lake in the central sector, and later, and more effectively, from No. 263 and a Hurricane Squadron (No. 46) in the north. The new task of Bomber Command thus became to damp down the activity of the 600–700 German aircraft which were ranging freely over Norway and rapidly bringing Norwegian resistance in the south close to collapse.

In the month between Hitler's invasion of Norway and his invasion of France and the Low Countries, Bomber Command raided the German-held airfields almost every twenty-four hours, usually with forces of from six to 12 aircraft. At no stage was it permitted to attack airfields (or for that matter, ports) in Germany itself, from which much of the German effort was coming; and at the outset attack by machine gun only was enjoined until it became clear – by 11 April – that the Germans themselves had dropped bombs on Norwegian airfields.

The airfields of most immediate importance to the campaign were those near Stavanger (Sola), Trondheim (Vaernes) and Oslo (Kjeller and Fornebu), together with Aalborg and Rye in Denmark. Most of these, however, were at extreme range – 700 miles or more – with the consequence that the main weight of attack fell on Stavanger-Sola. Even this involved a round trip of some 900 miles, but the airfield was on the coast and could be approached directly from the sea. As for results, whatever was accomplished was painfully insufficient to prevent heavy air attack on both the Norwegians and the Allied forces which had landed north and south of Trondheim. It did, however, help their escape by making Stavanger-Sola unserviceable except for emergency landings during the critical days of the evacuation – 28 Wellingtons and Whitleys attacked it on the night of 30 April/1 May, while 22 other aircraft attacked Aalborg and Rye,[13] and the assault was maintained during the next forty-eight hours.

The difficulties the crews encountered in attacking the more distant airfields are well described in G. L. 'Larry' Donnelly's *The Whitley Boys*. A wireless operator/air-gunner with No. 10 Squadron, Donnelly was detailed for a raid on Oslo-Kjeller airfield on the night of 18/19 April.

Leaving Dishforth at 20.15 hours we headed for Norway, hoping that the weather would be kind to us for a change, but it wasn't to be. As we proceeded over the North Sea cloud-cover increased, and the occasions when we could see the clear sky above and the sea below became less frequent . . .

. . . By the time we were on our way up Oslo fjord the weather conditions were very bad, and worsened as we attempted to find Kjeller airfield. The whole area was obscured by snowstorms and although we descended, sometimes as low as 500 feet, we were unable to locate the target. After searching the area for as long as our fuel stocks allowed we gave it up, and, frozen and fed up, set course for base. It was some thirty minutes after landing that any feeling returned to my numb nether regions. Only two of the other aircraft involved in our part of the operation were able to bomb . . .[14]

Donnelly's aircraft got home – unlike another Whitley, of 77 Squadron, briefed that night for a raid on shipping in Trondheim fjord. Its story serves for that of hundreds of Bomber Command airmen who, during the war, had to ditch in the North Sea. Some miles out from the coast, an engine had failed, and the aircraft lost height. The pilot, Raymond Chance, wrote a vivid account of what then happened:

Came to the conclusion ditching was inevitable and asked the crew who could swim. Two couldn't, so I told them to stick near me when we touched down . . . In an effort to maintain height everything movable was thrown out, but to no avail. Told everyone for ditching to get near the back door and brace themselves against the bulkhead. I went down the fuselage and chopped off the rear door with the fire axe, then went back to the pilot's seat again. . . . Then suddenly the aircraft, which had been in a shallow gliding attitude, dived steeply towards the sea.

I knew we had only seconds to live, and trying to be as calm as possible, told the others we were levelling off. Then bang! She blew up and I was flung somewhere in the wreckage in the nose and knocked unconscious. I hallucinated . . .

. . . Suddenly the reality of the situation hit me . . . The engine and the wing were on fire with the fuel spreading from the ruptured tanks. I could see no one in the aircraft and was about to jump into the sea when I saw the dinghy still folded lying down towards the tail inside the fuselage . . . I knew the men were outside somewhere but hadn't got the dinghy. I dived for it like a rugger tackle, dragged it to the door, and . . . flung it with all my strength into the dark towards the tail and immediately plunged after it.

My Mae West shot me to the surface; I found the dinghy, pulled the cord, and it started to inflate. As it did the two who I understood couldn't swim . . . started to climb in – think they had been hanging on the tail. We were joined by . . . the bomb-aimer, who I was told was now hanging on the other side of the dinghy. I didn't know then that I had a crushed ankle, a broken leg, and a hair-line skull fracture.

There then followed the tense, desperate moments of superhuman effort to gain release from the cords of the dinghy, push it away from the flames of the sinking aircraft, and give succour to Pilot Officer Hall who was some fifty yards away crying for help.

I told the survivors I would have to wait to get my breath back before I would be able to get back into the dinghy. It may have been fifteen minutes before I could clamber in. Eventually I was hauled in and collapsed inside the rim of the dinghy. I hadn't the strength to lift my head out of the water in the bottom and was saved from drowning by one of the survivors putting his boot under my chin. I heard Pilot Officer Hall shouting, but more faintly, and conceived the idea of going over the side and trying to drag the dinghy towards him. I got up on one elbow, but fell back exhausted. I had the agony of listening to him drown . . .[15]

During the night, to keep up warmth and spirits, Chance led his crew in singing 'Roll out the Barrel'. Then, just before dawn came the miraculous appearance of a British destroyer. It had been chasing a U-boat, and its searchlight beamed on to the dinghy, at first mistaken for a floating mine. A whaler promptly rowed over and picked up the distressed airmen, who then summoned up their last strength to climb a rope-ladder on to the destroyer. There was no doctor aboard, but the crew laid out mattresses for the rescued men, wrapped Chance's foot, by then black and barely recognisable, in cotton wool, and thoughtfully placed a bottle of whisky and two hundred cigarettes by his side.

In his (unpublished) despatch on the Norwegian campaign[16] Portal stated that between 4 April and 10 May Bomber Command had flown 882 sorties, dropped some 150 tons of bombs and 169 mines, lost 31 aircraft through enemy action, and shot down 11 German planes. Considering the danger and difficulty of attacking warships, the distances covered, and the complete local air superiority enjoyed by the Luftwaffe, his overall loss of just under 3.7 per cent of sorties was remarkably light. By comparison with what was to come, the bomber effort, averaging about 24 sorties a day, was extremely small – but so then was the Command itself.* The scale of operation was certainly in conformity with the Air Ministry's general instructions to Portal – that while he was to do everything possible to help in Norway, he was also to conserve the bomber force for the moment when Hitler would launch his grand assault on France.

This policy of 'conservation', incidentally, seems neither to have been explained to, nor (in their happy ignorance) appreciated by, aircrews. When an order came for three aircraft at Scampton to take part in a raid on Aalborg, the first thought of the eager warrior Guy Gibson was 'Why not the whole squadron?'[18]

Portal's despatch recommended a number of improvements. These

---

* The average availability of serviceable aircraft with crews during April 1940 was about 200.[17]

included better radio methods to link a shadowing aircraft with a striking force, a better weapon than the High Explosive Semi-Armour-Piercing bomb (which lost accuracy by having to be dropped from too great a height), and a specialised anti-shipping bomber force, perhaps equipped with a properly designed dive-bomber.* He also urged that to lessen the strain on aircrew undertaking long flights over sea, the Air Ministry should provide the best possible distress and rescue equipment. It is clear from the despatch that coordination between Bomber Command and Coastal Command, and the relationship between Bomber Command and the Air Ministry, both needed consideration. A pointed passage ran: 'The control of the operations of my Command was virtually assumed by the Air Ministry. Although my advice was often sought, I was not responsible for the selection of objectives, nor for deciding the effort to be employed against each.'[19]

Portal did not in fact emphasise the three biggest lessons of the campaign – either because they were too obvious or because they were outside his immediate province. These were the new dimension introduced into warfare by the Germans' use of paratroops and large-scale air transport; the need for the British authorities to coordinate their information from all sources and establish a stronger intelligence structure; and the folly of despatching military expeditions without adequate air support.

Despite the fact that Bomber Command had been able to achieve little, Portal himself emerged from the campaign with an undiminished, possibly enhanced, reputation. Basil Embry wrote of Portal's visit to Wattisham during the campaign: 'He made a great impression on the aircrew, to each of whom he spoke personally. He was alive to our problems and it seemed clear from the questions he asked that he was completely master of the situation. I wondered whether he appreciated the tremendous impact of his personality on the squadron's personnel, and the confidence which he inspired.'[20]

This confidence was felt in full measure by Portal's headquarters staff. Hugh Pughe Lloyd, Group Captain Operations, himself destined after the war to take charge of Bomber Command, began to keep a diary in April. His entries were characteristically forthright. He began with an assessment of Portal's predecessor: 'Ludlow . . . most knowledgeable, very sound on paper . . . As a Commander, a hopeless bungler and fuddler . . . unable to make up his mind, and will change

---

* The British had not yet experienced the remarkable accuracy of the German Ju 87 'Stuka' dive-bomber. Fortunately this was offset by its extreme vulnerability.

it five times in as many minutes . . . Never leaves an item to Group Commanders . . . On the other hand, he can be a very big man . . . His main trouble . . . he fussed the Commanders – they never knew where they stood.'

With obvious relief, on 15 April Lloyd recorded: 'I like the new Commander, Portal: young, friendly, active, and makes up his mind quickly. Not unapproachable like Mount Everest (Ludlow).' Twelve days later he enlarged on this theme: 'What a difference – Portal and Ludlow-Hewitt. No fuss, no bother, no changes of mind, no vacillation, no peevishness or excitement. I have never served with anyone as indecisive as Ludlow-Hewitt. The Staff would have been frantic had L-H stayed for this party, and the Groups would have been crazy . . .'[21]

With all its deficiencies, Bomber Command was in safe hands, as it needed to be. It had come through the trial of the Norwegian campaign more or less intact, to be confronted now with an ordeal far greater.

5

Against the Flood: France

After Norway – France, and the tragedy of the Battles.
On 10 May 1940, when Hitler at last attacked in the West, the Advanced Air Striking Force in France consisted of ten bomber squadrons and two – soon to be three – fighter squadrons. Two of the bomber squadrons had by then received Blenheims, but the rest were still on Battles.*

The Battle, with which the AASF is forever associated, was designed by the Fairey Aviation Company to meet an Air Ministry specification of 1932. The first Battles came into service in mid-1937, and within a year there were no fewer than 15 squadrons of them in Bomber Command. This unwontedly large provision of one bomber type happened partly because initial impressions of the aircraft were favourable; partly because Battles were easy to produce – Austin Motors manufactured nearly half the total output under the 'shadow factory' scheme; and partly because repeat orders were placed with Austin to keep their workforce in being while more advanced aircraft were in preparation.[1] By the outbreak of war Battles were reckoned obsolescent, but they were still by far the most numerous aircraft in Bomber Command. Including immediate reserves, the Command held twice as many of them as it did of Wellingtons, or Whitleys, or Hampdens.

* In January the AASF had been severed from Bomber Command and linked with the RAF Component of the British Expeditionary Force under a new higher command known as British Air Forces in France. The AASF's fate is recounted here because Bomber Command had not only given it birth but was soon to receive back its remnants.

When the Battles first appeared they seemed stunningly modern. All-metal stressed-skin monoplanes with retractable undercarriages and carrying a three-man crew, they were sleekness itself compared with the Hart and Hind biplanes they replaced. They were also much faster – at 240 mph, half as fast again – and they carried twice the bomb-load twice as far. 'At last,' exclaimed the journalist-pundit C. G. Grey, 'the RAF have a real aeroplane.' But it soon became clear that their single engine (the fine new Rolls-Royce Merlin) gave barely enough power in the climb, that there was not room for the observer and the air-gunner to be fully active at the same time, and that the two guns – a fixed Browning .303 forward and a manually aimed Vickers 'K' .303 aft – were utterly inadequate for defence. This last weakness was shown up in the very first month of the war when Me 109s on one occasion shot down two out of three, and on another occasion four out of five, Battles engaged on reconnaissance near the German frontier.[2]

Just as there were efforts during the month before the German attack to improve the aircraft of Bomber Command – notably by streamlining (which gave the Blenheim an extra 15 mph), adding more guns and armour, and coating petrol tanks with self-sealing dope, so there were efforts to improve the armament of the Battle. With the pilot firing only a fixed gun forward, and the gunner at the rear of the long cockpit greatly restricted in his field of fire, defence against attack from below was virtually nonexistent. In a desperate effort to remedy this, Fairey's designed an additional gun position, the description of which in the Bomber Command Headquarters Record Book amply explains why it was not widely adopted: 'To enable the gunner to fire the gun backward behind the tail, the gun swivels on a mounting fixed in the bombing aperture and is made capable of firing upside down, being provided with extra sights which will work in this position. The gunner wears a special harness enabling him to assume an almost upside-down position . . .'[3]

The work which the AASF and Bomber Command were expected to do in the event of a German attack had been much discussed between the British and the French. The task of the AASF was quite clear: it was to collaborate with the Allied armies in halting the invasion, mainly by attacking communication bottlenecks on the probable lines of the German advance. Also given this role, and also under the operational control of Air Marshal A. S. ('Ugly') Barratt at HQ British Air Forces in France, were the seven Blenheim squadrons of 2 Group, Bomber Command, together with two of 4 Group's Whitley squadrons. The latter were expected to deliver night attacks on German communications farther back.

The employment of the rest of Bomber Command – the Wellingtons, the Hampdens and the remaining Whitleys – was not so readily agreed. Barratt had no operational control over these squadrons: he could request their help, but not demand it. Very reluctantly the French (ever fearful of retaliation, and at heart wanting all the Allied air effort to be applied near the battlefield) had accepted, on 23 April 1940, the British Air Staff's preferred plan: that a German invasion of France or the Low Countries should be the moment for launching the RAF 'heavies' against German industrial targets, and particularly oil plants in the Ruhr.[4] Direct flight over Belgium would then for the first time become possible: the Germans would not have had time to organise forward air defences: and oil, essential for military success, was known to be a weak spot in the German war economy. This Anglo-French agreement was clear enough. The question was whether it would stick when the crunch came.

As the planning progressed, Portal at Bomber Command became increasingly concerned that his Blenheims might be called upon to attack the advancing enemy columns, rather than communications. Two days before the German invasion he wrote to the Chief of the Air Staff, Air Chief Marshal Sir Cyril Newall, in exceptionally strong terms:

> I am convinced that the proposed employment of these units is fundamentally unsound, and that if it is persisted in it is likely to have disastrous consequences . . . at the enemy's chosen moment for the advance the area concerned will be literally swarming with enemy fighters, and we should be lucky if we see again as many as half the aircraft we send out each time . . . I can say with certainty that really accurate bombing under the conditions I visualize is not to be expected, and I feel justified in expressing serious doubt whether the attacks of fifty Blenheims, based on information necessarily some hours out of date, are likely to make as much difference to the ultimate course of the war as to justify the losses I expect them to sustain.[5]

In the light of even the operational experience then available, Portal's own preferred plan, that the Blenheims should deliver harassing attacks against German industry when there was suitable cloud cover, seems singularly unlikely to have achieved much in the way of results. But his warning about high losses among the Blenheims if they operated directly against the German advance was more than justified; and anything he said about the Blenheims could have been said still more strongly about the Battles.

The German onslaught on 10 May, by attacking France through neutral Holland and Belgium, carefully avoided the powerful defences of the Maginot Line. The offensive combined two main armoured thrusts, each supported by concentrations of air power: one in the north through Maastricht, the other farther south through Luxembourg and the Ardennes. The AASF's first task that day was to attack the more southerly German columns, in Luxembourg. Thirty-two Battles, in two raids, went in at low level – 250 feet – to avoid interception by fighters. They met instead anti-aircraft fire so intense that it shot down 13 of the 32, and damaged all the rest.

The next day an early German air raid caught one of the two AASF Blenheim squadrons – No. 114 – on the ground, effectively putting it out of action for the rest of the campaign. Later, eight Battles tried again to attack German columns entering Luxembourg. Seven were shot down, the eighth crashed on return.

On 12 May the more northerly thrust seemed to be posing the greater danger. Soon after dawn nine Blenheims of 139 Squadron took off in search of a column on the Maastricht–Tongres road. Their orders this time were to attack at 6000 feet to avoid the worst of the light flak. They met fighters. Only two of the Blenheims survived.

Later in the morning came the much-described but ill-documented attack by Battles of 12 Squadron against two undemolished bridges over the Albert Canal, west of Maastricht. The area was known to be a hotbed of flak and fighters, and Barratt called for six volunteer crews. All the squadron pilots volunteered, and five aircraft eventually took off. Four succumbed to the enemy defences. The fifth, heavily damaged, and without two of the crew, who had been ordered to bale out, struggled back to a forced landing.[6]

For their extreme gallantry in successfully pressing home their attack – for in a dive from 6000 feet they broke one of the bridges – Flying Officer Donald Garland, the pilot of the leading aircraft, and his observer, Sergeant Tom Gray, received posthumous awards of the Victoria Cross. They were the first members of the Royal Air Force in the Second World War to be so honoured. Regrettably, the authorities found no way of recognising the third member of the crew, the wireless operator/air-gunner, Leading Aircraftman Roy Reynolds.

To coincide with this heroic action against the Albert Canal bridges, two Blenheim squadrons of Bomber Command attacked bridges and road junctions in Maastricht. Twenty-four aircraft took off. Only 14 returned.

These bare figures show that the work being demanded of the Battle and Blenheim crews was virtually suicidal. Two days were enough for Barratt and Newall to realise that it could not continue. Counting aircraft destroyed or written off, 40 per cent of the Battle sorties had been lost on 10 May, 100 per cent on 11 May, 62 per cent on 12 May. Within forty-eight hours the number of serviceable bombers in the AASF had shrunk from 135 to 72.[7]

But with the French Ninth Army opposite the southern thrust collapsing, the pressure from the French High Command to persist in such attacks became irresistible. The climax came on 14 May, when the AASF was called on for an all-out effort against the bridgeheads which the Germans had established the previous day over the Meuse. In a series of raids during the afternoon, 63 Battles and eight Blenheims strove to bomb bridges and columns near Sedan. More than half – 40 – went down to the German flak and fighters.[8] One crew member – Aircraftman First Class Leonard Clarke, wireless operator/air-gunner of 12 Squadron – was on his very first operation. He baled out from his blazing aircraft – to become a prisoner of war for the next five years.[9]

Reduced within four days to less than a quarter of its initial strength, the AASF was saved from extinction by a drastic change of policy. For the rest of the campaign the Battles bombed mainly at night, attacking communication centres with indeterminate results but gratifyingly light losses. In the daylight raids from 10 to 14 May, one Battle had been lost from every two sorties. In the night attacks which followed, from 15 May to 5 June, the loss was one in every 200.[10]

Crisis point for the Blenheims of Bomber Command soon followed. In the late afternoon of 14 May, following the disastrous raids a few hours earlier by the AASF, Wing Commander Basil Embry led two squadrons from Wattisham against the bridgeheads near Sedan. Fighter protection over the target area was supplied by RAF Component Hurricanes, and for once worked well. But there was still the flak. 'We began our bomb run on to the target,' wrote Embry later, 'and once again we were met by a terrific barrage of fire. By the law of averages our survival was impossible. The enemy certainly knew how to spread this means of destruction into the air and it came up all sizes, shapes and colours, and in such density that no aircraft could escape damage except by the grace of God.'[11] Five of the Blenheims were shot down, two more made forced landings, and at the end of the day Embry's squadron – 107 – had not a single aircraft serviceable.

The deciding blow came three days later. On 17 May No. 82 Squadron took off to attack columns near Gembloux. Fighter protection had been promised over the target area, but Me 109s intercepted. Eleven out of the 12 Blenheims failed to return,[12] and only the exceptional determination of the squadron commander, Wing Commander the Earl of Bandon, kept the squadron in being. Within forty-eight hours he led his remaining six aircraft on a night attack.*

One of the survivors of these desperate days, Peter Sarll, a pilot of 21 Squadron, wrote many years later of his Blenheim raid on 11 May: 'I don't remember how many we lost then, the awful moments I do remember were going back into the village of Watton where the young wives were waiting for their husbands who had not returned, and never would.'[13] Of 14 May he wrote:

I do not think that anyone who did not experience what we were called upon to perform this day could ever visualize the tremendous courage of our people, so many of whom died. We were three to a crew, twelve crews to a squadron, and our lives depended upon one another. We reached out to one another for strength and support: when one was low, we tried to boost him up. I remember seeing many of them vomiting before getting into the aircraft – a sure sign of physical and mental exhaustion. There was, too, the toll of the stand-bys, at 30-minute readiness in the aircraft, taxying to take-off, and then being recalled because the square that was chalked on the observer's map was the position of our own troops; and so back to dispersal, switch-off, and then that awful waiting again . . . Having a second tour on Lancasters and experiencing the smoothness of the higher organization and its tremendous efficiency, I used to look back on the old Blenheim days and wonder how any of us survived.[14]

The massacre of 82 Squadron on 17 May struck the final blow to

* The Earl of Bandon – in RAF parlance 'the Abandoned Earl', or more simply 'Paddy' – was one of many colourful characters, like the Atcherley brothers, from the pre-war RAF. Of the numerous stories told about him, one of the best comes from his time after the war as a commander of Allied forces in Europe. At the ceremonial opening of a swimming pool in Germany he ended his speech with the words 'And I hereby declare this pool open' – and dived into the water in his full Service dress.

the Air Staff's long-standing belief in the self-defending bomber formation. Complementary to this had been the conviction that fighter escort would be unnecessary. That belief had already been qualified by arrangements, in nearly all these operations, to provide fighter protection over the target area. But the 'protection' and the attacks had rarely coincided: either the handful of fighters available failed to arrive, or survive, or the bombers were intercepted before they could reach their objective. It became apparent that the fighters had to be with the bombers most or all of the way – and that meant far more fighters, and fighters of longer range, than the RAF as yet possessed.

Paradoxically, however, as the situation became worse in France and Belgium, so the Blenheim raids from England could receive better protection. By 21 May the panzer thrust through the Ardennes and across the Meuse had reached the mouth of the Somme at Abbeville, completely severing the main French armies south of this penetration from the British Expeditionary Force (BEF), the 1st French Army, and the Belgians on the north. Soon the BEF was left with only one hope – evacuation from Dunkirk. But as the struggle moved closer to the Channel coast, so it came – just – within the range of home-based Hurricanes and Spitfires. Escort – close escort – by fighters was now 'on' – if they could be spared from the as yet untried air defences of Britain.

While Guderian's tanks were forcing the Meuse the British War Cabinet was debating the merits of launching an air offensive against Germany. As already indicated, the Air Staff had long held the view that the moment for 'taking off the gloves' – which at that time meant nothing more than attacking precise industrial targets in the knowledge that stray bombs would inadvertently kill civilians – would be when the Germans invaded Holland or Belgium. But – the Cabinet wondered – were the Germans themselves killing enough civilians to justify such a course? All doubts were set at rest when the Germans bombed Rotterdam on 14 May. The following day the War Cabinet gave the go-ahead for the Air Staff's – and Bomber Command's – long-favoured plan.[15]

Up to this time the two squadrons of Whitleys allocated to 'collaboration' in the land battle had been bombing by night marshalling yards and communications in Germany, but only to the west of the Rhine. It was thought that the Germans would understand this to be fully legitimate, and non-provocative. Now this limitation was cast aside, and what was then considered a full-scale assault was aimed by night against oil plants, self-illuminating targets like coke ovens and blast furnaces, and marshalling yards and communications east of the Rhine. It was a period of bright moon, which at that time, before night-fighting was far advanced, favoured the bomber; and as an additional spur to the attack Sir Hugh Dowding of Fighter Command had pleaded that an air assault on Germany, by provoking the Germans into retaliation against Britain, would be the best means of relieving the French of the crippling attentions of the Luftwaffe.[16] (That way, too, Dowding could justifiably keep his remaining fighter squadrons in England, rather than see more of them wrenched away to be squandered – as he rightly thought – in France.)

So, on the night 15/16 May, the strategic offensive against Germany that was to last five years began. An unwontedly large force for the time – 96 Wellingtons, Whitleys and Hampdens – took off to attack industrial targets east of the Rhine. They departed, as was then the practice, at various intervals, the crews working out their own route and taking off throughout the night – some choosing to go early, some (perhaps in order not to miss a party or a 'date') much later. At intervals they then arrived, or failed to arrive, over their objectives. Of the 78 aircraft given oil installations as their primary target, only 23 (who managed several hits) claimed to have found them. For various reasons 16 failed to attack any objective at all.[17]

What was done that night had very little effect on German oil production, and still less on the advance of the German armies. Nor did it yet in any way divert German air attack from France to Britain. Its significance, disappointing to its advocates but still important, was purely that it was a beginning, and an inexpensive one. It did some small damage to the enemy, at a cost of only one British aircraft (which crashed into a hillside in France).

The intention was to persist with similar operations. By 16 May, however, the military situation in France had become so critical that Barratt, Lord Gort (C-in-C BEF) and the French were all pleading for Bomber Command's 'heavies' to concentrate on German communications directly behind the battlefronts. Against the strong pleadings of Portal at Bomber Command, who thought it would ruin the 'oil plan', most of the Wellingtons and Hampdens, as well as the Whitleys, were directed from 17 May to attack the Meuse crossings and other bottlenecks. This they duly did, with some, but only very brief, effect. Some of the bombers, however, continued to be sent against oil – in fact the major proportion when moonless nights began on 30 May, and Portal pointed out the difficulty of finding bridges in the misty French river valleys. (Targets in the Ruhr, it may be said, were not much easier; one pilot claimed to have made eight runs over Gelsenkirchen without finding the oil plant.)[18]

So it came about that on two nights during the height of the Dunkirk evacuation Bomber Command put forth its maximum effort not against communications in France but against oil in Germany. Hampered as it was by its limitations in size and navigational equipment, the Command, it would seem, was also suffering at this time from cross-currents in bombing policy.

There is evidence in the German army records that the British bombing attacks in the week before, and during, the Dunkirk evacuation did have a delaying effect. This applies to the night operations of the 'heavies' farther back, but even more to the work of the 2 Group Blenheims by day in the forward areas. With Fighter Command able to supply escort and to fly offensive patrols along the line of the French Channel ports, the Germans became aware for the first time that they were not completely masters of the sky. British troops, heavily bombed and unaware of any air activity which took place outside their own immediate view, returned reviling the RAF for its absence. It had, however, been very much present – not only in the Fighter Command patrols but also in the repeated attacks by the Blenheims against German columns and communications. The delays these imposed on German progress rarely lasted more than an hour or two; but in the context of holding back the enemy until Operation DYNAMO – the evacuation from Dunkirk – could be completed, every hour counted.

All told, in the fortnight from 20 May, when the BEF began its withdrawal, until the end of the evacuation on 3–4 June, Bomber Command Blenheims flew nearly 750 sorties to delay the German advance. They did this with impressive economy. In the opening seven days of the campaign, from 10–17 May, 39 Blenheims had been lost from 181 sorties – over 20 per cent. Now, operating directly to help the BEF, they lost only 16 in the 750 sorties – little more than 2 per cent.[19] Three things accounted for this dramatically improved performance: losses among the German fighters as the campaign progressed, the dilution of the Germans' flak defences as their armies spread through France, and – above all – the provision of stronger fighter support.

*   *   *

It was during one of the Blenheim attacks on 27 May that the dauntless Basil Embry, who had brought home a damaged aeroplane on fifteen occasions in the previous fortnight, was shot down. His ensuing adventures included escaping, though wounded, from a prisoner-of-war column, knocking out his gaolers when recaptured, hiding in a manure heap, pretending to be a refugee Irish Republican terrorist and speaking Urdu when told to talk in Gaelic, and eventually reaching the south of France on a bicycle.[20] His experiences were to be an education to later aircrew in the possibilities of escape and evasion.

The Battle of France now loomed ahead. Bomber Command faced two tasks: continuing 'collaboration' with the armies, and the attack on German industry.

The new German offensive struck south across the Somme on 5 June. The French were at once in trouble, and, as before, the Blenheims and the AASF Battles strove to attack columns and communications. In the rapidly heightening crisis the Battles were called upon to resume daylight attacks. From then on, with better fighter protection – two more fighter squadrons had joined the AASF's original three – they lost 9 per cent of sorties:[21] grievous enough, but less murderous than the 50 per cent of 10–14 May.

Within a week, however, the German advance was threatening the AASF bases. The Battles hastily left – somehow finding space in the by now fantastically overcrowded airfields around Nantes and Saumur. Some flew a last operation on 15 June, then all that remained were ordered back to England. About 60 of them, the majority unfit for further operations, took off for Abingdon,[22] where they became the nucleus of Bomber Command's immediately re-formed No. 1 Group.

On one of the last Battle operations, on 14 June, Flight Lieutenant Ronald Hawkins, of 105 Squadron, was shot down attacking tanks in a wood near Evreux. He hid his parachute, walked south at night by the stars, was captured, escaped, stole tools from a French army camp, lost his trousers and his money in swimming a river, and after eight days reached Trouville. Making his way west along the coast in search of a small boat he eventually, after another eight days, found a canvas canoe at Carteret and rowed the fifteen miles across to Jersey. That very day German forces arrived to occupy the island, so he rowed back to France, stole a bicycle, entered the unoccupied zone and by 11 July reached Vichy. Finding little help he made for Marseille, left there hurriedly when the police began rounding up foreigners, climbed over the Pyrenees, was captured by Spanish soldiers, and finally secured release and transfer to Gibraltar. On 7 October, four months after he had extricated himself from his parachute, he stepped out of a Sunderland on to his native soil.[23]

Of such stuff were the crews of the Battles.*

After a rest of only one day – of unfavourable weather – Bomber Command's Blenheims on 5 June resumed their attacks on German troops and communications. Until the end of the campaign they flew an average of about 50 sorties a day, including a special effort on 6 June to help the 51st (Highland) Division on its brave and fruitless march to St Valéry. From 14 June they also attacked German-held airfields – such as those at Flushing, Schipol, Merville and Rouen – in the hope of damping down German night-raiding over England, which had begun in a scattered way on 1/2 June. With the same object, a few Blenheims were also sent, under cloud cover, to bomb airfields and aircraft factories in north-west Germany – with less success.

Like the Battles, the Blenheims suffered fewer losses in the later stages of the campaign. Between 10 and 18 May they lost over 20 per cent of sorties. Between 20 May and 4 June, including the Dunkirk period, when fighter protection was at its strongest, they lost only 3 per cent. In the final phase, and overall, they lost something over 7 per cent.[24]

All told, during the German onslaught against France and the Low Countries, the AASF lost, from all causes, 137 Battles and 37 Blenheims. Number 2 Group, Bomber Command, lost 98 Blenheims.[25] Together, this was the equivalent of about 15 squadrons lost to Bomber Command – in terms of aircraft, half its strength at the outset of the campaign. For Bomber Command's hopes, and plans, of expansion, it was indeed fortunate that the Germans completed their conquest within no more than six weeks.

During the Battle of France most of the 'heavies', too, attacked the German armies' lines of communication. At first a lesser number also operated against oil plants in Germany, but by 8 June the

---

* Three years later Ron Hawkins was shot down and killed while leading No. 3 Squadron in an attack on a petrol refinery in Ghent.

situation in France was deemed so critical that oil disappeared from the target-list.[26] For the next nine nights everything was put into the attack on communications, with a peak of over 160 sorties by the Wellingtons, Whitleys and Hampdens on 13/14 June. 'Communications', however, covered a wide spectrum. In addition to the bombing of road and river crossings in France and Belgium and marshalling yards in western Germany, there were attempts to mine the Rhine and to fire forests. The Hampdens, too, kept up their by now regular quota of coastal minelaying.

It was on a raid against the riverside docks at Duisburg on 8/9 June that perhaps the greatest of all bomber pilots, Leonard Cheshire, had an early experience of German anti-aircraft fire. He was flying 'second Dicky' – second pilot – on a 102 Squadron Whitley, and later wrote memorably how the flak came up 'bursting all round, a series of crashes and groans and jerks: sometimes bright flashes and small black mushroom puffs'.[27] As his pilot took violent evasive action and a few pieces of shell came through the fuselage, Cheshire had a momentary sinking feeling, and then:

> ... the floodgates shut. I felt a surge in my heart. The engines sounded defiant, as though they were saying 'We are the top. That is what we are built for. If there were no opposition we did not have to be so strongly built. This is our life ... give us more.'
> ... I understood suddenly the attraction, the flipping, priceless attraction of night-bombing. Without ack-ack these flights were just another cross-country: they were dull, something you might find any time, anywhere: but with ack-ack they changed into something worth having, something that only war could give. And I at least understood this much: that I was not afraid of ack-ack. I am afraid of many things, small stupid things, and God knows I have suffered real, hopeless fear – but I am not afraid of ack-ack.[28]

This was, of course, the reaction of a very exceptional man: few bomber pilots can have regarded flak in precisely that way. Cheshire's nerve was to remain unshaken through far worse fire than he encountered that night over Duisburg. But one has to wonder – had he been a Battle or Blenheim pilot diving through the flak over the Albert Canal or the Meuse four weeks earlier, would his feelings have been the same, and would he have survived to become the master 'Master Bomber'?

On 10 June Mussolini, greedy for easy pickings from stricken France and anxious to keep in with the victorious Hitler, entered the conflict and at once added to Bomber Command's tasks. Italy's participation had been foreseen, and on 11/12 June 34 Whitleys took off precariously from 800-yard runways in the Channel Islands, where they had refuelled, to attack the Fiat works in Turin. Seven claimed to have found and hit this primary target, four others bombed alternatives, and the rest turned back, finding the storms and severe icing over the Alps too much for their labouring engines. One of the aircrew who 'aborted', Larry Donnelly, later described his experience:

> Lightning flashed constantly around us and ice built up on the leading edges of the wings and tailplane. We were thrown about like a pea in a bucket by the turbulence, and as the conditions got progressively worse we were unable to climb to an altitude that enabled us to cross the mountains. Our effort terminated suddenly when there was a blinding flash and an audible bang, which we discovered later had been lightning strike. It resulted in an 'about turn' and we scrambled back to Guernsey after being airborne for six hours.[29]

Among those who actually got to Turin, and bombed, was Douglas Mourton of 102 Squadron. He has described how his crew made it back – not to where they intended:

> The met. forecast was completely wrong. All across France it was 10/10ths cloud, and we could not get W/T assistance. On ETA [Estimated Time of Arrival] England we dived to 500 ft without breaking cloud. We stooged around until several bursts of flak came too close for comfort, and our petrol ran out. We abandoned the aircraft not sure whether we were over France, England or the Channel. I landed two miles over the coast somewhere near Tangmere.[30]

The Whitleys' efforts were meant to be supplemented by those of a squadron of Wellingtons sent out to hastily prepared airfields in the south of France. During the afternoon of 11 June 12 aircraft duly arrived at Salon, near Marseille, and were made ready for an attack that evening. But the French, who had agreed to such operations at the Supreme War Council on 31 May, now had second thoughts as they reflected on the defencelessness of the area and the likelihood of Italian retaliation. More and more urgent telephone messages from their various military, naval and air authorities began to pour into Salon demanding the cancellation of the attack. The RAF officer in charge, however, fortified by reference to British Air Forces in France headquarters and thence to Winston Churchill, refused to abandon the project. Shortly after midnight the first Wellingtons taxied into position – whereupon a fleet of French army lorries drove on to the airfield and dispersed itself strategically to prevent take-off.[31]

Four nights later, after high-level sortings-out, eight Wellingtons did take off from Salon against the Piaggio and Anseldo works at Genoa. They met storms *en route* and found conditions impossible over Genoa. Most of them returned with their bombs undropped – a depressing conclusion to a venture which had throughout operated under a depressing code-name (HADDOCK).

It is evident from these early attempts that Bomber Command was not yet able to bomb Italy – even northern Italy – effectively. The opportunity was there: Italian air defences against night attack were rudimentary, and the morale of the Italian people fragile. But the long journey with mountains to cross and a worthwhile bomb-load to carry, was simply asking too much from the aircraft available – unless the weather, for once, was entirely favourable.

Different considerations applied to north-west Germany, where the main difficulty lay in finding any targets unless they were adjacent to water. In particular, the constant industrial haze over the Ruhr presented an obstacle only to be fully overcome later with electronic aids to navigation and bombing. There was also of course the intense anti-aircraft fire, which inhibited loitering-about looking for the target. A later, and possibly greater, deterrent was, however, not yet much in evidence. Alan Nicoll, the young observer with 44 Squadron, who did 30 'ops' by September 1940, recorded: 'Bombing by night . . . leaflet-dropping . . . minelaying . . . I saw plenty of the flak. We were hit once . . . serious damage. But never saw a single fighter.'[32]

So the night operations by the 'heavies', whatever they were achieving – which was not very much, but cannot be accurately ascertained (and could not at the time, for lack of photographic reconnaissance) – were at least being conducted inexpensively. In the six weeks from 10 May–20 June only 69 Wellingtons, Whitleys and Hampdens were lost, or less than 2 per cent of the sorties. The contrast with the daylight operations of the Battles and Blenheims could hardly be more striking.[33]

As soon as the fighting in France showed signs of ending, the Air Staff, urged on by Portal at Bomber Command, promptly switched the whole weight of attack back on to the embryonic offensive against oil. On 17/18 June, the night after the French requested an armistice, but before the fighting stopped, the Command put forth its maximum effort – no fewer than 138 aircraft – against targets in Germany. Of these, 102 operated against oil targets – and in the clear weather all but 14 claimed attacks. The rest bombed railway yards or tried to mine the Rhine. From the whole night's work only one aircraft failed to return.[34]

Guy Gibson and 83 Squadron were on one of these attacks on oil during June, against the small Hermann Goering refinery near Hanover. Like many other pilots that night, Gibson was in no doubt about the effectiveness of his attack:

> The boys came romping in and soon the foundry area was one mass of bomb bursts. One by one the buildings caught fire and glowed red like a smouldering charcoal fire 500 yards below us. But we waited, Watty and I. We had a plan. At last, when we thought that all the boys had bombed and gone home, we cut off our engines and glided towards the oil storage tanks . . . When we were about 300 feet high Watty began to let go, trying if possible to put a separate bomb in each tank. Then, seconds later, there was a woomph!, and every tank blew up. The most wonderful sight that any man could ever hope to see, especially when you are responsible for it, and even more especially when they belong to Hermann Goering.[35]

The campaign in France and the Low Countries cost the RAF dear. The losses in all Commands included over 950 aircraft, much valuable equipment, 321 pilots and 359 other aircrew killed, 115 pilots and 120 other aircrew taken prisoner. The depletion in the ranks of other Commands, which had to be filled, affected the projected build-up of Bomber Command, just as did the depletion in the ranks of Bomber Command itself.

Much of the loss had been in vain, apart from the honourable fulfilment of obligation. No effort in the air by a force the size of Bomber Command, or of Bomber Command and the AASF and the gallant French and Belgian air forces, could possibly have compensated for the military weaknesses of France as revealed during the German attack. At the same time, however, the BEF had been helped to escape, and a beginning had been made with the bombing of Germany. Above all, some vital lessons had been learned. They included the need to give more thought to ways and means of supporting the British Army from the air, the comparative safety (as earlier foreseen) of bombing by night, and recognition of the fact that the daylight bombers needed fighter escort.

6

The Flood Stemmed: Britain

'W hen did the Battle of Britain begin?' asked the American historian Alfred Gollin. 'A not unreasonable answer', he suggested, would be 'when the Wright brothers flew'.[1] Disregarding such long perspectives, the Luftwaffe reckoned they began it on 13 August 1940, while the Air Ministry, reviewing the matter after the war, decided it started a month earlier, on 10 July. For Bomber Command, however, the Battle of Britain began on 19 June.

With France defeated, the Germans faced the prospect, welcome to their army and air force but dreaded by their Navy, of invading Britain. Preparations for that would take time, but the Luftwaffe might strike straight away. On 20 June the Air Ministry instructed Bomber Command that its 'primary offensive' must be against 'those objectives which will have the most immediate effect in reducing the scale of air attack on this country'.[2] This meant that the Wellingtons, Whitleys and Hampdens were to attack, as first priority, aircraft plants in Germany, while the Blenheims concentrated on the occupied airfields in France, the Low Countries and Norway.

No Air Ministry bombing directive of 1940, however, was quite as uncomplicated as that. Communications, oil, crops, forests were all listed as other suitable objects for attack; minelaying, too, was enjoined. Also the Commander-in-Chief, Portal, was told to be prepared 'at short notice to divert the bomber force, and particularly the medium bombers, to the attack of an enemy invading force at the ports of departure, and subsequently at sea or at the points of landing in this country'.

57

In anticipation of these orders, on 19 June Portal sent 30 Blenheims to raid German-held airfields at Rouen and Amiens. The Blenheims had no weapon as effective against this kind of target as the later fragmentation bomb, but they attacked successfully and suffered no losses. The following day 47 Blenheims bombed Rouen and Schipol airfields, again without loss. This was the start of Bomber Command's Battle of Britain, and for the next three weeks forces of six to 20 Blenheims struck repeatedly at the occupied air bases. Putting a few of these out of action for a day or two, however – quite a difficult task in itself – could hardly transform the situation: the number of airfields in use by the Luftwaffe was now about 400.[3]

Ordered to fly only under cloud cover when without escort – which led to much wasted effort when the cloud suddenly disappeared – the Blenheims now for the most part operated inexpensively. Occasionally, however, they paid an appalling price. On 9 July 12 Blenheims of Nos. 21 and 57 Squadrons took off to bomb a concentration of aircraft reported at Stavanger. Apprehensively the crews noted the absence of the forecast cloud as they approached the Norwegian coast, but they were under strict radio and wireless silence and could not confer; rather than break formation, they all pressed on. They delivered their attack, but almost at once 30 or more Me 109s and 110s rose in pursuit. 'I could see through my mirror,' wrote Sergeant T. Hudspeth of 57 Squadron,

> the enemy fighters manoeuvring to attack. On one occasion I saw six fighters queuing up getting ready for the kill. It was not long before casualties started to pile up. First I saw our port machine and its valiant crew smashed to smithereens when it was shot down and hit the sea. Then came the starboard machine's turn. He got a packet in the petrol tank and was burning like a torch. The pilot screamed out over his R/T that he was on fire, but there was little we could do about it. The Jerry fighter on his tail, with the usual Teutonic thoroughness, would not ease up in the slightest and continued to pour a stream of lead into the doomed machine, till I saw him, too, disintegrate into the sea, legs and arms and parts of the machine being scattered far and wide . . .[4]

Hudspeth's pilot finally found a friendly cloud, escaped, and made a successful belly-landing. Only four others of the 12, all badly damaged, managed to survive. Even worse was the incredible ill fortune of 82 Squadron – the squadron which on 17 May had lost 11 out of 12 aircraft on one operation. Now, on 13 August, 12 of the Squadron set out to bomb Hemsteds airfield, in Holland. Enemy fighters intervened.

For a second time, from a raid in squadron strength only one of 82 Squadron's Blenheims returned.[5]

In striking contrast to these disasters were the very small losses suffered at night, both by Blenheims attacking airfields and by 'heavies' attacking aircraft plants and other targets in Germany. In the fortnight 20 June–3/4 July the Wellingtons, Whitleys and Hampdens flew nearly 1200 sorties for the loss of only 17 aircraft.[6]

On 4 July the Air Ministry sent Portal a new directive. The high-flying Spitfires of the Photographic Reconnaissance Unit, operating under Coastal Command and stripped of their armament in the interests of speed, had picked up the first signs of movement by German barges towards the Dutch and Belgian ports. First priority for Bomber Command's attacks accordingly shifted from airfields and aircraft plants to German shipping, including warships, with the Blenheims of 2 Group concentrating on the self-propelled barges which would make up a large part of the German invasion fleet.[7] Again anticipating the formal order, on 3 July – a week before the Air Ministry's official date for the opening of the battle – Portal sent 24 Blenheims to attack barges in the Rhine approaching Rotterdam.

While the Blenheims struck at airfields and barges – the latter not yet greatly in evidence – the 'heavies' tried to hit ships in German ports. The crews could find ports at night with much less difficulty than most other places in Germany, and their bombing caused most damage in Hamburg, Kiel and Bremen, though rarely to the intended objectives. Their attempts to hit the warships *Scharnhorst* and *Deutschland* in Kiel all went narrowly astray, as did those to cripple the liners *Europa* and *Bremen*, intended for troop transports, in Hamburg. Guy Gibson, who tried to dive-bomb the *Scharnhorst* from 6000 feet on 1/2 July with the new 2000-lb bomb, later wrote: 'Each time we couldn't see a thing. In all we made six dives and on the last one this great bomb fell off too late and fell into the middle of Kiel town. This of course may have killed some civilians, but it was purely an accident as we had been told carefully to avoid the town.'[8]

Other classes of objective, however – oil, aircraft plants, communications – still featured in the directive of 4 July. In fact the choice was so wide that on 13 July the Air Ministry issued revised orders. Since there were still no great concentrations of shipping, priority was again to be given to aircraft plants and oil, with a greater weight of attack on fewer targets.[9]

This new directive moved Portal to protest – not at the priorities, but at the restriction in the choice of targets, and at some of the targets themselves. On 16 July he complained that of the ten main targets on the Air Staff's list, and assuming operations in moonlight, only three could be found by average crews. Some of the targets, he pointed out, were so far east that the crews would have no time for searching, if they were to clear the German defences before daybreak. Also – a point increasingly in Portal's mind – some targets were so isolated that no damage would be done by the bombs that missed them. Above all, he emphasised, he needed great flexibility in the choice of targets to allow for the vagaries of weather – a point to be strenuously echoed in later years by Sir Arthur Harris.[10]

From the foregoing it is evident that, apart from the decision to limit the 'heavies' to attacks by night, bombing policy in mid-1940 was not yet closely related to operational possibilities.

With the dream ever present in Hitler's mind of double-crossing his recent ally, Stalin, smashing Communism, and winning *Lebensraum* in eastern Europe, the German dictator was not disposed to attack Britain if she would agree quietly to his demands. On 19 July he made his so-called 'peace offer' in the Reichstag – and found it dismissed three days later by the British Foreign Secretary as 'a mere summons to capitulate'. Meanwhile, on the assumption that the British might not 'see reason', Hitler had already, on 2 July, instructed his armed forces to make full preparation for an invasion. At the same time, however, he laid down a precondition for the operation. In order to neutralise British sea power the Luftwaffe must first establish air superiority over the Channel and southern England.

Spurred on by the situation even more than by Churchill's eloquence, the British had been preparing, since Dunkirk, to meet the *furor teutonicus*. These were the weeks when they toiled for unwonted hours in the factories and mines, drilled with the newly formed Home Guard, built concrete roadblocks and pillboxes, removed road signs and the names of railway stations, stuck poles and old machinery in fields to prevent airborne landings, made seaside promenades bristle with guns, festooned the southern and eastern beaches with barbed wire. Inevitably – though the Chiefs of Staff could hardly gamble on it – a few weeks must elapse before the Luftwaffe could regroup and strike in strength, or before the German Navy could amass enough transports. On 16 July Hitler issued a provisional invasion directive to the Chiefs of his armed forces. On 1 August he decreed that all preparations for Operation SEALION must be complete by 15 September, thenceforth the target date for the invasion.[11]

While Fighter Command clashed with the Luftwaffe above the

Channel convoys, and Coastal Command scoured the ports and bays of north-west Europe, Bomber Command continued its attacks on Germany and the occupied airfields. During July the Blenheims flew about 300 sorties against airfields, and another 275 elsewhere, for a loss rate of 6.4 per cent. The 'heavies', flying that month 1826 night sorties of which 537 were against aircraft plants or airfields, lost only 2.3 per cent.[12]

On 12 August the Luftwaffe attacked some of the RAF's southern airfields and radar stations in preparation for the great *Adlerangriff* ('Eagle Attack') scheduled for the morrow. That night Bomber Command scored perhaps its greatest success in the war thus far. The Germans were by then making great use of the Dortmund–Ems Canal to move barges coastwards from the Rhineland. Near Münster this canal was carried over the River Ems by two aqueducts. Bomber Command had damaged the more modern of these on 25/26 July, but the older was still intact. On 12/13 August five Hampdens of Nos. 49 and 83 Squadrons, after intensive practice-bombing by night of canals in East Anglia, took off to attack this aqueduct. Other Hampdens meanwhile were to make diversionary raids.

First to bomb was Squadron Leader 'Jamie' Pitcairn-Hill DFC, of 83, who went in at 100 feet and somehow brought back his badly shot-up machine. Two Hampdens piloted by Australians followed: one managed to attack but both were shot down. The fourth Hampden went in next, bombed, was hit, and crawled back to England on one engine. Last of the five, through a storm of flak from guns lining both sides of the canal directly along his path, came the Hampden of Flight Lieutenant Roderick ('Babe') Learoyd, of 49 Squadron, who had already flown more than twenty operations. Though blinded by searchlights and having to trust to his bomb-aimer, Sergeant John Lewis, Learoyd attacked from 300 feet in a shallow dive and planted a special 'M' bomb, fused for ten minutes' delay, near the bank of the aqueduct. He then brought his badly damaged aircraft, with its hydraulics ruptured and flaps and undercarriage out of action, back to Scampton. It was 2 a.m., and he had to circle around for three hours before dawn broke and he could risk a belly-landing.[13] The VC he received for his gallantry and determination was the first of nineteen to be awarded to Bomber Command aircrew during the war.

Whether Learoyd or one or two of the others caused the crucial damage is uncertain; but between them they made the Dortmund–Ems Canal unusable for ten days, with serious consequences, according to the German official historian Admiral Assmann,[14] for Hitler's invasion preparations.

'Eagle Day', 13 August, dawned, and for a week, until bad weather intervened, the Luftwaffe tried desperately to drive the RAF from southern England and clear the way for invasion. It was during the first wave of attacks that the Germans struck one of the heaviest blows to fall on a Bomber Command airfield during the whole course of the war. On 15 August the Luftwaffe, for the first – and, since it turned out disastrously, last – time in the Battle of Britain, tried mass-raiding from Scandinavia. Some twenty Ju 88s from Denmark, survivors of a larger intercepted formation, forced their way over the Yorkshire coast to the 4 Group airfield at Driffield. Their bombs, besides killing 15 people and wounding 27, hit four hangars, burning out three, damaged other buildings, and destroyed ten Whitleys.[15]

On 24 August, after a few days of restricted activity, the Luftwaffe resumed its offensive in full force. Now the main weight of bombs fell, not on the coastal or fringe targets attacked earlier, but on the inner airfields guarding London and, most dangerously, on the vital 'sector' stations from which the British fighter squadrons were controlled. In a fortnight of violent action the Luftwaffe hit, among other Fighter Command airfields, Hornchurch, North Weald, Debden, Kenley and Biggin Hill – the last-named several times. Fighter Command still took a magnificent toll of the enemy, but now for the first time its own losses exceeded the output of replacement aircraft from the factories. Its strength was ebbing away, too, from the loss of experienced pilots and their replacement by novices. By the first week of September, crisis-point was looming ahead for Fighter Command.[16]

Throughout August Bomber Command had meanwhile kept up its attacks on Germany – oil plants, aircraft factories, airfields, communications, naval vessels – and had even sent small forces of Whitleys to raid works in Turin and Milan. It had continued minelaying, and had sent the Blenheims to attack airfields by night as well as by day – with a gratifying decline in their losses. But it had not yet spent much effort in attacking barges: after the first Blenheim raids the Germans had taken care not to concentrate their invasion craft prematurely.

Amid these multifarious, if often ineffective, operations in August, the raids on Berlin seem to have had, almost fortuitously, consequences of high strategic value. In addition to its main daylight assault the Luftwaffe had been making small raids on Britain by night, and on 24/25 August two or three of its aircraft, either through navigational error or jettisoning, dropped bombs on London – some in the southern suburbs, some in the City. This, though the British did not know it, was in accidental contravention of Hitler's long-standing order forbidding attacks on the British capital. In Churchill's view, there could be only one possible response – immediate retaliation against Berlin. The Air Staff was far from keen – Berlin was distant, and dangerous, and there were more important targets nearer home – but Portal had said such a raid was possible, if necessary at short notice, and Churchill's wishes carried the day.[17]

The notice was very short indeed – a matter of hours. The next night, 25/26 August, about 80 Wellingtons and Hampdens took off to attack precise objectives in Berlin. In cloudy conditions they failed to find or hit them, and further raids on these on the next four nights had little more success. The moral effect of the appearance of the British bombers over the German capital, however, seems to have been considerable. 'The Berliners,' wrote the American journalist W. L. Shirer, resident in Berlin at the time, 'are stunned. They did not think it could ever happen. Goering assured them it couldn't.'[18] More important, the attacks, coming on top of all those elsewhere in Germany, infuriated Hitler. On 30 August he not only withdrew his ban on bombing London but encouraged Goering to go ahead.[19] Five days later, before a wildly cheering audience consisting, according to Shirer, 'mostly of women nurses and social workers', he announced: 'The British will know that we are now giving our answer night after night. Since they attack our cities, we shall extirpate theirs.'[20]

This passion of Hitler's for revenge coincided precisely with the growing conviction of Kesselring, commander of the Luftwaffe forces attacking south-east England, that something more must be done to beat down Fighter Command's continuing resistance if the target date for the invasion, now postponed to 21 September, was to be met.[21] An attack on London must bring the full remaining resources of Fighter Command to battle, and so provide the opportunity for the Luftwaffe to shoot the last of its opponents from the skies. Also, the German leaders were agreed, there was no better plan than to create chaos in the British capital in the final run-up to the invasion.

This was a fatal decision, the true turning point in the Battle of Britain. Over London the Me 109s, with their limited endurance, could fly and fight for no more than ten minutes. Without proper protection, the German bombers became much easier to shoot down. Relieved from heavy attack, the sector stations breathed again. The ebbing away of Fighter Command's resources was staunched. Once more replacements from the factories exceeded losses.[22]

*   *   *

As the Luftwaffe prepared to switch its attacks on to London the German invasion craft made their way along the coasts and canals to the Channel ports. Very quickly, Coastal Command's Spitfires and Hudsons spotted the growing movement. On 31 August there were 18 barges in the port of Ostend, on 2 September 70, on 4 September 115, on 5 September 205.[23] Reconnaissance of Flushing, Dunkirk, Calais, showed similar concentrations. Photographs, too, revealed that Ju 87 dive-bombers were being assembled in the Pas de Calais, and ENIGMA decrypts – readings of the Luftwaffe's top-secret codes – confirmed that Kesselring's bombers were being reinforced. The decisive moment seemed at hand. On Saturday 7 September, as the first bombs of the Luftwaffe's great assault on London fell at Woolwich, the British Chiefs of Staff decided that invasion was imminent. The Royal Navy and the Royal Air Force were already at the highest state of readiness. That evening the issue of the code-word 'CROMWELL' brought the Army in south-east England to its battle stations.

Meanwhile, the assembly of the invasion craft was giving Bomber Command its opportunity. The Blenheims began to attack again from 5 September, and from 7/8 September the assault became intensive: while the Luftwaffe was raiding London's dockland Fairey Battles (now operating regularly again), Hampdens and Blenheims attacked docks and shipping at Calais and Ostend. From 13/14 September almost the whole of Bomber Command, together with bombers from Coastal Command, then began to join in.[24] On 14/15 September, and again on 18/19 and 19/20 September, over 170 bombers raided the invasion ports. The targets, for once, were easy to find, the flights brief, the results spectacular. 'The whole of "Blackpool Front", as we call the invasion coastline stretching west from Dunkirk,' wrote one of the Blenheim pilots, Flying Officer R. S. Gilmour, 'was now in near view . . . Calais docks were on fire. So was the waterfront at Boulogne, and glares extended for miles. The whole French coast seemed to be a barrier of flame broken only by intense white flashes of exploding bombs and vari-coloured incendiary tracers soaring and circling skywards.'[25]

Some of the crews on these cross-Channel attacks were new to operations. Sergeant Edwin Wheeler, a wireless operator with 150 Squadron, had flown with Battles, but the squadron had recently converted to Wellingtons. The night of 17/18 September saw not merely their first operation in a Wellington, but their first night flight in one.

*   *   *

We were briefed [wrote Wheeler] to fly in Wellington L7859, take-off at 2240 hours to attack invasion barge concentrations at Ostend. After the discomfort of flying in Battles, the 'Wimpy' was luxury indeed; I had a reasonable seat and warmth to operate the TR1154/55 radio receiver/transmitter. The security of having two pilots and armament at front and rear, and armour plate behind my seat gave me much more confidence than I had felt before. Ginger had the luxury of a seat and table to consult his maps and his log was at last glycol-free! We reached the target and sighted the rows of barges but Rocky must have had a lapse of memory as he put the Wimpy into a dive – must have thought he was still in Fairey Battles. The reaction from the crew was immediate! 'What the bloody hell!' was yelled from each crew position. It is a wonder that the wings were not torn off – such was the angle of dive! However, we survived and there were fewer barges when we left.[26]

Novices or veterans, all the crews were immensely impressed by the flak. Of a slightly later operation Group Captain Tom Sawyer wrote:

We were detailed for a 'barge-bashing' trip to Antwerp. These [trips] were quite enjoyed by all because they entailed a quick dash over the enemy coast and back without hours of stooging over blacked-out enemy territory . . . There was much searchlight activity with several aircraft obviously in the vicinity, and on our run-in a great increase in the amount of light flak tracer which seemed to be sprayed up all over the place almost indiscriminately and in all directions in prodigious quantities. Multicoloured strings of orange, red, and even green were hosed upwards, sometimes with a sort of 'S' bend in them as the gunners swung their barrels around. White and yellow blobs of fairy lights creeping up almost lazily at first, then with gradually increasing velocity to zip past the wings at terrific speed, and some a little too close for complacency.[27]

These attacks continued nightly, though less intensively towards the end of September, when photographic reconnaissance and ENIGMA decrypts indicated a lessening of the immediate threat. According to the German figures the British bombers sank, by 21 September, roughly 12.5 per cent of the 1865 transports and barges which the German Navy had succeeded in gathering together.[28] Twelve per cent may not seem at first sight an overwhelming figure but it was in fact quite enough, in little more than a week's intensive bombing, to convince the German naval authorities that they must disperse their painstakingly assembled craft – thereby ending any immediate prospect of invasion.

It was the combination of these attacks with Fighter Command's defeat of the Luftwaffe's daylight assault on London that convinced Hitler he could not go ahead with the invasion. On 13/14 September British bombing had destroyed no fewer than 80 barges. The next day Dowding's pilots won their greatest, immortal victory in defence of London. On 16/17 September Bomber Command struck in force again, 100 or more aircraft hammering the Channel ports. On 17 September Hitler, who had already deferred his target date from 21 to 24 September, postponed Operation SEALION indefinitely.[29] From mid-October he maintained the threats purely as bluff, for pressure purposes only. Though it did not seem so to Spitfire and Hurricane pilots chasing high-flying Me 109s throughout October and November, the Battle of Britain was effectively over.

An episode during one of Bomber Command's raids on the invasion ports typified the spirit of its crews. On 15/16 September a Hampden of 83 Squadron, piloted by a Canadian, Pilot Officer C. A. Connor, was attacking barges in Antwerp. As Connor came in and bombed on his second run, at 2000 feet, his aircraft was violently struck. Shells hit the bomb bay, the tail boom, the wing petrol tanks, and in an instant the rear interior was aflame. Quickly the aluminium floor then melted, leaving a large hole through which the rear-gunner had no option but to bale out. Sent back to see what was happening, the navigator from up front found himself unable to open the dividing door, saw that the gunner was gone and that the wireless operator, Sergeant John Hannah, was apparently on fire, and baled out too, expecting his pilot to follow. But Hannah, a determined Scot not yet nineteen years old, was able to smother the flames around him. Despite the fact that the stored ammunition was now bursting from the heat, he forced the jammed door open, grabbed an extinguisher and started to put out the remaining fires, beating at the last with his logbook when the second extinguisher ran out. Though burnt on the hands and face he then crawled forward to help the pilot, passing him maps and the navigator's log. With both wing tanks holed, Connor brought the aircraft back and made a successful landing.

Unhappily, these two brave men did not long survive. Connor, who received the DFC, was killed only a few weeks later; Hannah, the youngest airman ever to be awarded the VC, went on to instructional duties but never really recovered his health. He was invalided out in

1942 and died soon after the war, still in his twenties and leaving a widow and three young daughters.[30]

Bomber Command's contribution to the Battle of Britain would, of course, have been even greater had the Germans ever launched an expedition. Not only were all the operational squadrons under orders to attack the invasion forces at their embarkation points, on their sea-crossings, and at their landing places, but by the aptly-named Banquet Plan all the Command's resources in suitable training aircraft, instructors and even senior pupils, as well as similar resources from Training Command, were to join in too. When the plan was first drawn up, in May 1940, it embraced such vintage aircraft from the Service Flying Training Schools in Training Command as Audaxes and Harts, together with standard trainers such as Harvards, Oxfords, Masters and Ansons. Many of these were to be equipped, and their crews trained, for dive-bombing – they would be too inaccurate, it was thought, from anything above 200 or 300 feet.[31]

Later it became possible to omit the Audaxes from the scheme, but as the plan stood on 2 September no fewer than 218 aircraft (including 23 Battles, 71 Harvards and 51 Harts) from Training Command were to move, when the need arose, to Bomber Command stations, together with experienced pilots and air-gunners (they were to bring their own bedding, and were warned 'to expect to rough it'). In addition, from Bomber Command's own training resources (the Operational Training Units by then in Nos. 6 and 7 Groups), a staggering total of 519 aircraft, including 65 Battles and 124 Ansons, was also to move to the operational stations.[32]

Had all these ancillaries actually been called upon to attack the enemy their casualties would surely have been horrific; but, with equal certainty, they would have played their part unflinchingly. In company with their seniors and mentors, the operational squadrons, and under the protection of an undefeated Fighter Command, they would have made it extremely difficult for the Germans to maintain any foothold on British soil. In the words of John James: 'If the Germans had invaded using barges with jury-rigged anti-aircraft guns, and with their fighters kept busy upstairs, then we might be now talking about the wonderful Bomber Command and the gallant Fairey Battles which won the Battle of Britain.'[33]

As it is, the contribution of Bomber Command – its attacks on airfields and the invasion ports and barges, its bombing of Berlin and other German towns which helped to produce the Luftwaffe's fatal decision to attack London – is largely overlooked or forgotten. In one most hallowed place, however, it is not overlooked. The Battle of Britain Memorial Chapel in Westminster Abbey records the names of 537 of the gallant Few of Fighter Command who in 1940 lost their lives in saving Britain's freedom. It records alongside them the names of the 718 of Bomber Command and 230 of Coastal Command who, in the same struggle, made the same supreme sacrifice.

7

The Means of Victory?

'T he Navy can lose us the war, but only the Air Force can win
it. Therefore our supreme effort must be to gain overwhelming mastery in the air. The Fighters are our salvation, but
the Bombers alone provide the means of victory. We must therefore
develop the power to carry an ever-increasing volume of explosives to
Germany, so as to pulverize the entire industry and scientific structure
on which the war effort and economic life of the enemy depend, while
holding him at arm's length from our island . . .'[1]

Thus Winston Churchill to his Cabinet colleagues on 3 September
1940, at the height of the Battle of Britain. It would be long, he pointed
out, before the Army could return to the Continent; and the enemy's
conquests had 'blunted' the Navy's traditional weapon of blockade.
For the immediately foreseeable future, only bombing could seriously
injure Germany.

The Chiefs of Staff agreed, and as soon as the invasion threat
receded the order went out to Bomber Command to step up attacks
on Germany. On 30 October a detailed Air Staff directive followed.[2]
Minelaying should continue, together with raids on north Italian
industry and the big marshalling yards in western Germany. But
the main weight of the offensive should fall elsewhere. In the
moonlight periods most favourable for precise night-bombing – and
practicable in the virtual absence as yet of German night-fighters –
Bomber Command should try to knock out Germany's main plants
producing synthetic oil.

The darker nights, however, demanded a different policy. During these, Bomber Command must deliver 'regular concentrated attacks on objectives in large towns and centres of industry, with the primary aim of causing very heavy material destruction which will demonstrate to the enemy the power and severity of air bombardment and the hardship and dislocation which will result from it'. The targets listed for attack were still individual factories, and the like; but there was also a recommendation that the raiders should carry a high proportion of incendiaries. Under the impulse of a new Chief, the Air Staff were now both expecting and welcoming an overspill of bombs on to the surrounding industrial districts – the first step towards what would later be called 'area-bombing'.

Such were the orders under which Bomber Command, in the autumn of 1940, set out to 'pulverise' German industry. But how far, as yet, had it the numbers, the equipment, and the techniques to carry out the orders?

Numerically, Bomber Command at this time was no stronger than it had been a year earlier. Then it had deployed 23 operational squadrons, or 33 including the AASF. Now, with the relics of the AASF reabsorbed into a revived No. 1 Group (and converting from Battles to Wellingtons) the front line consisted of 29 operational squadrons. These officially comprised about 450 aircraft, but during November the average number of serviceable aircraft with crews was around 370, and of these 120 were Blenheims of limited range mainly committed to the nearer daylight tasks. So it was with the residual total of about 250 Wellingtons, Whitleys and Hampdens that Bomber Command had to pulverise German industry.[3]

There were many reasons why, despite ambitious plans for expansion, the Bomber Command striking force should still have been so small in the autumn of 1940. Crews and one or two squadrons were frequently 'on loan' to Coastal Command. The campaign in France had taken a heavy toll of the AASF and 2 Group's Blenheims. During the Battle of Britain bomber pilots had been transferred to Fighter Command, and German bombing had disrupted production – the raid of 14 September on Vickers at Weybridge alone caused an output loss of 125 Wellingtons. Following Mussolini's attack on Greece in October, two squadrons of Wellingtons – Nos. 37 and 38 – left Bomber Command for Egypt, and many Bomber Command crews ferried reinforcing aircraft to RAF Middle East, which quietly retained their services. The output of trained crews, too, was not yet smoothly geared to the output of aircraft: many squadrons were below their approved crew-strength. The foremost factor in keeping Bomber Command's front line small, however, was none of these. It was one which would give it far greater strength in the future – the formation of Operational Training Units.

Bomber Command could in fact expand its front line only by first contracting it. In peacetime, pilots who had completed their basic flying training had been posted direct to the squadrons, where under the guidance of the more experienced members they learned operational techniques. Observers (usually wireless operators who had taken the Air Observer's course) had also become operationally proficient on squadrons. The same had applied to wireless opera-tor/air-gunners, normally ground tradesmen in the rank of corporal or leading aircraftman who had volunteered for part-time flying duties. Drawing the princely bonus of 1/6d a day while so enrolled, they had not normally been part of a regular crew, but had been considered available to fly with any pilot, as required.

In 1938 it had been recognised that this relaxed system could not work in war, and that some stage of operational training must be interposed between the flying training schools and the squadrons. By the outbreak of hostilities some of Bomber Command's squadrons had been designated as Reserve, for operational use after further training, and others as Group Pool, to supply replacement crews to one or other of the five operational Groups. To administer the Reserve and Group Pool squadrons a new Group, No. 6,* came into being.

Before long the training in the Group Pool squadrons became more systematic for all classes of aircrew, and for crews as a whole. Wireless operators/air-gunners ceased to be part-time fliers and became regular crew members, their status much enhanced by the decision, announced in late May 1940, to accord all aircrew the basic rank of sergeant – from which, of course, large numbers would be commissioned. Meanwhile, in early April, the Group Pools had been reorganised and renamed. The squadrons within each Pool lost their identity, and their aircraft and crews became simply part of what was now called an Operational Training Unit.[4]

Under the command of a talented officer re-employed after retire-ment, Air Vice-Marshal W. F. MacNeece Foster,† No. 6 Group gradually established a common pattern of training in the bomber OTUs. In an eight-week course (longer in winter, to provide the

---

* Later renamed No. 91 Group.
† Unusually for an air marshal, Foster wrote verse. His 'Airman's Te Deum' was set to music by both Walford Davies and Martin Shaw.

same number of flying hours) the separate aircrew categories went through their own specialised training before coming together, for the final two weeks, as made-up crews – at which stage they undertook, in operation-type aircraft, such operational exercises as long-distance night navigation, formation-flying, bomb-aiming, firing, fighter 'affiliation' (i.e. 'dodging') and escape drill.

One of the most striking parts of this procedure, as it developed, was 'crewing-up'. In the course of the eight weeks, crews of three, four or five, depending on the type of aircraft, had to be formed from individuals nearly all unknown to each other. Surprisingly – in a Service context – but increasingly as time went on, this was done largely by free choice on the part of the airmen concerned. A pilot might strike up a friendship with an observer, the observer might have come across an agreeable and 'clued-up' wireless operator, and in next to no time they were the nucleus of a crew. If there were odd men left over, or required, the staff could always complete the process by allocation.

Jack Currie, pilot and author of a notable account of his wartime experiences, *Lancaster Target*, described how this worked for him, later on, in 1942.

> There were bomb-aimers, navigators, wireless-operators and gun-ners, and I needed one of each to form my crew. I didn't know any of them ... I had a sudden recollection of standing in a suburban dance-hall, wondering which girl I should approach. I remembered that it wasn't always the prettiest or the smartest girl who made the best companion for the evening. Anyway, this wasn't the same as choosing a dancing partner, it was more like picking out a sweetheart or a wife, for better or worse ...
>
> I hadn't realized the crewing-up procedure would be so haphaz-ard ... I'd imagined that the process would be just as impersonal as most others that we went through in the RAF. I thought I would simply see an order on the notice-board, detailing who was crewed with whom. But what had happened was quite different ... the Chief Ground Instructor got up on a dais. He wished us good morning, told us we were there for crewing-up and said: 'Right, chaps, sort yourselves out.'[5]

Ted Sweet, wireless operator, in his account of the same procedure, in *Enemy Below*, recorded a further instruction from the officer in charge – in his case, the Chief Flying Instructor: 'Remember, after today you are committed to the crew of your choice. There will be no swopping or changing after 1700 hours this evening.'[6]

Currie went on to describe how his crew came together:

I noticed that a wiry little Australian was looking at me anxiously. He took a few steps forward, eyes puckered up in a diffident smile, and spoke: 'Looking for a good navigator?' I walked to meet him. He was an officer. I looked down into his eyes and received an impression of honesty, intelligence and nervousness. He said: 'You needn't worry, I did all right on the course!' I held out my hand – 'Jack Currie.' 'I'm Jim Cassidy. Have you got a bomb-aimer? I know a real good one – he comes from Brisbane, like me. I'll fetch him over.'

The bomb-aimer had a gunner in tow, and while we were sizing each other up we were joined by a tall wireless-operator, who introduced himself in a gentle Northumbrian accent and suggested it was time for a cup of tea. As we walked to the canteen, I realized that I hadn't made a single conscious choice.[7]

'The choice today,' wrote Ted Sweet, 'was a matter of life and death. Some of these pilots would survive, some would be dead in a matter of weeks. How could you tell by looking at them? How could you make the right choice? Was it luck, judgement, or fate? As events turned out, it was fate – choice or judgement did not come into it.'[8] Whatever its basis, judgement or luck, the system worked amazingly well. In effect, the members of the crew came together on trust – a trust which, for the great majority, would remain their strongest bond and protection in all the dangers they were soon to face.

When the bomber OTUs were inaugurated, in April 1940, there were nine of them – Nos. 10 to 18 OTUs – of which No. 18 was for Polish crews training on Battles. Together they absorbed no fewer than 15 of the non-operational squadrons. During the summer of 1940 it became clear, however, that their output could not replace casualties and at the same time provide crews for new squadrons. It became necessary to form more bomber OTUs – a further eight by May 1941, with a new Group, No. 7,* to control them.[9] Every new OTU formed, however, inevitably drew on experienced crews for instructors and on operational-type aircraft for equipment. It also demanded one or more airfields and all the paraphernalia, often in short supply, of flying control.

Only in this way could Bomber Command expand, but for many months the formation of OTUs inevitably kept the front line smaller than had been expected – and much weaker than the Prime Minister

---

* Later renamed No. 92 Group.

was disposed to accept without complaint. On 20 October 1940 the Chief of the Air Staff received the following note:

> I am deeply concerned with the non-expansion, and indeed contraction, of our bomber forces which must be expected between now and April or May next, according to present policy. Surely an effort should be made to increase our bomb-dropping capacity during this period? Is it not possible to organize a Second Line Bomber Force which, especially in the dark of the moon, would discharge bombs from a considerable and safe height upon the nearest large built-up areas of Germany which contain military targets in abundance? The Ruhr, of course, is obviously indicated ... Could not crews from the training schools do occasional runs? Are none of the Lysander and Reconnaissance pilots capable of doing some of the simpler bombing?'[10]

Mercifully, the Air Staff were not disposed as yet to risk incompletely trained crews or *ad hoc* pilots on 'the simpler bombing' – least of all over the Ruhr, where the haze and flak ensured that no bombing was ever simple. A few days later Churchill tried again, deploring the negative response he had received and concluding: 'It is a scandal that so little use is made of the enormous mass of material provided. The discharge of bombs on Germany is pitifully small.'

As those at the head of the Air Ministry well knew, the Prime Minister, while always an inspiration, could frequently be a trial.

Though Bomber Command's striking force was still so small, in some respects it was growing stronger. In manpower it was beginning to receive a fine flow of superb volunteers from the Dominions. The gallant survivors of Allied air forces, too, were taking a place in the front line – a Czechoslovak squadron (No. 311) and two Polish squadrons (Nos. 300 and 301) all became operational in September 1940, by which time two more Polish squadrons (Nos. 304 and 305) were also forming. Moreover Bomber Command's aircraft, though the new generation of 'heavies' was not yet available, had undergone many improvements. All now had self-sealing tanks, most were better armoured, and the earliest marks of Wellington and Whitley were being relegated to the OTUs. Bigger bombs, filled with improved explosives, were coming into regular use, with the 500-lb medium-capacity largely replacing the earlier 250-lb general-purpose. New and bigger types of incendiary were available to supplement the standard four-pounder.

In one all-important matter, however, there was only hope, not improvement. The crews had as yet no better way of finding and hitting their targets at night in blacked-out Germany. Dead reckoning, 'astro-shots' when the skies were clear, occasional directional bearings or fixes by wireless on the return journey (if the set was working well) and even perhaps a beam at base – these remained the standard ways of navigating throughout 1940 and 1941. Before he left Bomber Command in October 1940 to succeed Sir Cyril Newall as Chief of the Air Staff, Portal had eagerly welcomed the prospect of the radar navigational aid GEE,* but another eighteen months were to pass before it was perfected and fitted for operations.

Meanwhile the crews were frequently in some doubt – to put it mildly – about their position. Pilot Officer (later Group Captain) Sam Hall, among the first batch of wartime New Zealand volunteers, was a young navigator/bomb-aimer with 9 Squadron. He was on one of the many raids against the marshalling yards at Hamm† in the Ruhr, in the autumn of 1940, and later wrote:

> Conditions were cloudy, and at ETA there was little to be seen below which was recognisable. Bertie [the pilot] was repeating 'Can you see the target' and I was replying with a laconic 'No' until he finally burst out, 'For Christ's sake bomb something! I want to get home for breakfast!' In the end I persuaded myself that a concentration of lights below could be the marshalling yards, but the evidence was meagre – a first practical lesson in realising that better methods and equipment would be needed before an accurate bombing campaign could be mounted.

This was only a very mild case of uncertainty. Group Captain Tom Sawyer recorded one of a far more serious kind. The crew of a Whitley, after getting lost over the Ruhr and dropping their bombs on what they thought to be an airfield in Holland, suddenly got a first-class DF fix which showed them to be over the Irish Sea. The aerodrome they had bombed, fortunately without much damage, was in Cambridgeshire. Sawyer writes generally of the autumn-winter months of 1940–41:

> So now our bombers were cruising all over Western Germany more or less every night in small numbers, and when the main target

---

* See pages 112–13.
† Announcements on the radio of raids against this target were so frequent in 1940–41 that they became something of a public joke.

could not be found during the thirty minutes or one hour we were usually given on each target to find it, the crews would then have to look round for a SEMO (self-evident military objective) or a MOPA (military objective previously attacked);* many were the surprised and indignant members of searchlight or flak batteries who suddenly received a parcel of bombs from a browned-off British bomber crew who hadn't been able to find any more valuable target ... And consequently on occasions in certain weather conditions we were not challenged at all, as the ground defence seemed to realize we were browsing around quite unable to find what we were looking for, and how right they were. By the end of December 1940 we had become less careful, and no one ever brought bombs back. We remembered the London blitz, Coventry, Southampton and Liverpool, which were very fresh in our minds.[11]

Portal's brief tenure of office at High Wycombe had seen crisis after crisis: Norway, France, Britain. Throughout all the turmoil of that fateful summer he had kept a cool head and a firm grip on his Command. His translation in October 1940 to Whitehall placed at the head of the Air Force a man of outstanding courage, intelligence, integrity and determination. It also placed there a man who was resolved to use, in the fullest possible way, the bombing weapon against Germany.

To succeed Portal at Bomber Command the Air Council appointed Air Marshal Sir Richard Peirse. He had flown with distinction in the First World War, and subsequently been Director of Operations and Intelligence at the Air Ministry. After commanding the British Forces in Palestine and Transjordan he had returned to the Air Ministry in 1937 and become Vice-Chief of the Air Staff. During the war thus far he had been closely concerned with bombing policy, and with his ability and experience he seemed an excellent choice to take over Bomber Command. His Service background – he was the son of an admiral – was no disadvantage, and his good looks and charm had not yet led him into undue difficulties.

From November 1940 until March 1941 Bomber Command's primary objective remained oil. The Ministry of Economic Warfare held the view that despite the big stocks captured by Germany during

---

* SEMO and MOPA were standard terms. They were also the names of two popular barmaids in York, rechristened by the crews.

Pilot, 1944

Air Marshal Sir Charles Portal, 1940.

Air Chief Marshal Sir Edgar Ludlow-Hewitt, 1937–40.

Air Marshal Sir Richard Peirse, 1940–1.

Air Chief Marshal Sir Arthur Harris, 1942–5, with his Deputy, Air Marshal Sir Robert Saundby (taken in 1942 before promotions).

Battles on
reconnaissance near the
German frontier, 1939.

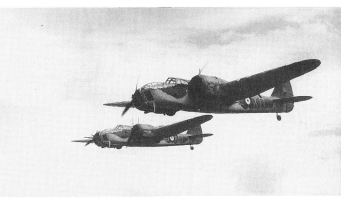

Blenheims of the AASF
on exercises, 1940.

Hampdens of No. 44
(Rhodesia) Squadron,
1940.

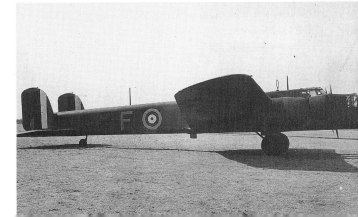

Whitley Mark V of
No. 10 Squadron, 1940.

Wellingtons Mark I of
No. 9 Squadron, 1940.

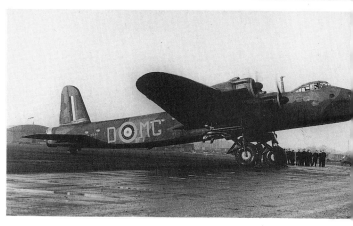

Stirling Mark I of No.
7 Squadron, 1941.

Halifax Mark V, 1942.

Lancaster B Mark I of
No. 467 Squadron
RAAF, 1944, being
loaded up for its 97th
operation.

Mosquito B Mark XVI
of No. 571 Squadron,
1944.

Bostons on low-level
approach, 1942.

Ventura Mark II of No.
464 Squadron, RAAF,
1943.

Mitchell B-25 Mark II
of No. 98 Squadron.

Halifax crew of No. 102 (Ceylon) Squadron before leaving on their 16th operation, 1943.

Boston crews with the Station commander, 1943.

Wireless Operator.

Flight Engineer.

Mid-upper-Gunner.

Rear-Gunner.

Navigator.

Bomb-Aimer.

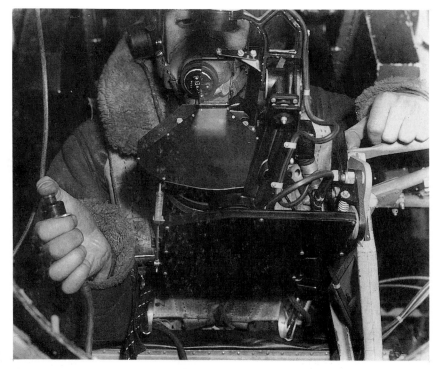

1940, her position was still extremely precarious. It believed, quite wrongly, that the attacks thus far had already reduced her stocks considerably, and that if the nine main plants producing synthetic oil could be put out of action Germany would enter a state of crisis. The attacks, however, must be completed by mid-1941, after which Germany's exploitation of Romanian oil would solve her problems. These considerations inspired a further detailed 'oil' directive sent to Bomber Command on 15 January 1941.[12]

Action, however, failed to live up to precept. In the five months November 1940–March 1941 Peirse managed to send only some 1200 sorties against oil, or an average of 55 a week – very little to deal with nine major plants, especially as many of the sorties would never find them. On 9/10 January 1941, in one of the attempts at a major raid, he sent out 135 aircraft, with the oil plants at Gelsenkirchen, in the Ruhr, among the main objectives. Only 56 crews claimed to have bombed their targets, and only one person was killed in Gelsenkirchen. In the opening two months of 1941 Peirse in fact found himself able to attack oil on only three nights. Bad weather, coupled with Admiralty requests for the bombing of naval targets, consistently frustrated him.

Progress against German oil might be slow and doubtful, but the other half of Peirse's remit – 'regular concentrated attacks on objectives in large towns and centres of industry' – showed more promise. During the three months November 1940–January 1941 Peirse mounted attacks of 50 aircraft on military or industrial objectives in – among other places – Berlin, Essen, Cologne, Düsseldorf, Duisburg, Kiel, Hamburg and Bremen. Some were failures, notably the attack by 63 aircraft on 7/8 November against the Krupps works at Essen, when many of the crews bombed decoy fires and the only night photograph taken showed an area of woodland. But others, and particularly those against the north German ports, where water made identification easier, were quite successful. On 15/16 November 67 Wellingtons, Whitleys and Hampdens, without loss, did extensive damage to Hamburg, including the Blohm and Voss shipyard. On 1/2 January more than 100 aircraft, again without loss – though four crashed on return – created large fires in Bremen and hit the Focke-Wulf factory and other industrial concerns.

The attack on Mannheim on 16/17 December, however, marked a new departure. The aiming-point this time was the centre of the town, not any individual building or industrial feature. It was a reprisal raid, approved as such by the War Cabinet,[13] in retaliation for the recent German attacks on Coventry and other British towns.

The largest number of aircraft yet sent against a single place – 134 – took part, and the crews returned with enthusiastic reports of their success. Great damage was done, but from the German records it appears that the first 14 Wellingtons, sent with incendiary loads in an elementary 'pathfinder' role, bombed some way from the centre of the city. At a cost of three aircraft lost and four more crashed on return, the raid destroyed or damaged 476 buildings, killed 47 people, and made 1266 homeless.

Mannheim was the first purely 'urban area' attack, but it did not immediately inaugurate a systematic campaign of urban area-bombing. Factories and other specific objectives, usually chosen because they were in industrial areas, continued to be the standard aiming-points until well into 1941. Meanwhile, however, the dictates of the war at sea were forcing Peirse and Bomber Command off their earlier prescribed course. In January 1941 Peirse had to send more sorties against German naval vessels and ports than against oil plants. Six attacks between 8/9 and 29/30 January on the *Tirpitz*, nearing completion in Wilhelmshaven, testified to the strength of the Admiralty's demands and influence, as did attacks on warships in Emden and Brest. Wilhelmshaven suffered severely; but the *Tirpitz* was still able to sail in mid-March.

During February 1941 Peirse, circumscribed as before by the weather, made three more attempts to bomb oil plants without much success. By far the heaviest raid of the month took place against an industrial area target, Hanover, on 10/11 February. No fewer than 222 aircraft, the largest number yet sent against a single objective, took part, and apparently did great damage – no German reports are available. The raid cost four bombers destroyed over Germany, but enemy 'intruders' awaited the raiders' return and got three more over England.[14]

At this stage Peirse had hopes that his Command might now enjoy an uninterrupted run against the two main target systems of his directive – oil plants and industry in populous areas. His forces were at last getting bigger – by the end of March 1941 17 squadrons had been added to the 29 of mid-November – and the first of the new heavy bombers specified in 1936 were trickling into service. The four-engined Short Stirling made its operational début on 10/11 February 1941, the twin-engined Avro Manchester on 24/25 February, and the four-engined Handley Page Halifax on 10/11 March. All were first tried out against 'fringe' targets in occupied territory.

Unfortunately, Peirse's expectations of these newcomers were soon to be disappointed. The Stirling, with a maximum speed of 270 mph, was faster than the Wellington, Whitley or Hampden, and it carried a much bigger bomb-load – though no bomb bigger than the biggest of 1941, the '2000-pounder'. It was well armed with eight to ten Browning .303 machine guns, and despite the great height of its front fuselage from the ground – a source of some danger to fitters working on the wings or engines – it was fairly popular with its seven or eight crew members for its spaciousness. An early weakness lay in the tail-wheel assembly, which had to be redesigned; but its vital and never remedied defect soon proved to be its low ceiling, possibly deriving from its comparatively short wings. Theoretically, it could reach 17,000 feet. In practice, even with a medium bomb-load, pilots found themselves struggling to reach more than 14,000 feet – at which height they were vulnerable not only to anti-aircraft fire but also, when raids became more concentrated, to bombs from their comrades above in other types of aircraft.

The Stirling, though it was withdrawn from routine operations over Germany in 1943, subsequently had a long and honourable career as a radio-countermeasures aircraft, a glider tug, and a troop transport. No such length of life attended the Manchester – not, at least, in its original form. Its twin Rolls-Royce Vulture engines soon proved unreliable, as well as giving inadequate power for an aircraft of such great size. After no more than 209 had been manufactured, and eight squadrons equipped, production ceased in November 1941. Long before that, however, its defects had become plain, and the happy genius of Roy Chadwick at Avro had produced a solution – basically a redesign with four Merlin engines and an enlarged wingspan. This was the famous Lancaster – in production and flying during 1941, but not operational until March 1942.

Meanwhile the third of the new 'heavies' built to the 1936 specification had come into service. At a very early stage, in 1937, Handley Page had switched from two Vulture engines to four Merlins and, unlike the Manchester, it had adequate power. Like the Stirling, its tail wheel assembly at first gave trouble. With a crew of seven, and up to ten .303 Brownings (of which two were in a front turret, four in a rear turret), the Mark I flew no faster than 265 mph but had a ceiling of some 22,000 feet. It proved to be, however, an aircraft susceptible to great improvement. Eventually it was to become, and remain, one of the outstanding bombers of the war. But in 1941 the Halifaxes, like the Stirlings and the Manchesters, were still a minor part of Peirse's night-bombing force in comparison with the faithful Wellingtons, Whitleys and Hampdens.

The Air Ministry's hopes of a sustained campaign against German oil had been frustrated by the weather and then, in January 1941, by 'diversions' on to naval targets. In March these hopes were completely shattered. Ever since Hitler's conquests had given him control over the coasts of Europe from the North Cape to the Pyrenees, the war at sea had been running in his favour. During the last seven months of 1940 the Germans sank, by U-boats, surface vessels, aircraft and mines, a monthly average of 450,000 tons of British, Allied and neutral shipping – far more than could be replaced in the time. Soon the sinkings became worse still. New ocean-going U-boats, the surface raiders, and more long-range German aircraft between them sent the shipping losses up to 532,000 tons in March, 664,000 tons in April. At this rate Germany could win the war simply by starving Britain of supplies and making it impossible for her ever to build up for an offensive.

Churchill's 'Battle of the Atlantic' directive of 6 March 1941 signalled the intention of now giving supreme priority to defeating this menace. New orders instructed Peirse that Bomber Command's main effort must be applied to the war at sea. The outcome was the transfer of Blenheims to Coastal Command for reconnaissance, and a series of attacks on the German North Sea ports, the U-boat bases in France, and the *Scharnhorst* and *Gneisenau* sheltering in Brest.

Apart from one last big raid on Gelsenkirchen on 14/15 March, which scored several hits and temporarily halted production, attacks on German oil now dwindled right away. The need of the moment was to give more direct support to the Navy and Coastal Command. This Bomber Command did, the most welcome part of its activity, in Peirse's view, being intensified bombing of the north German ports. In the next two months 20 attacks at an average strength of around 100 aircraft were aimed at one or other of the three main ports – Hamburg, Kiel and Bremen – and in June there were three more on Kiel and five on Bremen.

These places were among the least difficult to find in Germany, and the damage inflicted – at a cost of about two per cent of the sorties – was considerable. At Hamburg the raids caused over 500 fires, made some 3700 people homeless, and twice hit the Blohm and Voss U-boat yards. At Kiel, which on 7/8 April suffered an attack by 229 aircraft – the largest number yet sent against a single place – bombs destroyed the accommodation of some 8000 naval personnel and civilians and damaged the Deutsche Werke and Germania U-boat production yards, halting production for several days. At Bremen, twelve bombs hit the Focke-Wulf works manufacturing the long-distance Condors which preyed on Atlantic shipping, and others sank a floating dock.

The raid on Bremen on 27/28 June, however, saw a disturbing new development – German night-fighters operating in some numbers. The result was the highest total of bombers lost in a night raid thus far – 14 out of 108. Five of these went down to night-fighters. Events two nights later confirmed this fresh danger. In a raid on Hamburg by 28 aircraft including some of the new Stirlings, Manchesters and Halifaxes, three of the six aircraft lost fell to night-fighters.

Attacks on German ports, however, were only one of Bomber Command's ways of helping in the Battle of the Atlantic. From the time the *Scharnhorst* and *Gneisenau* took refuge in Brest at the end of March 1941 after their successful Atlantic foray, Peirse directed repeated attacks against the two warships – and on the *Prinz Eugen* when it joined them in June. By 6/7 July he had sent out some 20 raids, mostly by more than 50 aircraft, against these difficult and well defended targets. The cost at this time, contrary to the later general impression, was surprisingly light – seven aircraft out of some 1400 sorties. This, however, was partly because the vessels were so frequently obscured by cloud or smoke screens, or because the massive array of searchlights was so dazzling, that the crews were often unable to run in and bomb.

In general, the damage achieved by these attacks was hardly worth the effort expended. On 4/5 April, however, a bomb which fell near the *Gneisenau* in dry dock persuaded her captain that she would be safer in harbour – where Flying Officer Kenneth Campbell of Coastal Command, flying a Beaufort, at the cost of his life and that of his crew, lodged a torpedo in her stern.* On 10/11 April Bomber Command followed up with four hits which killed a large number of her crew. These two attacks put the *Gneisenau* out of action for months to come – a substantial success in the all-important campaign to safeguard Britain's lifelines.

Another requirement at this time was for Peirse to attack the U-boat base which the Germans had established at Lorient, and the lesser facilities at St Nazaire. He sent off four small raids before the end of May without much effect, the crews usually being frustrated

---

* Flying Officer Campbell was posthumously awarded the VC.

by bad visibility. The effort expended, by comparison with that against the warships in Brest, was small. The Admiralty called the shots, and at this time rated U-boats a lesser danger than surface raiders.

Bomber Command also answered Churchill's call by intensifying its minelaying, the Hampdens now extending their operations to the Biscay coast. In particular they tried to seal the ports of Brest, Lorient, St Nazaire and Bordeaux. More visible was the work of 2 Group's Blenheims, which in one-, two-, or three-squadron strength daily swept the enemy-held coasts in search of shipping at sea or 'fringe' targets along the shore – troops, gun-posts, radar stations and the like.

From early in 1941 the Blenheims had been flying what were known as CIRCUS operations – shallow penetrations of northern France and the Low Countries under strong fighter escort to attack objectives like airfields and power stations. On 28 April they also began to operate what was optimistically called the CHANNEL STOP – a determined attempt to prevent all German and enemy-controlled shipping moving through the Straits of Dover by day (the Navy, with its motor torpedo boats, took over at night). For this purpose first a flight of Blenheims, then two squadrons, were installed at Manston, a Fighter Command station. As if this were not enough, the hard-pressed Blenheims were also required on occasion to attack targets in north-west Germany, either by day under cloud cover or by night in conjunction with the main force.

The effect of the Blenheims' anti-shipping campaign and of the CIRCUS operation was not as great as had been hoped. The anti-shipping strikes (for which the aircraft were painted grey-green on the upper surfaces and duck-egg blue on the lower) were far more dangerous to the crews than the CIRCUSES – in which a dozen Blenheims, flying high, had the protection of perhaps forty fighters. Apart from asserting the offensive, the strategic intention behind the CIRCUSES was to force the Germans to maintain a strong fighter force in the West at a time when their armies were becoming increasingly involved in the East. In this the CIRCUS operations were only marginally successful, and in terms of attrition they were definitely unsuccessful. Between 14 June and 3 September Fighter Command lost 194 aircraft in these raids, and reckoned that its crews had shot down 437 of the enemy – whereas their actual haul was only 128. At least, however, the Blenheims in these operations escaped, for them, relatively lightly – 14 lost in some 520 sorties (2.7 per cent).

No such consolation attended the anti-shipping strikes. Most of the enemy-controlled coastal traffic sailed near the shore, and was well protected by batteries on land as well as by its own guns and accompanying flak-ships. Often, too, it had fighter cover. To have any chance of hitting a ship the Blenheim crews had to go in very low, at 50 feet or so – but not so low that they created a tell-tale wake in the water to attract enemy fighters. More than one pilot hit the top of a mast with fatal results. During April–June the rate of loss among the Blenheims despatched – 3.6 per cent – seemed just about sustainable, but the rate of loss of those actually attacking the ships was nearer an appalling 13 per cent. Unfortunately, too, contemporary assessments of strikings proved to be just as overestimated as those of German fighters destroyed. Bomber Command's belief was that between April and September 1941 the Blenheims sank or seriously damaged over 200 ships. Later in the year the Admiralty scaled this estimate down to 101. After the war, German records showed a total of 50.

Figures of enemy shipping losses, however, were not the essence of this matter. Figures of British, Allied and neutral shipping losses were. In June these figures, though less than those for April and May, were still grave – over 400,000 tons. But in July they fell sharply to 120,000 tons, and the improvement continued into August. The immediate crisis in the Battle of the Atlantic was over.

Towards this victory – very short-lived as it proved – Bomber Command had contributed by the 'loan' of crews and two squadrons to Coastal Command, and by its attacks on the enemy's warships, U-boat bases, merchant ships and ports. By July Peirse was free to apply the main weight of his offensive once more to the German homeland – his strong and frequently expressed preference.

Ten months had now passed since Churchill had seen 'the Bombers alone' as 'the means of victory'. Earlier, on 27 May 1940, the War Cabinet had approved the Chiefs of Staff view that even without allies the British Commonwealth and Empire might produce a critical situation in Germany by 'the middle of 1941': air attack, economic blockade, Resistance movements and the benevolent neutrality of the United States could see Britain through.[15] 'The middle of 1941' had now arrived, however, and Germany's collapse was as far off as ever. The bombers, though they had striven valiantly, had been neither numerous nor accurate enough to make much impression on the enemy. Britain had been saved, yet elsewhere – in Yugoslavia, Greece, Crete – the

Germans had coolly extended their conquests. But on 22 June 1941 came Hitler's insane attack on the Soviet Union, and the future held out other 'means of victory'. The Bombers were no longer alone.

8

'Transportation and Morale'

Hitler had attacked Russia; shipping losses in the Atlantic had declined; there was every reason, the Defence Committee thought, for Bomber Command to concentrate once more on Germany. On 9 July 1941 the new directive went out. Oil and naval targets (except in emergency) were no longer priority number one. Instead, the Command should apply its main effort towards 'dislocating the German transportation system and . . . destroying the morale of the civil population as a whole and of the industrial workers in particular'.[1]

'Dislocating the German transportation system' would clearly help the Russians. This would be especially so if, as was hoped, the great Ruhr–Rhineland industrial complex could be cut off from eastern Germany. But 'destroying the morale of the civil population' – what lay behind this, and what exactly did it mean?

The British Government, because of Germany's actions, had long considered itself morally freed from its initial commitment to bomb only military targets in the strictest sense. For a year Bomber Command had been attacking targets which might be called military-industrial. In the course of this, the incidental damage had clearly been much greater than the damage to the targets themselves. Recent attacks on specific points in Hamburg, Kiel and Bremen had resulted in much destruction of housing and public utilities, and there had been many reports from neutral sources of rising German discontent. If this discontent could be augmented by attacks actually designed to destroy whole industrial areas including the workers'

85

housing, it might help to lead to Germany's defeat. The directive of 9 July in effect elevated what had previously been an acceptable by-product of the bombing into one of the central features of the new bombing policy.

Though critics in recent years have tended to regard 'destroying morale' as a euphemism for 'killing', it was no part of this policy deliberately to slaughter civilians. Heavy civilian casualties would inevitably be involved, but the intention was to make it difficult or impossible for civilians, many of whom were an essential part of the war machine, to remain at their industrial or administrative jobs. It was hoped to break their will to do so by destroying their houses and all the comforts and necessities of a civilised urban life. If the civilians fled to the countryside, or the authorities managed to evacuate them from the major towns – as British mothers and children had been evacuated in the early days of the war – so much the better: the industrial desert could be created with less loss of life.

As a practical policy at this stage of the war attacking industrial centres and housing had one obvious merit: Bomber Command could hit urban areas with much less difficulty than individual factories. To make it effective, however, turned out to be a much harder and longer task than the Government and the Air Staff then thought. This was not simply because Bomber Command was limited in size and techniques, but because German morale was not in the least fragile, or impaired, as British Intelligence sources were reporting. Fed on conquests and the fruits of conquest, the Germans had hardly yet begun to feel the pinch of war. Lord Trenchard had given his opinion that in any 'bombing contest' the German people would cave in long before the British[2] – but this was only Lord Trenchard's opinion.* In fact, the Germans then, as at other times, were a brave, patriotic and disciplined people. They were not at all likely to panic and succumb quickly. Moreover, they had an additional spur to continue working despite the bombing of their cities: the Gestapo would regard them unfavourably if they did not. 'The Germans,' Harris was to observe later, 'are not allowed the luxury of morale.'

During the second half of 1941 Peirse duly struck at transportation as

---

* Trenchard was perhaps misled by the swiftness with which very minor RAF bombing, or the threat of bombing, had brought recalcitrant tribesmen to heel in the Middle East. During the 1920s he once began a paper for the Chiefs of Staff with the ringing assertion: 'The Egyptian is a chicken-hearted savage whose resistance will collapse at the *sound* of the first bomb.' (Author's italics)

his primary objective, 'morale' (i.e. industrial areas) as the secondary. Transportation occupied the moonlight nights – about a week each month – 'morale' the others. But there would also be 'morale' effects, of course, from the attacks on transportation, both from the hits and the misses.

At his disposal Peirse now had 45 operational squadrons, the average availability being around 450 aircraft with crews. Of these 45 squadrons no fewer than 21 were of Wellingtons, including four Polish, one Czech, one New Zealand and one Canadian. Some of these were in the original Wellington Group, No. 3, and the remainder in the revived No. 1 Group, with headquarters now at Bawtry and airfields in South Yorkshire and North Lincolnshire. The Whitley Group, No. 4, and the Hampden Group, No. 5, still held six squadrons apiece of their aircraft, but No. 2 Group was down to eight squadrons of Blenheims – the intention being to replace these by the end of the year with the faster American Bostons. In addition, Peirse had two squadrons each of the new Stirlings and Halifaxes, and two squadrons of Manchesters which periodically disappeared from the front line for modification. A few Fortresses from the USA were also to become operational during July. All the new British heavy bombers were arriving in disappointingly small quantities – during March–June, production had been only 54 per cent of that planned.[3]

This, then, was a force deeply in transition. The plan at this stage was to turn it into one composed entirely of the new 'heavies', discarding not only the old 'heavies', now called medium, but the old 'mediums', now called light (the Blenheims, or later the Bostons). Happily, however, the advent of a new phenomenon – though not for another year in the bomber squadrons – put paid to the idea of discarding light bombers. During 1941 the 'wooden wonder', the de Havilland Mosquito, proved itself. A 'private venture' of de Havillands' deriving from their 1934 Mildenhall–Australia race-winning *Comet*, it had encountered some opposition in the Air Ministry, but had been strongly supported from the start by the pre-war Director of Research and Development, Air Marshal Sir Wilfrid Freeman, especially as it used materials not in short supply. By the doubters who were horrified at the idea of an unarmed 'speed bomber' made of plywood, it had in fact become known as 'Freeman's Folly'. However, it soon became apparent that this machine – with only two crew, a top speed (in the earlier versions) of around 380 mph, a range of 1600 miles, a ceiling of 33,000 feet, and a bomb-load of 2000 lb – was a winner. The first call on it was obviously for strategic reconnaissance, but Peirse at once indented for the bomber version and in June 1941 was promised four squadrons for the following year.[4] Meanwhile the Blenheims soldiered on as the Command's light bombers, carrying the burden of nearly all the daylight raids.

On the personnel side, a shortage of trained crews which had threatened to hold up expansion had now been overcome, but only by the drastic expedient, adopted in April 1941, of shortening the standard summer courses in the OTUs from eight weeks to six. The drawback of this was soon evident. During the latter part of 1941 crews were arriving at the squadrons with barely sufficient training, and there was a sharp increase in both operational casualties and crashes. At the end of the year experience dictated a return to fuller training schedules.[5]

In the six months July–December 1941 Peirse managed to apply approximately 70 per cent of his Command's effort to Germany. His forces aimed about 7400 tons of bombs against transportation and other precise targets, and about 6400 tons against industrial areas. Nearly 45,000 tons, however, still went on naval targets.[6] Among the nine primary railway targets, Hamm, Soest and Schwerte repeatedly escaped because of the thick haze which overhung them. Others were hit, but no sufficient weight or continuity of attack fell on them to create any kind of obstacle which delayed movement for more than a few hours.

More impressive damage resulted from some of the area attacks, where railways were of course also involved. At Münster, during the July moon, attacks on four successive nights destroyed trains, tracks, a large part of the inland port, and another industrial area. At Aachen, on 9/10 July, a raid by 82 aircraft damaged the railway goods area and devastated about a fifth of the city. At Kassel, on 8/9 September, there was serious damage to railway buildings and the centre of the town.

Cologne, too, suffered much destruction. It happens that Cologne is one of the few places for which adequate German records exist covering this period. They show that from June 1941 to February 1942, in the course of 33 raids, only about 17 per cent of the bomb tonnage aimed actually fell within the city. The attacks caused 465 fires, and damaged 63 industrial plants, 41 transportation targets, and 10 military installations. They killed 138 people and temporarily displaced over 13,000.* The cost to Bomber Command in 'aircraft missing' was 2.6 per cent of sorties.[7]

It was while returning from one of the attacks on Münster, on 7/8

---

* In almost all respects these figures were to be exceeded during the single 'Thousand-Bomber' raid of 30/31 May 1942.

July, that the New Zealander Sergeant James Ward, of 75 (NZ) Squadron, before the war a young schoolmaster, performed a deed which earned him the Victoria Cross and which must surely be unsurpassed for calculated bravery. He was second pilot in a Wellington attacked by an Me 110 over the Zuider Zee. The rear-gunner was wounded, much damage done, the starboard wing set ablaze. The crew were preparing to abandon the aircraft when Ward volunteered to go out on the wing and try to smother the flames with a cockpit cover which had served in the plane as a cushion. Attached to a rope and with the help of the navigator he climbed through the narrow astro-hatch – far from easy in flying gear, even on the ground – put on his parachute, kicked holes in the Wellington's covering fabric to get foot- and hand-holds on the geodetic lattices, and descended three feet to the wing. He then worked his way along to behind the engine, and, despite the fierce slipstream from the propeller, managed while lying down to smother the fire. Isolated from the leaking petrol pipe, this later burnt itself out. Ward, exhausted, regained the astro-hatch with great difficulty: 'the hardest of the lot,' he wrote, 'was getting my right leg in. In the end the navigator reached out and pulled it in.' Despite all the damage, the crew got home to a safe landing – perhaps the most remarkable thing, apart from Ward's exploit, being the fact that the pilot had no idea at the time what Ward was doing. Sadly, Ward was killed on a Hamburg raid only ten weeks later – before he could even receive his Victoria Cross.[8]

Many pilots by now were nearing the end of their 'tour', which in most cases had become standardised at 30 operations. One was Sergeant Wheeler, a wireless-operator/air-gunner with No. 150 Squadron. His book, *Just to Get a Bed*, gives a glimpse of what completing a tour felt like:

On 8 August 1941 we were assembled in the C.O.'s office to be told at long last that our operation that night was to be our last and that we were to be rested at an OTU. The target was Hamburg, not the easiest of targets for our last excursion, and we all wished each other good luck and promised ourselves a party if we were fortunate enough to return. We had come to rely on each other so much over a period of one year and had become the staunchest of friends, we almost regretted the necessary split up to various stations after this last flight together. We reached the enemy coast and experienced flak for the last time, but as one engine was not functioning we were forced to abandon our task at Groningen. However disappointing this last sortie was, we had survived where so many crews had not, and when we taxied to our dispersal we climbed out of 'C' for Charlie, all kissed the ground in thankfulness, embraced our faithful ground crew and invited them to a final party to show our appreciation of their marvellous service and dedication . . .[9]

Despite a number of successes, the crews in general during the second half of 1941 still found it hard to locate their targets in Germany, and damaged them only slightly or moderately when they did. Their reports, on the whole, nevertheless conveyed an impression of substantial achievement, as did intelligence reports through neutral sources. But Bomber Command's aircraft were increasingly being equipped with night cameras, and photography was telling a different story.

The difficulty applying to targets in Germany also applied to targets in Italy. Scheduled for no more than occasional attention, these suffered attack from only some 300 sorties during the eighteen months July 1940–December 1941. The largest raiding force, on 10/11 September 1941, consisted of 76 aircraft including 20 of the new Stirlings and Halifaxes, and their targets were the marshalling yards, main railway station and Royal Arsenal at Turin. They managed to do some damage in the city centre but, misled by inaccurate incendiary leaders, mainly succeeded in hitting residential areas some miles further south. The smallest raid, a fortnight later against Genoa, was by a single Wellington of 311 (Czechoslovak) Squadron, piloted by Sergeant Musalka. It occurred because his aircraft failed to receive a message recalling the force when fog was suddenly forecast over base.*

Despite the length of the flight and the difficulty of identifying the main objectives, raids on Italy were not unpopular with the crews. They appreciated both the beauty of the Alps by moonlight and the absence of effective opposition over the target. The flak, they found, tended to die down with the first bombs. Of course there were many violations of Swiss airspace but the Swiss, at least in these early stages, were disposed to accept this with good grace. On 3 October 1940 the Foreign Secretary reported to the War Cabinet that the Swiss Minister had discussed the matter 'with complete good humour. If we had to pass over Switzerland he hoped that so far as possible we would use the Geneva route. Later on, the weather might make it impossible for us to

---

* A similar incident had occurred a year earlier when Wilfred Surtees, later a wing commander DFC, piloted a Whitley of 78 Squadron to Milan. Failing to receive the recall he carried on alone and returned to find thick fog over southern bases. With tanks almost empty he managed to land the aircraft intact in a small stubble cornfield near Winchester; he was 'mentioned in despatches' for saving his crew.

fly over his country, in which case he hoped we would make a virtue of necessity and draw attention to the correctness of our attitude'.

While the tried and trusted Wellingtons, Whitleys and Hampdens, aided by a few less well tried and trusted Stirlings, Manchesters and Halifaxes, did their best to destroy German transportation and morale, the Blenheims were still braving the enemy by day nearer home. But at times they were also required to join in night raids on the less distant German cities, or even to attack them by day under cloud cover.

An extreme example of this last, and most hazardous, type of operation was the raid on 4 July 1941 against targets in Bremen. Nine Blenheims of 105 Squadron and three of 107, led by the dashing and determined Australian, Wing Commander Hughie Edwards DFC, crossed the coast at Cuxhaven, ignoring the absence of the prescribed cloud cover. Sweeping between barrage balloons they bombed Bremen from chimneypot height – one aircraft collecting telephone wires around the tail wheel. Two bombs hit the Weser works, destroying many aircraft components, and another struck a minesweeper in the Atlas yard – where one of the Blenheims, riddled by flak, crashed down to inflict further damage. For his extreme gallantry in pressing home this attack successfully from so low a level Hughie Edwards, who himself flew beneath a high-tension cable, received the VC – the first Australian with the RAF to do so.[10] Immediate awards also went to five others. The cost of the raid, however, was very high – four aircraft of the 12 were shot down, and all the rest damaged. Churchill, praising the courage of the crews, compared it with that of the Light Brigade at Balaclava.[11] If he noted any other similarity between the two episodes, he forbore to point it out.

On 12 August Peirse tried another daylight operation of this kind, against what were said to be exceptionally important targets – power stations near Cologne. This was part of the strategy of trying to help the Russians by making the Germans keep a strong fighter force in the West. No fewer than 54 Blenheims set out, aided by diversionary raids and by fighters which accompanied them as far as Antwerp. Again it was a low-level attack, and again some hits were scored: the output of the power stations seems to have been reduced by about 10 per cent for nine days. But again the cost was appallingly high – ten aircraft out of the 54.

The final operation in this series came a fortnight later, on 26 August, when six Blenheims set out on a diversionary raid against Heligoland while others attacked shipping. None of the six found Heligoland, and four failed to return. Peirse absorbed the obvious lesson: the Blenheims made no more daylight trips to Germany.

Meanwhile, from 28 April, Peirse was experimenting with small numbers of the new heavy bombers in the daylight role. First were the Stirlings – but the cloud cover was rarely reliable enough. Then the few Fortresses of 90 Squadron tried to bomb from a great height – but they were beset with technical troubles, they produced giveaway contrails and the Sperry bombsight was not fully automatic over 20,000 feet; an American bomb-aiming expert, carried on one raid, failed to place a single bomb within the town of Bremen.[12] After some 50 mostly ineffectual sorties over Germany, and four losses, Peirse gave up in September and contemplated modifying the Fortress for work at night. Fortunately the Americans were soon to need them, and to develop them into formidable engines of war.

So, as the Manchesters were too unreliable, only the Halifaxes remained as possible daylight raiders over Germany. Six of them tried on 30 June, and five successfully bombed Kiel; but German fighters intercepted soon afterwards, and shot one down. Peirse did not call on them again to bomb Germany by day, and 1941 ended with the only daylight attacks on Germany being made by a few Hampdens. This was a waste: they had to be painted in day colours and could not be used for their normal – and more valuable – night operations.

Daylight raids over Germany in 1941 were an unsuccessful experiment, not unduly persisted in. The main daylight operations continued to be the Blenheims' CIRCUSES over France and the Low Countries and the anti-shipping strikes. On 16 July, for instance, after photographs had revealed a large number of ships, 36 Blenheims attacked the port of Rotterdam. Achieving complete surprise, they swept in at mast height in two waves line abreast, and were credited with destroying or damaging 22 vessels. German fighters, too late to intercept, were afterwards kept off by the Blenheims' escort. But, as usual, there were heavy casualties from flak – four of the 36. A repeat raid on 28 August, however, fared far worse. The Blenheims hit at least two ships, but of the 18 which set out, one crashed on take-off, and seven others failed to return.

Bomber Command's allotted coastal area at this time ran from Cherbourg to Texel, with Coastal Command responsible beyond those points. In addition to the attacks at Rotterdam, the Blenheims bombed shipping in Cherbourg, Le Havre, Boulogne and Ostend, but they were also constantly active against merchant shipping at sea. Particularly onerous was the operation of the CHANNEL STOP. On 18 July three Blenheims sank a trawler near Gravelines, but all three succumbed to flak. Two days later six Blenheims hit a tanker off Berck-sur-Mer; two were lost. So it went on through the summer of 1941 – success bought only at a heavy price. The losses in relation to sorties flown were no greater than the Blenheims were used to, but actually attacking the ships, as opposed to searching for them, was deadly work. In the later recollection of the AOC of 2 Group, every actual attack cost, in Blenheims destroyed or badly damaged, two-thirds of the striking force.[13] According to the German figures, the Germans lost 41 ships in the months July–December. The RAF lost 127 aircraft in its attacks – three aircraft lost for every ship sunk.

Fortunately during the autumn of 1941 a better instrument for this kind of work came to hand. Hurricanes had been successfully converted to carry bombs. On 29 November, after some experiments, the long-suffering Blenheim crews thankfully yielded the task of applying the CHANNEL STOP to Hurribombers of Fighter Command.

If there was one frequently demanded operation at this time more dangerous than attacking well-protected merchant ships, it was attacking units of the German Navy. The ever-present requirement to cripple the *Scharnhorst* and *Gneisenau* in Brest recurred in an acute form when they were joined at the beginning of June 1941 by the *Prinz Eugen*, escaped from the chase which sank the *Bismarck*. But the three warships were usually enveloped in smoke when the raiders arrived, and over 300 sorties flown against them in June did them no damage. 'Heavily protected ships in dock,' the Director of Bombing Operations at the Air Ministry explained for the benefit of the Secretary of State, 'will always be difficult to damage decisively. They cannot be sunk, the opportunities for underwater damage are absent, and full facilities for repair are always available.'[14] He went on to say, quite rightly, that the ships must have suffered damage to stay in Brest so long. But Air Vice-Marshal John ('Jack') Slessor, who early in 1941 had succeeded Harris in command of 5 Group, took a bleaker view. In a note to Peirse at the end of June he estimated that the odds against hitting the ships at night were 'as the national debt to a tintack'. 'Our bombs,' he added, 'either pitch into the water or a French town, and our crews do get very browned off with it.'[15] He suggested – as Portal had done after the Norwegian campaign – the formation of a specially trained and equipped squadron for such tasks. Less fruitfully, he also suggested trying a large-scale raid by daylight. Despite all difficulties, however, a raid by 52 Wellingtons on 1/2 July scored a hit on the *Prinz Eugen* and did serious damage to the vessel – and her crew.

On 22 July the *Scharnhorst* slipped out of Brest to La Pallice, where the following evening a Stirling, one of six despatched, claimed a hit. During the night 30 Wellingtons continued the attack, and together these raids prevented any immediate break-out. The next day, 24 July, Peirse tried the big daylight attack. He had planned it for Brest alone, but now had to extend it to both ports. At Brest, three high-flying Fortresses were meant to draw up the German fighters, while 18 Hampdens, escorted by long-range Spitfires, came in below. As the enemy fighters were refuelling, 79 Wellingtons would then arrive to do the major damage. Meanwhile 36 Blenheims would make a diversionary raid on the Cherbourg docks, to detain any fighters in that area.

The Blenheims did their job well at Cherbourg, and for once returned in the strength at which they had set out. At Brest, nothing went right. Flak broke up the Hampdens' formations, and Me 109s got in among them and the subsequent Wellingtons. Two Hampdens out of the 18, ten Wellingtons out of the 79, went down. At La Pallice, where the attack was entrusted to 15 unescorted Halifaxes, there were actually five hits on the *Scharnhorst*: two of the armour-piercing bombs failed to explode but the other three did damage which sent the battle cruiser, carrying some three thousand tons of sea-water, limping back to Brest next day for repairs.[16] But the cost was appallingly high – five of the 15 raiders, each carrying a crew of seven, lost, and all the rest damaged.

After this, Peirse forbore to attack again in strength by day. During September he tried two major attacks at night. Thereafter about 17 minor raids during October and November sufficed to keep the three warships in dock or harbour – for the time being.

At Bomber Command headquarters Peirse had long been worried by the number of sorties that failed to reach and identify, still less hit, their targets in Germany. Soon after he took over the Command he expressed his opinion that only one crew in five was finding the more distant targets, one crew in three the nearer ones.[17] Some of his Group commanders fully shared his concern. A few weeks afterwards, Coningham, AOC 4 Group, wrote to him: 'I have little idea what the Whitley boys do, and it causes me considerable anxiety.'[18] Coningham went on to suggest that the best crews should start fires for the others to bomb – which was what the Luftwaffe was doing at that time in

Britain, with the significant difference that the crack German fire raisers were being guided by radio beams. Coningham's idea – and others had the same – received consideration, but Peirse's best hopes for improved navigation were pinned to the arrival of GEE, the aid under development since the summer of 1940.

It was not only Peirse and Coningham who were worried about the target-finding, but also many of the crews, who knew the difficulties all the more acutely from firsthand experience. What one of the more thoughtful young pilots of 1941 felt is evident in the diary of Pilot Officer David Hardie of 101 Squadron, a public-school boy who had won a classics scholarship to Oxford but deferred taking it up in order to volunteer for flying duties. After a raid on 4/5 July 1941 he wrote:

Twelve 250s [bombs] on Rotterdam; but I don't think we got there – it was probably Dordrecht. It was Miller's [navigator] first trip, and really not very successful – on the way back we were stooging up the Thames estuary before we knew where we were, and when we did get to our own locality it took me time to find the aerodrome owing to trouble over the beam. There was one nasty moment when the port engine spluttered and gave out owing to lack of petrol, but we got things under control again and landed OK. Four hours on a trip scheduled to last two and a half.

Hardie's diary entry for 22 July shows an airman deeply concerned about operational shortcomings and over-optimism:

We were detailed to drive to Mannheim, but either because the kite wasn't feeling too well or because I was driving badly we couldn't get above 15000 ft. We ran into a bank of high cloud somewhere near Luxembourg and after turning back once or twice to try and get height Miller worked out that we would be over the target at 3 am. That wasn't pleasant, so we turned for Dunkirk or Ostend. By then we were hopelessly lost, and by the time we had got a fix over the sea it was too late to go for the ports. Stooging home, there was low cloud over E. Anglia, so anticipating trouble I jettisoned the eggs in the sea, only to find the mist broken over base. Such a thoroughly unsatisfactory trip that we all feel very badly about it. Even more infuriating is the suspicion that what with blokes like [—] who drop off a bomb or two on the enemy coast so as to get to safe height before bombing the edge of the flak, the majority of crews are shooting the hell of a line to all concerned when they get back from a trip. From my own experience I would think that

95

night bombing, unless on a heavy and prolonged scale, is likely to yield very few important results.*

Impressions of the success of the night-bombing at this time might have faded earlier had night photography been more advanced, or the supply of night cameras more adequate. By the end of April 1941 Bomber Command was scheduled to have 693 night cameras installed in its aircraft: it actually had 165.[19] Equally, success or otherwise might have been established by more daylight reconnaissance; but the Blenheims were short in range and had proved too vulnerable, and the high-flying stripped Spitfires of the Photographic Reconnaissance Unit were all too few and had been concentrating on the invasion threat. It was nevertheless these Spitfires' photographs, revealing much less damage than had been reported, that inspired Lord Cherwell, Churchill's personal scientific adviser, to instigate a systematic analysis of the bombers' own night photographs taken in June and July 1941.

The result was the famous Butt Report, completed in August 1941. D. M. Butt, of the War Cabinet Secretariat, examined about 630 photographs taken on night operations, together with the relevant orders and reports. He concluded that of all the aircraft recorded as having attacked their targets, only one-third had got within five miles of them. Naturally this proportion was much higher – two-thirds – over the nearer targets like the French ports; over the haze-shrouded Ruhr it dropped to one-tenth. In full moon, two-fifths of the aircraft reported as having attacked their targets had got within five miles of them. On moonless nights, only one-fifteenth.[20]

The Butt Report sent shock waves through the Air Ministry, Bomber Command, and Downing Street. If only a third of the attackers got within five miles of their objectives in Germany, how much of the bomb-load could possibly be falling on the targets? Clearly, very little.

---

* A few weeks later, returning from the disastrous raid on Berlin of 7/8 November (pp. 99–100), David Hardie was forced to ditch his Wellington in the North Sea, and he and all his crew were lost. His commanding officer wrote in the highest possible terms of his skill, courage, popularity and devotion to duty. There is a story to the diary. It was written in an exercise book, covered a few months of 1941, and ended abruptly. It bore no indications of its author, or of his squadron, though it was clear that he was operating on Wellingtons from Oakington, in Cambridgeshire. It was among a mass of papers in the bomber room at Binbrook, in Lincolnshire, about to be destroyed in 1947 when it was noticed and saved by Flight Lieutenant Neil St Clair l'Amie, who in 1991 brought it to my notice in connection with this book. It was possible to guess from some of the entries that the diarist's school might have been Charterhouse, and my Old Carthusian friend and neighbour, Ian Wallace, was able from the list and dates of OCs killed serving with the RAF, to point me towards Hardie's name and family. Through Neil St Clair l'Amie's kindness the diary is now in the possession of David Hardie's sister. D.R.

Peirse and Portal knew well enough that some of the bombing was going astray, but they had not imagined quite how much, or quite how far.

It would have been possible to criticise the Butt Report on some technical grounds, but, much to his credit, Portal did not waste time on this. Instead, he did all he could to accelerate the arrival of the new scientific aids. As one authoritative study put it: 'Realists within the Service accepted the irrefutable "evidence in camera" and, under the cloak of complacent publicity which kept the British people happy, went to work on schemes to improve matters and build up a force which would do what the optimists imagined was already being done.'[21]

Inevitably, however, the Butt findings could only detract from the prestige of the officer at the head of Bomber Command. Inevitably, too, they put doubt into the mind of Churchill about the whole strategy of a bombing offensive. If the bombers were so inaccurate, could they possibly provide, as he had forecast in 1940, the means of victory?

This doubt soon found strong expression. On 19 September 1941 Portal had placed before the Prime Minister a scheme for 'Coventry-scale' attacks on 45 of Germany's largest towns, indicating that decisive results might be obtained inside six months if a force of 4000 bombers could be built up and so employed. To this he got a sharp answer. 'It is very debatable,' Churchill wrote, 'whether bombing by itself will be a decisive factor in the present war . . . the British people have been stimulated and strengthened by the attacks made on them thus far . . . it seems very likely that the ground defences and night fighters will overtake the Air attack . . . it should be noted that only a quarter of our bombs hit the target. The most we can say is that it will be a heavy and I trust seriously increasing annoyance.'[22]

A Chief of the Air Staff of Portal's steely strength could not let this go unchallenged. The British Army was in no better position in 1941 than it had been in 1940, or than it would be in 1942, to liberate the Continent. The British official strategy of a major bombing offensive had not changed, yet here was the Prime Minister apparently striking at its very roots.

Portal's riposte, on 2 October, drew from the Secretary of State, Sir Archibald Sinclair, the delighted epithets 'Masterly! Audacious!' With characteristic tact Portal did not argue. He simply pointed out that the strategy had been constantly reaffirmed officially, and production planned to conform to it, and that if bombing was to be no more than 'a heavy and growing annoyance', the strategy and the production programmes had better be changed. And he reaffirmed his belief that, with technical improvements and the scale of attack the Air Staff visualised, decisive results could be obtained.[23]

This spiked Churchill's guns, for at that time there was no major offensive strategy open to the British Government other than bombing, and production was heavily geared to this. Nevertheless the Prime Minister, while assuring Portal that there was no intention of changing the existing policy, made some very prescient points in reply. On 7 October he wrote back:

> ... I deprecate placing unbounded confidence in this means of attack ... It is the most potent method of impairing the enemy's morale at the present time ... If the United States enters the war it would have to be supplemented in 1943 by simultaneous attacks by armoured forces ... Only in this way could a decision certainly be achieved. Even if all the towns in Germany were rendered largely uninhabitable, it does not follow that military control would be weakened or even that war industry could not be carried on ...
>
> It may well be that German morale will crack and that our bombing will play a very important part in bringing the result about. But all things are always on the move simultaneously, and it is quite possible that the Nazi war-making power in 1943 will be so widely spread throughout Europe as to be to a huge extent independent of the actual buildings in the homeland.
>
> A different picture would be presented if the enemy's Air Force were so far reduced as to enable heavy accurate daylight bombing of factories to take place. This, however, cannot be done outside the radius of Fighter protection according to what I am at present told.
>
> One has to do the best one can, but he is an unwise man who thinks there is any *certain* method of winning *this* war, or indeed any other war between equals in strength. The only plan is to persevere.
>
> I shall be delighted to discuss these general topics with you whenever you will.[24]

Duly assured that the policy held, Portal addressed himself to the tasks in hand, of which ensuring the expansion and greater accuracy of Bomber Command were among the foremost. Meanwhile the Prime Minister's wide-ranging mind encompassed the findings of the Butt Report, the fact that the Soviet Union had held out against Germany for more than the expected eight or ten weeks, and the possibility that sooner or later the United States would be drawn into the conflict.

There might be further ways, after all, of winning the war than only by bombing Germany.

On top of the disturbing effect of the Butt Report came the disastrous raid of 7/8 November on Berlin.

After the initial attacks in August 1940 which had so angered Hitler, Bomber Command had repeatedly sent forces against the German capital. With the exception of a major effort on 23/24 September, when 129 Wellingtons, Whitleys and Hampdens tried to hit 18 different power stations, gasworks and the like, all the raids in 1940 were by small forces. In all, there were 34 raids against Berlin during that year. The attacking aircraft dropped, on average, only half-a-ton of bombs apiece, and the casualty rate was high – 11 per cent.

In the spring of 1941, when Peirse mounted several raids on Berlin by around 70 aircraft, and one by over 100, there were some better results, but the tonnage dropped remained very small and the casualties high. Wilfrid Freeman, at that time Vice-Chief of the Air Staff, urged Portal in May to end what he called 'utter wastefulness and dissipation of our resources', but Portal declined to intervene. Berlin, after all, was on Peirse's directive and Portal himself thought it 'well worth sacrificing, say, ten tons of bombs from another target to get 4,000,000 people out of bed and into the shelters'.[25] In the next six raids after that, up to 25/26 July, less than half of the 55 aircraft despatched actually attacked, and nine were lost – over 16 per cent.

German records exist for eight raids delivered in 1941 on Berlin between 2/3 June and the ill-fated 7/8 November. In most of these attacks a few of the new heavy bombers took part, three or four Stirlings or up to six Halifaxes joining forces with some 20 or more Wellington IIs. This enabled some of the new 4000-lb ('block-buster' or 'cookie') bombs to be dropped. On some nights, notably 2/3 and 7/8 September, significant damage was done to important targets, such as railway stations, power stations and Tempelhof airfield, but in general the bombing was too widespread and (unintentionally) unselective to produce serious effects. Of the 630 bombers which took part, just over half claimed to have attacked. They dropped 1086 HE bombs, but the Germans recorded only a third of this number as having fallen within the city. The eight raids killed 135 people, made 4705 homeless, and cost Bomber Command 62 aircraft – nearly 10 per cent of sorties.

It was the raid of 7/8 November 1941 which put an end to this series. Perhaps in an effort, after the Butt Report, to show what Bomber Command could really do, Peirse had planned to send more aircraft out on this night than he had ever done before. No fewer than 169 took off for Berlin, and 223 for other targets. But the weather proved too formidable; of the Berlin contingent, fewer than a half reached their objective, and those did little damage. The German capital was in any case at extreme range for the Wellingtons and Whitleys which formed the bulk of the force; and with much more thick, ice-laden cloud and higher winds on the return journey than had been forecast, it was not only the inexperienced pilots who found their petrol running dangerously low. Of the 169 aircraft sent to Berlin, 21 – a shocking 12.5 per cent – failed to return.

One who long remembered that night was Bill Grierson-Jackson, a young graduate and recently commissioned navigator with 51 Squadron. It was only his second operation and he was under the captaincy of a much more experienced sergeant pilot. Unable to get a visual pinpoint or a wireless bearing after bombing Berlin, but eventually securing an astro-fix which placed him still over Germany, Grierson-Jackson decided to ignore the captain's firm instruction to follow the prescribed track home – by way of the Baltic and the North Sea – and instead gave a course across Germany and Holland. He did this because he was convinced that against headwinds of 95 mph the Whitley would run out of fuel, unless he took the shortest possible route home. He also trusted that the density and depth of cloud would conceal his deception from the pilot. Unfortunately for this hope, daylight arrived and the clouds parted before the aircraft had quite cleared Holland. The crew got back safely, but with no fuel margin at all; both tanks registered empty. The pilot, however, was aggrieved at the disregard of his instructions and at having been exposed to the danger of flying over enemy-occupied territory in daylight. He made his feelings known, and Grierson-Jackson's reward for a skilful piece of navigation in appallingly difficult circumstances was a severe castigation from the Squadron CO.*

The losses on the Berlin raid, however, were not the only disaster on 7/8 November. Fifty-five aircraft took off for Mannheim – seven (13 per cent) did not return. Another 43 went to the Ruhr, or mining; nine (21 per cent) were reported missing. Only the 133 sent against the nearer targets – Cologne, Ostend and Boulogne – got home intact.

The loss of 37 bombers in a single night – more than twice as many as in any previous night's operations – naturally resulted in enquiries. But

---

* Later in the war Grierson-Jackson became Senior Navigation Officer at the Pathfinders' Navigation Training Unit. He was awarded the DFC and the AFC. After the war Dr Grierson (as he then became known) was an agricultural scientist and university professor.

before their conclusions could reach the Prime Minister, Churchill had himself formed one of his own: such losses could not be tolerated when there was no evidence of decisive damage to the enemy. He insisted – and Portal and the other Chiefs of Staff agreed – that there should now be a period of 'conservation'. Bomber Command was Britain's only major offensive weapon: electronic aids to navigation and fine new aircraft – the Lancasters – were on their way: the Command must stop apparently unproductive losses of aircraft and crews and gather strength during the winter, to prepare for a new, heavier and more effective offensive in the spring of 1942.

Peirse demurred. This seemed like criticism of his handling of the force. If operations tailed off, disillusion might spread among his crews. 'It is damned hard,' he wrote, 'to fight a force like Bomber Command at a subdued tempo.'[26] Nevertheless, that, for the time being, is what he was told to do. Very promptly, on 13 November, a 'conservation' directive went out to Bomber Command.[27]

But of course a familiar demand soon reappeared to make this difficult. On 21 October 1941 – appropriately enough, Trafalgar Day – the First Sea Lord had pointed out that repairs to the three German warships at Brest must be nearing completion. He asked for heavy attack on the three warships, on the U-boat operating bases on the Biscay coast, and on the North Sea German ports, with special attention to the shipyards building and maintaining U-boats.

Peirse did his best. He was naturally more enthusiastic about attacking German ports than French ones, and in the next three months Bomber Command made 20 raids, involving some 1700 sorties, against these targets. The biggest, against Hamburg on 30 November/1 December, was proportionately the most expensive – 13 aircraft lost out of 181. The U-boat bases on the Biscay coast, which Peirse had also been asked to attack, were subjected to only three raids during November and December – and on each occasion mist prevented accurate bombing.

There remained the Admiralty's *bêtes noires*, the *Scharnhorst*, *Gneisenau* and *Prinz Eugen*, all in dock at Brest. After the damage inflicted in the summer, the 300-odd sorties a month flown against them at that period had been allowed to dwindle to a mere 50 sorties a month in October and November. But on 7 December Japanese aircraft wrecked the American Pacific Fleet at Pearl Harbor, and three days later sank the *Prince of Wales* and the *Repulse* off Malaya. Though Hitler's subsequent declaration of war on the United States was to give Britain a second great ally, the war at sea had entered a new and dangerous phase. It became more than ever important to keep the three German warships in Brest immobilised. During December Peirse directed ten raids against them, totalling 961 sorties – all without further success. There then followed a further 17 fruitless attempts, involving 961 sorties between 1 January and 12 February 1942 – when they escaped. Lesser raids meanwhile repeatedly attacked German shipping and minor naval units in the Channel ports, with the result that during January 1942 substantially more sorties were flown against French docks than against Hitler's Reich. It could certainly be said that the war at sea was providing useful anti-aircraft defence for the German homeland.

Meanwhile Portal had become dissatisfied with Peirse's replies to his enquiries about the losses on the night of 7/8 November. He had at first accepted Peirse's explanation that these arose from an inaccurate weather forecast. Then he had heard that Slessor, AOC 5 Group, unhappy at the forecast, had rung Command headquarters to say that his Hampdens could not take on long-range targets in such weather, and had received permission for them to bomb Cologne instead – which they had done without loss. Portal had also heard that one station commander, on account of the forecast, had permitted only his most experienced crews to go – and that they had arrived back with their tanks almost empty. The weather had undoubtedly turned out to be worse than anticipated; but, studying the forecast, Portal came to the conclusion that it contained enough danger signs to make large-scale, long-range operations inadvisable. Peirse, he thought, had made an error of judgement.

In the latter part of December Portal accompanied Churchill to the Washington Conference, the first of the great meetings with Roosevelt to discuss the strategy of the new Grand Alliance. Towards the end of the conference, on 4 January 1942, Portal showed the Prime Minister the papers relating to the Berlin and other raids of 7/8 November.[28] Four days later Peirse had a new appointment: to command the embryonic Allied air forces in South-East Asia.

9

Low Point: New Hopes: New Commander

U ntil Peirse's successor could take over at High Wycombe it fell to Air Vice-Marshal 'Jack' Baldwin, the well-liked commander of 3 Group, to act as AOC-in-C. It was his misfortune that during this brief period, on 12 February 1942, the three much-bombed German warships made their escape from Brest. It was also his misfortune that he was not at High Wycombe that morning, and that the Senior Air Staff Officer, the amiable and extremely efficient 'Sandy' Saundby, was not there either. Both were visiting the Air Ministry. It also happened that when the news broke, the Wing Commander Controller was out to lunch. However, a perfectly competent squadron leader was in charge, and it was he who initiated the agreed air action.[1]

During December 1941 the increased weight of attack on the three vessels at Brest, including a costly daylight raid by 47 of the new 'heavies', had convinced Hitler that they must be withdrawn. As he put it to his naval staff, the *Scharnhorst* and *Gneisenau* were 'like a patient having cancer, who is doomed unless he submits to an operation'.[2] The operation – the run for home – would inevitably be risky, but it was the only way to save the ships. Besides, he needed them, he thought, to guard against a British landing in Norway: a successful Combined-Operations raid on the island of Vaagsö on 27 December, much assisted by Bomber Command's diversionary attacks which cost eight aircraft out of the 29 involved, had planted in his mind an enduring illusion that the British might at any time invade Norway.*[3]

Early in February 1942 reconnaissance and other information revealed a break-out from Brest to be imminent, and the Admiralty correctly foretold that the route to Germany would probably be by way of the English Channel. From 3 February all available aircraft in Bomber Command were at two hours' notice, but as the days wore on this became impossible to sustain. On 10 February the force under warning was reduced to 100 aircraft at four hours' notice. Little more than twenty-four hours later the three vessels slipped out of Brest under cover of darkness. They would be passing through the Straits of Dover in broad daylight – the reverse of what the Admiralty expected.

The Germans had waited for a prolonged spell of cloud and rain, forecast with remarkable accuracy from reports by their Atlantic U-boats and far-ranging Condors. Everything went well for them. The standard Coastal Command patrols covering the western end of the Channel, suffering from unserviceable ASV (Air to Surface Vessel) radar, failed to detect the break-out; the numerous blips on the south-coast radar screens occasioned by the escorting minor vessels and aircraft aroused no immediate fears; and it was only the accidental appearance and sharp eyes of a fighter pilot, Group Captain Victor Beamish, station commander at Kenley, who on a 'quiet day' had decided, with a like-minded companion, to 'try and pick up a stray Hun', that finally ended the vessels' immunity from discovery. By that time the ships were off Le Touquet, only thirty miles short of Gris Nez. At 11.30 a.m. Fighter Command alerted Bomber Command, and at 1.35 p.m. the first bombers took off – two hours better than the four-hour notice required. By then the ships were past the Straits of Dover and visibility was appalling, with cloud eight-tenths to ten-tenths, in places down to 300 feet. In three successive waves between 3 p.m. and 6 p.m. a total of 242 bombers of all types, including a few of the new, fast, steady Bostons, set forth – the largest Bomber Command daylight operation thus far. But in such conditions all their efforts were in vain, as were those of Fighter and Coastal Command and a heroic suicidal attack by Swordfish of the Fleet Air Arm. Fifteen Bomber Command aircraft fell to the ships' guns or the accompanying fighters. In the murk, the vessels sailed on, unharmed.

* At a later stage in the war Winston Churchill would have turned the illusion into reality, but was restrained by the Chiefs of Staff.

Among those who might, with better luck, have interrupted their progress was Flight Lieutenant John Partridge, a pre-war pilot of 83 Squadron. Partridge had done seven operations on Hampdens, but this was his first on a Manchester. He later recalled:

> Very few aircraft found the ships but when we broke cloud we were right over them at under 100 feet. We encountered intense gunfire and received much damage. Unfortunately our hydraulics were hit and we were unable to open our bomb doors – or later to lower flaps or undercarriage. We had to set course for base with only one serviceable engine, and our rear-gunner was seriously injured and eventually died. We made for the nearest grass airfield and made a belly landing at Bircham Newton with all our bombs on board. We made a successful landing and came to a stop in a hedge at the edge of the airfield.[4]

The vessels sailed on, still unharmed by the bomber attacks, but they did not reach port unharmed. Mines laid previously by aircraft, or others dropped that evening by 5 Group in the projected path of the vessels, succeeded where bombing had failed: the *Scharnhorst* hit two and the *Gneisenau* one. Despite severe damage, they got home. However, there was an epilogue. A fortnight later, on 26/27 February, a direct hit on the *Gneisenau* in Kiel killed 116 of her crew and effectively ended her fighting career. No further bombs struck the *Scharnhorst*, but it was twelve months before she could again put to sea.[5]

The escape of the 'TOADS', as the battle cruisers were code-named (or the 'Salmon and Gluckstein', as they were more commonly referred to*), through waters historically regarded as a close preserve of the Royal Navy, was one of many humiliating incidents in a series of Allied reverses. The American Pacific Fleet had been crippled, American Pacific outposts besieged. The British had been chased out of Malaya and were shortly to be chased out of Burma. Three days after the battle cruisers' escape, the greatest mass capitulation in British history took place at Singapore. In North Africa, Auchinleck's advance had come to a halt and Rommel was about to strike back. In keeping with all this, Bomber Command, 'the means of victory', seemed as yet to have made no great impact on Germany, and was reduced to conserving its efforts – except against naval targets – until the approaching spring.

---

* From the name of a well-known chain of tobacconists.

Yet despite all this there were factors which pointed to brighter months ahead for the Allies. Undeniably, the British Commonwealth, the United States and the Soviet Union together commanded military and economic resources potentially far greater than those of Germany, Italy and Japan, bloated though these were by recent conquests. The Allies had suffered reverses, and would suffer more, but with the United States part of the team they were always the more likely victors in the long run.

Similarly, the outlook for Bomber Command was better than its recent history suggested. Beset with difficulties such as the production delays and teething troubles of the new heavy bombers, the drain of squadrons to Coastal Command and the Middle East, and the still unsolved problems of accurate navigation and bomb-aiming by night, the Command's performance had not thus far lived up to the expectations entertained at the start of the bombing campaign. Nevertheless it already had some solid achievements behind it, and among them, though it hardly seemed so at the time, was the long series of attacks against the warships now back in their home ports. Major Charles Carrington, Army GHQ Liaison Officer at High Wycombe, summed up in this way:

> Bomber Command had done better in its campaign against the TOADS than Fighter Command, or Coastal, or Fleet Air Arm, or ships of the Royal Navy. The Bombers had immobilized them for ten months in Brest and now put them out of action in their home waters. Yet no one regarded February 1942 as our finest hour . . .[6]

Whatever Bomber Command's shortcomings to date, it had certainly done enough damage to make the Germans regard its efforts very seriously. Paradoxically, perhaps its main achievement during 1941 was that it forced Germany to set up a much more elaborate night-fighter system. From the early days of the war the Germans had had powerful flak and searchlight defences for their big cities, but their first specialised night-fighter unit was formed only in June 1940 – in response to the RAF's early raids on the Ruhr. The following month Goering gave orders to expand this into a Night-Fighting Division, and within a year the Division grew into a whole *Fliegerkorps* (No. XII). Numerically, the German night-fighter force increased from three *Gruppen*, each with a notional strength of around 36 adapted day-fighters in the summer of 1940, to ten *Gruppen* by the end of 1941.[7]

Moreover the German night-fighter arm became much more technically advanced and better organised. At first the fighters had simply flown round in the dark in a 'standby' zone near a city, waiting for the searchlights to pick up a quarry and give them a fleeting chance to deliver an attack – during which the flak supposedly held its fire. But in the course of late 1940 and 1941 General Kammhuber, in charge of the force, built up around the frontiers open to RAF penetration, from Denmark through to Holland, a system of interception zones. In the RAF, though not in Germany, this was known as the Kammhuber line. The forward zone was divided into 'boxes' in each of which were stationed one early-warning FREYA radar and two close-range WÜRZBURG radars. After the FREYA had first picked up the oncoming bombers one of the WÜRZBURGS plotted it, while the other plotted the intercepting fighter. A controller on the ground with both displays before him could direct the fighter by R/T into the vicinity of the bomber. If the bomber penetrated through this radar zone he then came into a searchlight zone, later also assisted by radar, where the fighter could continue his attack. In either case there was no 'friendly' flak to disturb the fighter.[8]

The effect of this (and other) developments can be seen in the rising British losses as 1941 wore on. In 1940, according to German sources, night-fighters shot down 42 out of 271 British bombers destroyed attacking the Reich; in 1941 they shot down 421 out of 756.[9] In the first half of 1941 Bomber Command's casualty rate for aircraft missing at night was 2 per cent of sorties. In August it was 3.5 per cent and in November 4.8 per cent. Gone were the days, or rather nights, of which Alan Nicoll could write: 'I completed 47 trips . . . I saw plenty of flak, but never saw night fighters.'[10]

Instead, night-fighters now posed the greater danger.

On a return flight from Germany [wrote Group Captain Sawyer] I had the unhappy experience of seeing no fewer than five aircraft shot down around us in the distance over a period of about an hour while we were running up to the Dutch coast on the way home. It was grimly fascinating to see in each case the short burst of twinkling horizontal tracer – without any answering fire, unfortunately, so each must have been taken completely by surprise – followed by a small red fire, growing steadily into a larger red ball as seen from a distance. Then a slow, curving fall to a final vertical plummet earthwards as the stricken bombers disappeared into the haze below, or crashed burning on to the ground. Each incident happened so quickly, and I wondered each time if the crew had managed to bale out safely, as we ourselves droned on homewards knowing full well that there were other night fighters most probably stalking us too.[11]

Yet this increase in the German defences was in its way a tribute to the growing threat posed by the British offensive. One of the objectives of that offensive was, after all, to make the Germans deploy in Germany guns, fighters and other resources which they might otherwise be using against Russia. Bomber Command had begun the task, infinitely painful, of forcing the Germans on to the defensive in the air. Better, for the Allies, more of the Luftwaffe over Germany than over Russia – or Britain.

The winter of 1941–2 has been called 'the nadir of Bomber Command's fortunes'. If it was that, it was a nadir from which there was every chance of a rapid rise in the curve of success. Many lessons had been learned, and bombing policy had become more adjusted to operational possibility. The new electronic aid GEE would soon be available in quantity, the initial troubles with the Halifax were being remedied, the Lancasters would soon replace the underpowered Manchesters. Soon, too, there would be more favourable weather. The entry of the United States into the war had abruptly cut off the supply of American bombers, but in time this would be far outweighed by the Americans' own participation in the offensive.

Besides these favourable omens there was the fact that the system of operational training was now firmly and fully established, and that into the OTUs was flowing a fully adequate supply of superb young men trained under what was now called the Commonwealth Air Training Plan.* As the worst of the winter began to pass, the time seemed ripe for increased effort. Churchill, who had been foremost in calling a halt to intensive operations in November 1941, now agreed that a fuller offensive should be resumed. On 14 February – two days after the TOADS escaped – he wrote to Portal: 'The Brest question has settled itself by the escape of the enemy. I am entirely in favour of the resumption of the bombing of Germany, subject always, of course, to our not incurring heavy losses owing to bad weather and enemy opposition combined.'[12]

A week later the new Air Officer Commanding-in-Chief whom Portal had asked Churchill and Sinclair to approve arrived at High Wycombe. For its resumed offensive the Command needed a leader who was technically well-versed, physically untiring, of outstanding determination, and capable of inspiring others with his own confidence and relentless sense of purpose. In Air Marshal Arthur Travers Harris it got one.

*   *   *

* Previously known as the Empire Air Training Scheme.

The new commander at High Wycombe was 49 years old and already a little portly – reflecting, perhaps, his gastronomic interests and skills. Major Carrington, the Army GHQ Liaison Officer, described him on his arrival when he 'lived for a few days in the mess . . . until his official residence, a stockbrokerish villa called Springfield, three or four miles away, was ready to receive him. A large, sandy-haired, slow-moving man . . . he did not say much at first, though I was to learn that, like other strong, silent men he could be very talkative on occasion. Unlike Saundby, he was anything but matey . . .'[13]

When Harris took over Bomber Command he was already vastly experienced. The son of an engineer-architect in the Indian Civil Service, he had left his public school at 17 and insisted on going out to Rhodesia to make his own way in farming. On the way to securing a farm-manager job at the age of 21, he had earned his keep by, among other things, gold-mining, handling cattle, shooting for meat, tobacco-growing, and organising rural transport, including personally driving a team of sixteen mules. A few weeks after the outbreak of war in 1914 he had joined the 1st Rhodesian Regiment as a bugler – the only vacancy – and for six months had marched incessantly in pursuit of the Germans in South-West Africa. Anxious still to be of service after that campaign was concluded, but determined to do no more marching, he had returned to England, learned elementary flying in half an hour at Brooklands, been commissioned in the Royal Flying Corps, and become a night-fighter pilot in defence against the Zeppelins. As a fighter pilot and squadron commander he had also served on the Western Front.

Granted a permanent commission as a squadron leader in 1919, Harris had then commanded squadrons with success in India and Iraq. (In Iraq he adapted and trained his lumbering Virginia transports for night-bombing, and invented an electric truck for shifting them around on the ground, so that two men could accomplish work previously done by sixteen.) Back in England again, he had trained his new squadron, No. 58, in night-bombing – he later claimed that at that time No. 58 did more night-flying than all the rest of the world's air forces put together. He had also brought this squadron to the point where it won the RAF bombing championship – only to lose the trophy to No. 7 Squadron under Portal.*

In succession Harris had then passed through the Army Staff College, served on the RAF Middle East Air Staff, commanded No. 210 Squadron of flying boats and held appointments in the Air

---

* One of Harris's dicta in later life was: 'Anything you can do, Portal can do better.'

Ministry in charge, first, of Operations and Intelligence, and then of Plans. During this time he had strongly supported the concept of the new super-heavy bomber and had urged the development of mines for aircraft to lay at sea. A closer step towards Harris's final post had come in 1937 when he was given charge of the newly formed No. 4 Group in Bomber Command. This was the Whitley group, the only one at that time expected to specialise in night-bombing. But after a year he had been promoted air vice-marshal and sent out to command the RAF in Palestine and Transjordan.[14]

In Palestine Harris's health had suffered, and he had returned home in the summer of 1939. A week or so after the outbreak of war he had then become AOC of Bomber Command's No. 5 Group. During the ensuing year he had handled his problematical Hampdens well, initiating their successful mining campaign, contributing notably to the bombing of the invasion ports, and incurring a below-average rate of casualties. In November 1940 Portal, recently appointed Chief of the Air Staff, had summoned Harris to the Air Ministry as Deputy Chief, but had soon felt obliged to send him to the United States, where the purchase of aircraft and supplies was falling short of hopes and expectations. It seemed that Dowding, who had recently been the senior RAF officer there, had not been sticking entirely to his official brief. The Air Staff at that stage wanted, above all, bombers. Dowding had been heard to suggest that the Americans should concentrate above all on building fighters – and tanks.[15]

Harris had sorted out these difficulties and was confronting greater ones resulting from the United States' own needs following the Japanese aggression, when Portal, at the Washington Congress, told him he was to take over from Peirse at Bomber Command. Six weeks elapsed before he could do so.

On 22 February 1942 Harris assumed control of what was meant to be, but was not yet, the largest Command in the Royal Air Force. According to Charles Carrington at the Command headquarters, his impact was immediate: 'As a horse knows by instinct when his rider holds the reins with a firm hand, so Bomber Command knew that it had a master. The whole machine tautened up, seemed to move into a higher gear, and this though he rarely visited the squadrons and scorned to give pep talks.'[16]

One night in December 1940, shortly after he had become Deputy Chief of the Air Staff, Harris had called Portal up to the roof of the Air Ministry in King Charles Street, Westminster, to watch the 'Blitz' – 'the old city in flames – with St Paul's standing out in the midst of an ocean of fire . . . an incredible sight'. The two men gazed silently at the burning capital. Then Harris spoke: 'Well . . . they are sowing the wind.'[17]

It was the only time, he wrote later, that he felt vengeful. Vengeful or not, he would do his best to make sure the whirlwind followed.

10

Spring Offensive, 1942

O rders for a fresh offensive had already reached High Wycombe before Harris took over. On 14 February 1942 the Air Staff's new directive listed four towns which it classed as 'industrial areas' – Essen, Duisburg, Düsseldorf and Cologne. These were to be the primary targets, with another 14 towns named as alternatives.

This was a development in bombing policy. 'Area-bombing' had been standard practice on moonless nights since the summer of 1941, but it had not previously taken precedence during moonlight over attempted precision-bombing. The rapier, the Air Staff were plainly acknowledging, had not been striking home. Now it was time to try the bludgeon.

The hope was that area-bombing would not be purely material in its effects. With their homes, workplaces and neighbourhood amenities all destroyed, on top of all the privations they were thought to be already suffering, the German people were expected to lose their zeal not only for production but also for the Nazi regime. In cumbrous but clear enough terms the new directive instructed the Air Officer Commanding-in-Chief: 'The primary object of your operations should now be focused on the morale of the enemy civil population, and in particular of the industrial workers.'[1]

Despite this, the Air Staff still nourished hopes of later reverting to the rapier. The crucial question was how effective the new radio aid, GEE, would prove to be. If in practice it turned out to be simply a help to navigation, then area-bombing was likely to remain for some time the prime form of attack; but if it proved accurate enough for blind-bombing, at night or through cloud, then precision-bombing could again come into its own. In hopes of this, the directive of 14 February listed for destruction eight major industrial targets – four power stations, three oil plants and a synthetic rubber factory – within GEE range, and another four farther afield.

GEE, a name derived from the word 'grid', had originated in the mind of Robert Dippy, a young government scientist, as far back as 1937. Because of the concentration of early radar research on problems of air defence, he received little encouragement until, in 1940, the navigational difficulties in Bomber Command became too obvious to ignore. From the autumn of that year the GEE system was under active development at the Telecommunications Research Establishment (TRE), with the seriously ill Dippy playing a heroic part.*2 By the summer of 1941 it was fully proved in trials not only over England but over Germany. After a GEE-equipped Wellington had been shot down near Hanover in August, however, the Chief of the Air Staff had ruled that no more flights should be made over enemy territory until a substantial part of the bombing force was GEE-equipped and ready for action. He had in mind both the danger of the Germans developing countermeasures, and the loss of effectiveness by small-scale, premature use – as with British tanks in 1916.

Now, in February 1942, the moment had come. Over a third of Harris's aircraft carried a GEE box, misleadingly named T (transmitter) R (receiver) 1335, which by receiving radio pulses from England could enable an aircraft to follow a set course (particularly when 'homing', as the signals grew clearer) or at any time to determine its position on the track to the target.† Completely simple to operate, the system gave a very reliable fix, could be used by any number of aircraft, and involved no signals on to which enemy fighters could

* The Telecommunications Research Establishment was the renamed Air Ministry Research Establishment, which in turn derived from the Bawdsey Research Station set up by the Air Ministry in 1936 to investigate and develop radar. TRE was located at Worth Matravers, Dorset, from 1940–42, in which year it moved to Malvern, a place less accessible to enemy aircraft and landing parties.
† The system was based on the transmission of two sets of synchronised pulses from a 'master' (A) and two 'slave' (B and C) ground stations. The two 'slaves' were situated about 200 miles apart, with the 'master' in the middle, and the cathode ray display in the aircraft showed the differences in time taken to receive the AB and the AC signals. This made possible the calculation of the aircraft's position.
  As the GEE set received but did not echo back pulses, GEE was not what is normally considered a radar device, though it is often referred to as such.

home. Bomber Command's navigational problems, it seemed, might be over.

There was, of course, a range limitation to GEE – roughly 350 miles. It was also reckoned that within six months the Germans would discover how to jam the transmissions. Even so, Bomber Command had a revolutionary new device. With its help, Harris was now expected to carry out the first part of his task – to destroy the four great 'industrial areas' of Essen, Duisburg, Düsseldorf and Cologne.

The force at Harris's disposal for the work before him was much smaller than had been projected. The continual drain of bomber crews to the Middle East; the transfer of squadrons (six of them in 1942) to Coastal Command; the difficulties with the Stirling, Halifax and Manchester; the failure to meet production targets in the British aircraft industry; and the virtual cessation of bomber supply from the United States – all these had seriously restricted Bomber Command's growth. In addition, the steady conversion of 'medium' bomber squadrons to 'heavies', beneficial though it was, inevitably meant that many squadrons were non-operational for several weeks on end. At the beginning of March 1942 Harris commanded only 44½ operational squadrons, with another 8½ non-operational. Of the operational squadrons, 11 so far had the new heavies.[3] In terms of aircraft actually available with crews, Harris could rely during 1942 on an average nightly total of only about 350 suitable for operations over Germany.[4]

Though Harris's force was not as large as had been planned, it enjoyed several advantages denied to Peirse's a year earlier. Quite apart from the greater range and bomb-load of the new 'heavies', it had the benefit of all the work that had been done in 1941 in opening up and improving airfields. A standard system of airfield lighting – for perimeter, runways and approach 'funnel' in use – based on that evolved at Drem airfield had been introduced, which together with improvements in flying control had greatly reduced the likelihood of accidents. Above all, the all-grass bomber airfields of 1939 had become a thing of the past. On every station, old and new, there were, or soon would be, hard runways – a main one 2000 yards long and two subsidiaries of 1400 yards – and a series of hard perimeter tracks and dispersal standings, nearly all of concrete to a depth of 6 inches. Churned-up grass and mud were no longer an impediment to operations, or a hazard for the crews.

Harris also arrived at Bomber Command at a favourable moment in the evolution of operational training. Great difficulties were on the point of being overcome. During 1941 the number of pilots trained to full operational standard had fallen seriously behind requirements, and this in turn had disrupted the training schedule of other aircrew at the OTUs, where exercises for complete crews were final, and major, parts of the routine. The result was a general shortage of trained crews. All this, however, arose because the number of pilots to be trained in Bomber Command was so great: for all except the light bombers the policy was that every aircraft must carry two fully trained pilots. Even the slender Hampdens, which had no seat for a second pilot, carried one sitting behind as the navigator.*

To meet the heavy demand for pilots their courses in the OTUs had been shortened, as noted, but this merely resulted in a good supply of inadequately trained pilots. It was MacNeece Foster at No. 6 (later 91) Group who suggested and campaigned for the solution: drop the requirement for a second pilot, train the first one properly, and give some other member of the crew enough training to fly the aircraft home in an emergency. Also, as Harris insisted if Foster's plan (which he opposed) was to be adopted, install an automatic pilot ('George') in every bomber.

The 'single pilot' policy, the foremost feature of what became called the 'New Deal' in training, came into force in March 1942. As part of the same package, other important changes were made in crewing. The observer had been responsible both for navigation and, normally, for aiming the bombs. During the bombing run-up it was difficult for him to concentrate on navigation, with the result that he often became uncertain of the correct course for home. Known henceforth as the navigator, he was relieved of his bomb-aiming duty, which went to a new member of the crew, the air-bomber or bomb-aimer – who could also act in emergency as front-gunner. It was he in the medium bombers, and another new member of the crew soon afterwards introduced for the heavy bombers, the flight engineer, who now had to act as pilot's mate and learn to handle the aircraft in emergency. At the same time the requirement for two wireless operator/air-gunners in each medium or heavy bomber was

---

* For the second pilot navigator to change places with the first pilot in a Hampden was a tricky business. The first pilot let down the back of his seat and leaned over backwards while the second pilot moved forwards, sat astride of him, and reached for the control column. The first pilot meanwhile kept control of the rudder with his feet, until these were kicked away and replaced by those of the second pilot. The first pilot then wriggled or was pulled backwards into the second pilot's position.[5]

abandoned in favour of having one wireless operator/air-gunner and one 'straight' air-gunner.[6]

All this simplified training requirements, and produced a much smoother flow of trained crews from the OTUs. In so doing, it eased the formidable problems of replacement and expansion, and greatly strengthened Harris and the bomber force for the tasks that lay before them.

Harris was to be forever associated with area-bombing. But he began his campaign in the same way as he ended it – with precision attacks.

Bomber Command's targets on the first few nights after Harris took over were the docks at Wilhelmshaven and Kiel. On 26/27 February 1942, as already recorded, a raid on Kiel put the *Gneisenau* effectively out of action. This was not immediately known, but the next success was clear to all. On 3/4 March the largest number of Bomber Command aircraft until then despatched against an individual target – 235 – wrecked the huge Renault works at Billancourt.

Up to this point, attacks on French industrial plants working for the Germans had been made only in daylight. This was to avoid casualties to friendly civilians. On 2 February, however, the War Cabinet, after being advised that French public opinion would be in favour of such factories coming under heavier attack, gave permission for night raids on four of France's major industrial concerns.[7] The Renault complex astride the Seine just west of Paris headed the list. It was fairly near, easy to find, and lightly defended. It was also thought to be producing about 18,000 lorries a year for the Germans. To the Air Staff it seemed an ideal target on which to try out a new tactical plan: a very concentrated attack by the light of flares continuously dropped throughout the raid, so that the target would remain constantly visible.

Besides inflicting damage, encouraging French resistance, discouraging collaboration, and trying out massive flare-dropping, the attack on Billancourt was also designed to test other recent developments before applying them extensively over Germany. The most experienced crews among the heavy bombers, for instance, were to operate as raid leaders. Above all, as strongly recommended by the new Operational Research Section at Bomber Command, the attack was to be concentrated in time and space. If the greatest possible number of aircraft could be brought over the target in the shortest possible time, both the active and the passive defences might be completely overwhelmed. Night-fighters, ground-gunners, searchlight and radar operators, fire-fighters and rescue workers – all might be swamped by the sheer intensity of the attack.

Inevitably there were some initial doubts about the practicability of concentration. Could Flying Control at the bomber bases deal with large numbers of aircraft setting off and returning within a few minutes of each other, particularly if the weather closed in? Could so many aircraft keep to their prescribed tracks and arrive over the target at their exactly appointed times? Would the concentration over the target be so great that raiders would collide, or hit other raiders with their bombs?

In the event, almost everything went well. Of the 235 Wellingtons, Whitleys, Hampdens, Stirlings and Halifaxes despatched, no fewer than 224 dropped their bombs in the target area – in an attack which lasted only 1 hour 50 minutes. On average, two aircraft bombed every minute of the raid – an impressive figure at that time, though soon to be vastly exceeded. Bombing from low level under ample light from the flares and the moon, the raiders achieved great and unaccustomed accuracy – some 300 bombs fell on the various workshops. Photographs the next morning showed complete devastation. The Renault works, it seemed, might be 'out' for years to come, if not for ever.[8] Among those certainly satisfied with the night's work were Pilot Officer Harold Yeoman and his crew in a Wellington of 12 Squadron. Yeoman later wrote:

This one was so hush-hush that, in 12 Squadron at any rate, we were told we could only tell the rest of the crew once we were airborne ... It was to be a low-level attack, unheard of at that time, with lots of flares promised so that we could be 100% certain of hitting the target. Out at the aircraft that evening the wireless op. and the two gunners were in a ferment – why all the secrecy? where were we going? and so on. I remember pointing to the W/op's oxygen mask: 'You won't need that,' I told him cruelly. It did nothing for his peace of mind ...

[After crossing the French coast] Minutes later: 'Christ! it's not the bloody target on fire, is it?' It was. We ran in at 2500 ft from the south-west through a corridor of flares, about 40 of them. One light flak gun was dribbling tracer up into nothing about two miles to the south. He would stop, then start again – 'Gone down to the stores for more ammunition,' I suggested. The target was like a huge shovelful of hot ashes which someone had flung on the ground; we'd never seen anything quite like it. A Hampden, bomb-doors open, came charging at us at the same height. We bloody-fooled him and jinked out of his way. It was the proverbial piece of cake. Our first bomb hit the factory on the banana-shaped island in the Seine, the rest straddled the main buildings – 'every one a coconut', as the rear-gunner gleefully said. In the distance an aircraft went in near a bend of the river downstream – the only one to be lost, we believed. On the way home they were flashing V's from their skylights in Beauvais, an inspiring sight. We could still see the factory burning from the coast crossing out. We were tremendously excited about this one: it was a turning-point, we knew, and we knew from that night on things could only get better.[9]

The damage at Billancourt, it turned out, was not as terminal as at first believed. The wreckage could be, and was, cleared or patched up, the mostly undamaged machine tools reassembled, and after four months production was again in full swing. By unhappy chance, too, some of the bombs fell on workers' dwellings nearby, killing 367 people – more than twice as many as in any raid thus far on Germany. But that tragedy apart, the attack was a great success. There were no collisions; only one aircraft was lost; the new techniques worked; and the Germans were denied some thousands of French lorries.

Moreover, large numbers of French workers thenceforth absented themselves from evening and night shifts, in the Renault factories and elsewhere. Best of all, the French were not alienated, but encouraged in resistance to the Germans. Georges Gorse, one of de Gaulle's Free French and a post-war Mayor of Billancourt, later wrote: 'The workers of Boulogne–Billancourt truly saw in the raids of March a promise of liberation. And those who died have also brought "their own contribution to the coming of dawn".'[10]

The next step was to apply the raid techniques of Billancourt to a key objective in Germany, but using the new wonder-device, GEE. Almost inevitably the choice of target fell on the foremost of all German industrial centres, the town of Essen, with the enormous armaments complex of Krupps at its heart. It had been sought out a dozen or more times, but never effectively bombed: the constant industrial haze resulting from the outpourings of hundreds of chimneys in Germany's 'Black Country', coupled with a generous deployment of searchlights and anti-aircraft guns, had provided more than adequate defence. Now, with GEE-equipped aircraft to lead, Harris had high hopes of at last delivering a heavy blow.

On 8/9 March 211 bombers took off for Essen; on 9/10 March the number was 187, and on 10/11 March 126. Thanks to the GEE leaders, more found it than usual. But haze, or on the third night cloud, still baffled the attackers. Bombs fell on Essen, but other Ruhr towns received more – and Krupps remained untouched. GEE had proved itself an excellent navigational aid, outwards and homewards. But it was not precise enough for blind-bombing.

On 13/14 March, after a raid on Kiel which hit two U-boat building yards, Harris turned to another of his four major 'industrial areas' – Cologne. The plan was for a GEE-led attack, with the first raiders dropping mainly flares and incendiaries. The night turned out to be clear, and Cologne was readily identifiable by its position on the Rhine. As a result the force of 135 aircraft managed to start 237 separate fires and destroy or damage several factories, including one making synthetic rubber, and over 1500 houses. The Cologne local authorities at the time rated the raid as a heavy one.

However, Essen remained the official target number one, and between 25/26 March and 12/13 April Harris made five more attempts to hit it. On the first a decoy fire-site at Rheinberg, eighteen miles away, attracted much of the raiders' attention; but on the fifth some bombs (five HE, 200 incendiaries) at last landed on Krupps, causing a large fire. By 12/13 April Harris had launched eight GEE-led attacks on Essen, totalling over 1500 sorties. Two-thirds of the crews involved claimed to have attacked the city, but only one in ten of their bombing photographs showed features within five miles of it. And the eight raids had cost 64 aircraft – over 4 per cent of the attacking force.

Essen was an exceptionally hard nut to crack. Midway through the eight attacks Harris had fastened with relief on a much more easily approachable and identifiable target – the port of Lübeck, fourteen miles upriver from the Baltic. This old Hanseatic town was an industrial centre, a training station for U-boat crews and, above all, a key port for the import of iron ore from Sweden and for the supply of Germany's armies in the East. It also contained many late-medieval half-timbered houses inviting the kind of heavy incendiary attack with which the Air Staff was now keen to experiment. It was beyond GEE range, but GEE could help the leaders over much of the journey – out and home.

The raid took place on 28/29 March 1942 in almost full moon and good visibility. Of the 234 aircraft despatched, 191 claimed to have found and bombed the target. The defences were comparatively weak and the bombers were briefed to go in low. Twelve were lost, but the result was devastation on a scale never before inflicted by Bomber Command; the later raiders could see the conflagration a hundred miles ahead. Nearly a third of the built-up area disappeared in smoke and fire; some 16,000 people lost their homes; and the destruction extended to the central power station, several factories (including one making oxygen equipment for U-boats) and most of the city's fine old buildings. Many of the departing crews gazed awestruck at the inferno they had created. Harris himself later wrote the epitaph: 'On the night of 28/29 March, the first German city went up in flames.'[11]

The Lübeck raid was the first to cause real perturbation in Germany. Goebbels, among others, registered great dismay. Even a week later he was writing in his diary: 'The damage is really enormous. I have been shown a newsreel of the destruction. It is horrible. One can well imagine how such a bombardment affects the population. Thank God, it is a North German population . . .'[12] Goebbels was not exaggerating. The havoc was such that troops had to be called in to ensure the supply of food and clothing, and for three weeks the port was closed. The bomber offensive, till then more of a harassment than a mortal danger, had made its first serious impact on the German homeland.

Before Harris's next success there were the attacks on Essen already mentioned, and equally unrewarding operations against Cologne, Hamburg and Dortmund. On all these raids forecasts of favourable weather turned out to be false, either *en route* or over the target. There were also further night attacks on factories in occupied France – against the Ford motor factory at Poissy (twice), and the Gnome et Rhône engine factory at Paris–Gennevilliers. The former, already attacked by Bostons of 2 Group in daylight, suffered severely from the second night raid on 2/3 April, but the plant at Gennevilliers escaped – for the time being – undamaged.

In the midst of these by now routine operations, Harris tried a bold, possibly rash, experiment. He sent 12 of the new Lancasters on a daylight raid into Bavaria. The Lancasters' target could hardly have been more precise – the engine assembly shop within the MAN diesel engine manufacturing complex at Augsburg. Harris was anxious to show that he could best help in the Battle of the Atlantic by bombing factories in Germany rather than docks in France, and the MAN works produced engines for U-boats. The operation order stated, rather optimistically, 'The heavy bomber carries a powerful defensive armament, it is capable of comparatively high speeds, and it has a long range. Operating in daylight the fire-power of a section of three heavy bombers is such as to deter all but the most determined of enemy fighters.'[13]

However, Harris was hoping that the Lancasters would avoid, rather than engage, the enemy. To this end they were to fly very low across the Normandy coast to escape detection by radar, and continue flying low across France to make fighter attack difficult. When they entered south-west Germany, they were to feint for Munich, but then finally turn for Augsburg. Meanwhile, in the initial stages of their flight they would have had the benefit of diversionary raids over northern France by 30 Bostons and some hundreds of Fighter Command aircraft, intended to keep the German fighters there fully occupied. After a week of low-flying practice in formation, six Lancasters of 44 Squadron from Waddington and six of 97 Squadron from Woodhall Spa took off at 3 p.m. on 17 April 1942. They faced a round trip – if they were lucky – of 1250 miles. Their attack was timed for dusk, so that they could fly back under cover of darkness.

Unfortunately, things soon went wrong. By some confusion, the diversionary operations took place a little too soon to have their desired effect: the German fighters were not fully occupied at the critical time when the Lancasters thundered across Normandy. By unhappy chance the six of 44 Squadron, led by their South African flight commander Squadron Leader J. D. Nettleton, and apparently flying slightly north of their prescribed track, passed close to Beaumont-le-Roger airfield just as a German fighter pilot of II/JG2 was about to land there after vainly pursuing a diversionary raider. Recognising the huge bombers he at once sped upwards again, alerted his companions still in the air, and gave chase. The Me 109s were too fast for the Lancasters, and their cannon and machine-gun fire too deadly. Four of Nettleton's six went down; Nettleton and the other survivor, their aircraft badly damaged, escaped as their pursuers, fuel running low, turned for base. 'The time was 5.15 p.m. Of the 43 young men who had set out from Waddington at 3 o'clock, 21 were dead, and seven more were down, somewhere in the Plaine de St André.'[14]

Meanwhile Squadron Leader J. G. Sherwood, leading the six Lancasters of 97 Squadron, and still right on track, pressed on with his formation intact. On they roared across France, mostly at 50 feet and into Germany past Lake Constance. Seemingly heading for Munich, they abruptly turned north for Augsburg. Nettleton arrived first, and incredibly enough achieved surprise. But the anti-aircraft gunners soon sprang to life, and Nettleton's companion went down. So too did Sherwood (who survived as a prisoner) and another of his flight. Eight of the 12 Lancasters had reached Augsburg but only five would return home.

Between them the eight Lancasters landed 17 1000-lb bombs on the target. Five of these failed to explode. The rest did great damage, though more to the structures than to vital machinery.

When only four of Sherwood's flight returned to Woodhall Spa, and those all badly shot up, there was sorrow enough. But at Waddington, with five out of six lost, and Nettleton landing away from base, the grief was mixed with incredulity. Eric Howell, then a flight mechanic with 44 Squadron, had helped to prepare Nettleton's aircraft – *B Beer* – and with his fellow ground crew had waved him off. 'Next morning', he wrote many years later, 'when I reported for work at the dispersal area I was surprised that none of A Flight aircraft had returned. When I enquired at the Dispersal Office, Chief Gover said that all aircraft had been lost, except B-Beer which had landed away. There was absolute disbelief in the office at this piece of news, five aircraft missing out of six, it couldn't be true, but it was, as the empty panstands indicated. I won't elaborate, but . . . I do know that A/B Flight ground crew went into shock over their terrible loss.'[15]

Another who would never forget that morning was 'Pip' Beck, a WAAF at Waddington in Flying Control: 'There was no way to express the horror that I, like everyone on the station, felt. The whole camp seemed shocked and silent.'[16]

The Augsburg raid of 17 April 1942 was a remarkable achievement for which Nettleton received the VC, Sherwood (also recommended by Harris for the VC) the DSO, and others lesser awards. Apart from the damage it inflicted on the target, it gave notice that British bombers might penetrate the Reich at unexpected times and places, and so increased Germany's growing commitment to defence. But the cost was far too high – especially as it turned out that the MAN works was far from being the only one manufacturing diesels. The main lesson of the raid, however, was in any case clear. Lancasters in 1942 could no more brave the skies of Germany in daylight without crippling losses than could Blenheims or Wellingtons in 1939 and 1940.

The rest of Nettleton's story was of a sort heart-achingly familiar in Bomber Command. Promoted to command 44 Squadron, he lived up to his VC by putting himself down for the most difficult operations. Soon after Augsburg he married a WAAF officer. In July 1943 he was posted missing from a raid on Turin. Seven months later his widow gave birth to his son.

After raids on Hamburg and – more successfully – Cologne, Harris turned to the river port of Rostock, eight miles from the Baltic coast. Like Lübeck it was an old Hanseatic town, and like Lübeck it was beyond GEE range, but not difficult to find. It was also rich in timbered buildings which made it a suitable subject for incendiary attack. Disappointed in the results of a first raid on 23/24 April, Harris kept up the attack for three more successive nights. On each occasion the greater part of the force made a general attack on the main town area, while selected crews from No. 5 Group took on a precise objective: the Heinkel aircraft works in a southern suburb.

All told, Harris sent 521 sorties against Rostock. As at Lübeck, incendiaries made up a high proportion of the bomb-load. Reconnaissance after the last raid confirmed that the attack had scored hits on the Heinkel factory, and had laid most of the old town in ruins. The buildings destroyed, mainly by fire, included the law courts, the head post office, railway stations, storage depots and many fine late-medieval houses. Goebbels in his diary bewailed the destruction of 70 per cent of the city and waxed even more indignant than over Lübeck: 'He [the Führer] shares my opinion absolutely that [English] cultural centres, health resorts and civilization centres must be attacked now . . . There is no other way of bringing the English to their senses. They belong to a class of being to whom you can talk only after you have first knocked out their teeth . . .'*[17]

The Heinkel works recovered within weeks, the U-boat building yards suffered no great harm, and the citizens of Rostock, having fled in their thousands, soon returned to restore their shattered town to life. Nevertheless, vast damage had been done, and all at singularly little cost – 11 aircraft and their crews, or little more than 2 per cent of those despatched. The British Official History, *The Strategic Air Offensive Against Germany*, which rigorously eschewed panegyric, described the final raid, when thirteen of the bombing photographs showed the Heinkel works and every single one the target area, as 'a masterpiece'. 'Bomber Command,' it concluded, 'had won another great victory.'[18]

*   *   *

---

* The Germans promptly retaliated by attacks on, among other places, Bath, Exeter and Norwich – the so-called 'Baedeker' raids.

Fires were still raging in Rostock when nearly a hundred Wellingtons, Stirlings and Halifaxes heaped further destruction on Cologne. An area attack, however, was not to be Bomber Command's only work that night of 27/28 April 1942. The battleship *Tirpitz* and her attendant destroyers were lying in Aalsfiord, near Trondheim, and the Admiralty had requested action.

Attacking Germany's major warships was about the most difficult and dangerous of all the duties regularly expected of Bomber Command. On this occasion the attackers, frustrated by the enemy's smoke screen, scored no hits on the *Tirpitz*. But five of the 43 Halifaxes and Lancasters fell to the German guns.

Among those who narrowly escaped death that night was the Australian Wing Commander D. C. T. Bennett, the future chief of the Pathfinders. Leading No. 10 Squadron, Bennett had been briefed to drop a spherical mine on the steep bank of the Aalsfiord so that it would roll down and explode beneath the *Tirpitz*, anchored only 50 feet from shore. In this optimistic scenario, insufficient allowance had been made for the strength and accuracy of the ship's guns. Bennett ran into a storm of fire which set his Halifax ablaze and forced the crew to bale out. With one companion and the help of some Norwegians selflessly prepared to risk death or imprisonment, Bennett then made his way on foot right across Norway into neutral Sweden. Interned there, he managed with characteristic aplomb and determination to short-circuit diplomatic procedures. A month later he was back in England to continue the fight.[19]

The night after Bennett was shot down, 34 Halifaxes and Lancasters again tried to bomb the *Tirpitz*. They failed, but another raid damaged three shipyards in Kiel. With the April moon ending, Harris then returned to area attacks. Hamburg suffered on 3/4 May, but on the three succeeding nights Stuttgart, especially important for its Bosch magneto and dynamo works, escaped with very little harm from the efforts of nearly 300 aircraft. This south German city was distant, well-hidden geographically, and cleverly served by decoy fires.

The minelaying – increasingly now by the Wellingtons, Stirlings and Halifaxes rather than Hampdens – continued as ever; the Bostons made their daylight cross-Channel raids on factories, railways and power stations; twice a larger force tried to strike by night at the Gnome et Rhône aero-engine works outside Paris; but otherwise Bomber Command's activities declined as May 1942 wore on. In the twelve nights from 8/9 May to 19/20 May, Harris launched only two area attacks. Both were against distant targets – Warnemünde and Mannheim – and neither was very successful. Harris had not, however, lost his drive or his nerve. He was mustering his forces for an attack far bigger than any until that time launched, or even contemplated, in the history of air warfare.

I I

'Millennium'

Not the least remarkable thing about the first 'Thousand-Bomber' raid was the brief time between conception and execution. Early in May 1942 Harris told Saundby how he yearned to strike a really massive, spectacularly heavy blow against some major German city – not only for the harm it would do the enemy but for the good it would do at home. Bomber Command was being criticised for ineffectiveness, and the Army and the Navy were making demands for air resources on a scale impossible to reconcile with the planned growth of the strategic bomber force. If Bomber Command could bring off some specially impressive attack, the critics might be won over, or at least silenced.

Apparently Saundby then asked Harris how many bombers he had in mind for such a venture, and Harris promptly replied, 'A thousand.' His thoughts were running on the ideal rather than the practical, for he well knew that his entire front line amounted to only about 600 aircraft, and that the number available with crews each night for operations averaged no more than 350. Saundby went away and shortly returned with a scheme by which Harris might achieve the seemingly impossible. If operations were restricted for a few nights beforehand, aircrew leave stopped, and special efforts made to achieve maximum serviceability, and if operational-type aircraft and instructors were brought in from the Heavy Conversion Units and the bomber OTUs, around 700 aircraft and crews might be mustered from within Bomber Command. And if other Commands, particularly Coastal, would join in with their bombers,

126

something like the magic figure of a thousand might possibly be reached.[1]

On 18 May Harris broached his idea to Portal, who warmly approved. The following night Harris put it to Churchill at Chequers and found him equally enthusiastic. When the Prime Minister asked how many of the thousand might not return and Harris replied that he thought possibly forty or fifty, Churchill assured him that he would be prepared for a loss of a hundred.

On 20 May Harris received Portal's written confirmation. That same day he wrote to seek the cooperation of the heads of Coastal Command, Army Cooperation Command, and Flying Training Command, and to outline the project to his Group commanders. 'It is proposed,' he explained, 'at about the full moon to put over the maximum force of bombers on a single and extremely important town in Germany, with a view to wiping it out in one night, or at least two.'[2]

By return he received the reply he most wanted. Sir Philip Joubert at Coastal Command, expressing warm support, offered around 250 bombers, including the four Wellington and Whitley squadrons which he had 'on loan' from Bomber Command. This by itself brought the total up to about 950. Operation MILLENNIUM, as the venture was grimly code-named, was 'on'.

The next few days saw the operational plans drawn up and the ground crews everywhere working long hours – up to 18 in the day – to make the aircraft ready. Among other things about 100 GEE sets had to be conjured out of various establishments and fitted, mainly to the Conversion Unit aircraft, and the navigators trained in their use.[3] The town chosen for destruction was to be Hamburg (Harris's preference, to show the Admiralty how he was fighting the Battle of the Atlantic), or failing that, Cologne (which was within much easier GEE range). To saturate the defences, active and passive, the whole vast force was to pass over the target within 90 minutes – an unheard-of concentration of over 660 raiders an hour, or 11 bomb-loads falling every minute.

Naturally there was much concern about the risk of collisions, but Operational Research produced figures to show that the casualties from these were likely to be fewer than those saved by saturating the defences. If the force were divided into three parallel streams, approaching from the same direction and at different heights, with three separate aiming-points in the centre, north and south of the town, Operational Research reckoned that not more than two bombers would be lost through collision. Among other features of the plan, all available GEE-equipped Wellingtons and Stirlings of 1 and 3 Groups were to attack during the first 15 minutes, and all available Halifaxes and Lancasters of 4 and 5 Groups in the last 15 minutes, with the OTU crews among those attacking in between. Bombing was to be from a minimum height of 8000 feet, to avoid the light flak, and crews were to carry the maximum load of incendiaries – including the 4-lb X which produced a delayed explosion to deter fire-fighters.[4]

Full moonlight, essential for the success of the operation, was due to begin on 27/28 May and end on 31 May/1 June. From 22 May there was unparalleled activity throughout Bomber Command as hundreds of aircraft were serviced, tested, modified or flown to different airfields. The Command, wrote its chief radar officer, Wing Commander Dudley Saward, was 'like a beehive'. All was going well when on 26 May, only thirty-six hours before possible take-off, came a drastic set-back. Fearing that aircraft useful in the Battle of the Atlantic might be lost, and possibly also reluctant to give a boost to Harris's strategic offensive, the Admiralty had intervened.[5] Possessing operational control over Coastal Command, it had refused permission for the use of Joubert's 250 bombers.

Not entirely surprised, Harris and Saundby called on the only possible replacements. With the eager cooperation of the commanders and units concerned, they made up the numbers from the two or three reserve aircraft with each squadron, from the Heavy Conversion Flights, and from the bomber OTUs. This meant that there would be a much greater number of instructors and senior pupils than originally intended: on the raid, no fewer than 49 pupils flew as pilots. In the end, because the weather proved unsuitable for 27 to 29 May and three more days could be spent in preparation, the total of aircraft amassed reached 1047. With the exception of four Wellingtons from Flying Training Command, the entire force came from within Bomber Command. More than a third of the aircraft came from the two OTU Groups, with MacNeece Foster's 91 Group contributing 259 of these.[6]

Two other RAF Commands undertook to cooperate in a different way. To damp down opposition to the bomber stream on its way to the target, long-range fighters from Fighter Command and some Blenheims from Army Cooperation Command were to join with 2 Group's Blenheims in attacking the German night-fighter airfields which lay along the route.

The nights of full moon were passing, and the weather over north-west Germany remained persistently cloudy. The force could not stand idly by for long, with both training and the normal operational programme disrupted. At last on 30 May came a half-favourable met. report – more favourable over Cologne than Hamburg – but with some bad weather *en route*. Dudley Saward has described the moment of decision, when the fate of perhaps 6000 British aircrew and half a million German civilians lay in one man's hands:

> The C-in-C sat down heavily in his chair and leant back to allow the meteorological synoptic charts to be placed on his desk in front of him. Not a muscle moved and no sign of expression stirred his face while the forecast for the next 24 hours was outlined to him by that meticulous and worthy Meteorological Officer, Mr Magnus Spence.
>
> It was not a forecast which held much promise for good operational conditions . . . I held my breath, for this was probably the last possible night for the great operation, unless it were undertaken another month hence . . .
>
> The C-in-C moved at last. Slowly he pulled an American cigarette carton from his pocket and, flicking the bottom with his thumb, selected the protruding Lucky Strike. He lit the cigarette and then drew from his right breast-pocket a short, stocky cigarette holder. Very deliberately he pressed the cigarette into the end of the holder and grasped it firmly between his teeth. He continued to stare at the charts and then slowly his forefinger moved across the continent of Europe and came to rest on a town in Germany. The pressure on his finger bent back the end joint and drove the blood from the top of his finger-nail, leaving a half-circle of white. He turned to the Senior Staff Air Officer, his face still expressionless. 'The 1000 Plan to-night.' His finger was pressing on Cologne.[7]

Soon after noon the order: 'Thousand Plan to-night. Target Cologne' flashed to the Groups, the stations, the squadrons. Harris followed up with a special message to the crews: '. . . the force of which you form a part to-night is at least twice the size and has more than four times the carrying capacity of the largest air force ever before concentrated on one objective. You have an opportunity, therefore, to strike a blow at the enemy which will resound not only throughout Germany but throughout the world . . .'[8] Well aware for days beforehand that something special was in the wind, the crews responded with unwonted enthusiasm when they heard the target and intended scale of attack. 'The whole briefing room,' wrote one observer, 'exploded into an uproar as hardened aircrew crew jumped to their feet and threw their hats in the air.'[9]

So the air tests were flown, the pre-op meals devoured – or toyed with – the last checks made, the aircraft acceptance 'forms 700' signed by the pilots, and on some 40 airfields an astonishing array of 602

Wellingtons, 131 Halifaxes, 88 Stirlings, 79 Hampdens, 73 Lancasters, 46 Manchesters and 28 Whitleys stood ready. It was around 9 p.m. on 30 May 1942, and Bomber Command was about to launch the attack which would more than square Britain's bombing account with Germany, and which might make or break the fortunes of the whole bomber offensive.

> . . . a thousand aircraft on Cologne
> God help the bods below;
> With a full moon and a clear sky
> God help the sods that go.
> The banter crackles back and forth,
> Weak jokes that mask strong fears,
> And so we saunter to the flights,
> Each with his thoughts alone.
> Warsaw, Rotterdam, London burned
> For them – to-night – Cologne!
>
> George Cocker,
> 218 Squadron[10]

The raid went well – for Bomber Command. The analysis afterwards raised few points of criticism. The INTRUDER operations against enemy airfields by 95 fighters and Blenheims, costing three aircraft, were thought not to have been very effective; and stragglers extended the streams over the target longer than intended. Otherwise, the attack more or less conformed to plan: nearly 900 of the raiders claimed to have dropped their bombs (915 tons of incendiaries, 840 tons of high explosive) on target, there was only one collision, and the total loss was 41 aircraft, or about 3.9 per cent of the raiders. This was slightly above the recent rate of loss for attacks on Cologne, but lower than that in general over western Germany in clear skies and full moonlight.[11]

Among those who flew with the crews that night without being required to were Air Vice-Marshal John Baldwin, AOC of 3 Group, and Group Captain Hugh Constantine, 'station master' at Elsham Wolds and later a fine AOC of 4 Group. Of the many acts of courage in the air, one became well known from the award of a posthumous Victoria Cross. Flying Officer L. T. Manser, a 20-year-old pilot of 50 Squadron, was coned by searchlights – a most frightening and bewildering experience in itself – as his Manchester neared Cologne. Quickly the radar-predicted flak struck. But despite serious damage Manser flew on and bombed the target, only for his aircraft to be hit again and fire to break out, briefly, in the starboard engine. The Manchester lost height badly, but Manser was determined to bring it, and his crew, back to England. He delayed giving the order to bale out until, over Belgium, he could no longer avoid a crash. He then managed to hold the bomber steady until all his crew had jumped, but in so doing sacrificed his own chance to escape.[12]

The following day the first Mosquito flights over Germany reconnoitred and attacked the stricken city. The smoke was too dense for photography, but photographic reconnaissance four days later showed complete devastation over some 600 acres, including 300 acres in the centre. Contemporary German reports reveal that among the buildings destroyed or seriously damaged, besides hundreds of smaller factories and workshops, were 328 of the larger factories – including rubber and chemical works, an oil storage plant, and a manufactory of engines and accumulators for U-boats. The number of fires caused was some 2500, water mains, gas mains, electricity and telephone cables were all badly affected, and railway services from the centre ceased for seven days. Considering the scale of the attack, surprisingly few of the inhabitants were killed – 469 – but 12,840 buildings were destroyed or damaged and 45,132 people made homeless.[13]

The overall loss of war production in the city was later estimated to be between one and two months' normal output. Scores of thousands of the inhabitants temporarily fled, but as usual the Germans showed a great capacity for recovery and rushed in skilled workers from other towns to speed the repairs. The apartments were patched up, the services were restored, and the town returned to life and production, but at its heart was a great void. Marie ('Missy') Vassiltchikov, the young Russian *émigré* aristocrat whose *Berlin Diaries 1940–45* give so remarkable a picture of life among the air raids in the German capital, visited the Rhineland three months after the raid. She wrote, 'We passed through the *Ruhrgebiet* [Ruhr region] which is the industrial heartland of Germany, and where many towns are now mile after mile of ruins. In Cologne, only the cathedral was still standing.'[14]

The 'Thousand-Bomber' raid on Cologne did more damage to that city than all the previous 70 or more raids put together. It profoundly disturbed the Germans – Goering simply would not believe the report of the Police-President of Cologne, calling it a 'stinking lie'[15] – and it gave a powerful upward surge to British morale. Harris's gigantic gamble, in which he had committed to battle, unlike almost any other commander in history, not only his entire front line and his reserves, but also much of his training organisation, had come off. He had demonstrated to Downing Street, Parliament, British public opinion, the Admiralty, the War Office, the Americans, the Russians and the Germans that Bomber Command could strike serious, in time possibly decisive, blows at Germany. The Renault factory, Lübeck, Rostock and now Cologne – these were to be Harris's 'commercial traveller's wares' (as he called them) in the near future as he 'sold' further investment in Bomber Command to the War Cabinet. 'My own opinion,' he wrote later, 'is that we should never have had a real bomber offensive if it had not been for the 1000 bomber attack on Cologne, an irrefutable demonstration of the power of what was to all intents and purposes a new and untried weapon.'[16]

If possible, Harris intended to strike twice while the great force was still assembled. On 1/2 June, the last possible night for good moonlight, he sent 956 aircraft against what was still the top-priority target – Essen. The attack was to be on the so-called Shaker pattern: picked leading crews dropping flares, then another picked contingent dropping incendiaries by the light of the flares, then the main force dropping bombs on or near the resulting fires. But clouds overlay the town, and bafflingly reflected the light of the flares, which also became diffused in the local haze. As a result, few of the raiders saw what they were supposed to be aiming at. At the cost of 31 aircraft, a few bombs fell on Essen – where people remained unaware that they were being subjected to a major air attack – but a large number fell on eleven other towns in the Ruhr.[17]

With characteristic persistence, Harris sent four more raids, totalling 640 sorties, against Essen in the next fortnight. None of them had any significant success. Nor were two of the four raids during the course of June on the river port of Emden, terminus of the Dortmund–Ems Canal, any more profitable. The other two, however, on 6/7 and 20/23 June, between them damaged the docks and destroyed some hundreds of houses. The cost of these eight raids on Essen and Emden was 85 bombers, or nearly 6 per cent of the attacking force – a dangerously high figure.

Next in Harris's sights was the great commercial and industrial centre of Bremen, on the Weser, some forty miles from its more modern seaport of Bremerhaven. Since 5 May, when the Air Staff sent Harris an additional directive, it had been high in the target-list for its importance in the manufacture of fighters. Already attacked some three dozen times, it had been most recently raided on 3/4 June, when 170 aircraft did heavy damage to the town and docks but very little to the two special objects of attention – the Focke-Wulf factory and the U-boat construction yards. That, however, was but a preliminary to the massive operation now planned for

25/26 June – the third, and last, of the 'Thousand-Bomber' raids of 1942.

For this venture Bomber Command largely reassembled the force which had bombed Cologne and Essen, but now received the help of 102 Wellingtons and Hudsons from Coastal Command. The Admiralty had not so much relented over its previous refusal to cooperate as had given way to Churchill's objurations; also it had been assumed that the Coastal bombers would attack a specifically naval-industrial target. This brought the grand total of aircraft up to 1004, of ten different types, all of which were to make their attack within the space of 65 minutes. The 5 Group aircraft were to concentrate on the Focke-Wulf factory, Coastal Command on the Deschim AG U-boat shipyard, and 20 Blenheims of 2 Group on the AG Weser shipyard. The rest were to make an area attack on the town and dockyards. In addition another 59 aircraft – Blenheims, Bostons, Mosquitoes – were briefed for INTRUDER operations against German fighter airfields.

As so often, the decisive factor proved to be the weather. The forecast was for the cloud over Bremen to clear, but the wind changed and the cloud remained. Very few of the raiders in consequence saw Bremen. The GEE sets of the leaders, however, had led them accurately to the town, and the blind-bombing that ensued started fires on which the main force piled their bombs. The attack was not as successful as that on Cologne, but much more so than that on Essen. The raid put parts of the Focke-Wulf works out of action, did considerable damage to docks and shipyards, destroyed or damaged some 6500 houses and rendered about 2400 people homeless. The cost to both Bomber and Coastal Command was 5 per cent of their participating forces – more than they could, in the long run, safely sustain. Two of 15 Army Cooperation Command Blenheims were also lost, on the INTRUDER operations.[18]

One disquieting feature of the Bremen raid emerged as soon as the survivors landed. Against Cologne the OTU crews, concentrated in the middle of the main streams, had fared no worse than most of the squadron crews – indeed, they had incurred a lower rate of loss than the raid leaders. But against Bremen they had suffered disproportionately. Number 91 (OTU) Group had put up 198 Wellingtons and Whitleys; 23 – over 11 per cent – had failed to return. The main reason was clearly that, because of the greater distance and the thick cloud, the raid on Bremen had turned out to be much more difficult than that on Cologne. In consequence inexperienced pupil crews, flying older aircraft which had been relegated to training work, not surprisingly suffered heavy casualties.

In the euphoria generated by the success of the 'Thousand' raid on Cologne, Harris devised a plan for concentrating the main offensive against Germany into two such mammoth operations each month, with some lesser operations in between. This of course was with the intention of 'saturating' the defences by an overwhelming number of aircraft attacking within a minimum of time. But the plan also, in 1942, inevitably involved drawing on the OTUs and the Heavy Conversion Units to make up the numbers. To this the Air Staff, with some opposition from the Director of Organisation, agreed.[19] In the next three months these training elements duly took part in five major operations – none of which, however, remotely approached the scale of the 'Thousand' raids.

During this period Bomber Command continued its assault on Bremen, making three raids within a week. These notably failed to wipe out the city, but at least increased the damage: in particular the raid of 29/30 June by 253 aircraft scored further hits on the Focke-Wulf factory and the AG Weser U-boat construction yards. Then, interspersed with single raids on Wilhelmshaven and Vegesack, came a determined assault on the heavy-engineering town of Duisburg. Five times between 13/14 July and 6/7 August forces of around 200 or 300 aircraft attacked this vital industrial centre on the River Ruhr. Only once, on 22/23 July, did they achieve significant industrial damage. Beneath frequent cloud and constant haze, Duisburg proved almost as difficult a target as Essen.

Another town to feel the increasing weight of Bomber Command's attacks during the summer of 1942 was Hamburg. On 26/27 July a raid by 403 aircraft destroyed or damaged some 6000 houses, killed 337 people, and made 14,000 homeless. Two nights later, however, bad weather largely frustrated a second operation. It caused the OTU aircraft to be recalled during the outward flight, and contributed to the very heavy casualties – over 15 per cent – suffered by the 3 Group Wellingtons and Stirlings which carried on with the raid.[20]

Heaviest of all the raids in this period, and heavier than any other to be made during the rest of 1942, was the attack by 630 aircraft on 31 July/1 August against the big inland port and industrial centre of Düsseldorf, on the Rhine below Cologne. Though some of the attack went astray, the raid started 954 fires in the city and its suburb Neuss, across the river, destroyed or damaged more than 1500 buildings and caused some 12,000 people to be 'bombed out'. The losses were again very heavy among the training units – 11 aircraft and crews out of the 105 taking part.

OTU crews flew in further operations during the summer of 1942, notably on 10/11 September against Düsseldorf and the following night against Bremen. By that time, however, Harris was losing his earlier enthusiasm for using them. They had not always been able to contribute greatly to the bombing, and their casualties tended to be high unless the force was very large – which was difficult to achieve – and the weather conditions ideal. Also, there was the disruption to training both by their absence on operations and, still more, if they failed to return. Wisely, Harris gave up using OTU crews over Germany from mid-September. Until enemy opposition was greatly reduced, a leaflet raid or two over France in the final stages of OTU training would be sufficient.

During the summer of 1942 Harris was in fact experimenting with the still quite inadequate force under his command. The 'Thousand' raids, apart from their demonstration value, were a colossal and successful experiment in concentration to overwhelm the defences. The use of OTU resources over Germany was another bold experiment, fortunately soon discontinued. There were even experimental raids by Lancasters at dusk – the disastrous one against the MAN works at Augsburg in April, and another, more successful, against the far distant and unexpected target of the U-boat yards at Danzig. There was a small daylight Mosquito raid, too, successful but costly, against U-boat yards at Flensburg.

In every way Harris was showing skill and flexibility in the handling of his force, but he remained acutely conscious of its still limited impact on Germany. For this, it was clear in the minds of Harris and the Air Staff alike, there were two main reasons. One was the fact that his force, while fast growing in bomb-carrying capacity through the steady conversion to four-engined aircraft, had not as yet significantly increased in numbers of aircraft. The other reason, despite the great improvement in navigation brought about by GEE, was the continued prevalence of inaccurate bombing, particularly when the target was obscured – a weakness which would be all the more fatal as the growth of the German night-fighter force increased the hazards of operating in moonlight. Greater accuracy was indeed the next essential. As Harris himself later wrote: 'There is not much difference between the load of a medium bomber which misses the target and the load of a heavy bomber which also misses it.'[21]

Until Bomber Command could gain significantly in both numbers and accuracy it would hammer away at Germany, keep the fight alive, and win victories – but never decisive ones.

12

Policy and the USAAF

1942 was the year of transformation. In the opening months all was disaster for the Allies, but by the end of the year the balance had swung firmly the other way: the Japanese had been stopped, the German Sixth Army was trapped at Stalingrad, Egypt and Cyrenaica had been cleared, French North Africa invaded. Such developments vindicated the strategy agreed between the British and the Americans in their 1941 staff talks and at the first Washington Conference – an 'all-arms' strategy directed first towards victory in Europe.[1] But before the improvement set in – and afterwards – there was much debate on the part to be played by the long-range bombers.

Since the fall of France, Britain's only major offensive weapon against Germany had been Bomber Command. In the absence of any likelihood that British and Commonwealth armies could liberate the Continent unaided, great hopes had been pinned on the bomber offensive, and plans made for a huge expansion of the bomber force. At the beginning of 1942 the currently approved programme, Target Force E, envisaged for Bomber Command a front-line strength of no fewer than 4000 heavy and medium bombers by mid-1943.[2] This goal, however, could be attained only with very extensive help from American production. When the United States became involved in the war, that help could no longer be given on anything like the intended scale: with certain excepted categories, American planes were to be flown by American crews. This dealt the deathblow to Bomber Command's hopes of ever reaching the 4000 target.

There was, however, a massive compensation. The Americans were resolved to build up their own long-range bomber forces and operate alongside Bomber Command in the European theatre. Such an arrangement had been agreed in staff discussions before the United States entered the war and was formally ratified at the Washington Conference on 13 January 1942. The participation envisaged was enormous: the Americans planned to establish in Britain by April 1943 a force of over 3500 aircraft.[3] This was more than the entire home strength of the RAF at the time of the decision.

In these circumstances, the RAF's Target Force E gave place in July 1942 to a more modest goal, Target Force G. This visualised for Bomber Command a front line of 125 squadrons, or about 2000 aircraft, by December 1943 – about half the previous total contemplated, to be achieved over a period six months longer.[4]

Towards this total of 125 squadrons Harris had only 44 when he took over in February 1942, and fewer than that – though a higher proportion of heavy bombers – seven months later. This was not the fault of the training arrangements. In June 1942 a third OTU Group (No. 93) had been formed, and by the following August there were 22 bomber OTUs. These had been producing bomber crews beyond casualty replacement needs, but large numbers of them had been going, either as spare crews or formed into squadrons, to man Coastal Command, Army Cooperation Command, and RAF Middle East. In 1941 all 17 squadrons raised from the Bomber Command OTUs had been allocated to other Commands, and in 1942 all but three of the 19 raised followed the same paths, either permanently or 'on loan'.[5] These 'diversions' (as Harris called them), coupled with shortfalls in planned aircraft production, inevitably sent even the reduced expansion scheme for Bomber Command seriously awry.

The transfers to other Commands were made in response to genuine strategic needs. As always, it was a question of deciding priorities. But some further demands in 1942 emanating from the Admiralty and the War Office would, if satisfied, have killed off the strategic bombing offensive completely. This was not the declared intention, for in the Chiefs of Staff Committee the heads of all three Services were always united on its necessity. In 1942, however, Dudley Pound's pleas for local 'Coastal Commands', home and overseas, under Admiralty control, would have absorbed 2000 aircraft, while Alan Brooke's demands for Army Cooperation Command, or preferably a separate Army Air Arm, would have taken up another 4000.[6] As Portal pointed out in a masterly Chiefs of Staff paper in May 1942, these demands, amounting in total to more than the entire strength of the Luftwaffe, 'would absorb into limited and specialized roles the greater part of our total foreseeable strength in the air. To meet them would automatically extinguish any hope of development of that bomber offensive which has been postulated by the British and American Chiefs of Staff as one of the essential measures for winning the war, as opposed merely to not losing it . . .'[7] Portal's logic carried the day: Pound and Brooke got what they needed in the way of air support as more aircraft became available, but not the large, specialised detached forces of their wishes.

It was against the background of these demands, of the 'diversions', and of criticism from Sir Stafford Cripps and others that Portal, with immense tact and skill in Whitehall, and Harris, battering away from High Wycombe, strove to defend Bomber Command and build it up to its approved strength. Like most airmen, they passionately believed that the bomber, by striking at the enemy's vitals in his own homeland, could shorten the war and obviate the need for long-drawn-out military campaigns and mass battlefield slaughter in the manner of 1914–18. As yet, in May 1942, there were no settled plans for a military landing in Europe, only an intention and alternative possibilities, and so the case for a powerful strategic air offensive was all the stronger.

Fortunately the leaders of the United States Army Air Forces (USAAF), General Henry ('Hap') Arnold and his principal lieutenant for Europe, Major General Carl ('Tooey') Spaatz, were just as ardent for strategic bombing as were Portal and Harris. They also believed that their multi-gunned B-17 Flying Fortress with the newest Norden bombsight, capable, according to legend, of putting a bomb into a pickle barrel from 20,000 feet, was the ideal instrument for its execution. Ever anxious to escape from what they regarded as restrictive and uninformed Army control, they had jumped at the chance to send bomber groups to England in advance of any American armies.

The B-17 was a daylight bomber, and if it could succeed in penetrating Germany – which was at first by no means certain – its operations would ideally complement those of Bomber Command by night. Harris, while doubting if the Americans would have any more success than his own forces in bombing Germany by day, naturally gave his new allies the warmest of welcomes. He had the problem of finding some of the many airfields they would need, but this he addressed enthusiastically and, among other things, gave over the whole ground resources of a new Bomber Group which had been about to form. Brigadier General Ira Eaker, the commander designate of the American VIII Bomber Command, the advance formation of the new US Eighth Air Force, arrived with half-a-dozen officers at High

Wycombe only a day or two after Harris took up his appointment, and immediately found himself treated as a personal friend. He stayed as a guest for some weeks in Harris's house and then, after the arrival of a large staff group, in May set up VIII Bomber Command headquarters (code-named PINETREE) in the commandeered Wycombe Abbey Girls' School, five miles away from Harris's own HQ (SOUTHDOWN). His superior, General Spaatz, set up US Eighth Air Force headquarters the following month at Bushy Park, Teddington (WIDEWING).

Raymond Daniell of the *New York Times* saw Harris and his American counterpart some time later. He noted the contrasts between the two, and their underlying compatibility:

Harris, who had been a gold miner and tobacco planter in Rhodesia, is a hulking giant of a man – tall with shoulders to match – having a lusty, mordant sense of humour. He is bluff and hearty for an Englishman – a provocative, stimulating conversationalist. He has the appearance of a successful Middle Western farmer and the manner of a rather crusty county judge who has seen much of life and has enjoyed every minute of it.

Eaker is a soft-spoken Texan with an agile, athletic body. His features, like those of so many men who have devoted most of their lives to flying, have set themselves into sharp, firm lines that make one think of an eagle. He is modest and retiring almost to the point of shyness and he has that unconsciously thoughtful courtesy usually associated with the antebellum South . . .

Of the two Harris is the more studious. He likes to read history and books on farming, to which he hopes to return after the war. Eaker is restless and fidgety unless he is doing something. He is a confirmed believer in the value of exercise. He spends his few spare moments of daylight playing golf, tennis and softball, and after dark he enjoys a game of gin rummy, bridge or poker – a contest at which he is so expert that he sometimes has trouble finding anyone to gamble with him. Harris likes cocktails and highballs but Eaker hardly ever touches anything but a glass of sherry for sociability's sake.

General Eaker arrived with only one preconceived notion about Britain – namely, that it was his job to get along with the British. He has found that to be an easy and pleasant task . . . And the British have found that they like this cool, efficient American general who is as different from the traditional caricature as Air Marshal Harris is unlike the American conception of a monocled upper-class Englishman . . .[8]

In the opening days of July 1942 the first B-17s, late on schedule, flew in across the Atlantic. A month of training, familiarisation, and formation practice flying followed. In the afternoon of 17 August, watched by a large crowd of journalists, 18 of them took off on their inaugural European mission – 12, under heavy RAF Spitfire escort, to bomb from high level the extensive marshalling yards at Rouen–Sotteville, the others on a diversionary operation. At the head of the second six of those attacking the marshalling yards was General Eaker, in *Yankee Doodle*. The bombing was good, and all the Fortresses returned safely. The Eighth Air Force was in business. RAF Bomber Command had a valorous, powerful and – as it proved – essential partner.

The arrival of the Eighth Air Force diminished rather than increased Harris's own resources, and he was characteristically vigorous in pleading for more. On 17 June 1942 he wrote a trenchant letter to the Prime Minister expressing his views on future strategy – how air power, if built up, could obviate the need for a long and bloody military campaign in the West – and asking for the return of his 'diverted' squadrons and top priority in aircraft manufacture for heavy bombers. 'The utter destruction,' he asserted, 'of Lübeck and Rostock, the practical destruction of Cologne (a leading asset to Germany turned in one night into a vast liability) point the certain, the obvious, the quickest and the easiest way to overwhelming victory.'[9]

Not for the first or last time, Harris was exaggerating, and the Prime Minister told him so. While agreeing with Harris that a heavier bombing offensive was necessary, he did not think it could end the war virtually by itself. 'Only by ever-growing, ever more accurate and ever more far-ranging Bomber attacks on Germany,' wrote Churchill, 'can we prepare the conditions which will be favourable to the major military operation on which we are resolved.'[10] Bomber Command's function, in Churchill's eyes, was to weaken Germany, not (as had been desperately hoped while Britain 'stood alone') to try to beat her down single-handed. He fully agreed that the momentum of the bomber programme must be restored. 'We must observe with sorrow and alarm,' he wrote to the War Cabinet on 21 July 1942, 'the woeful shrinkage of air plans for Bomber expansion.'[11] Two months later, on 17 September, he ruled that some of the 'diverted' squadrons should be returned to Bomber Command, that the production of aircraft for the Command should have temporary priority, and that the 35 operational squadrons to which the Command had fallen should be built up to at least 50 by the end of the year.[12] Though his larger ideas had been rejected, Harris had at least ensured a limited expansion.

By that time, however, the Allies had decided on their next move.

Further study, and the fact that the Russians were still holding out, deleted from the British list of projects the desperately risky SLEDGEHAMMER – an emergency lodgement in France during 1942. Instead, on the combined impetus of the British and of Roosevelt, who was anxious to see American troops in action in the European theatre before the end of 1942, the decision was taken on 24 July to invade French North Africa (the former projected Operation GYMNAST, now renamed TORCH).[13] This was a bitter disappointment to Roosevelt's Chief of Staff, General Marshall, who enthusiastically championed a major invasion of France in 1943 (Operation ROUND-UP), and who rightly sensed that the decision for North Africa in 1942 might make this impossible.

So TORCH was on, but no one yet knew whether it could be effectively carried out, or to what it would lead. In this interim period Portal again put the case for concentrating on a massive bombing offensive. On 30 September 1942 he sent a memorandum to his fellow Chiefs of Staff claiming that there were three ways of beating Germany – by building up a big bomber force, by building up big armies, or by compromising between the two. He pointed out the length of time needed to amass great armies, and the danger that compromise would leave both elements too weak to achieve victory. He argued for the first solution – in effect, victory by air power, at least to the point where only a small military force would finally be needed. If, he asserted, a force of 4000–6000* heavy bombers, British and American, could be built up in England by April of 1944, it could obtain decisive results within that year.[14]

Portal's advocacy was so persuasive that he was actually able to obtain the agreement in principle of Dudley Pound and Alan Brooke, and on 30 October 1942 his proposals were circulated as an official Chiefs of Staff recommendation.[15] Asked to state what the operation of such a force would achieve in terms of physical destruction, Portal drew on figures from the German bombing of Britain, multiplied by the greater tonnage that would fall on Germany. On this basis, 6,000,000 German houses, with a proportionate number of factories and transport and power facilities would be destroyed, the destruction encompassing at least one-third of German industry. In the course of this, 25,000,000 Germans would be rendered homeless, 900,000 killed and another 1,000,000 injured.[16]

When he studied the Chiefs of Staff paper Churchill was far from convinced. By that time the Anglo-American landings in French North

---

* This has always struck me as a curiously wide disparity. D.R.

Africa under General Eisenhower had gone well, and there were good prospects that the last Axis forces in Africa might be expelled and Italy threatened. The Prime Minister could even visualise the opening of a 'Second Front' in Europe in 1943, as he had personally promised Stalin. He was all in favour of a powerful bombing offensive, but had no intention of placing almost exclusive reliance on it. Nor, when they thought about it further, had Pound or Brooke. Portal for his part had been flying a kite rather than nailing his colours to the mast, and he was quite ready to accept the 'compromise' strategy. So what finally emerged as the agreed aim of the bombing offensive was a formula which was carried forward to the next great Anglo-American conference, at Casablanca in January 1943, and there approved by both nations: 'the progressive destruction and dislocation of the enemy's war industrial and economic system to a point where his capacity for armed resistance is fatally weakened.'[17] From this aim Portal thereafter never deviated. Harris, however, continued to nurture visions of winning the war virtually by bombing alone – if he and the Americans were given big enough forces.

A contributory, though much lesser, factor in Churchill's reluctance to rely predominantly on bombers for the defeat of Hitler was the limited scope of USAAF VIII Bomber Command's initial operations. After the beginning against Rouen–Sotteville on 17 August Eaker's forces flew regular missions, but in 20 operations over France before the end of October they did not venture beyond Lille. By the end of 1942 they had still not penetrated Germany, and it was not until 27 January 1943 that they attacked their first German target – a 'fringe' one at Wilhelmshaven.

There was in fact every reason for this delay. In the haste to send over forces, many of the American airmen had arrived with quite inadequate training, and this had to be rectified. Then, when the decision was taken for TORCH, several of the best-trained elements of the Eighth Air Force were incorporated in the Twelfth Air Force for service in North Africa. And finally, the self-defending Fortresses had needed fighter escort over France – how would they fare over Germany when the Allies had as yet no effective long-range fighters? All these factors amply explain why the Americans rightly took their time before attacking the Reich itself.

In the interim, not only Harris but also Portal wondered whether the great ideal of the daylight precision-bombing of Germany would ever be attained – whether the Americans would not do better to turn over to night-bombing, lengthy as this transition might be. Portal's doubts did not last: he soon became convinced, for reasons both of strategy – the merits of 24-hour 'round the clock' bombing were obvious – and of diplomacy, that the Americans must be encouraged to make their great experiment. But long after Portal had lined himself up firmly behind the American concepts, Churchill's doubts remained. On 29 November 1942 he wrote to General Ismay, military secretary of the Chiefs of Staff Committee, about the undesirability of bringing into Britain 'masses of air groundsmen while the United States Air Forces have not shown themselves possessed of any machines capable of bombing Germany either by night or by day'. It would be, he thought, 'the greatest pity to choke up all our best airfields', and he would far sooner see the arrival of 'half-a-dozen extra American divisions'. It was to take all the persuasive powers of Spaatz and Eaker at Casablanca in January 1943 to make Churchill support their concept by – as he himself described it – 'giving up opposing them'.

It was as well that Churchill's reservations were overcome. The American bombers were not designed for a night role, nor were their crews trained for it. Had he persisted in his attitude, a possible American reaction might have been to transfer most of their British-based air units to the Pacific. In that case, or had they stayed in Europe and operated by night, they and Bomber Command would assuredly never have achieved what they did achieve – 'the progressive destruction and dislocation of the enemy's war industrial and economic system' to the point where Germany's capacity for armed resistance was 'fatally weakened'.

13

The Advent of the Pathfinders

For many months selected aircrews of Bomber Command had led the night raids, lighting up, as best they could, what they took to be the target area, and raising fires for later arrivals to bomb. All the same, much of the bombing had gone astray. During November 1941 the newly appointed Deputy Director of Bomber Operations at the Air Ministry, Group Captain Sydney Bufton, had proposed a radical solution. He had suggested that instead of raid leaders being selected at station or Group level for particular operations, a Target Finding Force should be formed from picked crews and located in a given area. This force would not only provide the raid leaders but would also study the techniques and equipment necessary for efficient raid-leading.[1]

Bufton was not theorising from inexperience. He had been an effective and popular squadron commander in 4 Group on Whitleys and Halifaxes, and was one of the very few members of the Air Staff who had taken part in recent operations.

Nothing had come of Bufton's proposal during the last weeks of Peirse's regime, so he put it forward again as soon as Harris took over at High Wycombe. It met with instant rejection. Harris, and all his Group commanders, were firmly convinced that the formation of a target-finding *corps d'élite*, in addition to raising administrative problems, would be detrimental to squadron morale: the squadrons would resent, and suffer from, having their best crews taken away, and the crews themselves would lose opportunities of promotion within their squadrons.

Exchanges and meetings followed, and Harris yielded a little ground. Well aware of the high proportion of bombs missing their targets, he proposed that all squadrons should be assessed each month for bombing accuracy on the evidence of their bombing photographs, and that those with the best results should act as the raid leaders the next month. This, he thought, would stimulate competition and lead to improvement. The suggestion obviously failed to meet Bufton's point that only a separate Target Finding Force, with its units close together and devoting themselves continuously to all aspects of the problem, could bring about the maximum possible improvement.[2]

Three months had now passed since Bufton's first approach to Harris, and Portal, who wholeheartedly backed Bufton, decided that the time was ripe for action. In June 1942 he saw Harris and secured his reluctant compliance.[3] Within two months the Target Finding Force came into being.

Harris, however, was not entirely defeated. He managed to weaken the original intention. Instead of four new target-finding squadrons being formed in large part from the best crews of all squadrons, he allowed the commanders of the four Groups – Nos. 1, 3, 4 and 5 – primarily concerned with night-bombing over Germany each to nominate one squadron from his Group. There were some transfers of crew but in general the squadron went *en bloc*. This produced a Target Finding Force, but not one initially composed only of outstanding crews.

Harris also won some concessions officially. To make up for their lost opportunities of promotion, and for the fact that they would be required to do a tour of 60 operations (including those already flown), the target-finders were to be accorded, after they had proved themselves, an acting rank one higher than that they already held. Reluctantly the Treasury agreed that sergeants could become flight sergeants, flight sergeants warrant officers, and so on.[4] Moreover Harris was allowed to give his own, and better, choice of name to the new organisation – the Pathfinder Force (PFF). And finally he secured for the Pathfinders – oddly in view of his objections to a *corps d'élite*, but very sensibly – an emblem of their special function, the Pathfinder Badge (an eagle).

The Pathfinder Force came into official existence on 11 August 1942. Six days later its first four squadrons gathered on their allotted airfields in Cambridgeshire and Huntingdonshire. They had a rare mixture of aircraft: No. 7 Squadron with Stirlings, 35 Squadron with Halifaxes and Lancasters, 83 Squadron with Lancasters and 156 Squadron with Wellingtons. In addition, 109 Squadron, as yet only affiliated, had

Mosquitoes. For replacement crews they were to rely on their parent Groups; but their operational orders were to come, through 3 Group channels, direct from Bomber Command.

To command the new force Harris made an unorthodox choice. He asked for, and got, Donald Bennett, the Australian who had but recently returned from Sweden after being shot down over Norway. An aviator of quite exceptional qualifications and experience, Bennett was to receive in Harris's memoirs the accolade: 'He was, and is, the most efficient airman I have ever met.'

Though aged only 31, Bennett already had an impressive list of achievements behind him. After learning to fly with the RAAF he had transferred to the RAF and in England had been successively a fighter pilot, a flying-boat pilot (Harris was his CO in 210 Squadron) and a lecturer at the RAF School of Navigation. In preparation for a later career in civil aviation he had acquired the First Class Navigator's Licence – there were only six other holders at the time – the Pilot's 'B' Licence, the Wireless Operator's Licence, and in three categories the Engineer Ground Officer's Licence. After leaving the RAF in 1935 he had then written a standard work on navigation and become a flying-boat pilot for Imperial Airways. He had established the flying-boat long-distance flight record, been much concerned with the Mayo composite aircraft and flight refuelling, and in 1939 had piloted for the new British Overseas Airways Corporation the inaugural transatlantic flights.

After the outbreak of war Bennett had continued in civil aviation but now with a military purpose. He had become Flying Superintendent of the Atlantic Ferry Organisation, flying American aircraft across to Britain: in his eleven-month tour of duty, only one aircraft was lost in the crossing. On the formation of RAF Ferry Command to take over this work Bennett had then returned to England, re-entered the RAF as an acting wing commander and successively commanded two bomber squadrons. He was within an hour or two of departing with 10 Squadron for the Middle East when Harris summoned him to High Wycombe.[5]

This extremely able and widely experienced young airman was not considered senior enough to become at once an Air Officer Commanding. He was promoted to acting group captain, and at first commanded the Pathfinder Force by virtue of a position on the staff at Bomber Command HQ. Soon, however, in January 1943, when the initial four squadrons had grown to six, the new force became constituted as a separate Group – No. 8 – with Air Commodore Bennett as AOC.

Bennett at once set himself to tackle what he considered the heart of the problem – the equipment of his squadrons for their task. New flares were needed for illuminating, target-indicator bombs and a range of pyrotechnics for marking. On the navigational and blind-bombing side, two new radar systems under development at the Telecommunications Research Establishment had to be tested under operational conditions, and their production and fitting speeded up. All this Bennett set in train, while also planning and supervising the Pathfinder operations.

Bennett possibly swung into action all the more vigorously from the conviction that he was the sole originator of the whole Pathfinder idea. In his book *Pathfinder*, he described how, while still working with the Atlantic Ferry early in 1941, he had been invited to the Directorate of Bomber Operations at the Air Ministry to give his views on what could be done to improve current standards of navigation and bombing:

> I looked at the assembled company and I simply asked a question. 'You are all experienced general duties officers; you have been flying a lifetime. Could you get into an aircraft on a pitch-black night, fly for three or four hours on a compass and an air-speed indicator, find a pinpoint in central Germany, avoid spoofs and dummies, not be put off by night fighters, flak and searchlights, and guarantee success?' They looked at each other and then looked at me and replied, 'Of course not; we are pilots, not navigators.' I pointed out that they had had twenty years or more in the air, whereas those boys they were sending out over Germany had had no practical experience whatever of genuine operational flying. They had only had the aircrew training which was carried out in distant and peaceful parts of the world, and in the circumstances their chances of success were remote. I pointed out, however, that if a force of experienced navigators were to lead the crews, and if such navigators were to be given somewhat better equipment than that available in ordinary bomber aircraft, the chances of success were relatively high, and if they were then given fireworks of some description with which to attract the main force to the target it should be possible for them to act effectively as leaders and to get the whole of the bomber effort on to at least some targets. We discussed the scheme in considerable detail before I returned to Montreal. It was the first seed which I sowed on the subject of the Pathfinder Force which was subsequently to turn Bomber Command from failure to success.[6]

Bennett, as Harris later wrote, 'could not suffer fools gladly, and by his own high standards there were many fools'. Undue modesty was not one of his faults. He was young, he had risen fast, he was too self-assured to be universally popular. But he had knowledge, intelligence, enterprise, experience, vigour and unlimited courage. He was unquestionably an inspired choice to form and lead the Pathfinders.

The Pathfinder Force started with no advantage in equipment over the other squadrons, and not much in general level of skill. Moreover, its advent coincided with the Germans' first success in jamming GEE – which remained invaluable for navigation up to about 200 miles from base, but lost most of its effectiveness over Germany. Not surprisingly, the initial Pathfinder-led operations showed no great improvement in bombing accuracy. And if the Pathfinders' marking went wrong, the whole raid now went wrong.

The first Pathfinder operation, on 17/18 August 1942, went sadly astray. Over 100 aircraft, led by 31 Pathfinders, took off to bomb Flensburg, a U-boat construction centre in a Baltic inlet a few miles south of the Danish border. But the winds were not as forecast, and despite claims made by many of the crews, no bombs hit Flensburg. Instead they fell near a similar inlet several miles to the north, in Denmark.

Little more success marked the next Pathfinder-led raid, against Frankfurt. On 27/28 August, however, in better conditions, Pathfinders led an effective attack by some 300 aircraft on Kassel. Unfortunately the severe damage they inflicted, including some to the Henschel and the Fieseler aircraft works, was offset by the loss of 31 aircraft – more than 10 per cent of the attackers. That same night, nine Lancasters of 106 Squadron in 5 Group – Harris's old Command, which he tended to prefer for special operations – set out for distant Gdynia to attack the new German aircraft carrier, *Graf Zeppelin*. Seven of the Lancasters got there and back – nearly 2000 miles – without loss, but the *Graf Zeppelin*, enshrouded in haze, suffered no harm.

The last big operation of August 1942, on the night 28/29, showed how far Bomber Command still was from being consistently effective. While 113 bombers made a scattered and mainly unrewarding attack on relatively near and lightly defended Saarbrücken, a larger force of Pathfinder-led aircraft penetrated much more deeply into Germany. Their objective was Nuremberg, dear to the Nazis as the scene of their great pre-war rallies. Using for the first time an improvised target-indicator bomb – an ordinary 250-lb bomb casing filled with incendiary material – the Pathfinders marked quite accurately. This resulted in heavy damage to the town; but 25 of the attacking force – more than 13 per cent – failed to return.

Losses of this order could not possibly be sustained for any great length of time. They had fallen especially heavily on the older aircraft, the Wellingtons. Of 41 Wellingtons which set out for Nuremberg, 14 failed to make the journey back – and this on top of a disaster the previous night to 142 Squadron, which had lost five of its 15 Wellingtons raiding Kassel. The Blenheims had already been withdrawn from operating over Germany, and the Hampdens were shortly to follow. Now it looked as though the trusted Wellingtons, still equipping over a third of the operational squadrons, were also becoming easy prey to the ever more numerous German night-fighters.

The raid on the first night of September 1942 gave even less cause for complacency. On this occasion the losses were light, but the bombing went entirely astray. The Pathfinders intended to mark the capital of the Saar coalfield, Saarbrücken. Instead they marked the much less industrialised town of Saarlouis (Saarlautern), thirteen miles away. The main force piled down its bombs on the markers, and Saarlouis escaped heavier casualties only because the disused fortifications of the Siegfried Line nearby made excellent air-raid shelters.

Very soon, however, as Bennett weeded out the less efficient crews, his leadership began to show results. On 2/3 September the Pathfinders led a very successful operation against Karlsruhe, and three nights later a damaging attack on Bremen, with hits on the Atlas shipyard and the Weser aircraft factory. For this raid they used what was to become the basis of their most frequently employed technique. First an advance party, soon to be known as the 'illuminators', found the target area and lit it up with lanes of white flares. Then a second group, the 'visual markers', identified the actual target and marked it by dropping coloured flares. This group was quickly followed by a third, 'the backers-up', which dropped incendiaries on the coloured flares. After all these came the main force, with high explosives and further incendiaries to bomb the fires created by the backers-up. Many refinements of ground- and sky-markings were to develop later, but this remained the broad pattern. Greater and greater effectiveness was to come in 1943 with new hooded flares to reduce dazzle, barometric fuses to ensure that the flares exploded at the right height, properly designed target-indicator bombs, and further navigational aids.

Later in September 1942 Bomber Command made heavy and mainly successful attacks on Duisburg, Düsseldorf, Bremen again, and Wilhelmshaven. The raid on Düsseldorf by 479 aircraft on 10/11 September, which resulted in nearly 20,000 of the inhabitants being 'bombed out', saw the first use by the Pathfinders of a new gigantic marking bomb – an ordinary 'cookie' (4000-lb bomb) casing filled with incendiary material and popularly known as a 'Pink Pansy'. It tended, however, to burn out too quickly for its purpose. The same raid also saw, for nearly the last time, OTU crews operating over Germany in large numbers: no fewer than 176 OTU aircraft took part, though not without casualties: one OTU (No. 16) lost five of the 13 Wellingtons it contributed. The raid on Bremen three nights later by 446 aircraft, 139 of which were manned by OTU crews, was, however, less costly and equally effective. It did further damage to the Focke-Wulf aircraft factory, halted production in the Lloyd dynamo factory for two weeks, and left the usual wreckage of residential, commercial and historic buildings.[7]

These were big efforts, as was the attack on Essen by 369 aircraft on 16/17 September. For once this most difficult of targets suffered: 15 bombs and one crashing bomber landed on Krupps, but the cost was very high – more than 10 per cent of the aircraft despatched. Good results, by a smaller force, were also achieved on 23/24 September against the U-boat building yards at Wismar and the Dornier aircraft factory nearby, but other raids during the month, especially against distant targets like Frankfurt and Munich, were comparative failures.

In this category must also be placed the gallant attempt by four Mosquitoes of 105 Squadron to destroy the Gestapo headquarters in Oslo on 25 September during daylight. The raid, intended to coincide with a parade by Norwegian 'Quislings' (collaborators), met German fighters as it swept in at low level. These quickly shot down one of the Mosquitoes, but could not prevent four bombs hitting the intended target. Unfortunately the skill and daring of the attackers was ill rewarded. All four bombs, three of which passed right through the building, failed to explode.

The first raids of October 1942 were little more successful. Against Krefeld, on 2/3 October, the Pathfinders marked late and most of the bombing went astray. Three nights later bad weather spoiled an attack by 257 aircraft on Aachen: Charlemagne's capital suffered, but many of the aircraft dropped their bombs on Lutterade, in Holland, seventeen miles away. Eighty-three of its inhabitants lost their lives, 3,000 their homes.

Much more successful were raids by over 200 aircraft against Osnabrück on 6/7 October and Kiel a week later. Some of the bombers hit Kiel heavily, but, even so, many bombed instead a large decoy fire in the open countryside. This kind of error happened again on 16/17 October, during an attack on Cologne.

For incomplete success after superb endeavour, however, the most remarkable operation of this period was undoubtedly the dusk raid on 17 October against the great Schneider armament works at Le Creusot and an associated transformer station five miles away. A daylight operation gave the best chance of avoiding heavy casualties among the local population, and tactically the raid was all that could have been hoped for. Flying in pairs for mutual support, 94 Lancasters from 5 Group headed out from Land's End, crossed the Biscay coast south of St Nazaire, swept through central France at below 500 feet, met no fighters, and bombed with only light opposition from flak. Except for one aircraft which crashed into the transformer station and virtually destroyed it, all returned safely. Had the bombing been more completely accurate, the operation would have been a truly outstanding feat of arms. As it was, the damage inflicted on the Schneider works – which was considerable – still left most of the plant intact, and several bombs, misaimed in the failing light, fell with tragic results on the workers' estate nearby.[8]

Before October 1942 was out, a new set of targets assumed priority. With Montgomery's offensive at El Alamein due to begin on 23 October, and the Anglo-American landings in French North Africa on 11 November, the heat had now to be turned on Italy. On 22/23 October Bomber Command began with Genoa, 105 Lancasters of 5 Group led by 8 Pathfinders leaving a trail of devastation in the eastern docks. All the raiders returned safely. But, characteristically for the time, a repeat raid the following night, in much worse weather, went astray and instead bombed Savona, thirty miles distant along the coast. Two raids on Milan then followed within the next twenty-four hours. On 24 October, in the first daylight raid on Italy from home bases, 88 Lancasters from 5 Group caught Milan completely by surprise. They hit, among other objectives, the Caproni aircraft factory, and lost only three of their number. At dusk another 71 bombers set out to increase the damage, but storms intervened and Milan escaped lightly.

During November the main weight of the bombing continued to fall on Italy, only Hamburg and Stuttgart in Germany being attacked in strength. Four more raids on Genoa, followed by four on Turin – two by over 200 aircraft – kept up the pressure. The cost was light, the effect on Italian morale considerable, and in Turin the heavy damage extended to the Fiat works, the Lancia works, the State Railway works and the Royal Arsenal. In all, between 22 October and 11/12 December Bomber Command flew 1646 sorties against Italian targets and lost 62 aircraft – around 3.7 per cent.[9]

The crews regarded these long trips to Italy as vastly preferable to shorter runs into Germany, simply because the Italian defences were so much weaker. But there was still ample room for heroism, as the Australian Flight Sergeant R. H. Middleton and his crew showed. *En route* to Turin on 28/29 November, Middleton coaxed his labouring Stirling over the Alps only with great difficulty and heavy consumption of fuel. Despite this he pressed on, and determinedly set about identifying his target. On his third run, at 2000 feet, anti-aircraft fire twice caught the Stirling, and one shell burst in the cockpit. Fragments struck Middleton in the leg, the chest, and the face, destroying his right eye. He slumped back unconscious and the aircraft plunged down to within 800 feet of the ground before the second pilot, Flight Sergeant L. A. Hyder, though also badly wounded in the legs and head, managed to regain control. Incredibly enough, he completed the bombing. Over Turin the flak struck again, but Middleton came round, and insisted on relieving his wounded comrade at the controls. Though there were great holes in the main planes and the windscreen was gone, Middleton managed to bring the Stirling back over the Alps, only to be hit again as he crossed out over France. Somehow the Stirling gained the coast of Kent, by which time hardly any fuel remained. With the aircraft so badly damaged, and both pilots wounded, Middleton felt that a safe landing was impossible. He turned along the shore and ordered the crew to bale out. Five did so successfully. He himself was too weak to jump, and he was apparently intending to ditch just off land when, with the last fuel running out, the aircraft plunged into the sea. Middleton, who was posthumously awarded the VC, perished, together with two of the crew who had insisted on staying to help him.[10]

During December 1942 bad weather greatly restricted activity. Crews had hard work finding Frankfurt and Mannheim, but managed to deliver heavy attacks on Duisburg and Turin. The outstanding operation of the month was undoubtedly OYSTER, the daylight attack by almost the entire forces of 2 Group on 6 December against the vast Philips' Radio, and Lamp and Valve, factories at Eindhoven. Occupying 77 and 15 acres respectively, these were thought to be supplying about a third of Germany's radio component requirements. In the first big concentrated operation by the Group, no fewer than 93 aircraft took part: 36 Bostons, 10 Mosquitoes, and 47 of the newly acquired Venturas – twin-engined American aircraft of indifferent performance which filled a gap before Mitchells and more Mosquitoes became available. Only fifty miles short of the Ruhr, Eindhoven was beyond the current limits of fighter escort, but Spitfires and Mosquitoes and USAAF Fortresses flew diversions. The bomber formations sped across Holland at low level and, despite harrying by German fighters and some mutual interference, hit both the factory complexes hard. The raiders' work lasted: not until six months had passed did Philips regain full production.[11]

In achieving this great success, however, 2 Group paid a heavy price – 15 per cent of the attacking force. There was, too, another cause for sadness, revealed later. Although the raid was in daylight and on a Sunday, to avoid injuring the Dutch workers, 148 of those who dwelt nearby lost their lives.

As 1942 drew to a close Harris could reflect that, in bomb-lift if not yet greatly in numbers, his force was now much stronger; that the Pathfinder Force, the creation of which he had resisted, had proved itself – bombing photographs showed an increase in accuracy of almost one-third; and that, though operations had frequently gone wrong, his Command had struck some notably heavy and hurtful blows. He could also contemplate the fact that in the US VIII Bomber Command he now had an ally of huge potential power. And he could think with satisfaction of the new devices just introduced, or about to be introduced, into Bomber Command: RCM (radio countermeasures, to confuse the enemy radio and radar) and, above all, the two remarkable new aids to navigation and blind-bombing – OBOE and H2S. The struggle would still be hard and long, but with these the blows delivered at such human and material cost would now regularly, though not infallibly, strike home.

Harris, in writing of his first year at Bomber Command, summed the situation up in his usual vigorous fashion:

So ended a year of preparation in which very little material damage had been done to the enemy which he could not repair from his resources, but in which we had obtained or had in near prospect what we required to strike him to the ground, and learned how to use it.[12]

14

Towards the Main Offensive

I n the winter of 1942–3 crews in Bomber Command became aware that OBOE and H2S were no longer just a musical instrument and a gas that smelled of rotten eggs. They were also new radar aids to night navigation and blind-bombing.

OBOE had been about two years in gestation. During 1940 the Luftwaffe had used wireless beams to navigate over Britain. As a countermeasure, Wellingtons attacking a source of these transmissions near Cherbourg had flown along a beam emitted from one of the south-coast radar stations – which had plotted their progress and signalled when to bomb. In this largely unsuccessful experiment the note heard in the aircraft from the modulated continuous wave transmission gave rise to the name OBOE. Though this was a far cry from what later developed, by the beginning of 1941 the RAF had become seriously interested in long-distance wireless guidance for its bombers, and the code-name OBOE had been born.*

In May 1941 a team at TRE under A. M. Reeves began intensive work on OBOE. This resulted in December in some experimental blind-bombing against the *Scharnhorst* and *Gneisenau* at Brest. Stirlings of 7 and 15 Squadrons flew along a beam (known as the Baillie beam) laid over Brest from a transmitter in Cornwall, while an impromptu OBOE station in south Devon plotted the aircraft by radar and gave the

---

* The RAF was already experienced in the use of *short*-distance wireless beams – for landing aircraft. At most bomber stations the Standard Beam Approach (SBA) system was in place by 1940. Many pilots had cause to be grateful for it, but others distrusted it or their own proficiency and avoided practising SBA landings.

signal when to bomb. Operation TRINITY, as this was called, taught the scientists a great deal, but it was only partly on these principles that OBOE then developed. The OBOE system, as it emerged, departed from the use of beams and was based on pulses. Amplified in the aircraft, these were echoed back to the source of origin, on the true radar principle – unlike GEE.

In the developed OBOE system the bomber navigated to within ten minutes' flying-time of its target by a variety of means – often by GEE or a Baillie beam. At that point it picked up the main OBOE transmission. It then flew on an arc leading to the target at a constant range from the transmitting station (dubbed the CAT). Knowing the bomber's prearranged height and speed, the CAT could measure the aircraft's distance from it by the time taken to receive back the echoes. It could therefore inform the pilot by dots or dashes in his earphones whether he was veering to one side or the other of the constant arc track. If he was flying correctly, he heard a strong continuous note – OBOE – and knew he was on a sure path to the target area. Meanwhile a second ground station (the MOUSE), situated about 100 miles away from the CAT, was plotting the passage of the bomber along the arc of constant range. As the bomber reached the correct point for aiming near the target itself, the MOUSE cut in with a distinctive sharp signal, and the bomb-aimer released his load.

Though OBOE seemed likely to achieve far more accurate blind-bombing than any previous aid, it had some obvious weaknesses. Its range, dictated by the curvature of the earth, was at first only some 260–270 miles – good enough for the Ruhr, but certainly not for Berlin. Also, since the bomber echoed back signals, enemy fighters could 'home' on to it – a drawback soon countered by mounting OBOE in Mosquitoes, which could outfly the German fighters.*

The main operational weakness of OBOE at first appeared to be something apart from either of these. A pair of ground stations could deal with only one OBOE aircraft at a time. The process of final guidance and bombing instruction took about ten minutes, which meant that the pair of stations could handle only six aircraft in every hour. By December 1942 a second pair of ground stations had been built – one of each pair was near Cromer, the other in Kent. This still meant, however, that only 12 aircraft in every hour could fly under OBOE control.†

---

* The high ceiling of Mosquitoes also extended the OBOE range.
† A third pair of stations opened in July 1943, so enabling 18 aircraft in every hour to fly under OBOE control.

A major policy decision overcame, or bypassed, this serious limitation. OBOE, it was decided, would be fitted to the Pathfinder squadrons, but not the main force. If it could help the Pathfinders to mark more accurately, particularly when the target was obscured, the main force following would inevitably bomb more accurately. Moreover, reserving OBOE for the Pathfinders saved casualties among the main force. OBOE aircraft had to fly straight and level for the last stages of their bombing run. The fast Mosquitoes of the PFF could get away with this far better than the generality of Wellingtons, Stirlings, Halifaxes and Lancasters.

The first OBOE operation, a trial only, took place on 20/21 December 1942. Six OBOE Mosquitoes set out to bomb the power station at Lutterade, in Holland, and three succeeded. But subsequent photographs could not distinguish between the craters caused then, and others resulting from the earlier accidental attack on the town,* so the operation left Bomber Command little the wiser about the accuracy of the new equipment.

Within a few nights, however, a more satisfactory trial followed. Word had come that a German night-fighter unit had its headquarters near an airfield outside Florennes, in Belgium. On 31 December 1942/1 January 1943 two OBOE Mosquitoes, bombing from 28,000 feet and through clouds, managed to score a hit on the headquarters and two near misses. Success was clearly established. Previously alerted Belgian Resistance workers, at some risk to themselves, measured the distance of the craters from the target and sent the exact results to London.[1]

By mid-January 1943 the Pathfinders had flown nine other operational trials with OBOE, including several over the Ruhr. The main force squadrons, too, were beginning to follow up: raids of 50 or so Lancasters, led by three or four Pathfinder OBOE Mosquitoes, had found and attacked Düsseldorf, Duisburg and Essen. They had even done some damage to Krupps. But success was by no means yet complete, or guaranteed. Cloud or haze were nearly always present to prevent 'ground-marking'; and 'sky-marking', with the flares soon blown adrift by the wind, was very much a second best. Also, in these early operations, it was rare for all the OBOE Pathfinders to arrive at their appointed times, or for one or more of their sets not to go U/S *en route*.[2]

*　　*　　*

* See page 151.

Meanwhile the other new radar aid, H2S, was also under development. Because of the urgency of air defence against the Luftwaffe, radar work in Britain during 1937–9 had concentrated largely on providing early-warning ground stations – the Chain Home (CH) and the Chain Home Low (CHL). But the radar pioneers, and notably Dr E. G. Bowen, first at Bawdsey and then at TRE, had early visualised forms of airborne radar. The first of these were AI (Airborne Interception), for use in night-fighters, and ASV (Air to Surface Vessel), for the detection of ships and submarines at sea. In the course of developing these Dr Bowen became well aware that an airborne radar set, scanning ahead and registering the echoes on a cathode ray display, might be invaluable to bombers as an aid to navigation and possibly bomb-aiming. Indeed the early ASV sets could distinguish coastline from sea, built-up areas from countryside. But these sets were all badly needed for Coastal Command, and it was not until the autumn of 1941, with the Butt Report, that the full extent of Bomber Command's navigational problems became plain.

Priorities then changed. In the closing months of 1941 intensive work on airborne radar for blind navigation began at TRE under the direction of Professor P. I. Dee and Dr A. C. B. Lovell.* It soon became apparent that, if the aerial array on the bomber was not to be too cumbersome, and recognisable outlines of towns were to be obtained, the sets would work best on a short, centrimetric wavelength. This could be produced by the new, extremely powerful and highly secret valve, the cavity magnetron; but for security's sake it was hoped to make do, in a more developed form, with the well-known Klystron valve, which powered the existing ASV sets on a wavelength of 1.5 metres. By June 1942 this hope had to be abandoned; with the Klystron there was neither adequate range nor clear enough definition. Development then proceeded using the magnetron (producing a 9.1-centimetre wavelength, usually known as 10 cms). A scanner at the front of the aircraft searched the area ahead, and the responses appeared in the aircraft on the form of cathode ray screen known as a Plan Position Indicator. On this, a skilful operator could detect rudimentary indications of a town ahead – which he might recognise all the better if, for purposes of comparison, he had at hand an up-to-date plan of the town concerned.

With technical details settled, the next step was to start a 'crash' programme to produce the sets, install them in the aircraft – beginning with some Halifaxes, which were the easiest to fit – and train the

* Later Sir Bernard Lovell, the Astronomer Royal.

operators. The programme soon fell into arrears, but at least by December 1942 HQ Bomber Command could report confidently: 'The accuracy of bombing with H2S in blind conditions will produce a concentration of bombs about the aiming-point comparable with the best results that can be achieved at present by crews in perfect visibility.'[3]

It seemed that at least a few Pathfinders equipped with H2S would now be ready by the close of 1942. But during December the Admiralty intervened with a plea that no bomber aircraft carrying H2S should operate until the first week in March 1943: the U-boats were in the ascendant again, and Coastal Command needed the new centimetric magnetron-powered ASV to counter them. For two months at least, the Admiralty urged, the secrets of the magnetron should not be compromised by the use of H2S aircraft over Germany. This plea won only a short delay. On 22 December 1942 the Prime Minister came down on the side of the Air Ministry, and on 8 January 1943 the Combined Chiefs of Staff, against Admiralty wishes, agreed to the immediate use of H2S over enemy territory.

The weather, as usual, had the last word. It was not until 30/31 January 1943 that the first H2S operation took place. A few H2S Halifaxes and Stirlings led a force of Lancasters against Hamburg – a target near the coastline chosen for ease of identification. But the weather was poor, and the raid not much more successful than previous ones. More discouraging, only two nights later an H2S Stirling crashed in Holland, immediately yielding the Germans a set for examination. From this they were able – though not for several months – to develop a device, NAXOS, by which their fighters could home on to H2S transmissions.

Though the initial H2S operations were not particularly successful, Bomber Command clearly had an invaluable new aid. Some crews reported that they had been able to navigate by H2S throughout their whole trip, and that it had picked out towns at an average distance of some 25 miles ahead. In no doubt that he had a winner, Harris soon pressed for H2S to be fitted to the entire main force. But production was slow, and fitting the Lancasters was no easy task. For the first five months of 1943 Harris had to be content with only two flights of H2S aircraft, one of Stirlings and the other of Halifaxes, as part of the Pathfinder Force.[*4]

*   *   *

---

* There has been much debate about the origin of the name H2S, the chemical formula for the gas sulphuretted hydrogen. Dr R. V. Jones relates that the scientists at TRE dubbed it this after Professor Lindemann had dismissed their excuse for slow progress with the words 'It stinks'. But they told Lindemann that it stood for 'Home Sweet Home'.

By the beginning of 1943 Harris could contemplate the benefits to be derived not only from OBOE and H2S but also from an increasing number of countermeasures to the Germans' own radio and radar devices. The first such countermeasure, of extremely dubious effect, was for the bomber pilot to switch on his IFF (Identification, Friend or Foe) set when caught by a radar-assisted searchlight.* Scores of pilots – even including Leonard Cheshire – became convinced that the IFF had a jamming effect on the enemy's radar; they reported that it caused the master (i.e. radar-assisted) searchlight, bluer in tone than the others, either to be switched off or to lose coherent direction. Acting on these reports, Bomber Command HQ endorsed the practice, and even provided a special timed switch for the purpose – much to the dismay of the Assistant Director of Scientific Intelligence at the Air Ministry, Dr R. V. Jones. Jones pointed out that the German night-fighters were bound to home on to IFF transmissions from the bomber, but it was nearly two years before his point was proved and the practice forbidden.[5]

Whether IFF worked over Germany as the pilots thought it did, or not, it was clearly not doing enough to confuse the German defences. During 1942 Bomber Command's losses over the Reich had steadily increased. From around 2 per cent of sorties at the beginning of the year, the loss rate had risen to a peak of 6.7 per cent in August. From all the evidence of the crews it was apparent that losses from flak remained fairly constant at around 1.25 to 1.75 per cent of sorties. The increase arose from the German night-fighters.

In August 1942 Harris accordingly asked the Air Ministry to consider measures to confuse the German radar, both ground and airborne. By the end of the year a number of devices were in operation. One of the most long-lasting was MANDREL – a jamming device against the early-warning FREYAS on the coasts. A few bombers in every squadron carried this, as did some Defiants of Fighter Command – who patrolled off the French coast and set up a MANDREL screen. These jamming efforts were aided by GROUND MANDREL transmitted from Kent.

MANDREL was far from exhausting the ingenuity of the countermeasures experts. They also produced SHIVER, a device to increase the effect of IFF by making it 'squitter'; TINSEL, a microphone amplification of the bomber's engine noise, to drown the German fighters' R/T communications; and BOOZER, a set carried in the bomber to warn

---

* IFF sets, normally switched on when approaching British shores, produced a distinctive blip on the screens at the British radar chain stations, so identifying the aircraft as 'friendly'.

the pilot when he was tracked by enemy radar. All these helped: the loss rate declined for a while as each was introduced. But the Germans were good at countermeasures to countermeasures. The war, as it turned out, was more than halfway through by the end of 1942; but the radar battle of wits was still in its early stages.[6]

With OBOE, H2S, RCM (Radio Countermeasures) and a properly designed target-indicator bomb all available, Harris now looked forward to dealing Germany some crushing blows. His force, increasing at last in numbers as well as bomb-lift, now included eight squadrons of the Royal Canadian Air Force in a separate Group (No. 6) and four-and-a-half squadrons of Pathfinders. All told, by 3 February 1943 Harris had 59½ squadrons operational, of which 33½ were the new 'heavies', as opposed to only 15 of these a year before.[7]

Other developments, too, were by then giving Bomber Command additional strength. By the end of 1942 nearly all the satellite airfields had been brought up to full station standard, in flying facilities if not in domestic amenities. With the growth of the force, however, the Group headquarters had found it difficult to deal directly with the increased number of stations. In March 1943 the Command accordingly introduced the 'Base' system: except in the two smallest Groups – the Pathfinders and the Canadians – three airfields, each holding two squadrons, became linked to form a 'Base' under the command of an air commodore. Group headquarters thereafter dealt directly on most matters with the 'Base', leaving the latter to deal with its stations and squadrons. The new system not only created a new intermediate formation between the Group HQ and the station; it also concentrated many specialised facilities and personnel at the Base HQ airfield. In aircraft servicing and minor repairs, for instance, the Base airfield took over nearly all tasks except the daily ones. At the cost of perhaps some weakening of 'squadron spirit' this was to make a much more economical use of scarce equipment and skills.

Another major organisational improvement was occurring at the same time in the growth of the Heavy Conversion Units (HCUs). The equipment of the bomber force with four-engined aircraft had demanded an additional stage of training beyond the OTUs, and at first four of the new machines had been assigned to each heavy bomber squadron for training purposes. Then Heavy Conversion Flights had also been created at Group disposal. All this, however, had proved inadequate, so these resources were being amalgamated to form Heavy Conversion Units. Each of these had 32 four-engined bombers and its own airfield, services, and extremely experienced instructors. This growth was essential to the efficiency of the Command but made an enormous call on resources.*

Most encouraging of all in the early months of 1943 was the fact that the US Eighth Air Force began operating against Germany. On 23 January it flew its first German mission – against Wilhelmshaven. Bomber Command could now look forward to Eaker's ardent and increasingly powerful contribution to the assault on the Reich. But just when Harris was preparing to strike with unprecedented force against Hitler's industrial towns, demands for attacks on other targets supervened.

During 1942 suggestions had been made, mainly by the Admiralty but also by Coastal Command, that Bomber Command should bomb the main U-boat bases on the Biscay coast – Lorient, St Nazaire, La Pallice, Brest. At one point, in April, after the Germans had started to cover the U-boat pens with massive layers of concrete, Harris himself proposed an attack.[8] But any such action would inevitably take the form of area-bombing by night, and the Air Staff doubted whether this would greatly affect the U-boat sailings. Moreover there would be heavy casualties to French civilians. The Foreign Office, too, was strongly against, on both political and humanitarian grounds. So for months nothing was done. Meanwhile the Germans made the pens virtually indestructible by any bomb which then existed.

As, however, the Allied and neutral shipping losses rose in the autumn of 1942 – from 476,000 tons in July to 729,000 tons in December – so the Admiralty's pressure naturally increased. On 7 January 1943 the First Lord put in a strong plea to the War Cabinet for the bombing of the four ports, arguing that although not much damage might be done to the U-boats in their pens, the destruction of the bases as a whole would affect maintenance and drive away faint-hearted labour. He pressed for a heavy scale of attack, on high priority, employing – according to the weather – both precision- and area-bombing.[9]

Four days later the War Cabinet accepted this policy in principle. The Combined Chiefs of Staff then approved it for inclusion in the Casablanca directive of 21 January 1943. This listed German U-boat

---

* By the autumn of 1944 there were 20 HCUs and shorter-course Finishing Schools. They were established on 20 airfields and utilised the services of about 700 heavy bombers and 27,000 personnel.

construction yards as the top-priority objective long term, and the U-boat operating bases on the Biscay coast as a prime target for the shorter term. Meanwhile on 14 January the Air Ministry told Harris of the War Cabinet's decision and ordered him to attack at night 'the whole area in which are located the submarines, their maintenance facilities and the services, power, water, light, communications etc and other resources on which their operations depend'.[10]

Subject to the possibilities of mounting an effective raid against Berlin, or a raid on an important German or Italian objective by more than 200 bombers, Harris was to attack the Biscay bases 'as first priority at the earliest possible date'. Beginning with Lorient, on the heaviest scale, he was to proceed in turn, after an assessment of results, to St Nazaire, Brest and La Pallice. In the existing state of the art of bombing, that in effect meant wiping out four French towns.

Harris fumed, but obeyed his orders swiftly. That night he sent 122 bombers, Pathfinder-led, against Lorient. The following night, by which time most of Lorient's inhabitants had fled to neighbouring villages, he sent another 157. Between then and 16/17 February he piled on seven more area attacks, one all-incendiary. On 7/8 February the force of 323 bombers included 100 Wellingtons; on 13/14 February the attackers numbered no fewer than 466, including 144 Lancasters. In all, the nine attacks involved nearly 2000 sorties – fortunately at a loss rate of under 1.5 per cent. According to a French army report, by 16 February about 3500 of the 4500 houses in the town had been completely destroyed, and most of the rest were uninhabitable.[11]

Harris then moved on to the next port on his list. On 28 February/1 March he sent 437 bombers, including 294 'heavies' and 119 Wellingtons, against St Nazaire. Repeat attacks by 357 aircraft on 22/23 March and by 323 on 28/29 March followed. A final, lesser, attack on 2/3 April on both Lorient and St Nazaire concluded the series, leaving both places in ruins. Three days later, after wireless intercepts had revealed that the bombing had made little difference to the U-boats' use of these two havens, a fresh directive relieved Harris of this unwelcome task.[12]

During all this time the US Eighth Air Force had been collaborating in the assault, but with a far lesser weight of attack. Between 16 February and 3 April it sent 63 sorties against Lorient, 65 against St Nazaire and 75 against Brest. It dropped about 460 tons of bombs as compared with Bomber Command's 6000 tons. The American bombing was, of course, meant to make up in precision what it lacked in weight; but it was no more effective than that of Bomber Command in destroying the concrete pens – which proved to have full repair facilities and power services within them. On 4 May Admiral Dönitz was able to tell his colleagues: 'The towns of St Nazaire and Lorient have been rubbed out as main submarine bases. No dog or cat is left in these towns. Nothing but the submarine shelters remains. The Todt Organization built them because of far-sighted orders by the Führer, and the submarines are repaired in them. The enemy has shifted his fight,* since he realizes he cannot achieve anything by the air raids.'[13]

Harris in his *Bomber Offensive* referred to these attacks on the Biscay ports, which absorbed some 3000 sorties, as 'one of the most infuriating episodes in the whole course of the offensive'.[14] The official history of the strategic air offensive, fully agreeing with Harris, called them 'a gross misdirection of the force'.[15] It is not difficult to be wise after the event; but merchant shipping was being lost at a desperately dangerous rate, and the Allies did not know at the time how self-contained the pens were. Harris, however, said that they would be, and that they could not be destroyed by the bombs available.† He, at least, was wise before the event.

The order to launch massive attacks on the Biscay ports galled Harris deeply – 'the only effect they had on the course of the war was to delay . . . the main bomber offensive against Germany by nearly two months,' he complained later.[16] However, he was still able during this period to deal some sharp blows against more congenial targets. The Casablanca directive enjoined, in certain circumstances, the bombing of Berlin, Genoa, Milan and Turin. During January and February 1943 Harris enthusiastically attacked them all.

Raids on Berlin at this time were meant to hearten the Russians during their victorious struggle at Stalingrad. On 16/17 January, taking advantage of the long hours of darkness, Harris sent 201 Lancasters and Halifaxes against the German capital – the first visit by the RAF since the disastrous night of 7/8 November 1941, which had contributed to Peirse's departure. But Berlin was far beyond OBOE range, H2S was not yet available, and success still depended largely on human eyesight and accurate navigation by dead reckoning. The Pathfinders, briefed for an elaborate system of illuminating and marking, now carried for the first time properly designed indicator

---

* i.e. out to sea again.
† The largest general purpose bomb available was one of 4000 lb. The 8000-lb bombs of the time were high capacity, with thin cases and blunt noses, for blast effect, not penetration.

bombs to drop when the target area had been verified visually; but as the skies were dense with cloud and snow, the bomb-aimers failed to pinpoint anything at all. Nevertheless the raid created great alarm among the Berliners and substantial damage in the Tempelhof area. One episode caused much local comment. When the alarm sounded, several thousand spectators were watching a circus performance in the Deutschlandhalle. They evacuated the building under orders – just minutes before incendiaries came crashing down on the roof and set the whole vast structure ablaze.[17]

Encouraged by the loss of only one bomber, Harris repeated the raid the following night. But though the weather was clearer, the bombing was still widely scattered. Reconnaissance later suggested that bombs had hit the Daimler-Benz aero-engine works, and intelligence sources reported damage to other large concerns including the Lorenz radio factory. This may or may not have been the case: post-war German confirmation is lacking. But one thing was certain: this time the defences had not been caught unawares. Of the 187 Lancasters and Halifaxes which set out, 22 – a frightening 11.8 per cent – failed to return.[18]

Apart from two audacious daylight raids on 30 January, each by three Mosquitoes, to interrupt high-level Nazi celebrations, Harris then left Berlin alone until he could rely on having available at least a dozen H2S Pathfinders. By the beginning of March that time had come. On 1/2 March 16 H2S Halifaxes and Stirlings led some 300 bombers against the German capital. Though still very widely scattered, the resulting damage, notably to the railway repair shops at Tempelhof and some twenty factories in the south and west of the city, was far heavier than any inflicted on Berlin before. The price was 17 aircraft – at 5.6 per cent of sorties about standard for Berlin, but still too high to be acceptable.[19]

The raids on northern Italy in the first two months of 1943 took place because the weather on those nights made operations impossible over Germany. On 4/5 February, for the loss of three Lancasters, an attack by 188 aircraft inflicted heavy damage on Turin. Ten nights later 142 Lancasters, enjoying similar clear weather, hit Milan. Reconnaissance revealed no fewer than 27 factories destroyed, and again the loss to Bomber Command was minimal – two aircraft.[20]

Only two more attacks on north Italian targets took place in the first half of 1943. They occurred not because of bad weather over Germany but because the Admiralty pressed for heavy attacks on the naval base of La Spezia, which was then holding three Italian battleships. On 13/14 April Harris reluctantly complied, sending 211

H2S-led heavy bombers. They 'blitzed' the town and dockyard, but missed the smoke-protected warships. Four Lancasters failed to return, and three more judged it safer to fly on to captured airfields in North Africa – a new facility. Five nights later Harris tried again. The 178 bombers, nearly all Lancasters, added to the damage in the town and sank a destroyer but left the major warships unharmed. Meanwhile other Lancasters mined the waters outside the harbour.[21]

In addition to the raids on Berlin, Harris made several attacks on other German cities during the time of the Biscay commitment. Three assaults on Cologne in February involved in total no fewer than 832 sorties. With OBOE Mosquitoes and H2S 'heavies' as Pathfinders, these attacks added substantially to the existing damage and made many thousands of people homeless. But they also showed how dependent the raiders still were on good visibility. Heavy cloud restricted the ground-marking, and a high proportion of the bombs fell outside the city.[22]

Much the same thing happened in two attacks on Hamburg. On 3/4 February 263 aircraft achieved only scattered bombing; and on 3/4 March some of the Pathfinders leading a force of 417 aircraft missed their target area completely. As a result, most of the bombs hit the township of Wedel thirteen miles downstream, where by chance they did as much damage to factories and docks as if they had fallen on the target intended.[23]

Perhaps the most venturesome operation of this period was the raid by 337 'heavies' on 25/26 February against Nuremberg. The weather was poor, some of the Pathfinders arrived late, and most of the bombs fell outside the city. But only nine aircraft – 2.7 per cent – failed to return from this very deep penetration.

By far the most effective raid of the period was the first of four in February against Wilhelmshaven. The other three, involving 648 sorties, were largely failures – though inexpensive ones. The initial raid of the series, however, an attack by 177 Lancasters, Halifaxes and Stirlings on 11/12 February, was a brilliant success. The weather was thick, parachute flares for sky-marking had to be dropped on H2S indications alone, and the bombing was completely 'blind'. Nevertheless much of it fell on the harbour area, and a bomb or bombs hit a naval ammunition depot. This blew up with such force as to devastate some 120 acres of the town and dockyards – the first notable triumph for H2S in blind-bombing.[24]

All these operations provided useful tests of navigation, and often blind-bombing, by OBOE or H2S. With the experience thus gained, and the Biscay commitment slackening, Harris was at last able to begin – in his own phrase – 'the main offensive'. It fell initially, and almost inevitably, on what had been Bomber Command's number one target ever since May 1940: the Ruhr. And within the Ruhr, Essen; and within Essen, at long last, Krupps.

15

'The Battle of the Ruhr'

At dusk on 5 March 1943 442 Bomber Command aircraft stood ready to begin what Harris called 'the Battle of the Ruhr'. Ever since May 1940 the Command had been – on and off – attacking, or trying to attack, what the crews characteristically dubbed 'the Happy Valley'. The moments of major success had been few. Now, however, the prospects were much brighter. With many more four-engined bombers available, the weight of bombs dropped could be far greater than in the preceding year. And since the Pathfinders now had OBOE and H2S and a range of target-indicator bombs, the increased tonnage could be dropped far more accurately.

The target on 5/6 March was the biggest town in the Ruhr, Essen – and especially the two square miles covered by the main works of Krupps. Five OBOE Mosquitoes of 109 Squadron led the attack – three others turned back when their apparatus failed. The five, spaced out over forty minutes under OBOE control, first dropped yellow indicator flares 15 miles short of Essen to mark the route inward. The night was clear, but haze still shrouded the town. Over Krupps, purely on the OBOE signals, the five then in turn dropped red indicators. Meanwhile, at one- or two-minute intervals, 22 H2S Pathfinders – Stirlings and Halifaxes – acted as 'backers-up'. They first reinforced the yellow markers along the approach route and then, over the target area, aimed green indicators (plus some explosive and incendiaries) at the red indicators dropped by the Mosquitoes.

Led by other H2S Pathfinders, the main force followed in three waves. Their instructions were to bomb the red indicators, or, if these were invisible, the green. First the Halifaxes put in an attack which lasted 18 minutes. Then, with this still in progress, the Stirlings and Wellingtons delivered a ten-minute assault. Finally, as the last Halifaxes were departing, the Lancasters streamed in, to add a further ten minutes of death and destruction. In each case the bomb-load was one-third high explosive (some fused for long delay) and two-thirds incendiary. As many as 56 aircraft turned back before reaching the target area, mainly on account of technical failures, but the rest mostly kept well to their scheduled times. The whole violent incursion took little more than the planned 40 minutes – a concentration which overwhelmed both the active and the passive defences.

Many crews reported big explosions and vast fires, and reconnaissance later showed that OBOE and H2S had without doubt set new standards of bombing accuracy. Over 160 acres of the town lay devastated, with a further 450 acres extensively damaged. At Krupps, bombs had hit no fewer than 53 buildings. In the town 3000 houses had been reduced to rubble, and there was great damage to, among other things, a sulphuric acid factory, a sawmill, three coalmines, transport facilities, a power station and the gasworks. Much machinery within the shattered buildings, however, escaped serious harm, and the Germans were adept at coping with bomb damage. Though it took the local authorities more than a month to restore full power supplies to Essen as a whole, they had electricity flowing to the main factories by the next day.

From this raid, by far the most effective which Bomber Command had ever made against a Ruhr target, 14 aircraft failed to return – 3.2 per cent of the force despatched. It was a heartening start to 'the battle', which would in fact be a five-month-long campaign.[1]

Harris waged 'the Battle of the Ruhr' from that opening attack of 5/6 March 1943 until the end of July. But during that period, for tactical and other reasons, he also attacked many objectives outside the Ruhr. This he did most frequently in the first two months, when the longer hours of darkness allowed deeper penetration into the Reich.

Among these wider-ranging ventures in March, apart from those against St Nazaire, were raids by forces averaging 300 aircraft against Nuremberg, Munich and Stuttgart. The attack on Munich was extremely successful, the others much less so. In each case the rate of loss was sustainable – never more than 3.5 per cent. All these places were far beyond OBOE range, but H2S proved a useful, if much less precise substitute.*

Farther ranging still were two raids on Berlin on 27/28 and 29/30 March for which the Prime Minister had been pressing. The first, by 396 aircraft, was inexpensive, but the bombs fell for the most part miles short of the city. A lucky hit, however, wrecked a Luftwaffe stores eleven miles away from the prescribed aiming-point. The second raid, by 329 Lancasters, Halifaxes and Stirlings, was no more successful, and cost a dangerously high 6.4 per cent of the force despatched.

In the following month, April, Harris laid on at least two attacks against other parts of Germany for every one on the Ruhr. Apart from the raids on St Nazaire, Lorient and La Spezia, he launched major assaults by around 500 aircraft against Kiel, Frankfurt and Stuttgart. The first and second of these, in difficult weather, were failures, and the third suffered from the common phenomenon of 'creep-back' – the later aircraft bombed the first target indicators they saw and, as the raid proceeded, the bombs fell more and more short. This raid, on 14/15 April, damaged the Stuttgart suburbs but unfortunately, by a direct hit on a shelter, killed 400 French and Russian prisoners of war.

Outside the Ruhr, other attacks in April fell on Mannheim, where 41 factories lost production and nearly 7000 people their homes, and on Stettin and Rostock. At Stettin, in good visibility on 20/21 April, a force of 339 aircraft wrecked about 100 acres of the town. At Rostock, on the same night, 86 Stirlings failed to find their target – the Heinkel factory nearby. Much the most distant and costly of these operations, however, was the attempt by 327 Lancasters and Halifaxes on 16/17 April to bomb the great Skoda armament works at Pilsen. The works escaped unscathed, a large asylum seven miles away received many of the bombs, and 36 of the raiders failed to return – a grievous 11 per cent.

In the Ruhr itself, the towns most frequently attacked during the opening two months of the battle were Essen and Duisburg. After the initial 'blitz' three more raids, totalling 1100 sorties, struck Essen. All were successful, and inflicted further damage on Krupps. Much less

---

* Returning from the raid on Nuremberg on 8/9 March, D. R. Spanton, a gunner in a Pathfinder Stirling squadron, found himself alone in the aircraft over England. He had not heard the order to jump when the rest of the crew baled out – to drown, most unfortunately, in the Channel. Spanton parachuted successfully down over Kent, but lost his life three months later in a raid on the Ruhr.[2]

effective, mainly on account of bad weather or OBOE failure, were a raid against Essen's neighbour Bochum, an important centre of coal and steel production, and four raids against Duisburg, near the junction of Ruhr and Rhine – the biggest inland port in Europe.

With the shortening of the nights, Harris increasingly concentrated on the Ruhr and the less distant targets. Between the beginning of May and the end of July 1943 he launched 21 major attacks* against Ruhr or Rhineland towns as compared with only nine against all other objectives, including ill-fated Hamburg.

Leaving aside Hamburg, only three objectives outside the Ruhr–Rhineland felt the full force of a Bomber Command attack during these three months. At Le Creusot on 19/20 June some of the 290 aircraft despatched succeeded, at the cost of only two of their number, in damaging the Schneider arms plant and the Breuil steelworks. Unfortunately they also damaged much residential property nearby. Turin, attacked on 12/13 July in an effort to speed up the collapse of Italy after the invasion of Sicily two days earlier, also suffered much damage and loss of civilian life. But it was at Aachen, on the following night, that the destruction was greatest, engulfing public buildings, factories and about 17,000 residential apartments. Nearly 300 people lost their lives, and '28,000 appear to have fled the town and were still absent when the new ration card was issued seven weeks later'.[3]

Meanwhile the major part of Bomber Command's offensive was falling on the Ruhr. At Dortmund, 'the forge of Germany', a centre of mining and ferrous metal enterprises employing huge numbers of men, raids by 596 aircraft on 4/5 May and 826 aircraft on 23/24 May wrought appalling destruction. The bombing demolished more than 3000 buildings, including important steelworks, and killed nearly 1300 people – including 200 prisoners of war. At Bochum, twice attacked by 450–500 aircraft, the tale was similar. Oberhausen, with one of the largest iron- and steelworks in the Ruhr, suffered likewise but not so severely as Mülheim, picturesquely situated on the river but equally industrial. An attack by 557 aircraft on 22/23 June destroyed nearly two-thirds of the entire built-up area.

Even more devastating were the two attacks on the heavily industrialised area of Wuppertal. On 29/30 May 719 aircraft concentrated on Barmen. They laid waste about 1000 acres, destroying nearly 4000 houses, seriously damaging more than 200 factories, and killing 3400 people. A month later, on 24/25 June, 630 aircraft wrecked the companion town of Elbefeld, obliterating 171 industrial premises

---

* Defining a major attack as one by at least 100 aircraft.

and some 3000 houses. Eighteen hundred of the inhabitants lost their lives.

Another notable success was against the key target of Duisburg, attacked many times since 1940 and heavily in 1942, but never until now with any great profit. On 12/13 May a force of 572 aircraft destroyed over 1300 buildings, damaged four of the Thyssen steel factories and 60 ships, and sank 34 barges. Shortly afterwards Duisburg's more elegant neighbour, Düsseldorf, suffered a similar fate. On 25/26 May a raid by 759 aircraft achieved little but on 11/12 June another by 783 aircraft made ample amends. Though a substantial part of the force went astray, the remainder destroyed about 130 acres of the city, including military establishments and civic headquarters. The local authorities listed no fewer than 8882 separate fires, of which 1444 were large. Many industrial firms ceased production. The dead numbered nearly 1300, the 'bombed out' 140,000.

Before the end of June Bomber Command had laid waste a large part of the Ruhr, and Harris was moving on to industrial targets in the neighbouring Rhineland. On 21/22 June 705 aircraft attacked Krefeld, just west of the Rhine. The moon was bright, the German night-fighters active, and 12 of the Pathfinders failed to return.* Nevertheless, the raid was fearfully effective. It set fire to almost half of the town's built-up area, and drove some 72,000 of the inhabitants from their homes. About 20,000 of these had to be evacuated to other towns.

Four nights later 603 aircraft attacked Cologne. Their efforts were even more effective than in the 'Thousand-Bomber' raid a year earlier. Apart from incidentally killing 4377 people, they destroyed nearly 50 industrial and military premises and 15,000 other buildings, and left around 230,000 of the inhabitants homeless.

A week later, on 3/4 July, a force of 653 aircraft added to Cologne's agony, driving a further 72,000 people from their homes. On this occasion, however, the raiders encountered a new defensive measure. German night-fighters usually operated under radar control in the approaches to the Reich and its big cities, but now they appeared over the target itself, operating individually by the light of the searchlights, the RAF's flares, and the fires below. These were the so-called *Wilde Sau*† fighters, and on this occasion they claimed at least six of the raiders.

---

* 35 Squadron had the great misfortune to lose six of its 19 Halifaxes.
† *Wilde Sau* = wild sow, but usually translated, more delicately, as 'wild boar'.

Air Vice-Marshal D. C. T. Bennett CBE, DSO.

Group Captain Basil Embry DSO and
2 Bars, AFC.

Squadron Leader H. B. ('Mick') Martin
DSO and Bar, DFC and 2 Bars, AFC.

Group Captain G. L. Cheshire VC, DSO and 2 Bars, DFC.

Wing Commander Guy Gibson VC, DSO and Bar, DFC and Bar.

AFTER THE DAMS RAID

Pilot Officer F. M. Spafford DFM, RAAF (centre) and Pilot Officer H. T. Taerum RCAF of 617 Squadron, the bomb-aimer and the navigator of Gibson's aircraft, at debriefing with an Intelligence officer. Looking on, Sir Arthur Harris and A. V-M. Ralph Cochrane.

Wing Commander Hughie I. Edwards
VC, DFC.

Squadron Leader John D. Nettleton
VC.

Squadron Leader Ian W. Bazalgette
VC, DFC.

Captain Edwin Swales VC, DFC,
SAAF.

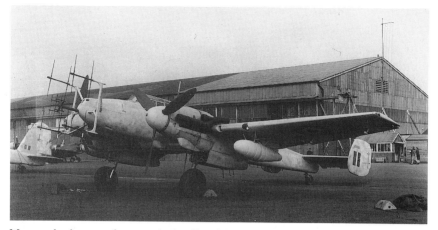

Messerschmitt 110, photographed at Farnborough in October 1945.

Dornier 217, 1942: a bomber developed into a not very successful night-fighter.
The Lichtenstein radar is visible in front.

A Junkers 88 which landed by mistake at Woodbridge in July 1944. Its Flensburg
and SN2 radars yielded useful information.

Getting ready to 'bomb up' a Halifax.

Refuelling a Halifax.

Halifaxes attacking the *Gneisenau* at Brest by daylight, 18 December 1941.

Philips' works, Eindhoven, under daylight attack, 6 December 1942.

BOMB DAMAGE
AT HAMBURG

Bomb damage at
Hamburg showing flak-
tower with four gun
positions.

Bomb damage, 1943.

Bomb damage,
including to midget
submarines, at Blohm
and Voss shipyards,
1945.

Breached by 617 Squadron, 16/17 May 1943.

Cologne's ordeal was still not over. Five nights later, on 8/9 July, a smaller force of 282 aircraft took a further toll of factories and houses and human lives, adding another 48,000 to the number of people 'bombed out'. In terms of a strategy mainly based, as Britain's was at this stage, on 'dehousing' the population of Germany's great industrial and administrative towns, this was success on a grand scale. In three raids within a fortnight 350,000 inhabitants of Cologne – over a third of the population – had been driven from their homes.

Amid these successes there were inevitably some failures. On 9/10 July 418 aircraft set out to attack Gelsenkirchen, one of the Ruhr's main centres of synthetic oil production. Largely on account of OBOE failures, the raid came to very little. But this was not the general pattern. By mid-July Harris had in effect won his Battle of the Ruhr–Rhineland, and was preparing his next great onslaught – against Hamburg.

Before July was out Harris dealt two final – for the time being – blows on the Ruhr. On 25/26 July, the night after the opening attack on Hamburg, he sent 705 aircraft against Essen in a raid which again fell heavily on Krupps. And five nights later, in what can be regarded as the last raid in the five-month battle, a force of 273 aircraft hit Remscheid, a Ruhr town not previously attacked. The bombs fell largely as intended, devastating four-fifths of the built-up area and putting over 100 industrial enterprises out of action. Local production virtually ceased for three months, and never fully recovered.

There can be no doubt that the Battle of the Ruhr–Rhineland was a major victory for Bomber Command. By the end of July 1943 most of Germany's largest industrial complex lay in ruins. This had been accomplished for a loss in aircraft, at around 5 per cent of sorties, which was extremely serious but still sustainable – more particularly because the rate of loss in other operations was lower. Unfortunately for the Allies, however, Germany was a large country, and the Germans a resourceful people. Their industries were wide-spread, and some, like aircraft manufacture, not too difficult to disperse. For the business of bringing about 'the progressive destruction and dislocation of the German military, industrial and economic system, and the undermining of the morale of the German people to a point where their capacity for armed resistance is fatally weakened', the Battle of the Ruhr was only a promising beginning.[4]

By far the best-known incident in the Battle of the Ruhr is Operation CHASTISE – the attack on the dams. The subject of many published accounts and a notable film, it was described in the normally restrained official history of the British Strategic Air Offensive as 'the most precise bombing attack ever delivered and a feat of arms which has never been excelled'.[5]

From at least 1937, British planning staff had pointed out the importance to the German economy of a dam on the Möhne and another on the Sorpe, two tributaries of the River Ruhr. The massive reservoirs created by these dams were used to control the level of the Ruhr, which supplied water for the numerous power stations, steelworks, coking ovens and other industrial enterprises in the area, as well as for domestic use. Five smaller dams on lesser streams flowing directly or indirectly into the Ruhr also attracted the interest of the planners, as did the bigger dam on the Eder, linked not to the Ruhr but to the Fulda. The water from this served the important railway manufacturing town of Kassel.

If the Möhne and the Sorpe dams could be breached, the planners thought extensive flooding would occur in the low-lying Ruhr valley, with a devastating effect on power supplies to the Ruhr industries. But, for long, any such project came up against the stark facts that Bomber Command would be most unlikely to hit such targets at night or, with the bombs available, destroy them if it did. Nor could the other obvious weapon be used: nets protected the dams against torpedoes. The structures to be destroyed were certainly no invitation to early action. The Möhne dam, holding back some 130 million tons of water, and the strategically less important Eder dam, restraining over 200 million tons, were both massive affairs of stone and concrete; the Möhne dam was 25 feet thick at the top and 112 feet thick at the bottom. The Sorpe dam was differently built, being of earth, stone-faced, sloping away on either side of a 30-foot-wide concrete core. But it seemed little more vulnerable than the other two to attack with the weapons available in the early years of the war.

It was the genius of Barnes Wallis of Vickers which saw a way through these difficulties. After playing with a scheme, which received no encouragement in the Air Ministry, for a new ten-ton bomb to be delivered by a new six-engined aircraft, he concentrated on the idea that the dams might be vulnerable to a depth charge exploded directly against them beneath the waterline. But how to deliver this when there were nets against torpedoes? His fertile brain soon produced the notion of a depth charge which skipped. Released from an aircraft below the dam and near the surface of the water, this might bounce over the torpedo nets and into the face of the dam, roll down, and then, at a predetermined depth beneath the surface, explode against the dam wall.

Given that such a depth charge could be produced – and Wallis soon saw to this – there would still be great difficulties in aiming it. The aircraft would have to fly very low for the so-called 'mine' (code-name UPKEEP) to skip rather than instantly submerge, and would also have to fly at a given speed and bomb at a precise distance from the dam – all probably in the face of anti-aircraft fire. To give better control over the release and ensure that the mine fell downwards when it hit the dam, rather than ride over the top, Wallis quickly concluded that a device must be incorporated in the aircraft to give the weapon backspin as it was dropped. This he tried out successfully with practice spheres at Chesil Beach in December 1942.

Events then moved with astonishing speed. For the best results an attack had to be made while the water level in the reservoirs behind the dams was at its height – i.e. in late May, before the summer set in. Though Harris was no enthusiast for the scheme, Portal was, and on 8 March 1943 the first orders were issued for the modification of a Lancaster to carry UPKEEP. A week later 24-year-old Wing Commander Guy Gibson DSO and bar, DFC and bar, who had completed two tours as a bomber pilot and one on night-fighters, amounting to some 170 operations, was given the task of forming a new squadron in 5 Group to carry out the attack. Before the end of the month No. 617 Squadron was in being at Scampton, in Lincolnshire, and training on borrowed Lancasters. Gibson, gifted, charismatic, tough and utterly determined, took care to 'vet' the crews, posted in from all over 5 Group. Ultimately, of the 133 aircrew that flew on the raid, no fewer than 29 were Canadian and 12 Australian.

There followed six weeks of intensive training, collectively involving some 2000 hours of flying, in which Gibson led his crews at very low level over English, Welsh and Scottish lakes and reservoirs, and in which tests of the developed weapon – ultimately a cylinder, not a sphere – took place at Reculver on the Kent coast. To avoid the breaking up of the mine and to produce the required skip, it was found that the release had to be made from as low as 60 feet – a highly dangerous business at night, since standard altimeters were unreliable at such a height. Fortunately there was a simple solution at hand, if one that was of some assistance to enemy gunners. The Director of Scientific Research at the Ministry of Aircraft Production, Ben Lockspeiser, came up with the idea of fixing a spotlight on each of the Lancaster's wings, with the beams set to converge at 60 feet below. When the point of convergence rested on the top of the water, the bomber was at its right height for the attack.

Around dusk on 16 May 1943 the first Lancasters, each heavily laden with its UPKEEP, took off laboriously from Scampton. The squadron had been fitted with the latest VHF R/T, so there was good intercommunication between the crews. The first wave to reach Germany, led by Gibson, left Scampton nine aircraft strong, and flew in separate vics of three. Keeping very low to avoid, as far as possible, detection by enemy radar and the attention of German fighters, Gibson reached the Möhne dam and gathered together his small force. One aircraft, caught by flak, failed to arrive. Gibson himself made the first run, only just missing the target, and then acted as what would later be termed a 'Master Bomber', calling in the others to attack in turn. Meanwhile he flew up and down the valley and across the reservoir to draw upon himself the enemy's anti-aircraft fire – from the shore as well as two towers on the dam. The Australian low-flying specialist, Flight Lieutenant 'Mick' Martin, after he too had attacked and narrowly missed, did likewise. Then, as the fifth aircraft made its run in, after one of the Lancasters had been badly hit and another shot down, the dam suddenly crumbled. Soon a huge torrent of water was pouring down the valley. 'Then we began to shout and scream,' wrote Gibson in *Enemy Coast Ahead*, 'and act like madmen over the R/T, for this was a tremendous sight, a sight which probably no man will ever see again.'[6]

After appointing Squadron Leader H. M. Young DFC and bar, whose attack had caused the final damage, as his deputy, Gibson then flew off towards the Eder dam, fifty miles away. He was accompanied by Young and by the three Lancasters which had not yet dropped their mines. By now Gibson's wireless operator had signalled back to 5 Group headquarters, where the AOC, Air Vice-Marshal Ralph Cochrane, was waiting anxiously with Harris and Barnes Wallis. His message was the agreed code-word for success at the Möhne – NIGGER, the name of Gibson's dog.* Amid the ensuing scenes of elation at Scampton, Harris was heard to remark to Barnes Wallis: 'I didn't believe a word of what you said when you came to see me, but now you could sell me a pink elephant.'[7]

Gibson, Young and the three with the unspent mines were by this time heading in the direction of the Eder dam. When they found it, the first aircraft to bomb scored either a hit or a near miss.

* Nigger had been most unfortunately run over and killed at Scampton the previous evening.

The second dropped its mine too late, directly on to the dam; the aircraft, probably fatally damaged from the explosion, was not seen again. The third aircraft, piloted by another Australian, Pilot Officer L. G. Knight, got the approach exactly right. The mine bounced three times, hit the dam just right of centre and made a large breach 30 feet below the top. Soon a great cascade was sweeping down the valley, swallowing up cars whose lights the crews saw disappearing beneath the water.

Their work well done, Gibson's surviving six – two of them direct from the Möhne – headed home to base. Only five got there. Young and his crew did not make it back.

Meanwhile another wave, five aircraft strong, their target the vitally important Sorpe dam, had run into deep trouble. One turned back early, damaged by flak. Another lost its mine from flying too low over the sea. Two more succumbed to anti-aircraft fire *en route*. Only the Lancaster of the American pilot, Flight Lieutenant J. C. McCarthy DFC, who had taken off late and separately, reached the Sorpe and returned safely. Owing to the different construction of the dam his task was to attack it directly, lengthwise, for which purpose the spinning cylinder was by no means ideal. McCarthy nevertheless scored a hit, and the top of the dam crumbled. But the breach was too small to cause a collapse.

There were still five more Lancasters, the third wave or reserve. They left Scampton about two-and-a-half hours after Gibson and company, briefed to attack the Möhne, the Eder, or any of the other dams which 5 Group might specify by wireless while they were airborne. They were not to be blessed by good fortune – perhaps scarcely surprising considering that the earlier waves must have alerted the German defences. Flak shot down two of them before they could reach their target area. A third, piloted by a Canadian, Flight Sergeant Ken Brown, received orders in the air to bomb the Sorpe dam. In misty weather he made five runs before, on his sixth, successfully planting his mine on the dam. But, as he himself saw, no breach ensued. Of the two remaining Lancasters, one attacked the smaller Ennope dam unsuccessfully; the other, damaged and with the crew uncertain of their position, returned to Scampton with its mine still on board.

In sum, 19 aircraft had taken off; 11 had actually attacked, between them causing serious damage to the Möhne and Eder dams and minor damage to the Sorpe; and eight had failed to return. Of the 133 aircrew who had set out, 53 had been killed, and three had become prisoners of war.

The dramatic nature of the raid, with waters flooding down the Ruhr and Eder valleys, coupled with the extreme skill and courage shown by the attackers, naturally made a big impact in Britain and captured the headlines in the press. The Air Ministry and Bomber Command headquarters, stressing the uniqueness of the feat, gave it the full publicity treatment, while taking care not to reveal the nature of Barnes Wallis's weapon. Not surprisingly, decorations in unusual numbers descended upon the crews. Gibson received the VC, and the 34 awards included five of the DSO, four of a bar to the DFC, ten of the DFC, and 11 of the DFM. Among the recipients, one was American, six Canadian, eight Australian, and one from New Zealand.

It is impossible to state the raid's exact effect on the German economy. Local German sources for the Möhne episode indicated that 1294 people were dead or missing (including 573 foreigners, mostly Ukrainian women workers) and that about 1000 houses had been destroyed or damaged. Among other results, 11 factories had been destroyed and 114 damaged, 2822 hectares of farmland ruined, 6316 cattle and pigs killed, 25 road bridges destroyed and 10 damaged, and various power stations, pumping stations, water and gas facilities put out of action. All this inevitably affected production in the Ruhr through temporary loss of power and water, but not nearly as much as was at first thought. Duplicated sources of electric power, and water from the intact Sorpe reservoir, made up for most of the deficiency and prevented any catastrophic fall in industrial output.

The breaching of the Eder dam had no direct effect in the Ruhr, but it caused floodwater six feet high to reach Kassel, over twenty miles distant. There, however, the important Henschel aircraft works escaped damage. The chief effect seems to have been the ruination of agricultural land and riverside villages.

Summing up, the British Official History states that, in regard to both the physical and the moral impact on Germany, 'the total effect was small'.[8] But though the damage was certainly less irreparable than the first British claims and newspaper reports suggested, and though the Germans undoubtedly displayed their usual vigour in recovery, it is difficult to accept this as a sufficient verdict. Hitler and Goebbels would hardly have been so upset – as records show they were – if the damage had been only of a minor or fleeting nature; nor would huge labour corps have been drafted in and set to the work of repair – including 20,000 from the Todt Organisation then working on the West Wall defences against an Allied cross-Channel invasion. Nor again, if the damage had not been severe, would the Germans have troubled to install anti-aircraft defences and torpedo nets at dams which had previously lacked them. All the evidence seems to be that the damage was indeed serious, but that the Germans showed immense vigour in restoring lost facilities and industrial capacity.

This should be taken into account when considering No. 617 Squadron's losses. Eight lost out of 19 was indeed a horrifying proportion of the squadron; it is little wonder that the sensitive Barnes Wallis, after his first elation at the news of the breaching of the Möhne, was soon in tears. However, if the loss is seen, not in relation to the number of participants, but to the normal loss on an operation which inflicted comparable (or lesser) harm on the enemy, it appears in a different light. There were few RAF raids on Germany in 1943 which did so much damage for the loss of eight aircraft.

Moreover, as the official history stresses, the raid was a landmark in the development of precision-bombing by night. Number 617 Squadron's exploit proved that in certain circumstances, and with sufficient skill, determination and training, it could be done. This was immensely important for the future. The ultimate result was to be seen in the precision attacks of 1944–5 which destroyed V-weapon sites, the *Tirpitz*, German communications, German oil.[9]

16

Mining: 2 Group: 'Pointblank'

Contrary to popular notions, Bomber Command was not exclusively engaged throughout the war in bombing German cities. Among its many other tasks, and an increasingly profitable one, was laying mines at sea.

The Command's involvement in minelaying had begun during the Norwegian campaign, when Hampdens of 5 Group mined the waters off Denmark. Later, after the fall of France, Hampdens had mined the French Atlantic coast, the seas off Holland and round the Frisians, Kiel Bay, and the estuary of the Elbe. All this, though regular, was small in scale. Together Bomber Command and Coastal Command during 1940 laid, on average, about 100 mines a month. Hampdens could carry only one 1500-lb mine; on any night only five or six usually operated; and the crews were mainly freshmen, getting operational experience less riskily than over Germany. Up to the end of 1940 these mines, according to German records, sank 82 merchant ships totalling 81,277 tons and damaged another 55. The cost to the RAF was 30 aircraft, 2 per cent of the sorties involved.[1]

Minelaying on a slightly lesser scale continued throughout 1941. Between 1 January 1941 and the end of the year, by which time Coastal Command was playing only a minor part, the RAF's air-laid mines sank 45 ships totalling 51,004 tons.[2] The cost – 3.5 per cent of sorties – was higher than in the previous year. But in February 1942, just before Harris took over as AOC-in-C, Manchesters carrying four mines joined in and the month's total of mines sown showed a sharp increase to over 300. This included those laid in the attempts to pin the *Scharnhorst* and *Gneisenau* into their French anchorages, and then to halt them on their homeward dash – in which both ships suffered hits from mines laid earlier or dropped in their path.

A total of 300 mines a month, however, was far too little for the Admiralty, who pressed for a much greater effort. This suited Harris, always keen on minelaying as long as it did not interfere with the bombing of Germany. Making two stipulations – that major minelaying should take place only when the weather precluded attacks on Germany, and that on such occasions fully trained crews should take part as well as the novices – he was soon able to reach agreement with the Admiralty and the Air Staff. In July 1942 Bomber Command became committed to drop around 1000 mines a month, or ten times more than in 1941–2.[3]

The obsolescent Hampdens could not of course cope with this by themselves, and the disappointing Manchesters had been withdrawn from operations in June. In 5 Group the new Lancasters, as they arrived, replaced the Hampdens and could carry many more mines – six, as opposed to the Hampden's one. But Harris also, with Air Ministry approval, committed the whole of his main force to the task.[4] Within a few weeks Stirlings and Wellingtons were being adapted to carry mines, and by the autumn the Halifaxes too. Apart from the Pathfinders and 2 Group, the entire front line of Bomber Command became equipped for minelaying.

This soon resulted in a vastly increased number of mines laid. In May 1942 the monthly total exceeded 1000 for the first time; in September acoustic mines became available to supplement the existing magnetic mines; and in November, when Bomber Command's minelaying hampered U-boat movements from the Biscay ports during the Allied invasion of French North Africa, the total of mines laid rose to 1219. All told, air-laid mines during 1942 sank 163 German-controlled vessels, or nearly 174,000 tons of shipping.[5] The cost to Bomber Command, which laid all but 141 of the 9669 mines dropped from the air in North-Western waters during the year, was 165 aircraft, or almost 3.3 per cent of sorties. This was less lethal than operating over Germany at the time but by no means the 'easy ride' that minelaying was often thought to be.

The Battle of the Ruhr saw no slackening of this campaign. Coastal Command had by this time ceased regular minelaying, but Bomber Command more than compensated. From January to July 1943 it dropped on average more than 1100 mines a month, with a peak of 1809 in April.

This very high total came about because a new firing unit in the mines, incorporating both acoustic and magnetic fuses, became available, and the Admiralty wished to exploit the factor of surprise. On 27/28 April 1943 123 Bomber Command aircraft, out of 160 which took off, laid 458 mines off the French Atlantic ports and around the Frisian Islands. The losses were confined to a single Lancaster. An even bigger venture the following night, however, fared less well. Of over 200 aircraft which took off, 167 succeeded in laying mines off Heligoland, in the Elbe estuary, and in the Great and Little Belts between western and eastern Denmark. Between them they dropped 593 mines – the highest total on any night of the war. But the dropping zones presented greater hazards than those of the previous night, and the number of aircraft lost – 22 – was also the highest in any night's minelaying.[6]

Altogether during 1943, mines laid by Bomber Command sank 133 ships totalling 96,286 tons and damaged 92 others at a cost of under 3 per cent of the sorties.[7] The reduced aircraft casualty rate arose primarily from the fact that in June 1943 Bomber Command found the means of dropping mines effectively from a greater height – 6000 feet instead of the previous 2000–3000 feet.

The results of minelaying contrasted favourably with those of another of Bomber Command's maritime tasks at this time – direct attack on shipping. Between 1 January 1942 and 30 June 1943 the RAF's air-laid mines sank 275 merchant vessels. This cost 283 aircraft. During the same period, direct air attack by 2 Group – the light bomber component of Bomber Command – and Coastal Command sank 68 ships. This cost 369 aircraft.[8] In terms of tonnage sunk for each aircraft lost, minelaying was proving to be three times more effective than direct air attack. Nevertheless the latter still paid dividends by restricting the Germans' Channel traffic, and by forcing them to provide fighter cover for their ships.

Fortunately for the health of the crews, 2 Group's main activity in 1942 and through to the summer of 1943 consisted not of shipping strikes but of CIRCUSES and RAMRODS. Both types of operation took place in daylight over France and the Low Countries. In a CIRCUS the 2 Group bombers – Bostons, the new Venturas, and still a few Blenheims – were merely bait, to draw the Luftwaffe into the sky: the intention was to induce a battle in which the bombers' escorts would wear down the German defenders, and so force the Luftwaffe to bring in fighter reinforcements from Russia. In a RAMROD, on the contrary, the idea was for escorted 2 Group bombers to do serious harm to important objectives on the ground, such as airfields, factories, power supplies, and communications.

In general the CIRCUS operations, which had begun in 1941, continued to be no more than a partial success.[9] They compelled the Germans to keep many of their best fighters – the FW 190s – in France and the Low Countries, but they completely failed to make the Luftwaffe withdraw fighter units from Russia to reinforce these territories; any fighters pulled back from the Eastern Front went to strengthen the air defences of the Reich itself. Also, contrary to British beliefs at the time, the balance of losses in the air-fighting was markedly unfavourable to the RAF.*

The operations against ground targets had their moments of triumph, notably the biggest one, the raid on the Philips works at Eindhoven on 6 December 1942.† In the first half of 1943 the Venturas, for all their unhandiness and lack of speed, made several effective attacks. On more than one occasion, however, they suffered heavily, and on 3 May 1943 a New Zealand Ventura squadron – No. 487 – met disaster.

That afternoon 12 of 487's aircraft, under escort, took off to bomb a power station at Amsterdam. One, losing its escape hatch, quickly turned back; the other 11 carried on. But unfortunately a pre-arranged diversionary sweep by Spitfires had taken place half an hour too soon, and had alerted the German defences: FW 190s were consequently waiting to deal with the Spitfire escort, Me 109s with the Venturas. Remorselessly, over the sea and then over Holland, the 109s picked the Venturas off, until only the leading aircraft, piloted by Squadron Leader L. H. Trent, survived. In desperate straits Trent still pressed on and attacked the target – only to overshoot. Then his aircraft, too, succumbed: bullets tore into the controls and the Ventura plunged to earth, hurling Trent and his navigator out at 7000 feet. Mercifully both managed to pull their ripcords, to become prisoners of war. Of the 11 Venturas which had crossed the Channel, only one, badly shot up, made the journey back.‡[10]

As well as taking part in CIRCUSES and RAMRODS, 2 Group during 1942–3 also flew INTRUDER patrols by night to restrict Luftwaffe

---

* e.g. From 31 March to 30 June 1942 the RAF lost 314 fighters and bombers in these cross-Channel operations, the Luftwaffe 90 fighters.

† See page 153.

‡ When details of Squadron Leader Trent's exceptionally gallant and determined leadership became known after the war, he was awarded the Victoria Cross.

operations from airfields across the Channel. During the 'Thousand-Bomber' raid on Cologne, for instance, 34 Blenheims intruded, or attempted to intrude, over airfields in Holland. The last Blenheims in 2 Group went on doing this work until August 1942, when their honourable and at times excessively perilous service with Bomber Command ended.

The 2 Group operations which promised best in 1943 were those undertaken by its two Mosquito squadrons – Nos. 105 and 139. These carried out raids at night and, more frequently, by day at low level under cloud cover. On 25 February 1943 20 Mosquitoes made an outstandingly successful attack on a naval stores depot at Rennes; and on 3 March ten Mosquitoes hit the flotation plant of the molybdenum mines at Knaben, in Norway, causing months of lost production. 'Mosquito stings judiciously placed are very painful,' signalled Harris to the crews.[11] Before the end of March 2 Group Mosquitoes had also successfully attacked the Renault factories at Armage, near Le Mans, a steel plant at Liège, a locomotive works at Nantes, and engine sheds at Paderborn as well as other railway targets in Germany. On 27 May 14 Mosquitoes, at the unwontedly heavy cost of three missing, made a successful attack on the Zeiss optical works in Jena.

On 1 June 1943 No. 2 Group passed from Bomber Command to Fighter Command, before becoming part of the 2nd Tactical Air Force created for the re-entry into France. It had done noble, if not always very profitable, work with Bomber Command; and now it would revert, with brilliant success, to the role for which it had originally been created – direct air support to the Army.

In agreeing to relinquish control of 2 Group Harris characteristic-ally and successfully fought to retain the two Mosquito squadrons. They had been bombing precise and often distant targets with heartening accuracy and their expertise could be well employed in the role of Pathfinders. They would also form the nucleus of an increasingly effective, and amazingly economical, Light Night Striking Force.

The Casablanca directive of January 1943 had stated the task of Bomber Command and the US Eighth Air Force in broad but clear terms: 'the progressive destruction and dislocation of the German military, industrial and economic system, and the undermining of the morale of the German people, to a point where their capacity for armed resistance is fatally weakened.' Within that general concept, the directive had listed U-boat construction yards as the first-priority target, the German aircraft industry as the second. In the ensuing months an Eighth Air Force committee with British participation drew up plans for a Combined Bomber Offensive, indicating the forces needed for the Eighth Air Force and the target systems recommended for attack. In this plan, U-boat construction yards still ranked as target system number one, with the addition now of the main U-boat bases, while the German aircraft industry in general still ranked as target system number two. Special attention, however, was called to the urgent need to reduce German fighter-strength, and this was singled out as an 'intermediate' objective, to be achieved before the others. In all, there were six target systems recommended for attack, the other four being ball bearings, oil, synthetic rubber, and military transport vehicles.[12]

The Combined Bomber Offensive plan, strongly backed by Portal, received the endorsement of the Combined Chiefs of Staff at the TRIDENT Conference in Washington on 14 May 1943. While acknowledging the particular task of each air force – RAF Bomber Command to 'destroy German material facilities' and 'undermine the willingness and ability of the German worker to continue the war', US VIII Bomber Command to destroy 'specific essential industrial targets' – the plan also envisaged close cooperation between the two forces. It included, for instance, an instruction, or at least a recommendation, that 'when precision targets are bombed by the Eighth Air Force in daylight, the effect should be complemented and completed by RAF bombing attacks against the surrounding industrial areas at night'.[13]

The new bombing directive which emerged from the Air Ministry, however, did not impose quite such closely concerted action. It reflected, rather, Harris's desire to preserve maximum tactical flexibility, and was no doubt acceptable to Eaker because he was personally present or represented at Harris's daily conferences, and was happy with the collaboration as it stood.

At all events the new orders, known as the POINTBLANK directive, sent to Harris on 10 June 1943, gave him full freedom to continue the destruction of Germany's major towns. 'While the forces of the British Bomber Command,' the directive stated, 'will be employed in accordance with their main aim in the general disorganization of German industry, their action will be designed as far as practicable to be complementary to the operations of the Eighth Air Force'.[14] The 'as far as practicable' retained for Harris the operational flexibility he felt to be essential.

The main purpose of the POINTBLANK directive, however, was, as recommended in the Combined Bomber Offensive plan, to change the priorities for air attack laid down at Casablanca. While most of them remained in the same order, the new one – the German fighter force and its associated industries[15] – took precedence over all. Its description as an 'intermediate' objective meant in effect that it had to be accomplished before the other objectives became possible.

The elevation of this target system into 'top priority' reflected recent developments. In May 1943 the Allies had achieved great success in the Battle of the Atlantic, but this victory was too recent and possibly too temporary to explain the change in priority. That occurred to some extent because the German night-fighters had been taking an increasing toll of the British bombers, shooting down three for every one which fell to the flak. But it arose above all because the German day-fighters were threatening the American intention of bombing precise targets throughout Germany.

The US VIII Bomber Command had been operating for five months from its English bases before it became sufficiently strong and well-trained to attempt a raid on Germany. In bad weather on 27 January 1943 about 55 Fortresses and Liberators, out of 91 which set out, attacked the docks and U-boat yards at Wilhelmshaven. During the next month Eaker's airmen made three more raids on Germany, but still on coastal targets only. On 4 March they tried for the first time a deeper penetration, to the marshalling yards at Hamm, and lost four out of 17 planes – 23.5 per cent. Much more encouraging was a shallower penetration, of 20 miles or so, a fortnight later to Vegesack, but April again brought disappointment. In the Command's only operation that month over Germany, on 17 April, 110 B-17s took off to attack the Focke-Wulf works outside Bremen, involving a penetration of some 40–50 miles. Sixteen of the Fortresses – 14.5 per cent – failed to return. For attacks on Germany in May, VIII Bomber Command then reverted to fringe targets only, but even so its losses were around 6 per cent.

These experiences made two things clear. If the Eighth Air Force was to penetrate deep into Germany without crippling losses, something had to be done about the fighter opposition: the 'self-defending' American formations were not self-defending enough. And unless the German fighter force could be drastically weakened, or preferably wiped out, the projected Allied invasion of France, now settled for 1944, might lack the degree of air superiority essential for its success.*

---

* At the TRIDENT Conference in Washington on 21 May 1943 Britain and the USA agreed that Operation OVERLORD should be launched by 1 May 1944.

In the weeks which followed, the Eighth Air Force made frequent and successful forays into France, often against fighter objectives, but until the last week in July its targets in Germany mostly involved no deep penetration. For his part, Harris was still preoccupied with the Battle of the Ruhr, but he struck at least one useful blow in the new campaign to weaken German fighter-strength. On 20/21 June, 56 Lancasters of 5 Group, helped by four Pathfinder Lancasters, attacked the Zeppelin works at Friedrichshafen, which were producing WÜRZBURG radar equipment for fighter control. Despite being compelled by flak to bomb from a greater height than intended, they did considerable damage and suffered no losses. It was a raid which had three novel features. One was that a 'Master Bomber' – not yet called that – controlled the attack. Another was that because of the distance from England the raiders flew on to captured bases near Algiers and bombed La Spezia on their way back three nights later. And a third was that when smoke obscured the whole target area, part of the attacking force bombed on a 'timed run' from a prominent point near the objective – a technique in which 5 Group was later to specialise.[16]

Another Bomber Command raid in the following month against an objective important to the German fighter force was much less successful. On 15/16 July 165 Halifaxes, including 31 from the Pathfinder Force, set out to attack the Peugeot works at Montbéliard, in France, some twenty miles west of the Swiss border. Unfortunately the main concentration of marker bombs fell some 700 yards away from the factory, with the result – according to a local report – that while 30 bombs hit the factory, 600 hit the town. Production was not affected, and 123 civilians lost their lives.[17]

The raids on Friedrichshafen and Montbéliard were gestures by Harris in the direction of the new priority, but the great weight of Bomber Command's efforts in June and July 1943 continued to be against German industry and urban existence generally. Shattered towns throughout the Ruhr and the Rhineland now bore eloquent testimony to the destructive power of Bomber Command, and Harris was eager to extend the devastation elsewhere. Already on 27 May he had issued an operation order to his Groups warning them to prepare for major raids on Hamburg. In it he had stressed the benefits that would accrue from 'the total destruction of this city'.[18] Ominously, the code-word chosen for the task was GOMORRAH.

17

Hamburg: Italy: Peenemünde

In 1943 Hamburg was the largest port in Europe and Germany's second biggest city, with a population of around one million. As if this alone would not have made it a prime target, it was also a main centre of submarine production – over a third of the U-boats launched during the war came from Hamburg. Of its numerous shipbuilding firms the most famous was Blohm and Voss, which before it went over mainly to U-boat construction had built Germany's crack liner, the *Europa*, and such formidable warships as the *Hipper* and the *Bismarck*. On the south side of the Elbe, separated by the river from the main residential, commercial and administrative quarters, were also important engineering works, oil plants, and factories manufacturing aircraft and aircraft components. In addition Hamburg had the attraction, from the Bomber Command point of view, of being readily identifiable by its position on a great river and by its extensive canals, lakes, docks and harbour. And as it was only fifty or so miles from the coast, the raiders would not be required to make any deep penetration inland.

By mid-1943, Hamburg had already suffered nearly a hundred visits from Bomber Command. They had begun on 17/18 May 1940 with an attempted attack by 48 Hampdens on oil refineries; had continued during 1941 with special attention to the Blohm and Voss shipyards, sometimes by forces of 100–180 aircraft; and more recently had included two area attacks each by over 400 bombers. Had the local weather been less cloudy at the time, Hamburg, rather than Cologne, would have been the target for the first 'Thousand-Bomber' raid.

188

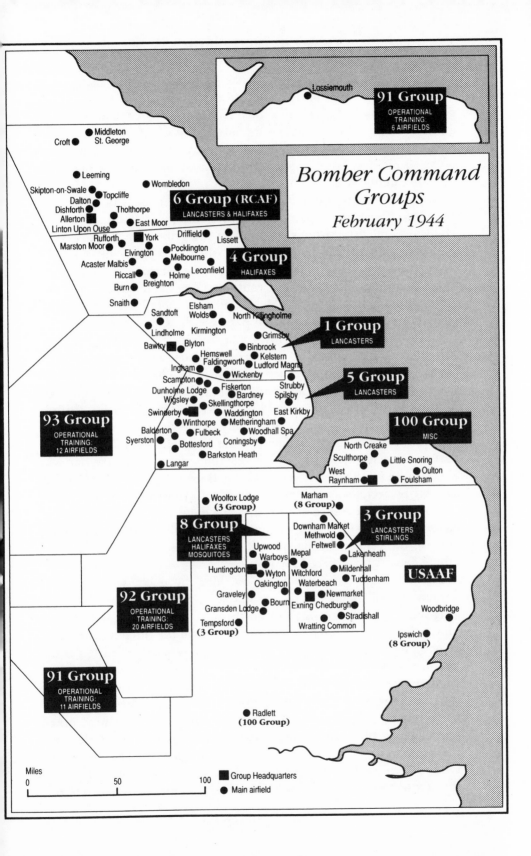

Bomber Command Groups
February 1944

91 Group
OPERATIONAL TRAINING: 6 AIRFIELDS

Lossiemouth

Middleton St. George
Croft
Leeming
Wombledon
Skipton-on-Swale
Topcliffe
Dalton
Dishforth
Tholthorpe
Allerton
East Moor
Linton Upon Ouse

6 Group (RCAF)
LANCASTERS & HALIFAXES

Rufforth
York
Driffield
Marston Moor
Lissett
Elvington
Pocklington
Acaster Malbis
Melbourne
Riccall
Leconfield
Holme
Burn
Breighton
Snaith

4 Group
HALIFAXES

Sandtoft
Elsham Wolds
North Killingholme
Lindholme
Kirmington
Bawtry
Blyton
Grimsby
Binbrook
1 Group
LANCASTERS
Hemswell
Kelstern
Ingham
Faldingworth
Ludford Magna
Scampton
Wickenby
Dunholme Lodge
Fiskerton
Strubby
5 Group
LANCASTERS
Wigsley
Bardney
Spilsby
Swinderby
Skellingthorpe
Waddington
East Kirkby
Winthorpe
Metheringham
Balderton
Fulbeck
Woodhall Spa
Syerston
Coningsby
Bottesford
Barkston Heath
Langar

100 Group
MISC

North Creake
Sculthorpe
Little Snoring
West Raynham
Oulton
Foulsham

93 Group
OPERATIONAL TRAINING: 12 AIRFIELDS

Woolfox Lodge
(3 Group)
Marham
(8 Group)

8 Group
LANCASTERS
HALIFAXES
MOSQUITOES

Downham Market
Methwold
Feltwell
Mepal

3 Group
LANCASTERS
STIRLINGS

Upwood
Warboys
Lakenheath
Huntingdon
Wyton
Witchford
Mildenhall
Oakington
Waterbeach
Tuddenham
Graveley
Bourn
Newmarket
Exning Chedburgh
Gransden Lodge
Stradishall
Tempsford
(3 Group)
Wratting Common

USAAF

Woodbridge

Ipswich
(8 Group)

92 Group
OPERATIONAL TRAINING: 20 AIRFIELDS

91 Group
OPERATIONAL TRAINING: 11 AIRFIELDS

Radlett
(100 Group)

Miles
0   50   100

■ Group Headquarters
● Main airfield

Despite all this, however, the damage inflicted by mid-1943, while substantial, had been in no way critical. In addition to wider fighter defence the city had excellent protection locally, with 278 anti-aircraft guns of 88 mm calibre or above, 24 batteries of searchlights, and three smoke generators.[1] Also its air-raid shelters, many in the basements of big buildings, were among the best and most comprehensively provided in all Germany.

Harris launched Operation GOMORRAH on the night of 24/25 July 1943. No fewer than 791 aircraft, including 347 Lancasters, 246 Halifaxes and 125 Stirlings, took off on the grim task of destruction. Flying in gaggles at different heights, they soon made up a stream some 200 miles long. Eighty miles from the German coast the H2S Pathfinders put down yellow route-markers, and soon the crews were dropping inoffensive-looking bundles of metallised paper strips, code-name WINDOW, designed to paralyse the German radar.

WINDOW had a fairly long history behind it. It had been produced, proved, and recommended for operational use as far back as April 1942. Then there had been second thoughts. The War Cabinet and the AOC-in-C Fighter Command feared that, if the Luftwaffe took to using it, Britain's cities would pay heavily. This defensive attitude persisted throughout 1942 – mistakenly in the view of the Chief of the Air Staff, since the great majority of the Luftwaffe's bombers were by that time safely engaged in Russia. By the spring of 1943 the ban was about to be lifted when it was reaffirmed for the period of the Allies' next big project, the invasion of Sicily. On 10 July the Anglo-American landings took place successfully, and five days later the Chiefs of Staff cleared WINDOW for operational use after 23 July. Even so, it took the voice of the Prime Minister to still the objections of the Minister for Home Security, Herbert Morrison.[2]

The WINDOW strips, each 27 cm long by 2 cm wide, were of aluminium foil on black paper and were tied in bundles of 2200 weighing 2 lb. The crews released them at the rate of one bundle a minute both on the run in to Hamburg and on the run out. Strenuous heaving by one, or sometimes two, of the crew was needed to get the bundles, with their strings cut, out of the aircraft: no special tube had yet been provided, and as they went down the narrow flare chute, there were not infrequent burstings-open and blow-backs, leading to some blackened faces in the aircraft.[3] However, the strips certainly worked – not against the long-distance FREYAS, which had already detected the bomber stream soon after take-off, but against the shorter-range WÜRZBURGS used for fighter, gun and searchlight control, and against the LICHTENSTEIN (AI) sets installed in the German fighters.

Fascinated, the raiders watched searchlights waving aimlessly, saw anti-aircraft shells burst in directions remote from the incoming stream, and heard over their R/T cries of alarm and frustration as the German controllers vainly strove to sort out significant blips on their screens from amid what appeared to be a heavy snowstorm.

With the German radar in utter confusion, the bombers had things very much their own way. All but 63 of the 791 aircraft managed to attack, between them dropping 1346 tons of high explosive and 931 tons of incendiaries; and though the bombing 'crept back' badly from the aiming point in the centre of the city it still fell on built-up areas. Residential districts suffered most, but bombs also hit, among other places, the town hall, the main telephone exchange, the main police station, various factories – and the Hagenbeck Zoo. At one point 55 miles of streets were ablaze; civil defence workers and fire-fighting teams were rushed in from neighbouring towns; and at 4 a.m. the local authorities declared a 'major catastrophe'. About 1500 people lost their lives, tens of thousands their homes. For Bomber Command the cost was extraordinarily light, considering the size of the operation. Of the 791 aircraft, only 12 failed to return – 1.5 per cent of the sorties.

In the spirit of POINTBLANK – though Hamburg was not primarily a 'fighter' target – the Eighth Air Force followed up promptly. During the day of 25 July 68 American bombers, out of the 127 directed there, attacked the docks area, hitting Blohm and Voss and another U-boat yard but losing 15 planes.[4] Throughout, smoke from the earlier Bomber Command raid hampered their operations. It was still so prevalent when night fell that Harris, who had contemplated another huge assault on Hamburg, sent his force off to Essen instead.*

On 26 July the Eighth Air Force tried again, only to encounter the same problem of smoke. Fifty-four aircraft attacked and this time only two failed to return.[5] The raiders damaged a U-boat yard and put one of the two main power stations out of action for a month. In conjunction with other B-17s which attacked Hanover successfully but suffered heavy losses, they claimed to have shot down 60 German fighters. This indeed would have been a victory. Unfortunately, however, the American claims, as often happened, were exaggerated, largely because of the number of gunners firing at what they took to be different German fighters, but which were in fact the same ones. Post-war research revealed that in countering these raids the Luftwaffe lost only four fighters, with another three damaged.

* See page 173.

Two nights later, on 27/28 July, Harris struck his second blow. Once more, nearly 800 aircraft took off, of which 729 actually attacked. Between them, they dropped 2326 tons of bombs. The Pathfinders, acting this time purely on H2S without visual checks, marked with an average error of two miles from the prescribed aiming-point, but the subsequent bombing was exceptionally well concentrated and did enormous damage, particularly to residential areas. The night was hot, there had been no recent rain, and many buildings were tinder-dry. Huge numbers of fires sprang up, doubly uncontrollable due to the fact that blocked streets prevented free movement of fire engines from the districts attacked earlier. Then, in the working-class area of Hammerbrook, the fires began joining up into one huge conflagration as the hot air above sucked in the surrounding cooler air to produce the phenomenon of a firestorm. Asphalt melted on the roads; the raging winds, strong enough to uproot 3-foot-thick trees, whirled people and goods into the flames; and thousands died in the shelters from the all-pervading invasion of carbon monoxide. All told, some 40,000 of Hamburg's inhabitants perished. The next day, tens of thousands of shaken survivors fled the city, their task all the harder because 15 of the 18 railway stations were out of action.[6]

The report written by 'the Police-President', or Chief of Police, of Hamburg and dated 1 December 1943[7] makes grim reading:

Only very shortly after the first bombs had fallen an enormous number of fires caused by a great concentration of incendiary bombs – mixed with HE bombs – sprang up. People who now attempted to leave their shelters to see what the situation was or to fight the fires were met by a sea of flames. Everything round them was on fire. There was no water, and with the huge number and size of the fires all attempts to extinguish them were hopeless from the start.

In the affected areas there were mostly large blocks of flats in narrow streets with numerous houses behind them, with terraces (inner courtyards) etc. These courtyards became in a very short time cauldrons of fire which were literally man-traps. The narrow streets became firelocks through which the tall flames were driven . . . The fires spread with incredible speed because owing to the concentration of HE bombs and land mines, roofs were torn off, walls blown in, windows and doors torn from their frames or smashed, and the fires were therefore fed unhindered.

People waited in the shelters until the heat and obvious danger compelled some immediate action . . . In many cases they were no longer able to act by themselves ... They were already dead or unconscious from C.O. poisoning. The house had collapsed, or all the exits had been blocked. The fire had become a hurricane which made it impossible in most cases to reach the open.

Many of these refugees then lost their lives through the heat. They fell suffocated, burnt, or ran deeper into the fire. Relatives lost one another. One was able to save himself, the others disappeared. Many wrapped themselves in wet blankets, or soaked their clothes, and thus reached safety. In a short time clothes and blankets became hot and dry. Anyone going any distance through this hell found that his clothes were in flames or the blanket caught fire and was blown away in the storm.

Numbers jumped into the canals and waterways and remained swimming or standing up to their necks in water for hours until the heat should die down. Even these suffered burns on their heads. They were obliged to wet their faces constantly or they perished from the heat.

A population ready and prepared for the alarm were literally overwhelmed by the fire, which reached its height in under an hour.

The raid was one which the Bomber Command crews, too, would never forget. The smoke rose to the height of their aircraft, and as they peered down through it, saw the sea of fire below, and heard the violent explosions, some felt as though they were gazing into a volcano. 'I looked down,' wrote one, 'fascinated and aghast, satisfied yet horrified.' Many were those who felt a mixture of contentment at a job well done and pity for 'those poor bastards' below.[8]

Delenda est Carthago: Hamburg must be destroyed. Two nights later Harris sent another huge force – 777 aircraft – to bomb parts of the city which had thus far escaped great harm. This they did, 707 aircraft dropping 2318 tons of bombs and bringing death and destruction to new areas, though mostly not those intended. In one incident carbon monoxide poisoning killed 370 people trapped in the basement shelter of a large store.

One more raid completed the onslaught. On 2/3 August 737 aircraft set off again, but this time thunderstorms and ice-laden clouds frustrated much of their effort. At High Wycombe the raid was reckoned a failure, but this was evidently not the opinion of the Hamburg Police-President, who wrote: 'the struggle against the fire as an overwhelming enemy ... reached its climax during the night of August 2/3, in which the detonation of exploding bombs, the peals of thunder and the crackling of the flames and ceaseless downpour of the rain formed a veritable inferno.'

'The Battle of Hamburg' was one of the most concentrated and successful series of operations undertaken by Bomber Command during the whole course of the war. In the four big raids – leaving aside the half-dozen Mosquito sorties flown each night to keep up the pressure – the Command flew over 3000 sorties and dropped, on and around Hamburg, over 8500 tons of bombs. Its losses – 87 aircraft – were amazingly light, and amounted to less than 2.5 per cent of the sorties. Noticeably, however, the German defences, after the first impact of WINDOW, regained some cohesion. By giving up attempts at close continuous control and instead merely steering 'Wild Sow' fighters in the direction of the bomber stream, and by bringing in more searchlights, they secured better results as the battle progressed. On the first big raid Bomber Command lost 1.5 per cent of the sorties; on the second, 2.2 per cent; on the third, 3.6 per cent; and on the fourth – but that was also the night of the thunderstorms – 4.1 per cent. At least three-quarters of these casualties fell to the German night-fighters.

In terms of destruction the results were unprecedented in air warfare and not to be exceeded until the Anglo-American bombing of Dresden and the American bombing of Japan. Of the 8382 acres of Hamburg that were closely built up, 6200 became uninhabitable for many months. Complete destruction befell more than half the city's dwelling units, and something like 900,000 people lost their homes. In the days following the firestorm more than a million left the city, about half of whom stayed away until the end of the war.[9]

The exact number of those killed can hardly be stated. In addition to the estimated 40,000 on the night of the firestorm about 4500 others, including 800 servicemen, perished. The difficulty of establishing a precise figure may be appreciated from the fact that in some of the shelters there were only piles of ashes, which doctors might variously estimate as representing the remains of perhaps 250, perhaps 350, human beings.

Though the residential quarters of Hamburg and the public buildings (436 of which were destroyed or damaged) fared worst, industrial concerns also suffered great damage. Complete destruction befell 186 of the 574 larger works, and 4118 of the 9068 smaller factories. Nearly half the workforce in the war industries remained absent for at least two months. However, the post-war bombing surveys put the overall loss of production in the larger concerns at no more than 1.8 months' output, with perhaps six months' output lost from the smaller concerns.

The damage to Hamburg's shipping was unquestionably heavy, as it also was to goods and food in warehouses. About 180,000 tons of shipping went to the bottom of the harbour, or was destroyed by fire. In addition the bombing, in conjunction with that of the Americans, robbed the German Navy, according to post-war estimates, of the probable accretion of 26 or 27 U-boats.

Patriotism, the German character and the SS were enough to ensure that in the absence for many months of further heavy raids, Hamburg made a remarkable recovery. Though the earlier levels of production were never fully regained, within five months the main war factories were up to four-fifths of their previous output. Nevertheless the impact of the raids on the rest of Germany was profound, as citizens from Hamburg arrived with their tales of horror. Minister of Armaments Albert Speer (who qualified his statement later, when he saw how Hamburg recovered) at first reckoned that another six similar raids might end Germany's capacity to continue the struggle.[10]

Bomber Command, however, was not yet in any position to apply the Hamburg treatment to the five or six cities whose destruction would now matter most to the German war effort: Berlin, Munich, Stuttgart, Frankfurt, Augsburg, Leipzig. To attack any of these demanded deep penetration, either directly into the Reich or through its defences in occupied territory. And that could not be done with a loss of only 2.5 per cent of sorties – as Harris was soon to confirm in 'the Battle of Berlin'.

Satisfied that Hamburg, if not completely destroyed, was at least so thoroughly wrecked that it would be a liability to the Reich for months to come, Harris moved on to his next task. The Allies were fighting their way across Sicily; Mussolini had been disowned by the Fascist Grand Council on 25 July and arrested the following day; and a new Italian government had been formed under Marshal Badoglio. Understandably fearful of the German reaction if he withdrew Italy from the war or changed sides, Badoglio at first kept up at least a pretence of continuing the struggle. On 31 July 1943 General Eisenhower, C-in-C of the Allied forces in North-West Africa, accordingly broadcast a warning that the penalty for Italy if she delayed in making peace would be further air bombardment. Three days earlier the British War Cabinet had agreed to this, and Portal had instructed Harris to 'do his best to heat up the fire'.[11] On 7/8 August Bomber Command duly began a new series of attacks on northern Italy.

The raids that night, by nearly 200 Lancasters, fell on Milan, Turin and Genoa. H2S Pathfinders led the way, the crews dropped WINDOW, and only two aircraft failed to return. At Turin, for the first time in an attack of more than squadron strength, a Master Bomber – as yet called an MC (Master of Ceremonies) – controlled the raid on the spot by VHF R/T. He was Wing Commander John Searby of No. 83 (PFF) Squadron, and he was able to halt an incipient 'creep-back' in the bombing. Together with their bombs, the raiders dropped leaflets. On the front of these the message was 'The Government of Rome says the war continues'; on the back, 'That is why our bombardment continues'.[12]

Five nights later no fewer than 504 aircraft, of which 477 actually attacked, operated against Milan, while another 152 bombed Turin. Forty-eight hours after that, on 14/15 August, 134 (of 140) Lancasters again attacked Milan, some concentrating on the Breda factories. The following night nearly 200 Lancasters hit the centre of the city. On 16/17 August 154 Lancasters and Stirlings (of 183 sent) attacked Turin. The Stirlings, which could not fly high anyway, had the task of bombing the Fiat works from 5000 to 8000 feet.

Meanwhile on 15 August Badoglio's emissary had arrived in Portugal to begin serious peace talks. Though an armistice was not signed until 3 September, the new government's wish to join the Allies soon became clear, and Bomber Command's operations were accordingly halted. Their physical results quickly became known from daylight reconnaissance. At Turin the most important objective, the Fiat works, had been hit on each occasion. In Milan, which suffered most, the bombing had destroyed or damaged about 40 per cent of the fully built-up areas and about 14 per cent of the rest. Industrially the toll of damage had extended to some 240 factories, including those of Alfa Romeo, Isotto-Fraschini, Breda and Pirelli. Railways and supplies of electricity, gas and water had all been badly affected, leading to a temporary paralysis of local industry.[13] Inevitably, in the destruction famous buildings, including La Scala opera house, suffered too. In the refectory of the Church of Santa Maria delle Grazie only one wall remained standing – the wall on which Leonardo da Vinci had painted *The Last Supper*.[14]

Frequently during these operations guns stopped firing and searchlights stood stationary as the attack began, betokening an overriding interest in survival among those who manned them. In the whole series of attacks the cost to Bomber Command was no more than 1.2 per cent of the forces involved, and the objective, that of speeding the unconditional surrender of Italy, was undoubtedly attained.

Harris, however, in his *Despatch*, was wide of the mark when he (or his Staff Officer) wrote: 'There is little doubt that it [the bombing] was the principal factor contributing to the downfall of Mussolini's regime.'[15] The bombing of 7/8 to 16/17 August, to which he was referring, could not have contributed to the fall of Mussolini since it took place afterwards. It is also obvious that the free-range bombing of southern Italy by the North-West African Allied Air Forces, which went on intensively until the end of August – largely to deny the Germans airfields and communications – must also have greatly influenced the Italian decision to capitulate. But undoubtedly, Bomber Command had played its part by showing clearly what was in store for Italy if surrender were rejected, or long delayed.

In 1937 the German Army established a Research and Experimental Station, and the Luftwaffe an airfield, at Peenemünde, a fishing village on the Baltic some sixty miles east of Rostock. Between then and the outbreak of war the resident scientists worked enthusiastically to develop long-range rockets. For brilliant young Wernher von Braun, deputy director of research, there was always the dream of firing one to the moon. Their immediate task, however, was to design and produce mammoth rockets as weapons of mass destruction.

An indication of a connection between Peenemünde and rockets first reached Britain in November 1939 in the so-called 'Oslo Report' – a seven-page typescript of unknown provenance which had been put through the letter-box of the British naval attaché in Oslo. It gave much information about German radar and weaponry, including a naval rocket, and mentioned Peenemünde. With the exception of Dr R. V. Jones, the youthful first occupier of the post of Assistant Director of Scientific Intelligence at the Air Ministry, few in the Intelligence organisation took it seriously. The general view at first was that it was a German hoax, designed to waste British time and energy in following false trails.[16]

Three years passed, and suddenly German long-range rockets began to seem all too real. In December 1942 a report from Stockholm told how a Danish engineer living in Berlin had overheard a conversation about a huge rocket being tested near Swinemünde. A month later a further message referred to the test-firing of rockets and mentioned Peenemünde. But it was not until late in March 1943 that the British authorities became alarmed. In a 'bugged' room at ASHBIN, the prisoner-of-war interrogation centre in Buckinghamshire, General von Thoma, lately captured in Africa, had been heard talking to a fellow German general. He had expressed surprise that the intended rocket attack on London had apparently not yet begun.[17]

Other information then flowed in, notably from Polish sources and from two Luxemburgers who had worked in Peenemünde. In mid-April, the alarm bells by now ringing loud, Duncan Sandys, Churchill's son-in-law, became entrusted with the task of coordinating the various efforts being made to investigate the danger. By that time the scientists at Peenemünde had already designed and test-fired a huge rocket with a one-ton warhead. Known at first as the A-4 and later, on Hitler's wishes, as the V-2 (for *Vergeltungswaffe* 2 – i.e. Revenge Weapon 2), it was about to go into series production. Hitler's ambition, it later transpired, was to build up supplies until 5000 could descend on London in rapid succession.[18]

In the course of the next two months Coastal Command Mosquitoes flew five photographic reconnaissances over Peenemünde. The fast-flying, unarmed 'wooden wonders' encountered no opposition: the defences, to preserve Peenemünde's secrecy, were under orders not to open fire on isolated aircraft. The second sortie, on 12 June, provided the sought-for confirmation – a photo of a V-2 lying on a trailer. The interpreter who first studied the photographs failed to detect the rocket, but Dr R. V. Jones picked it out six days later.[19]

Later photographs showed more rockets, and on 29 June the Defence Committee of the War Cabinet gave orders for Peenemünde to be bombed on the heaviest scale.[20] But the nights were as yet too short to give cover of darkness over so long a flight: Peenemünde was 700 miles from the British bases. So it was agreed that Harris should wait six weeks, until mid-August, before launching the attack. Meanwhile investigations were ordered into another threat now reported, though not as yet in connection with Peenemünde: the pilotless aircraft or flying bomb, *Vergeltungswaffe* 1 – the V-1.

On 17 August 1943 final orders went out from Bomber Command HQ for a massive raid that night. The stations had already been warned to prepare for a GOODWOOD – a maximum effort. The crews were told nothing about rockets, but were given to understand that they would be attacking an important radar experimental station, the destruction of which would greatly help the British bombing offensive. They were also told, most unusually, that if they did not destroy their targets that night, they would have to go back again until they did.[21] 'Not one of us,' later wrote Sergeant K. W. Rowe of 434 Squadron, 'had ever heard a message such as that to conclude a briefing.'[22]

At dusk 596 bombers, all four-engined, stood ready. The northern tip of Peenemünde promontory, where the Luftwaffe, unknown to the Allies, was testing its new pilotless aircraft, was not one of the objectives. The three targets for the force were all south of this. In south-to-north order, and in the order to be attacked, these were a housing estate on which lived most of the scientific, technical and administrative staff; a new rocket-production plant; and the Experimental Works, the scientific heart of the complex. For greater accuracy the attack was to take place in full moonlight and the bombs dropped from about 8000 feet, despite the risk to the raiders. Each of the three objectives was to be bombed for 15 minutes, which would mean moving the marking for the aiming-points during the course of a raid – an untried procedure. To assist this, and to control the raid generally, Group Captain John Searby, CO of 83 Squadron, was to act as Master Bomber – the new and definitive term for the role he had exercised over Turin.

Two ancillary operations formed an important part of the plan. To damp down fighter opposition *en route*, 38 Mosquitoes and Beaufighters of Fighter Command were to 'intrude' over enemy-occupied airfields in Holland. And to focus the attentions of the night-fighters in Germany elsewhere than over the true objectives, eight Mosquitoes of No. 139 Squadron were to make an attack on Berlin slightly earlier.

The chosen route across Denmark worked well, and Searby arrived over Peenemünde within thirty seconds of his appointed time. Other Pathfinders followed, to drop new marker bombs with ballistic properties; consisting of impregnated cotton wool in a 250-lb bomb casing, they burst at 3000 feet and lit up the ground below for ten minutes. But unhappily some of the initial Pathfinders marked nearly two miles south of the intended housing estate, and drew the attack instead on to a forced labour camp holding several thousand foreigners – mostly captured Poles and Russians. Within three minutes Searby managed to correct the aiming, but meanwhile bombs from the leading aircraft in the first wave had killed over 500 of the unfortunate slave workers.

By means of Searby's instructions and further and more accurate marking, the rest of the first wave (which numbered 244 aircraft, mainly Stirlings and Halifaxes of 3 and 4 Group) then dropped their bombs as intended – on the housing estate. They destroyed about three-quarters of the buildings but – owing to the soft ground and the excellence of the shelters – killed only about 170 of the 4000 residents. This was a much smaller total than the planners had hoped for. But among the dead were Dr Walter Thiel, chief engineer for rocket propulsion, and Dr Erich Walther, chief maintenance engineer in the rocket production works.[23]

The second wave – 131 aircraft of 1 Group, nearly all Lancasters – then arrived to blast the new rocket production and assembly factory. They did little damage to one of the two main shops but hit the other, used for storing completed rockets. Their bombs wrecked the roof and the rockets, but failed to destroy the main structure. In the course of the attack, a strong wind sprang up and blew the markers eastwards, with the result that several aircraft dropped bombs into the sea.

The objective for the third wave, the Experimental Works, consisted of over 70 small buildings. This complex contained vital scientific equipment and data, and within it lived the Director, General Dornberger, and his deputy, von Braun. The task of wrecking it had been entrusted to the Canadian Group, No. 6, with 52 Halifaxes and nine Lancasters, and to No. 5 Group, with 117 Lancasters. But by the time they arrived, half an hour after the first wave's assault on the housing estate, the situation had deteriorated sharply. Smoke, both from the bombing and the defenders' smoke generators, was obscuring the target area, clouds were developing, and German night-fighters, earlier lured to Berlin by the Mosquito attack, were arriving in force. The Canadians bombed on the Pathfinders' markers, some of which were by then too far east or south; but No. 5 Group came in on their AOC's favoured technique of a 'time-and-distance run' – gauging the wind, then setting the speed exactly to cover, in just over a minute, the four miles from Ruden Island.

A 'time-and-distance run' was a particularly good tactic for a smoke-obscured target, but Air Vice-Marshal Cochrane's men were also under orders to bomb on the markers they saw, unless these were obviously misplaced, or they received other orders from the Master Bomber. This resulted in some of their effort going astray. Nevertheless, despite the fact that important structures like the wind tunnel and the telemetry block survived intact, the attack did great damage, destroying a third of the buildings, including the headquarters office and the design block. The loss of the latter would have been a disaster to the Germans had they not duplicated their drawings and lodged them elsewhere after each day's work.

It was this third wave which met the full force of the German reaction, as the night-fighters arrived from chasing around over Berlin. In the first two stages of the attack only one or two bombers had succumbed, but in the last quarter-of-an-hour 28 went down. Some of these were victims of the new upward-firing twin cannon fitted to German fighters and known as *Schräge Musik* (harsh music). The fighters, however, did not go entirely scot-free. The bombers shot down five.

As the bombers recrossed Denmark on the way home they met a further challenge, and three more plunged to destruction. All told, Bomber Command's losses, omitting a Halifax which crashed on return, amounted to 40 aircraft, of which 23 were Lancasters, in the main raid, and one Mosquito from the diversion against Berlin. In addition, Fighter Command lost one of the 'intruder' Mosquitoes. On the other side, the Germans lost at least 12 night-fighters to the guns of the bombers and the intruders.

'And what good came of it at last?' The benefits to the Allied cause, and particularly to Britain, were considerable. Although Peenemünde survived for research and development, the Germans felt they had to move rocket-testing and production to somewhere safer – the testing to a site in Poland, the production to tunnels and underground galleries in the Kohnstein, one of the Harz mountains in central Germany.* These transfers saved the V-2 for Hitler, but caused a loss of at least two months' output.

The first V-2 finally arrived on London on 8 September 1944. Had the V-2s been available to Hitler three or even two months earlier to coincide with the initial invasion operations and the launching of the V-1 flying-bomb attacks on southern England, their impact would have been far more serious than it later proved to be. Even disregarding the fact that without the attack on Peenemünde V-2s would have been falling on Britain's south-coast ports in the vital invasion period of July 1944, the loss of two months' production was a deadly blow to Hitler's intentions. The Germans, aiming to produce 1800 V-2s a month, over the period January 1944 – March 1945 in fact produced about 6000, an average of 400 a month. At the lowest estimate, the Bomber Command attack saved London and Antwerp, the prime V-2 targets, from the fall of about 720 rockets and the slaughter of some 3,600 civilians. It was a great achievement, for which 245 aircrew of Bomber Command, including no fewer than 60 from Canada, paid with their lives.

* In this underground complex, code-named DORA, some 60,000 slave workers toiled, and 20,000 died, before the American liberation in April 1945.

18

'The Battle of Berlin'

L ike 'the Battle of the Ruhr', 'the Battle of Berlin' was no single battle but a whole campaign. And just as the Ruhr by no means monopolised Bomber Command's attentions in the spring and early summer of 1943, so in the following autumn and winter the Command concerned itself with many places besides Berlin.

As a target, Berlin had three great attractions. It was the administrative capital of the Reich; it was a key point in German communications, especially for the flow of troops and munitions to the Eastern Front; and it was a major centre of industry. Its importance in this last respect is evident from the many famous firms inside the city – AEG, Siemens, Telefunken, Lorenz, BMW, Daimler-Benz, Zeiss, Mauser, Henschel and Dornier. Between them they turned out massive quantities of articles essential to the German war effort: artillery, tanks, small arms, ammunition, railway engines and wagons, electrical and wireless apparatus and signals equipment of all kinds, aero-engines, aircraft.

There was no doubt about the importance of Berlin as a target. But there was equally little doubt about the difficulty of attacking it. In the first place there was the distance from the British bomber bases – some 650 miles. Since the survival of the raiders depended on the cover of the dark, they could not attack Berlin during the shorter nights of summer, when the weather might have been less of an extra hazard. Instead, they had to operate most intensively during the formidable months of November to February. Attacks on Berlin, unlike those on some other distant targets, involved very deep penetration into Germany. This meant that the Luftwaffe's single-engine night-fighters, skilled now in their new 'Wild Sow' tactics, had an excellent chance of rallying to the defence of the capital before the raiders got there.

There were further difficulties, not perhaps at first so well appreciated at High Wycombe. Berlin was a city of many wide streets and generous public spaces – on which incendiaries could fall harmlessly. Also it was vast, covering with its suburbs almost 900 square miles. Though some kind of damage could be inflicted almost anywhere, serious damage to specific districts was much harder to achieve. This was particularly so because the H2S Mark II available in the autumn of 1943, and used by the Pathfinders for navigation and marking, gave only the roughest indication of the urban maze below.

Another obstacle was the great strength of the local defences. A belt of searchlights some 30 miles from the centre of the city and another of anti-aircraft guns ten miles further in, ringed the capital. Some of these lights and guns could be, and were, moved for the close defence of particular areas as the battle wore on. Prominent among the regular inner defences were 24 large 128-mm guns mounted on three almost indestructible flak-towers. With a range of up to 45,000 feet, they provided a formidable high fire until the German fighters could arrive.

The passive defences, almost needless to add, were also well organised. Some 15 decoy sites beyond the suburbs tempted the raiders to unload their bombs on the wrong places; and wooden floats dotted about the lakes made the task of target identification more difficult by disguising these easy reference points. For the protection of the public there were excellent and extensive air-raid shelters in the Underground railway stations and beneath the many big residential and business blocks. These could not, of course, hold everybody, but pressure on them eased when the Berlin Gauleiter, Goebbels, alarmed by the fate of Hamburg, ordered the evacuation of all children and young mothers. By the time the main assault began, over three-quarters of a million 'useless mouths' had left the city.

With his predecessor's disastrous raid of 7/8 November 1941 doubtless in mind, Harris for long avoided taking action against the German capital. As he wrote in *Bomber Offensive*: 'In 1942 I refused, however much I was urged, to attack Berlin.' He felt that his four-engined aircraft, and especially his Lancasters, were as yet too few and their navigational aids inadequate for such a major task. Somewhat against his better judgement in January 1943 he at length sent a major force against Berlin. Results were disappointing, but the political pressure continued. On 16 February 1943 Portal instructed Harris: 'Recent events on the Russian front have made it most desirable, in the opinion of the Cabinet, that we should rub in the Russian victory [at Stalingrad] by further attacks on Berlin.'[1]

During March 1943 Harris duly mounted three more raids. Guided by H2S, they showed more promise than those of January; but they also stimulated the Germans into strengthening the inner defences of the city and improving air-raid precautions. During the shorter nights that followed, Harris concentrated on targets elsewhere.

Having dealt successfully with the Ruhr, the Rhineland, north Italy, Hamburg and Peenemünde, Harris reverted, by now more willingly, to Berlin. His forces were stronger, and the nights were lengthening. On 23/24 August he sent no fewer than 727 aircraft – Lancasters, Halifaxes, Stirlings and a few Mosquitoes – to bomb the German capital. The unwontedly large number of 70 turned back before they got there, but the rest, relying for the most part on the Pathfinders' blind-marking by H2S, inflicted much widely scattered damage. The intended target area escaped completely but every government building in the Wilhelmstrasse suffered, as did the Tempelhof airfield and district. In general, though, the efforts of the Master Bomber – in this case the tough Canadian Wing Commander 'Johnny' Fouquier – could not compensate for the crews' inability to see what was actually going on.

This raid of 23/24 August 1943 was the heaviest and most effective yet made on Berlin. It was also the most expensive. Nearly forty minutes before the planned beginning of the attack the Germans had realised the target, and fighters were hastening there. The result, together with the toll taken by the anti-aircraft guns, was the destruction of 57 of the raiders – not counting others which crashed on return. This represented an alarming overall loss-rate among the heavy bombers of 7.9 per cent. For the Halifaxes, who flew lower than the Lancasters, the rate was 10 per cent; for the Stirlings, who flew lowest of all, nearly 14 per cent.

Eight nights later, on 31 August/1 September, 613 heavy bombers with nine Mosquitoes for marking tried again. This time an even bigger number – 86 – failed to reach the target area. The great majority who did were in for an unpleasant surprise – German fighters had marked out the last stages of the approach route with brilliant white parachute flares. Several of the crews thus illuminated likened the experience to being caught naked in public. Their inevitable tendency was to bomb short of the target, and this 'creep-back' extended for nearly thirty miles. The losses amounted to 47 heavy bombers (7.7 per cent), little significant damage was done, and more than three times as many British aircrew lost their lives as did German civilians. But Goebbels took the raid seriously enough to speed up the evacuation of children and non-essential workers.

One further raid on Berlin, on 3/4 September, was all that Harris ventured at this stage. Since casualties among the Halifaxes and Stirlings had been so high, he limited the raiding force to 316 Lancasters, and planned to put them all over the target within sixteen minutes. Helped by four Mosquitoes which carried out 'spoof' attacks – i.e. dropped flares and the odd bombs at various places to mislead the German fighters – they did great damage to factories and public utilities. And, of course, to houses: something like 35,000 more Berliners joined the ranks of the 'bombed out'. But the cost was again heavy: over 6 per cent of the raiding force. Fortunately the casualties did not include the BBC's airborne reporter, Wynford Vaughan Thomas, who, despite the attack of a German fighter, recorded a memorable description of what was happening around him.

In these three raids Bomber Command had sent out some 1700 sorties, from which 125 aircraft and over 850 aircrew had not come back. If a loss rate of over 7 per cent had to be accepted – and, if so, it could only be for a short time – then it was more imperative than ever that the bombs should fall in the right places. Many of the bombs dropped on Berlin thus far had caused damage, but mainly in districts remote from the aiming-points. In the knowledge that a more accurate H2S – the Mark III, using a wavelength of only three centimetres – was promised for the autumn, and in the hope that longer nights would mean fewer casualties, Harris now 'laid off' Berlin for the next eleven weeks.

Before he turned to Berlin again, in mid-November 1943, Harris launched several heavy raids against other distant, but less daunting, targets. He had already twice attacked Nuremberg, on the first occasion (10/11 August) inflicting great damage at low cost. Now, in October, using forces of 300–400 Lancasters, he aimed crushing blows at Stuttgart and Leipzig. At Stuttgart the missing rate was only 1.2 per cent. But on the Leipzig raid, involving deep penetration in appalling weather, it reached a more normal 4.5 per cent.

Not surprisingly the heaviest blows fell on the nearer targets, and especially those within OBOE range. Forces of from 250 to 700 aircraft rained destruction down on München-Gladbach and Rheydt,

Mannheim and Ludwigshafen, Frankfurt and Hanover, Bochum and Hagen. Once, against Kassel on 22/23 October, the missing rate reached an alarming 7.8 per cent, and once, against Hagen on 1/2 October, it fell to an almost unbelievably low 0.8 per cent. Over the whole series of attacks at this time it averaged 3.6 per cent – too high for complacency, but sustainable.

Some of the heavier blows in these months fell on Mannheim and Ludwigshafen, towns on opposite sides of the Rhine. Bombs, high explosive or incendiary, hit scores of industrial premises, including the great I.G. Farben chemical works; thousands of fires sprang up; the 'bombed out' numbered more than 50,000. Equally destructive was the assault on Hanover, important for the rubber industry and the manufacture of aircraft tyres. It was attacked four times during September and October in raids involving 2253 sorties. The first two attempts were not specially effective, but the third, on 8/9 October, devastated the centre of the city. In clear conditions the attack became well concentrated, bombs fell on important industrial concerns like the Continental rubber company and the Hanomeg machine works, and fires quickly gained a hold. Nearly 4000 buildings went up in smoke and flame, and 30,000 more suffered damage. Over 5 per cent of the raiders failed to return, but happily there were no losses among the 26 Wellingtons, the last of these sturdy and reliable machines to operate over Germany.

The single most destructive attack in this period was on Kassel, important for its fighter assembly plants. The town had already been raided once in October, without great success apart from hits on the Henschel and Fieseler aircraft factories. Now, on 22/23 October, when visual markers were able to correct the initial 'blind' H2S marking, the result was complete devastation. As at Hamburg, though on a lesser scale, a firestorm developed; 155 industrial premises were completely or partially wrecked, and three Henschel factories, by this time making flying bombs, suffered damage which set back the launching of Hitler's V-1 campaign. Harshest of all was the blow to the town's housing, with over 26,000 flats and apartments totally destroyed and as many more made uninhabitable. The dead and missing numbered nearly 9000, the 'bombed out' over 100,000.

It was on one of the last big raids of this series, against Düsseldorf, on 3/4 November, that Flight Lieutenant William Reid of 61 Squadron became the eleventh member of Bomber Command to win the Victoria Cross. Two hundred miles from Düsseldorf his aircraft encountered a Messerschmitt 110 night-fighter and then, when he shook that off, a Focke-Wulf 190. Their attacks shattered Reid's cockpit windows;

put the intercom, the oxygen supply, the mid-upper turret, and the compasses out of action; wounded the flight engineer in the arm and Reid in the head and chest; mortally wounded the wireless operator; and killed the navigator. Despite all this, Reid pressed on, bombed the target accurately, and then, steering by the pole star and the moon, set about bringing the aircraft home. At one point he lost consciousness, and the wounded flight engineer had to operate the controls. Recovering, Reid then took over again. Despite mist, a partial collapse of the undercarriage and blood running into his eyes from his head wound, he put down successfully at an airfield in Norfolk.[2]

In all, Bomber Command made 25 major attacks on targets in Germany between the final Hamburg raid of 3/4 August 1943 and the opening of the major offensive against Berlin on 18/19 November. In the course of these it flew 12,700 sorties and lost 588 aircraft – just over 4.6 per cent. During the same period it made six substantial attacks on north Italian towns, one (unsuccessfully) on long-range gun positions near Boulogne, and three on railway centres (Modane and Cannes) on the lines linking France with Italy. It also delivered a very heavy and completely effective attack by moonlight on the Dunlop rubber factory at Montluçon, in central France. From these major raids outside Germany, involving 1146 sorties, only 19 bombers failed to return – slightly over 1.6 per cent. It was little wonder that a ribbon leading to Turin on the briefing map was a more popular sight with aircrew than one leading to Berlin or the Ruhr.

During this period of heavy attacks before the renewed assault on Berlin, Bomber Command also maintained its usual lesser routines. New crews gained operational experience by minelaying; crews still at OTU dropped leaflets over France; small forces of six to 12 Mosquitoes made independent attacks or cooperated in major raids by flying diversionary sorties to mislead the German fighters.

The minor attacks within OBOE range by Mosquitoes were significant for the future of the bombing offensive. They showed that much greater precision in bombing by night was becoming possible. As yet, however, Bomber Command Mosquitoes were few in number, and the bomb tonnage they could deliver was small. And when Harris, after a lapse of four months since the raid on the dams, sent heavy bombers into Germany to attack a precise target, the result was still much as before. On 15/16 September eight Lancasters of 617 Squadron set out to bomb the important Dortmund–Ems Canal, the object of Learoyd's successful attentions during the Battle of Britain. They encountered mist, flak and fighters. Only three returned. To Harris the lesson was clear. Over Germany, and for some time to come, Bomber Command must continue waging war by area-bombing.[3]

By November 1943 the time seemed right for a more sustained assault on Berlin. The nights would be at their longest; some of the Pathfinders would be carrying the new H2S Mark III; and the force regularly available with crews – around 800 four-engined bombers and 40 Mosquitoes – could deliver a greater bomb-load than ever before. Huge stretches of Germany's more accessible industrial towns had been reduced to rubble. Now was the moment, Harris thought, to extend similar treatment to the German capital.

In words which have been often quoted – usually against him – Harris on 3 November 1943 expressed his hopes to the Prime Minister. After claiming that Bomber Command had virtually destroyed 19 of Germany's major industrial cities and seriously damaged a further 19, he went on to urge that the highest priority target should now be Berlin. 'I await promised USAAF help in this, the greatest of air battles,' he wrote, 'but I would not propose to wait for ever, or for long if opportunity serves . . . We can wreck Berlin from end to end if the USAAF will come in on it. It will cost between us 400–500 aircraft. It will cost Germany the war.'[4]

As many critics have pointed out, things did not work out in this way. The US VIII Bomber Command, lacking until very recently long-range fighter escort, had found deep penetration of Germany inordinately expensive: in November 1943 it was not yet ready to take on Berlin. Considering this, the Air Staff advised Harris on 13 November that he should not count on American participation, or plan for a sustained and probably costly series of assaults. Instead he should attack Berlin by seizing suitable occasions when the weather and other tactical conditions seemed to offer the best chances of success.[5] Attacking Berlin, in other words, was to be one further step in weakening Germany. It was not to be, as Harris had hoped it might be, an attempt to bring Germany directly to the edge of submission. The Air Staff had no desire to see the British and American strategic air forces blunted by heavy casualties just before they gave their indispensable help to the great enterprise scheduled for summer 1944 – the cross-Channel invasion.

From the frequency with which Bomber Command during the next three months attacked Berlin, usually in conditions of weather which were far from ideal, it has appeared to some commentators that Harris nevertheless disregarded the Air Staff's instructions and followed his own ideas. He certainly continued to nourish the hope that his attacks would be more decisive than they actually proved to be. But he can hardly be convicted of deliberately exceeding his brief. There was never any complete certainty about the weather to be expected, either over Germany or over England on return; and Berlin *was* a major target, high on the Chiefs of Staff approved priority-list ever since the Casablanca directive of January 1943. So long as he did not blunt his forces in attacking it, he would remain within the bounds of official policy.

Harris struck his first blow in the new campaign on 18/19 November 1943. While nearly 400 Halifaxes, Stirlings and Lancasters attacked Mannheim/Ludwigshafen, 440 Lancasters and a few Mosquitoes operated against Berlin. Twenty-six of the Berlin aircraft were carrying the new H2S, so no tell-tale route markers were used; but as cloud covered the target area completely and 21 of the 26 sets failed *en route*, the bombing was far from concentrated. The railways, a gasworks, 15 chemical or explosives factories, and several thousand homes suffered damage, but possibly the most satisfactory feature of the raid was the low casualty rate: only nine of the Lancasters – 2 per cent – failed to return. This was because the dense cloud hampered the defenders quite as much as the attackers.

The next night 266 aircraft took off to raid Leverkusen, important for its I.G. Farben chemicals plant. Results were poor, but losses few. Then on 22/23 it was Berlin again. Once more the cloud was thick, but this time the huge force of 764 aircraft inflicted enormous damage. Its losses were light, and Harris was encouraged to strike again the following night. Another success resulted; but the Germans had their single-engine night-fighters waiting above the capital, and over 5 per cent of the Lancasters failed to return.

These two raids hit Berlin far more heavily than all the previous attacks put together. 'I just can't understand,' wrote Goebbels in his diary, 'how the English are able to do so much damage to the Reich capital in one air raid. The picture that greeted my eye in the Wilhelmsplatz was one of utter desolation . . . Blazing fires everywhere . . . Hell itself seems to have broken loose over us. Mines and explosive bombs keep hurtling down upon the government quarter. One after another of the most important buildings begins to blaze . . .'6

Among those 'important buildings' was Speer's Armaments Ministry, which he saw burning when he ventured out on to the platform of one of the flak-towers. He promptly drove over to the scene. 'In place of my private office,' he later wrote, 'I found nothing but a huge bomb crater.' His description of one aspect of the raids is memorable:

'From the flak-tower the air raids on Berlin were an unforgettable sight, and I had constantly to be reminded of the cruel reality in order not to be completely entranced by the scene: the illumination of the parachute flares, which the Berliners called 'Christmas trees', followed by flashes of explosions which were caught by the clouds of smoke, the innumerable probing searchlights, the excitement when a plane was caught and tried to escape the cone of light, the brief flashing torch when it was hit. No doubt about it, this apocalypse provided a magnificent spectacle.'[7]

The raids of 22/23 and 23/24 November completely destroyed more than 30 major industrial premises, and damaged scores more. They also killed or injured some 9000 Berliners and, for longer or shorter periods, deprived about 200,000 of their homes. The extent of the disaster to Berlin may be gauged from the fact that the authorities rushed in 50,000 troops, two-and-a-half army divisions, to help clear the wreckage.[8]

Three nights later, after a moderately successful raid on Frankfurt, Harris struck again at Berlin. On 26/27 November he despatched a force of 433 Lancasters, with seven Mosquitoes for pathfinding. A big diversionary raid of 178 aircraft, mainly Halifaxes, against Stuttgart successfully drew off many of the German fighters; but others, mainly twin-engined aircraft, operating in what was called 'Tame Sow' fashion, caught up with the main stream and mingled with it on its return journey. That night the 'missing rate' rose to 6.2 per cent, with a further 14 aircraft crashing in England. In Berlin, bombs hit many unintended places such as the zoo, where leopards and other wild beasts escaped to add to the terrors of the night. But the damage, which included the complete destruction of 38 plants producing war material, was again huge.

Especially grievous to the Germans were the hits on the Rheinmetall Borsig works (by 25 high-explosive bombs and more than 10,000 incendiaries) and on the Alkett works producing tanks and guns – one of the most important munitions plants in all Germany. Hearing this was ablaze, Hitler personally intervened and ordered fire engines to the site in such profusion that, according to Speer, they completely blocked the surrounding streets and prevented attention to other fires.[9] Goebbels in his diary recorded: 'That is a heavy blow. The Führer, too, is much depressed . . . The situation has become ever more alarming since one industrial plant after another has been set on fire.'[10]

According to a German report the raids on Berlin in the latter part of November resulted, apart from the industrial damage, in the deaths of 4430 people and the 'bombing out', for periods of more than a month, of nearly 418,000. Four big assaults had by that time been delivered, and a fifth was soon to follow. On 2/3 December 458 aircraft took off for Berlin. But incorrectly forecast winds blew some of the markings astray, and the scattered damage scarcely compensated for a 'missing rate' of 8.7 per cent. Among the casualties were two of the new breed of war reporter, from the *Daily Mail* and the *Sydney Sun*. They were in one of the five aircraft of 460 (Australian) Squadron to be shot down that night.

For some time now Harris had been pressing the Air Ministry to give him greater control over the ancillary forces increasingly involved in the raids. The Ministry met his wishes, and on 3 December 1943 a new Group, No. 100 (Bomber Support), formed within Bomber Command. Its task was partly to fly INTRUDER operations against the German night-fighters and their airfields (undertaken thus far mainly by aircraft of Fighter Command) and partly to develop and operate RCM (radio countermeasures) against the enemy air forces. Originally the RAF had developed these for defensive purposes – the ground stations of No. 80 Wing of Fighter Command, for instance, had distorted, or more popularly 'bent', the Luftwaffe's navigational beams during its night attacks on Britain. With the changing course of the war, however, RCM had by now become a potent weapon in the British bomber offensive.

The new Group, under the command of the signals expert, Air Vice-Marshal E. B. Addison, took over 80 Wing (which Addison had previously commanded) and three INTRUDER Squadrons (Nos. 141, 169 and 239) from Fighter Command. These were mainly of Mosquitoes, though one still had a few Beaufighters. In addition, the Group included among its flying units No. 192 Squadron, mainly of Wellingtons, which had been accompanying the bomber stream and investigating the enemy's radar and the efficiency of the RAF's countermeasures. Of the many devices, ground-based or airborne, that the Group was to employ, some were well established, such as MANDREL, for jamming the German early-warning radar, and others were soon to be developed. In December 1943 100 Group's most pressing task, apart from flying the offensive INTRUDER operations, was to jam German night-fighter communications. One important new device used for homing on to the enemy fighters' radar emissions was SERRATE. In the months to come, SERRATE patrols*, usually by no

---

* One SERRATE duo, Harry White and Mike Allen of 141 Squadron, both of whom earned a DFC and 2 Bars, was credited with the destruction of no fewer than twelve enemy aircraft.

more than half-a-dozen Mosquitoes, were to make an increasingly useful contribution to the bomber offensive. And many other devices with arcane code-names would also help – CORONA, for instance, for jamming the German night-fighters' High Frequency R/T, or CIGAR, ground and airborne, which jammed their Very High Frequencies.

On 7 December, a few days after 100 Group came into being, Harris addressed a long letter to the Air Ministry. In it he recounted progress, and made a remarkable claim. Evidently impressed by the achievements against Berlin thus far, and not discouraged by the heavy loss on 2/3 December, he asserted that if three conditions were fulfilled his Lancasters could virtually win the war by themselves. The conditions were that Lancaster production and repair should be given top priority, to increase the present slender margin between production and wastage; that the promised supply of navigational aids should be maintained; and that the rate of loss should not average more than 5 per cent. If these conditions were met, Harris considered that 'the Lancaster force alone should be sufficient, but only just sufficient, to produce in Germany by April 1st 1944 a state of devastation in which surrender is inevitable'.[11]

Harris's hopes found little echo in the Air Ministry. The Air Staff view remained the same – that raids on Berlin or other towns would weaken but not in themselves defeat Germany. Undeterred, Harris went on to mount ten more major attacks on Berlin within the next eleven weeks. During this period, however, he also delivered weighty assaults elsewhere, with particular success against Leipzig on 2/3 December. After this raid Goebbels wrote in his diary: '. . . whole rows of houses went up in smoke. The centre of the city was especially hard hit. Almost all public buildings, theatres, the University, the Supreme Court, the Exhibition Halls* etc. have either been completely destroyed or seriously damaged. About 150,000–200,000 people are without shelter.'[12]

The second half of December saw three more major attacks on Berlin. All inflicted great damage, but not as much as those in November. Two were achieved inexpensively, but the raid on 16/17 December proved costly. The 'missing rate' was no more than 5 per cent, but large numbers of the bombers returned to find low clouds overhanging their airfields. Some crews took to their parachutes, and altogether 29 of the Lancasters crashed, with the loss of at least 140 aircrew.

Summing up the position at the end of 1943, Harris reckoned that

---

* Some of the Exhibition Halls had become factories for Junkers aircraft.

from March of that year ten times more damage had been done to Germany's industrial cities than during all the preceding period of the war. He could also claim that the missing rate had been lower in 1943 than in 1942, while the tonnage of bombs dropped had been two-and-a-half times greater.[13]

The new year, 1944, opened with raids on Berlin by 421 aircraft on 1/2 January and 383 the following night. By the standards of 22/23 November they were relatively ineffective, and incurred losses of around 7 per cent. A successful raid on Stettin and an unsuccessful one on Brunswick then followed before, on 20/21 January, another huge force – 769 aircraft – took off for Berlin. Some 70 failed to get there, but the rest inflicted massive damage on factories, railways and power stations. Their 'missing rate' was 4.8 per cent – too high for satisfaction but much more sustainable than the 8.8 per cent incurred in a raid on Magdeburg the following night.

January 1944 then ended with three more full-scale attacks on Berlin, each by over 500 aircraft. The concentration by now achieved was such that 20 or more aircraft were attacking during each minute of the raid. Immense damage resulted to public buildings (including Hitler's new Chancellery and Goebbels's Propaganda Ministry), to industrial premises, and, as usual, to housing – for longer or shorter periods some 200,000 more people lost their homes. But all this was effected only at a high price. The percentage of aircraft missing from the three raids – 6.8 – was beyond Harris's acceptable average for the success of the campaign.

These three raids took place within the space of four nights, between 27/28 and 30/31 January. To send such large forces at such short intervals to so distant and fiercely defended a target as Berlin was indeed pressing Bomber Command hard. Some of the scheduled aircraft could not be made ready in time, and many of the crews had a bare few hours' rest between the operations. All this tended to damp the spirits of the squadrons hardest hit. There was never any danger of a collapse in morale; but the combination of the winter weather, the recent extreme demands, and the disappearance of so many fellow aircrew made January–February 1944 a bleak time for many in the Command.

The pressures of the winter of 1943–4 may be seen in the logbook of Pilot Officer Michael Beetham, who survived to become in the fullness of time Marshal of the Royal Air Force Sir Michael Beetham and Chief of the Air Staff. After joining 50 Squadron as a newly fledged pilot Beetham made the customary initiatory trip as 'second dicky' – in his case to Düsseldorf – and then faced his first operation with his own crew. The squadron was detailed for the 18/19 November 1943 raid on Berlin, but his commanding officer left Beetham's name off the list, telling him that Berlin was 'a bit tough for a new pilot'. However, the squadron's next assignment, on 22/23 November was again Berlin, so Beetham had to go with the rest – his CO explaining: 'it looks like being all Berlin from now on.' Beetham went on to do nine more raids on Berlin in the ensuing weeks.

With bad weather greatly restricting operations over Germany, the most significant of Bomber Command's attacks during the first half of February 1944 were on precise targets in France. On 8/9 February 12 Lancasters of 617 Squadron, the 'Dambusters', led by their new commanding officer, Wing Commander Leonard Cheshire, destroyed most of the Gnome et Rhône aero-engine factory at Limoges. The attack, made at low level – like Cheshire's marking, which took place at 50–100 feet – was extraordinarily successful. By three runs over the target Cheshire first warned the night shift at the factory of the attack, so that they could take shelter. Then ten of the Lancasters planted a bomb each – some of them the new 12,000-lb High Capacity – on the factory, completely crippling production for some months to come. To crown their feat, the whole squadron returned safely.*

This raid showed that Bomber Command could now attack at night with a new degree of accuracy. The circumstances, however, had been favourable. The target had been in occupied France, not Germany; fighters had not intervened; and the close defences of the factory had consisted of only two machine guns. An attack of a similar nature attempted by 617 Squadron four nights later against the Antheor viaduct in the south of France showed that no magic transformation had yet taken place. The viaduct, difficult to approach and heavily defended, remained intact.

By this time small forces of Mosquitoes guided by OBOE Mark III or the new navigational aid GH† had for some three months been attempting precision attacks by night on targets in Germany. Delivered from high level, these had proved remarkably economical but had not yet achieved any great success in destroying key plants. These attacks and the expertise of 617 Squadron nevertheless encouraged the belief that greater precision in night-bombing was becoming possible. Moreover the Air Staff were also beginning to question whether Harris was

---

* The 12,000-lb HC was a blast bomb formed from three 4000-lb 'cookies'.
† For a note on GH, see pp. 245–5.

sufficiently coordinating the area offensive with the more selective attacks of the Americans. On 14 January the Deputy Chief of the Air Staff, Air Marshal Norman Bottomley, had sent Harris a letter calling his attention to the POINTBLANK directive of the previous June, under which Harris was to direct Bomber Command's actions, as far as practicable, 'against industrial centres associated with those industries selected for precise attack by the American bomber forces'. Bottomley asked Harris to 'adhere to the spirit' of this directive, and in particular to attack 'those industrial centres associated with the German fighter air-frame factories and ball-bearing industry'.[14]

This reminder from Bottomley appears to have made little difference to Harris's immediate actions. During the rest of January he had continued to attack Berlin (which of course remained officially a priority target) and had launched a big raid against Magdeburg (which was not on the priority-list at all). On 28 January the Air Ministry accordingly instructed him in more precise terms. To complement the Americans' attacks on particular plants Bomber Command's first-priority targets should be six German towns particularly associated with the production of ball bearings or fighters. In order of importance they were Schweinfurt, Leipzig, Brunswick, Regensburg, Augsburg and Gotha. Berlin was to be attacked, but only when the conditions were not suitable for operations against these six towns.[15]

In the first fortnight of February bad weather prevented major operations over Germany. The Americans, who had prepared a massive onslaught against German fighter-strength, had to bide their time. Then, on the first sign of suitable weather, Harris once more struck – against Berlin. On 15/16 February he despatched the largest force yet sent against the German capital – no fewer than 891 aircraft. They dropped 2645 tons of bombs, did enormous damage and returned with less than 5 per cent missing. Had this been Harris's last big blow in the campaign, historians would possibly have drawn up the Battle of Berlin balance sheet more in his favour. Unfortunately, there was one more big attack still to come.

In accordance with the Air Staff instructions Harris then integrated his operations more closely with those of the Americans. With notable exceptions, such as the effective but costly raid against Schweinfurt on 14 October 1943 when 60 out of 228 bombers failed to return, the US Eighth Air Force had thus far operated over Germany against 'fringe' targets, such as the north German ports. This was because on missions of deeper penetration the 'self-defending' formations of Fortresses or Liberators had suffered too heavily from the attacks of the German fighters. During the autumn of 1943, however, longer-range escort fighters with drop tanks had gradually become available, at first the P-47 Thunderbolt and then with greater range the P-38 Lightning. The Lightnings had begun to provide escort as far as the North Sea ports; but the Lightning in turn was surpassed by the P-51 Mustang with Merlin engine, which with drop tanks could provide escort to Berlin. In January 1944 the Americans allocated their Mustangs exclusively to work with the Eighth Air Force, and by the following month this could call on about a hundred of them. Together with the (as yet) far more numerous P-47s and 38s, they transformed the situation in the air over Germany and made profitable the great series of attacks on German fighter production which became known as 'Big Week'. In these the 'Mighty Eighth' was aided both by the US Fifteenth Air Force from Italy and by RAF Bomber Command.

It was Bomber Command which in fact began 'Big Week' on the night of 19/20 February, when 823 aircraft set out to bomb Leipzig, home of four Messerschmitt factories and a ball-bearings plant. Cloud completely covered the city, the bombing was on sky-markers, results could not be seen, and 9.5 per cent of the force failed to return. But the next day, with the skies at last clear, some 200 bombers of the Eighth Air Force, with close fighter escort, followed up the attack. Subsequent photographs showed serious damage to five of the ten main targets.

All told, over 1000 American bombers took off that day in a series of attacks which ranged from the aircraft factories in Leipzig to others in Gotha, Brunswick and Rostock. Harris promptly followed up the next night, 20/21 February, by a massive and inexpensive (1.5 per cent missing) raid on Stuttgart, inflicting heavy damage not only on the city centre but more importantly on the Bosch dynamo and magneto works. Then the following day, with 861 aircraft, and the day after that, with 600, the Americans were out again, attacking Brunswick, a Junkers factory at Halberstadt, and Luftwaffe aircraft parks and airfields.

On 24 February, as well as attacking Gotha and Rostock, the Eighth Air Force took on the ball-bearings plant at Schweinfurt once again. This time Bomber Command followed the Americans, 734 aircraft making an area attack in two separate waves during the ensuing night. Schweinfurt was a target to which Harris had strongly objected, and he attacked it now only after the Air Staff had given it an unequivocal 'top priority' and ordered him to make an attempt as soon as possible. He had argued that the town was distant and difficult to find, and that anyway the ball-bearings industry was one of the Ministry of Economic Warfare's 'panacea' targets, the destruction of which was always expected to cripple the enemy at a stroke but never did. In the event, the huge Bomber Command force which attacked the town suffered no more than moderate losses – 4.5 per cent missing. But though the orginal marking was accurate the actual bombing 'crept back' by up to six miles. Probably most of the considerable damage later photographed was done by the Americans the day before. And, as Harris had predicted, the raid, though serious for the Germans, proved to be no panacea. Since the American attack of 14 October 1943 the Germans had dispersed some of the industry, established priorities in the use of ball bearings, extended the use of substitutes, and discovered large reserves of ball bearings held by manufacturing firms.

While the Americans the following day went on to deliver attacks on aircraft or aircraft-related factories in Augsburg, Stuttgart, Regensburg and Brunswick, Harris prepared his further contribution to 'Big Week'. On 25/26 February, in clear weather, nearly 600 bombers made a devastating attack on Augsburg. At a moderate cost – 3.6 per cent missing – they seriously damaged an engineering works and an aircraft components factory, at the same time obliterating most of the historic centre of the city and making some 85,000 people homeless.

This was a 'Combined Bomber Offensive' of a more integrated kind than before. The following month the close coordination continued, with an increasing weight of bombs falling on targets in France. On German towns important to the aircraft industry Bomber Command made four huge raids between 1/2 and 22/23 March, three times with over 800 aircraft. The attacks fell twice on Stuttgart, with serious damage not only to the town but also to the Bosch and the Daimler-Benz works, and twice on Frankfurt. In all cases the losses were sustainable, varying from 0.7 to 4.3 per cent. At Frankfurt, where some 55,000 people were 'bombed out', the industrial areas as well as the city centre suffered badly, and within thirty-six hours 162 American B-17s added to the devastation. A municipal report recorded that the three raids had dealt 'a blow which simply ended the existence of the Frankfurt which had been built up since the Middle Ages'.

The recent massive American daylight operations, coupled to a lesser degree with Bomber Command's attacks on Augsburg, Stuttgart and Frankfurt, had inflicted wounds from which the German aircraft industry would never fully recover. It was put under Speer's direction and went on producing ever more fighters, but only at the expense of other aircraft types. In the course of combat the Americans, though their own losses were severe, had made sharp inroads into the strength of the German day-fighters. But nothing had happened as yet which immediately reduced the strength of the German night-fighters, of which there were by January 1943 about 1000 operational – mainly Ju 88Cs and the faster Me 110Gs. Disorganised at first by WINDOW and the collapse of the Kammhuber system, they had partially recovered through their 'Wild Sow' tactics and improved airborne radar, and their formidable 20-mm cannon and other weapons continued to outmatch the British bombers' machine guns. Bomber Command still had much to suffer from them.

On 24/25 March, after concentrating on other targets for five weeks, Harris ordered another great raid on Berlin – which the Americans themselves had by now twice attacked under Mustang escort. Whether he considered the weather unsuitable over all the six other towns of high priority in his directive, or whether he was eager to strike one more crushing blow before his operations became geared to the re-entry into France, is not clear. At all events, a huge force of 811 aircraft set forth, only to find the north wind far stronger than predicted, and stronger than the corrected versions transmitted to the aircraft in flight. The bomber stream became scattered, some aircraft finding themselves over Germany when they were meant to be approaching over Denmark, and others on the return journey tangling with the defences of the Ruhr. The raid inflicted great damage on industry and homes alike, but German fighters wrought havoc with the stream on its homeward flight, and 44 Lancasters and 28 Halifaxes – nearly 9 per cent of the force – failed to return. Of the aircrew involved, 392 lost their lives, 131 became prisoners of war, and four were shot down but managed to avoid capture.

Only two nights later Bomber Command was nevertheless able to make a devastating attack on Essen, using 683 Lancasters and 22 Mosquitoes, and at a cost of only nine aircraft missing. But this success was immediately followed by a disaster. On 30/31 March 795 bombers took off for Nuremberg, a centre not only of administration but of the aircraft manufacturing industry. The night was moonlit, but there was a forecast of protective high cloud for the outward journey. This failed to materialise. Instead German 'Tame Sow' fighters appeared in great numbers, with the result that no fewer than 85 of the bombers went down on their way to, or over, the target. Little damage befell Nuremberg, and the total of 95 aircraft failing to return was the heaviest loss in one raid ever recorded in the history of air warfare. The human cost to Bomber Command was 540 aircrew killed, 25 wounded, and 148 made prisoners of war.

Among the many acts of heroic determination that night one seemed outstanding, and was fittingly recognised by the award of a posthumous Victoria Cross. The Halifax of Pilot Officer C. J. Barton, of 578 Squadron, suffered heavy damage in a fighter attack before reaching Nuremberg. Owing to a misunderstanding over the intercom, the navigator, the wireless operator and another member of the crew then baled out. Barton nevertheless carried on to the target, bombed, and on three engines set course for home. Reaching the Durham coast just as his petrol ran out, he made a forced landing which cost him his life, but from which the three remaining members of the crew escaped only slightly injured.

The costly final attack on Berlin, followed by the disaster of Nuremberg, cast a shadow over Bomber Command's considerable achievements in the last weeks before it came under General Eisenhower's higher control for the re-entry into France. The heavy toll exacted by the German defences, and particularly by the night-fighters, has persuaded some historians, and most notably the authors of the British official history, *The Strategic Air Offensive Against Germany*, that only the incidence of the Normandy invasion saved Bomber Command from humiliation – or, at least, saved it for its later tasks in the war. Of the Battle of Berlin the official history writes: 'From the operational point of view, it was more than a failure. It was a defeat.'

One should note here the careful qualification 'from the operational point of view'. The official historians do not suggest that the defeat was strategical. It was indeed a defeat for Harris's higher hopes; but it was not a defeat for the agreed Allied strategy, which envisaged no more than weakening the German war economy and war machine, and so helping the Russians and improving the chances of a successful cross-Channel invasion.

But was the Battle of Berlin in fact a tactical, or operational, defeat for Bomber Command? From nearly 8700 sorties in the sixteen major raids between 18/19 November 1943 and 24/25 March 1944, roughly 500 failed to return – a 'missing rate' of 5.8 per cent. This was 0.8 per cent outside Harris's parameter, but on other operations during the period, especially those over France, the missing rate was much lower, and so the overall loss became sustainable. Bomber Command's raids on Berlin were certainly expensive, and on the whole increasingly so, but they ceased – except for persistent minor attacks by Mosquitoes – not because the losses had become insupportable but because Harris's forces were needed in the preparations for the cross-Channel invasion.

The strength of the German defence organisation, the skill and valour of the Luftwaffe night-fighter pilots, and the courage and stoicism of the civil population, coupled with the sheer size of the capital, ensured that Berlin continued to function, and even, with rationalisation, to increase production in priority categories. The cessation of major Bomber Command raids after March 1944 also, of course, permitted recovery. But though Bomber Command had paid a heavy price, it had inflicted enormous damage – on factories, power stations, gasworks, public buildings, railways and, inevitably, housing; a German record places the total of Berliners rendered homeless at 1½ million. Moreover Bomber Command remained strong enough not only to play its part in the great cross-Channel venture later, but also, more immediately, to cooperate with the Americans in the intensive assault on German fighter-strength which they launched in late February, and which was to prove a turning point in the air battle over Germany.

Whatever the Berlin raids failed to achieve, they certainly injured the German war economy and forced the Germans to devote to local defensive purposes guns and fighters which they could have used elsewhere – against, for instance, the Russians. If the Battle of Berlin cannot be listed with those of the Ruhr and Hamburg as an outright victory for Bomber Command, it nevertheless played its part in the grim business of 'progressively weakening' Germany.[16]

19

Prelude to 'Overlord'

O n 17 August 1943, as Harris's bombers streamed east for Peenemünde, the British and American Chiefs of Staff were conferring at Quebec. There they approved the outline plans for OVERLORD, the great cross-Channel invasion heralding the liberation of western Europe.[1] At the same time they confirmed 1 May 1944 as the target date for the landings – but warned that the demands of forthcoming operations in Italy might set these back to June or July.*

In the next three months the plans were elaborated, the forces allocated, the commanders selected. An early appointment, confirmed on 15 November, was that of Air Marshal Sir Trafford Leigh-Mallory, head of Fighter Command, to be Air Commander-in-Chief of the specially created Allied Expeditionary Air Force (AEAF).† This new formation, intended to support and later accompany the invading forces, was well provided with fighters, fighter-bombers, light bombers, medium bombers and reconnaissance aircraft. It had no heavy bombers – but could request their support.

Not unnaturally, Leigh-Mallory quickly pointed out that so vague

---

* The outline plans were the work of an Allied team in London under Lieutenant-General Frederick Morgan – COSSAC (Chief of Staff to the – as yet unnamed – Supreme Allied Commander).

† AEAF was a combination of the US Ninth Air Force and the recently created RAF 2nd Tactical Air Force (which included fighters and fighter-bombers from Fighter Command, and the medium bombers of No. 2 Group from Bomber Command). Also under AEAF was the remaining 'stay-at-home' part of Fighter Command, which was renamed Air Defence of Great Britain.

an arrangement about heavy bombers was unsatisfactory, since he would certainly need their help for his operations to succeed. The planners had in fact not been unaware of this. Their difficulty had been how to arrange for it without disrupting the strategic bombing offensive against Germany – or, for that matter, offending the susceptibilities of Harris and General Spaatz.

All the RAF's heavy bombers were under Harris in Bomber Command. All the American heavy bombers in the European theatre were, from 6 January 1944, under Spaatz in USSAFE, later USSTAF, (United States Strategical Air Forces in Europe) – a new upper command covering the US Eighth Air Force in England and the US Fifteenth Air Force in North Africa and Italy. Equally ardent champions of strategical air operations, Harris had long favoured the destruction of German industrial towns, Spaatz the bombing of selected targets such as aircraft factories and oil refineries. Neither would willingly contemplate the transfer of any part of his forces to tactical work with the armies, and least of all to an organisation commanded by an airman with no experience of heavy bombers and little recent experience of military operations – Leigh-Mallory.

The two bomber commanders made their views, along with their objections, very plain. While accepting that OVERLORD was settled policy, they urged that their forces should still be used in distinctively strategic roles. Spaatz forcefully and persistently advocated sustained offensives against oil and the German Air Force – offensives, he thought, which would rapidly paralyse the whole German war machine. Harris was also true to form. On 13 January 1944 he addressed a long letter to Portal, Leigh-Mallory, and General Montgomery (by now commander-designate of the land forces in the initial operations). In it he stressed that his bombers had to operate by night, could not be expected to hit small targets, were extremely dependent on weather, and needed several hours' notice before they could take off. Moreover, if they were diverted from their normal tasks to help the armies, German industry would rapidly recover from the damage it had thus far suffered. He concluded:

> It is clear that the best and indeed the only effective support which Bomber Command can give OVERLORD is the intensification of attacks on suitable industrial centres in Germany as and when the opportunity offers. If we attempt to substitute for this process attacks on gun emplacements, beach defences, communications, or drops in occupied territory, we shall commit the irremediable error of diverting our best weapon from a military function for

which it has been equipped and trained to tasks which it cannot effectively carry out. Though this might give a specious appearance of supporting the Army, in reality it would be the greatest disservice we could do them. It would lead directly to disaster.[2]

The British Chiefs of Staff were keen enough on the bombing of Germany, but they could not accept Harris's view that it must still take precedence even during OVERLORD. On 30 January 1944 Portal replied tactfully but firmly:

> The United Nations are irrevocably committed to OVERLORD and I am sure that both before and during that operation Bomber Command will wish to help to the utmost, even if this means trying new techniques and tactics against the kind of targets which you rightly consider to be outside the scope of normal night-bomber operations ... The extent to which the support of Bomber Command will be required in the various stages of OVERLORD will be determined by the Combined Chiefs of Staff after they have considered General Eisenhower's recommendations. The advice which your representatives can afford the Supreme Commander's planning staff should do much to ensure that the tasks Bomber Command will be asked to perform will be reasonable and practicable.[3]

Meanwhile Harris's fears that his force might be misemployed had been lessened by the appointment on 17 January 1944 of Air Chief Marshal Sir Arthur Tedder as Deputy to the newly announced Supreme Commander of the Allied Expeditionary Force, General Eisenhower. At Supreme Headquarters, Tedder would be primarily responsible for air matters; and in Tedder, Harris knew that he would be dealing with an airman of wide views, sharp intelligence, and a proven track record from 1941 onwards in the campaigns of the Middle East, North Africa and the Mediterranean.

Into the planning for OVERLORD obtruded a far less welcome concern – the threat from the German V-weapons. The attack on Peenemünde on 17 August 1943 had temporarily, at least, disrupted the German Army's long-range V-2 rocket programme, but it had done little to interfere with the development of the Luftwaffe's pilotless aircraft, the V-1 flying bomb. Indeed the existence of this, though it had been more than once reported by agents since the first mention in June 1943 of a 'bomb with wings', had not been established with certainty by the Allies until late August, when a prototype V-1 crashed on the German-occupied Danish island of Bornholm. Further evidence had then accumulated, notably from the French Resistance, and by 25 September 1943 Dr R. V. Jones was warning the Chiefs of Staff: 'It is probable that the German Air Force has been developing a pilotless aircraft for long-range bombardment in competition with the rocket, and it is very possible that the aircraft will arrive first.'[4] By this time some very large concrete emplacements had begun to appear in northern France, and it was not difficult to deduce some connection between these and a forthcoming V-weapon attack. On 27 August 1943 B-17s of the US Eighth Air Force began countermeasures, attacking the first structure at Watten, near St Omer.

The purpose of these 'large sites' (as the Allies termed them), which – though they did not know it – had underground chambers big enough to hold tens of thousands of people, in fact varied. The general British assumption at the time was that the sites were for storing and launching rockets. In fact, of the seven identified, four were apparently for the assembly, storing and firing of flying bombs, one for the storing and firing of rockets, one for housing batteries of long-range guns, and one for the manufacture of the chemicals used in firing the V-weapons.[5] In any case, they clearly called for attack, and the work fell on the Eighth Air Force and the AEAF.

Very soon, however, another type of concrete site began to appear in northern France. Its main features, apart from five or six steel and concrete buildings with massive walls, were two structures each nearly 100 yards long and shaped like skis. They seemed obviously intended – and were indeed intended – for the storage and launching of flying bombs. By the end of November 1943 79 of these 'ski sites', as they became known, had been spotted, including seven in the Cherbourg peninsula. All, and many more under construction, were within 130 miles of London, on which they were aligned.

The time was now obviously ripe for major countermeasures. In view of the large number of sites, and the fact that bad weather had restricted attacks by the AEAF, Bomber Command was required to help. By this time further reconnaissance of the Luftwaffe airfield at Peenemünde had revealed similar ski structures, with a flying bomb on one, and so had clearly established the function of the ski sites. In a joint programme of destruction in which he reluctantly joined, Harris had the task of attacking eight of the sites. Between 16/17 December 1943 and 25/26 January 1944, he in fact attacked seven of the eight, several more than once, using forces of an average strength of 50–60 aircraft and mainly employing Stirlings – by now deemed unfit for operations over Germany. Losses were extraordinarily light – only one aircraft from over 400 sorties – but success was not invariable, and at the end of January Harris managed to extricate his Command from the task. The CROSSBOW attacks – as countermeasures against V-weapon sites were termed – nonetheless continued, with the Mosquitoes of 2 Group playing a notable part. By the end of May 1944 combined American and British effort had destroyed 103 of the 140 ski sites identified.[6]

The attacks by the AEAF, and to a lesser extent by Bomber Command, were cumulatively so effective that the Germans abandoned their ski-site programme and began to build sites which were smaller and much better concealed. These became known to the Allies as the 'modified' sites. Photographic reconnaissance first discovered one on 27 April 1944, and then twenty more within the next fortnight. Clearly the Allies' attacks had to be switched from what were in fact abandoned ski sites to the modified sites. But this, as Harris pointed out, was far from ideal work for his heavy bombers. Bomber Command accordingly took no more part in operations against the launching sites – until, in mid-June, flying bombs actually began to reach England. Nevertheless by its attacks on Germany, most notably the raid on Peenemünde, and by its operations against the ski sites, it had already done much to delay the opening of the V-weapon onslaught.

The proposed bombing policy for OVERLORD, in the preparatory as in the assault phases, emanated from Leigh-Mallory's headquarters and quickly secured the support of Tedder. Soon known as the 'Transportation Plan', it was aimed at the German armies' known dependence on rail transport. In the final stages before the landings there would be attacks on coastal batteries, radar stations, and specific railway routes and bridges; but by then the bomber forces would have created, it was hoped, a 'railway desert' between western Germany and the French coast. This was to be done by attacking a large number of railway centres – 83, finally – at which locomotives and wagons were maintained and repaired. Such depots would have tracks and marshalling yards which would also be usefully damaged, but the paralysis was expected to result from the destruction of the repair facilities, especially in combination later with attacks by fighter-bombers on moving locomotives.

In the formulation of this plan, Tedder's former scientific adviser in North Africa, the distinguished zoologist Professor Zuckerman, had played a leading part. It met with strong opposition from both Harris and Spaatz, whose forces would be expected to help carry it out. It also raised grave doubts in the minds of Churchill and other members of the War Cabinet, who thought that the incidental, and inevitable, casualties among French and Belgian civilians would harm the Allied cause. To assist a final decision, Harris was told to carry out some trial attacks.

On 6/7 March 1944 261 Halifaxes and 6 Mosquitoes duly took off against the railway centre at Trappes, south-west of Paris. Without loss to themselves, they did enormous damage to sheds, track and rolling stock. The following night 304 bombers raided a similar centre at Le Mans with equal success and again without loss. On 13/14 March the trial continued with another attack on Le Mans, resulting in the destruction of 15 locomotives and some 800 coaches. Then, on 15/16 and 16/17 March, followed two attacks on the yards at Amiens, again with impressive damage and few losses. From the five operations the cost in French lives proved to be around 110, far fewer than had been feared.

Though a further operation against the yards at Laon had less success, the Transportation Plan clearly promised well. Spaatz still remained resolutely opposed, but in the light of experience Harris swung round: the OBOE-directed attacks had so obviously been both accurate and inexpensive. At a meeting with Eisenhower, Tedder and the main air commanders on 25 March, Portal, too, who had previously favoured attacking targets in Germany for a longer period, gave it his support.[7] Thenceforth 'Transportation' attacks continued apace, though Churchill and the Foreign Office still expressed great anxiety about repercussions from the deaths of friendly civilians. Indeed Churchill secured revision of the target-list to eliminate all attacks likely to result in the deaths of more than 100–150 of the local population and insisted that the total fatal casualties during the execution of the plan should not exceed 10,000.

Also in the last week of March, Portal accepted a new and clearer arrangement for the higher control of the heavy bombers. Thus far this power had resided in him as the agent of the Combined Chiefs of Staff. For the duration of OVERLORD, however, including the preparatory phase, Eisenhower had insisted that it be vested in his own hands as Supreme Allied Commander, but had also stated that it would be exercised through Tedder. With this assurance, Portal was content to accept the change. Officially Bomber Command, like USSTAF, came under the 'direction' – the word was tactfully preferred to 'command' or 'control' – of Eisenhower at SHAEF (Supreme Headquarters Allied Expeditionary Force) from 14 April 1944.[8] In practice Harris

– though not Spaatz – had by then already been operating on the SHAEF-backed Transportation Plan for five weeks.

In the final allocation of tasks in connection with the Transportation Plan, Bomber Command emerged with the heaviest burden. Harris in the end dealt with 37 of the railway centres, the Eighth Air Force 26, and AEAF 20. Bomber Command dropped nearly 45,000 tons of bombs on the centres, or twice as much as the other two formations put together. Harris, initially so opposed to the plan, prided himself on his Command's effort and the accuracy of the attacks. In his *Bomber Offensive* he explained that the targets were only lightly defended and could therefore be bombed at a lower level than usual. He wrote: 'This of course made for increased accuracy of attack . . . In fact I may as well say outright that Bomber Command's night bombing, from this point onwards, proved to be rather more accurate, much heavier in weight, and more concentrated, than the American daylight attacks, a fact which was afterwards clearly recognized by SHAEF when the time came for the bombing of German troop concentrations within a mile or so of our own troops.'[9]

In all, from the opening assault on Trappes on 6/7 March until the final pre-D-Day blow against the same target on 2/3 June, Bomber Command put in 69 such attacks, involving nearly 9000 sorties. In the course of these it lost only 198 aircraft, or 1.8 per cent. The damage it did was enormous. From Cologne and Aachen, through Ghent and Courtrai to the centres around Paris such as Gennevilliers and Vaires, to as far afield as Le Mans, Orléans, Tours and Saumur, the railway targets became scenes of desolation. In the end about two-thirds of Harris's 37 were classed as completely out of action for a month or more and the remainder as needing only some further attention from the fighter-bombers.

Several times, unhappily, the toll of friendly civilian lives was greater than the prescribed limit of 100–150 for each attack. At Courtrai on 26/27 March 252 people lost their lives; at Lille on 9/10 April 456; and at Ghent the following night, 482.[10] A much more frequent total, however, was around 50; and when a seriously perturbed Churchill raised the point with Roosevelt on 7 May whether, for fear of otherwise alienating the French and Belgians, the Transportation Plan should be dropped, the President gave a firm reply. He was 'not prepared to impose from this distance any restraint on military action by the responsible commanders that in their opinion might militate against the success of OVERLORD.'[11] The Transportation Plan held good.

In the end, the number of French and Belgian civilians killed was much smaller than the 10,000 'limit'. And, as Eisenhower pointed out, it was, sadly, part of the price that France and Belgium had to pay for their liberation – something which he felt sure their patriotic peoples would understand. Fortunately there was no doubt about the effectiveness of the bombing, memorably described in Harris's post-war *Despatch*: 'In most of the attacks the bombing accuracy was of a high, and in many of an outstandingly high, order. For instance, at two important centres near Paris – Juvisy and La Chapelle – the whole railway complex was almost annihilated as the result of single attacks; engine roundhouses and depots, marshalling yards, rolling stock and nearly all other facilities had almost entirely disappeared. Reconnaissance showed complete wildernesses resembling nothing so much as a telescopic view of the extinct craters of the moon.'[12]

The attacks on rail centres by Bomber Command, AEAF and the Eighth Air Force proved catastrophic for the Germans. After two months the number of serviceable wagons in the region affected had been reduced from some 70,000 to 10,000; and by D-Day, following further attacks by the tactical air forces on moving trains, only about 12 per cent of the rolling stock in the Nord system remained fit for use.[13] The result was seen in the immense difficulty the Germans then experienced in bringing up reinforcements to meet the Allied invasion. This problem was exemplified in the movement of a division which was rushed across from Poland. It arrived in western Germany within three days, only to take another four weeks reaching the Normandy battlefront.[14]

Though the railway centres accounted for much of Bomber Command's effort during April and May 1944, they were far from being its only targets. Harris also kept up the pressure on German air power by attacking airfields in France – notably at Montdidier, Tours, Nantes, Rennes and Brest – and aircraft factories. A particularly important raid, both in technique and results, was that on 5/6 April against the Gnome et Rhône aero-works at Toulouse. The attacking force of 144 Lancasters came entirely from 5 Group, with Leonard Cheshire of 617 Squadron doing the initial marking at low level from a Mosquito. Two Lancasters of 617 Squadron followed on to reinforce the marking with great accuracy, and this led to a raid which completely destroyed the factory. Harris had already found it necessary, for tactical reasons, to operate 'split' raids over Germany – i.e. against two or more objectives on the same night – and the accuracy now displayed by 5 Group led him to a further decision. Thenceforth he normally entrusted the Group, the largest in the Command, with its own marking, independent of the Pathfinder Force.[15]

Among Bomber Command's other cross-Channel targets during the OVERLORD preparatory period were ammunition dumps and military camps. At Mouilly-le-Camp on 3/4 May a raid by 360 bombers severely damaged about 150 buildings, destroyed 37 tanks and scores of vehicles, and killed some 200 German soldiers, many of them panzer NCOs. Unfortunately German fighters came up before the attack was over and 42 of the bombers – 11.7 per cent – failed to return. Equally effective, and much less costly, was an attack by 331 aircraft on 27/28 May against a camp at Bourg Leopold, in Belgium.

Though targets in France and Belgium bore the brunt of Bomber Command's pre-OVERLORD attacks, Harris also managed to operate farther afield. The always profitable minelaying continued – sometimes by more than 100 aircraft – and Germany itself was not neglected. Fortunately for their harmonious relationship, Tedder and Harris were in complete agreement that if the weight of attack were lifted entirely from Germany she would not only make speedy industrial recovery but would also transfer anti-aircraft guns and fighters from the Reich to invasion-threatened France and Belgium.

Bomber Command's most constant, though not heaviest, form of attack on Germany during April and May 1944 was by small forces of 30 or so Mosquitoes. These kept up an offensive night after night against German cities and particular objectives within them. At least a dozen towns – Berlin, Cologne, Hamburg and Düsseldorf among them – suffered these nuisance raids, with Berlin the target many times. From all these Mosquito operations the losses were extraordinarily light – not more than one or two aircraft during the whole two months.

More surprisingly, Bomber Command during April and May managed to deliver 14 major attacks on German cities. The most heavily hit – three times by raids totalling nearly 1000 sorties – was Aachen, primarily as a railway centre. The first attack, on 11/12 April, in which over 1500 of the townspeople died, cost Bomber Command only 2.6 per cent of the 362 sorties; but the third, on 27/28 May, although the raid was all over in twelve minutes, resulted in a missing rate nearly three times as great.

Other major onslaughts during April were directed at Cologne, with only four aircraft failing to return out of 379, and Düsseldorf, with 29 aircraft lost out of 596. At Karlsruhe, on 24/25 April, a huge force of 627 Lancasters and Halifaxes, with a few Mosquitoes for marking, achieved only scattered damage; but during the same night another 260 aircraft, nearly all from 5 Group, wrought havoc at Munich and left 30,000 of the inhabitants 'bombed out'. On this occasion low-level initial marking by Cheshire of 617 Squadron led to very accurate bombing, and a variety of diversionary and support operations helped to keep losses to a moderate level. Among these auxiliary measures 165 OTU aircraft carried out a sweep to within 75 miles of the German coast; a flight from 617 Squadron made a 'spoof' attack on Milan; and No. 100 Group flew radio-jamming intruder and SERRATE* patrols.

The most completely successful of Bomber Command's nine major attacks on German towns during April 1944 was that on Essen. On 26/27 April a force of 493 bombers did enormous damage there for the loss of only six Lancasters and a Halifax. Equally effective, though at heavier cost, was the raid the following night on Friedrichshafen where 323 aircraft devastated something like two-thirds of the Zeppelin works, at that time partly engaged in producing components for V-2 rockets. By contrast, the least profitable raid of the month – no surprise to Harris – was another attempt to hit Schweinfurt. On the same night as the raid on Essen 225 aircraft took off to seek out this well-concealed and defended centre of the ball-bearing industry. Once again it proved difficult to find and to subject to any concentrated form of attack. And once again the defences took a heavy toll – 9.5 per cent – of the raiders.

During this raid on Schweinfurt there occurred an act of bravery comparable with that of the New Zealander Sergeant Ward in 1941. Sergeant Norman Jackson was the flight engineer in an aircraft of 103 Squadron. After successfully bombing Schweinfurt the Lancaster came under attack from a fighter, which scored many hits. Fire soon broke out on the upper surface of the Lancaster's starboard wing between the fuselage and the inner engine, and near a petrol tank. Though wounded, Sergeant Jackson volunteered to try to put out the flames. With his captain's permission, he jettisoned the hood and climbed out on to the fuselage. He had stuffed a hand fire-extinguisher into his jacket and clipped on his parachute, but the parachute began to open before he could get to the fire, and the straps and part of the canopy trailed back into the cockpit. Still he persisted, while two of the crew held on to the rigging lines. Then Jackson slipped, and lost the fire-extinguisher, but saved himself by clutching an air intake on the wing leading-edge. By that time the flames were licking at his hands and face, his parachute was burning, and he was swept over the wing.

---

* Homing on to the enemy night-fighters' radar emissions.

Seeing what was happening, his comrades released his rigging, and themselves baled out shortly afterwards.

Despite his wounds, his burns, and a broken ankle on landing, Jackson got down still alive. At daybreak he crawled to the nearest village and was taken prisoner, to spend the next ten months in hospital. Later he tried to escape, the second time successfully. Recognition of his extreme courage and determination came after the war, with the award of the Victoria Cross.*[16]

As the date for OVERLORD drew nearer, Bomber Command inevitably sent fewer aircraft over Germany. Nevertheless, during the moonless period of May Harris still contrived to make massive and successful raids against Duisburg and Dortmund, as well as an unsuccessful one against Brunswick. These were all accomplished at around the marginally acceptable 5 per cent rate of loss. In addition there were the two more expensive, but well rewarded, attacks on Aachen as a railway centre.

In sum, the strategy of maintaining a limited air offensive against targets in Germany, while concentrating primarily on 'Transportation' and other objectives in France and Belgium, worked well. The Germans were kept guessing as to where the Allies would invade, and they were unable to transfer guns and fighters freely to France. Berlin indeed escaped heavy attack from Bomber Command – though not entirely from the Americans – for some months to come, but elsewhere great damage was done and all at sustainable cost. In the 14 major attacks on targets in Germany in April–May 1944 Bomber Command flew over 5000 sorties and suffered an overall 'missing rate' of just above 4 per cent. Taken in conjunction with the lighter losses over France and the extraordinary economy of the harassing raids by Mosquitoes over Germany – some 600 bombing sorties during the two months, and scarcely an aircraft lost – this was a good omen for the future. It meant that Bomber Command could not only continue with its attacks but while doing so could gather further strength. On 9 March 1944 it had 65½ squadrons operational. By D-Day, three months later, it had ten more.

---

* In an interview after the war Jackson revealed the source of his strength: 'Nobody prayed harder before we took off and after we landed.' He added: 'So did all the rest of them, though nobody mentioned it.'

20

Normandy and the V-weapons

B y the beginning of June 1944 all was set for the great invasion, which awaited only a favourable weather forecast. Strong disturbances had set in and on the evening of the target date, Saturday 3 June, Eisenhower postponed the operation for twenty-four hours. In the afternoon of Sunday 4 June the weather slightly improved, and by the early hours of the following day the met. men could hold out the prospect of 'a short spell of fairly clear sky, diminished wind and good visibility, from the early hours of Tuesday (6th) until possibly the evening or early morning of the 7th'.[1] It was only a 24–36-hour break that was forecast, but Eisenhower seized his chance. That night the foremost invasion troops, who had been cooped up in their vessels for three days or more, sailed for their beaches in Normandy. Shortly after midnight the airborne contingents began to land at, or near, their appointed places. At 6.31 a.m. on Tuesday 6 June the first seaborne troops, Americans, were pouring from their landing craft on to OMAHA beach. D-Day had at last arrived, and all, or almost all, was going well.

As the great event had drawn near, Bomber Command had switched from the longer-term OVERLORD objectives like railway centres to more immediate tasks. Among the new targets were railway junctions. Starting on 26/27 May with a small raid on Lison, by D-Day Harris's bombers had done serious damage to Angers, Laval, Saumur and Nantes – all key junctions for German reinforcement of Normandy from the west and south.

In the week preceding D-Day the Command had also put out of

action four important wireless or radio stations. Each time the raiding force, about 100 aircraft strong, had operated by a 'controlled OBOE technique', the marking being directed by OBOE and subsequently checked by a Master Bomber. The bombing had been extraordinarily accurate. On 31 May/1 June heavy attacks had hit two objectives near the invasion coast – a wireless transmitting station at Au Fevre and an R/T jamming station at Mont Couple (a jamming station with no fewer than 60 transmitters). Two nights later four Mosquitoes had led 103 Lancasters to wreck another radio jamming station at Bruneval, near Dieppe. Finally, after an earlier raid had left most of it intact, No. 5 Group Lancasters on 3/4 June had devastated a wireless and radio listening station at Ferme d'Urville – a station which turned out to be a headquarters of the German 'Y' (Intercept) Service.

Bomber Command's biggest task immediately before the invasion, however, had been to help silence the enemy's coastal batteries. As with the offensive against railway targets, airfields and wireless stations, this was work shared with AEAF and the Eighth Air Force. Harris's bombers had been attacking coastal batteries on most nights since 24/25 May, but for deception purposes many of these raids had been made outside the intended invasion area. As D-Day approached, so the assault had been stepped up. On 2/3 June 271 bombers had attacked four batteries in the area where the Germans most expected the invasion – the Pas de Calais. The following night 135 bombers had fuelled this expectation by attacking batteries at Calais and Wimereux. On 4/5 June 257 aircraft had operated similarly – though this time one of the four targets was in the planned lodgement area. Then on 5/6 June, as the invasion fleet was under way, Bomber Command had moved on to 'maximum effort' – a massive operation by 1136 aircraft, of which 1047 attacked, against ten of the main batteries on the actual invasion coast. Whether Bomber Command, other air formations or naval bombardment put the greater number of these out of action is uncertain, but between them they rendered nine of the ten batteries incapable of sustained fire against the invasion forces.[2] Bomber Command's 5000+ tons of bombs – the heaviest load yet dropped during any night of the war – had certainly helped.

There were other ways, too, in which the Command had contributed to the success of the landings. Thirty-six of its bombers had dropped dummy parachutists and set off explosions to create the illusion of an airborne landing where no landing was intended. And, very importantly, Bomber Command aircraft, in conjunction with Coastal Command, had laid mines to guard the flanks of the invasion fleets, and to bottle up the E-boats and U-boats in their harbours.

The Radio Counter-Measures squadrons of 100 Group, too, had played an invaluable part against the Germans' radar and wireless. A MANDREL screen of 20 Stirlings from No. 199 Squadron, together with an American squadron, had orbited for five-and-a-half hours round twelve points in the Channel, jamming such coastal radar stations as had survived the bombing. Two squadrons had also jammed the R/T control of the German night-fighters, and the INTRUDER squadrons had made their unwelcome presence felt at the German airfields.

Most ingeniously, two bomber formations with accompanying naval craft had also simulated approaches to coastal areas other than that being attacked. One of their bluffs, against Boulogne by Stirlings of 218 Squadron, drew a lively response. The other, apparently, did not. Intended to simulate a large convoy moving towards the beaches on either side of the Cap d'Antifer, it was carried out by 16 Lancasters of No. 617 Squadron performing 30 orbits round a group of surface craft. Each orbit took the aircraft 0.82 miles nearer France. As they orbited they dropped a special type of WINDOW to produce on the German radar screen the effect of a large seaborne convoy moving slowly towards the coast.[3]

It has to be recorded that this particular deception was not challenged, and so may not have been noticed. Perhaps the local radar had been too well jammed. But at all events the German High Command remained convinced for some days that the landings in Normandy were but the prelude to bigger happenings in the Pas de Calais. It was an illusion in the creation of which Bomber Command had played a useful part.

In the week after D-Day Bomber Command repeatedly attacked communications, mostly railways, to prevent German reinforcements reaching the battlefront. During these few days it flew some 3500 sorties to this end, with great effect and at a 'missing rate' of no more than 2.5 per cent. One of the most skilful of all these attacks, undertaken to stop the forward movement of a panzer unit by train, took place on 8/9 June against a railway tunnel at Saumur. Lancasters of 83 Squadron first dropped flares to illuminate the target, so that it could be accurately marked by Mosquitoes. Then 25 Lancasters of 617 Squadron followed, each dropping the new, enormously powerful and deeply penetrative 12,000-lb 'Tallboy' bomb designed by Barnes Wallis. At least one bomb hit the tunnel, and others blocked the approaches. The panzers were duly delayed.[4]

It was on one of these attacks on communications, at Cambrai on

12/13 June, that an episode occurred typifying the utter selflessness in face of danger of so many of the bomber crews. A German fighter caught a Lancaster of 419 Squadron, RCAF, and riddled it with bullets from below and astern. With the port engines out of action and the aircraft ablaze in two places, the pilot ordered the crew to bale out. The mid-upper-gunner, Pilot Officer Andrew Mynarski from Winnipeg, was about to leave the aircraft when he saw that the rear-gunner was trapped in his turret. He made his way to the rear turret through flames, but all his efforts to move it were in vain and his clothing and parachute caught fire. The rear-gunner, recognising the hopelessness of the attempt, then waved Mynarski away, making signs that he should bale out. Returning through flames to the escape hatch, and with his clothing still on fire, Mynarski turned round to face his trapped comrade, stood to attention, saluted, and left the aircraft. He died soon after he reached the ground; but the rear-gunner by a miracle survived the crash of the aircraft, and it was his report that led to the posthumous award to Mynarski of the Victoria Cross.[5]

The day after Mynarski lost his life a German Air Ministry report afforded striking testimony to the success of the whole railway Transportation Plan. Had they been able to read it at the time, Leigh-Mallory and the OVERLORD planners would surely have glowed with pride: 'The raids carried out in recent weeks have caused the breakdown of all main lines: the coastal defences have been cut off from the supply bases in the interior, thus producing a situation which threatens to have serious consequences. Although even the transportation of essential supplies for the civilian population has been stopped for the time being and only the most vital railway traffic is moved, large-scale strategic movement of German troops by rail is practically impossible at the present time and must remain so while attacks are maintained at their present intensity.'[6]

It was rare, however, for Bomber Command to be committed so completely to one set of tasks that it did not take on others. The night of 12/13 June that saw the attack on railways at Cambrai also saw the bomber crews returning in force to Germany for the first time since 27/28 May. They did so against a class of objective – German oil plants – which had been sanctioned in an unusually informal way.

Though outvoted on the pre-OVERLORD bombing policy, General Spaatz had not lost his conviction that the key to the rapid defeat of Germany was an all-out assault on her oil supplies. It was a view with which Portal and the British Air Staff, though not Harris, had much sympathy. In the two months before OVERLORD Spaatz had used his position as commander of the United States Strategic Air Forces in Europe to initiate a campaign against German oil without proclaiming the fact: in April the US Fifteenth Air Force, operating from Italy, had attacked marshalling yards at Ploesti in Romania and taken care to spill its bombs on to the adjoining oilfields, and in May the US Eighth Air Force had dealt three devastating blows against synthetic oil plants in Germany in the course of attacks officially designed to generate air battles and wear down the German fighter force. So successful were these attacks that Spaatz had little difficulty in securing the approval of Arnold, Eisenhower, Tedder and Portal to their continuation. An offensive against oil, as yet subsidiary and not enjoined in any formal directive, had thus come into being before the first Allied troops landed in Normandy, and was officially acknowledged soon afterwards.

On 12/13 June, though 671 Bomber Command aircraft were attacking communications in France, Harris was able to dispatch a considerable force for his first contribution to this new offensive. No fewer than 286 Lancasters, guided by ground-marking Mosquitoes equipped with the latest type of OBOE, set out to attack the Nordstern synthetic oil plant near Gelsenkirchen. They did enormous damage. According to German records some 1500 bombs fell in the plant area, all production ceased, and 1000 tons of aviation fuel, as well as other fuels, were lost every day for several weeks. But unhappily for the Lancasters the Reich defences were as active as ever, and over 6 per cent failed to return.[7]

It was not this rate of loss, however, but other demands which limited Bomber Command's attacks on German oil to only three in the next five weeks. The first of these, by 321 aircraft against the synthetic oil plant at Sterkrade/Holten on 16/17 June, did little damage owing to low cloud. The raiders suffered heavily, with a 'missing rate' of nearly 10 per cent and with No. 77 Squadron losing seven of its 23 Halifaxes. The other two attacks, each by about 130 bombers, took place five nights later against the plants at Wesseling and Scholven-Buer. There were conflicting reports of their success, some suggesting little damage and others a great deal. There was no doubt, however, about the price paid. At Scholven-Buer it was 6.5 per cent of the Lancasters missing, at Wesseling a horrifying 27.8 per cent. Such losses did nothing to persuade Harris that bombing German oil plants was a more profitable operation of war than obliterating German cities.

*   *   *

Fortunately for Bomber Command, the requirements of the struggle in Normandy took precedence over attacks on Germany, and the Command was soon called on for further help to OVERLORD. German E-boats – fast torpedo boats – and other light naval craft in the northern French ports were well placed to interrupt the flow of Allied troops and supplies across the Channel. On 14 June 221 Lancasters, Mosquito-led, accordingly bombed Le Havre. They killed about 1000 German sailors and did great damage to the naval craft, the pens and, unfortunately, the town. The following day an even larger force wrought similar havoc at Boulogne. Between them, the two attacks put about 130 vessels out of action and virtually ended the E-boat threat in the Channel.[8] And only two of the bombers failed to return.

A notable feature of these operations, apart from their success, was that they took place in daylight under Spitfire escort. They were in fact Bomber Command's first major raids by day since the end of May 1943, when No. 2 Group had left the Command to be absorbed in due course into the AEAF. They marked the beginning of a new flexibility in the Command's operations, and a significant increase in its powers of attack.

In the midst of the onslaught against railways, fuel, ammunition dumps and E-boats, Harris found himself also required to undertake close battlefield support. This of course was everyday work for the light and medium bombers of the AEAF, but was new to the 'heavies' of Bomber Command. Heavy bombers – American B-17s – had indeed tried it earlier in the year at Monte Cassino during the Italian campaign, but their efforts had impeded the Allies almost as much as the enemy. Now it was up to Harris to use heavy bombers in such situations more effectively.

During the struggle in Normandy there were eight occasions on which Bomber Command was required to operate in strength over, or very close to, the battlefield. The first was on 14/15 June, at the request of the British Second Army, when 337 bombers successfully and without loss attacked German troops and vehicles at Aunay and Evrecy, near Caen. A fortnight later, on 30 June, came the first intervention in daylight. Under Spitfire escort, 266 aircraft – Lancasters and Halifaxes with a few Mosquitoes leading – bombed a road junction at Villers-Bocage from 4000 feet and frustrated a panzer attack.

Next, on the evening of 7 July, 467 bombers tried to break the deadlock between the armies north of Caen. Accurate bombing and the loss of only one aircraft, however, failed to compensate for the fact that the target area had been poorly chosen – the raid did more damage to the northern quarters of Caen than to the shaken, but still surviving, German defenders. British troops were able to force their way into Caen's heavily cratered streets – but not beyond them.

Of Bomber Command's five other attacks in close support of the Allied armies, the biggest, in the early evening of 18 July, was operation GOODWOOD.* It was a gigantic affair, with 863 bombers of AEAF and the US Eighth Air Force taking part as well as 1056 of Bomber Command. The intention was for the air forces to help the ground troops in a push south-east of Caen towards Falaise; but after three days and the dropping of several thousand tons of bombs, the combination of bad weather and unsubdued anti-tank guns brought the offensive to a halt. At the farthest point of advance it had penetrated only six miles beyond Caen, and the air forces were inclined to think that greater advantage might have been taken of their massive air support. Montgomery, however, was ready to explain, what had not been clear at the time, that from the start he had intended only a limited advance.

Disappointing though GOODWOOD seemed to Tedder, the Allied air forces' part in it had made a strong enough impression on the German High Command. Von Kluge, who had just succeeded Rommel after the latter's narrow escape from death during a Spitfire attack on his car, took an early opportunity of explaining the situation to Hitler. On 21 July, in terms which more or less sealed his own fate,† he wrote to Hitler:

> There is no way by which, in the face of the enemy air forces' complete command of the air, we can discover a form of strategy which will counterbalance its annihilating effects unless we withdraw from the battlefield. Whole armoured formations allotted to the counterattack were caught beneath bomb carpets of the greatest intensity so that they could be got out of the torn-up ground only by prolonged effort . . . The psychological effect of such a mass of bombs coming down with all the power of elemental nature on the fighting forces, especially the infantry, is a factor which has to be taken into very serious consideration. It is immaterial whether such a carpet catches good troops or bad. They are more or less annihilated, and above all their equipment is shattered . . .[10]

Another huge and successful Bomber Command battlefield intervention was a night raid by 1019 aircraft on 7/8 August against five

---

* This had earlier been a code-name to denote a raid with all available forces.
† He committed suicide a month later when Hitler (who was also suspicious of him after Stauffenberg's assassination attempt of 20 July) would not sanction a strategic withdrawal.

points in advance of the Allied troops. This powerful support helped the Canadian First Army to open the way towards Falaise. But such attacks also revealed that the military and Bomber Command – and, for that matter, the Eighth Air Force – had much to learn together about army–air cooperation. For Bomber Command there was a distressing incident a few days later, on 14 August, when 811 aircraft were to attack enemy positions 2000 yards in front of the Canadians. Unfortunately some of the troops lit yellow recognition flares which 77 of the bombers mistook for yellow target indicators. Their bombs killed 80 Canadian soldiers and destroyed much equipment.[11]

In the eight major close-support operations from 14/15 June to 14 August, Bomber Command flew over 4700 sorties and dropped over 25,300 tons of bombs. In welcome contrast to operations over Germany, it lost only 26 aircraft. There was no doubt about the effectiveness of the attacks; they subjected the German troops to a profoundly terrifying experience and in nearly every case made possible an advance. Too often, however, the broken roads and villages prevented the rapid bringing-up of supplies, and the Allied ground forces could not sustain the momentum of their attack.

So overwhelming was the air superiority of the Allies, with some 14,000 aircraft at their disposal as against the 1000 or so that the Luftwaffe could finally bring to bear, that once substantial ground forces and their supplies had been successfully landed and positioned for battle, the issue could hardly be in doubt. When the Germans failed to destroy the invasion in its early days and at the same time kept potential reinforcements waiting for the landings in the Pas de Calais that never came, they in effect lost Normandy – and the war.

For six weeks that was not so apparent as it later became. The Germans held resolutely on to Caen – which the Allies had planned to take on the very first day – and on to the positions behind it. But to do so they concentrated too much of their available strength in those sectors, leaving inadequate forces farther to the west to hold the Americans. On 25 July, having thus far penetrated little beyond Caen, Montgomery gave the Americans on the right of the Allied line their chance. They took it nobly, broke through at Avranches on 31 July, and but for a diversion to deal with Brest would have been streaming east and south-east across France even faster than they did. Meanwhile the outflanked Germans behind Caen, denied by Hitler the chance of an earlier retreat to a possibly tenable line, headed helter-skelter towards and across the Seine. By 25 August Paris was free. On 3 September spearheads of the British Second Army, after driving forward 75 miles in a single day, arrived in Brussels.

Bomber Command had not been idle during these exhilarating movements. It had helped not only by weakening enemy resistance at particular points, but also by continuing attacks on railways and supply dumps, and by special operations like the sinking of ships in Brest to prevent their being used to block the harbour entrance. From 18/19 July Harris had also been able to resume his attacks on Germany, beginning that night with highly successful raids on the synthetic oil plants at Wesseling and Scholven-Buer. Such attacks would have been heavier and more frequent still – a joint Anglo-American Oil Targets Committee had been set up on 9 July – but for the intervention of another urgent task. The V-1s – the flying bombs – were bringing death and destruction to southern England, and Bomber Command's help was needed in the fight against them.

Hitler had hoped to launch his V-1 campaign against London in the opening days of 1944 – a 'New Year's present', as he playfully expressed it. This would have been well before the Allies could invade France. However, the destruction of the ski sites, the damage done by Bomber Command to the Fieseler works at Kassel and, above all, the difficulties experienced by the Germans in getting mass-production versions of the bomb to behave with reasonable reliability and accuracy, had set back the first launchings. These had been rescheduled for 15 February, and then postponed again to mid-June. By that time Colonel Wachtel, in charge of Flak Regiment 155W in France, was nearly but not quite ready. He had plenty of the new 'modified' sites, mainly in the Pas de Calais, as replacements for the battered and abandoned ski sites, but to avoid detection from the air many of these had not yet been fitted with their telltale catapult launchers. Also the Allied bombing of the railway centres had held up the delivery of these and some of the bomb components.

When the Allies landed on 6 June Wachtel's superiors declined to give him the time necessary for proper final preparations, and called for instant action: no more than six days must pass before the firing of the first bomb.[12] On the night 12/13 June the attack accordingly began – falteringly: seven of the 55 sites supposedly ready managed to fire between them ten bombs, only three of which reached England. But within a very short time Wachtel's regiment was performing altogether differently. Between 15/16 and 16/17 June 144 flying bombs crossed the Kentish coast and 73 reached London.

This stung the British authorities into vigorous action, and Eisenhower agreed that CROSSBOW operations, as they were called, should rank second in priority only to the urgent needs of the battlefield. The US Eighth Air Force, AEAF, and Bomber Command were all required to join in the offensive. From mid-June to mid-August attacks on V-weapon objectives became one of Bomber Command's major concerns, absorbing about 40 per cent of its effort and correspondingly reducing its ability to bomb Germany.

The CROSSBOW targets were of three main kinds. There were the new 'modified' launching sites with rails and catapult gear, difficult to spot and difficult for heavy bombers to hit. There were depots for the supply and assembly of the bombs, easier targets except for those that had been hidden underground in caves and tunnels. And there were still the few 'large sites', whose purposes were not fully understood by the Allies but were assumed to be for V-weapons and particularly rockets. All of these Bomber Command attacked, beginning on 16/17 June with raids against four launching sites in the Pas de Calais.

From 19 June Bomber Command operated against flying-bomb targets not only by day, but almost every day, and many times by night. At first the attacks fell mainly on the launching sites, but from early July they were increasingly directed against the larger targets, such as the assembly and storage depots. Among the storage points attacked three times or more were the 'large sites' at Wizernes (in a quarry, and actually for V-2s) and at Siracourt, and two smaller depots – one in the Forêt de Nieppe and the other in tunnels at St Leu d'Esserent. In each case the bombers did great damage, and usually at little cost. An unhappy exception was the attack on 7/8 July against St Leu d'Esserent. The raid blocked the tunnels, but German night-fighters intercepted and 31 of the 221 bombers failed to return. One squadron, No. 106, lost five of its 16 Lancasters, and No. 630 Squadron lost its commanding officer, Wing Commander W. J. Deas, who was on his 69th operation.[13]

In the course of one of these attacks, against a launching site at Trossy St Maximin on 4 August, Squadron Leader Ian Bazalgette of 635 Squadron displayed such heroic determination as to be awarded posthumously the Victoria Cross. Flak hit Bazalgette's Lancaster as he neared his target: the bullets put both starboard engines out of action, started fires in the starboard wing and the fuselage, and seriously wounded the bomb-aimer. Bazalgette nevertheless pressed on, and his accurate marking and bombing led to the success of the whole attack. By the time it was over one of his port engines, too, had failed, the starboard wing was completely ablaze, and the mid-upper-gunner had been overcome by fumes. Bazalgette ordered those of his crew who could to bale out, and then, in an attempt to save the helpless two still aboard, brought the blazing aircraft down on some clear ground. Unhappily it exploded, killing him and the men he had tried to save.[14]

A month before Bazalgette's self-sacrifice a pilot in Bomber Command, Leonard Cheshire, had completed his 100th operation. It had been a raid by 617 Squadron, with Cheshire leading, against the 'large site' at Mimoyecques, which turned out to be the shelter for Hitler's V-3 – a giant 25-barrel long-range gun capable of shelling London. Cheshire's AOC in 5 Group, Air Vice-Marshal Ralph Cochrane, deciding that 'enough was enough', thereupon took Cheshire off operations, so preserving a truly remarkable man for – as it turned out – a lifetime of near-saintly service to fellow men in ill-health or distress. His Victoria Cross, awarded in September 1944, related not to any one action but to his whole career as a bomber pilot. The citation stressed how he had developed low-level marking, and rightly stated that 'his careful planning, brilliant execution, and contempt for danger' had 'established for Wing Commander Cheshire a reputation second to none in Bomber Command'.[15]

After mid-August the need for Harris to devote so much effort to destroying V-weapon sites lessened. In the third week of July the defences in Britain had been redeployed, with the guns moving forward to the coast and the fighters operating in front of them and behind. This, and the introduction of shells with proximity fuses, had greatly reduced the number of bombs reaching London, which fell from around 50 per cent of those launched in the early days of the attack to less than 20 per cent in its later stages.

All told, in the two months from mid-June to mid-August, which saw nearly all of the renewed CROSSBOW offensive, Bomber Command flew over 16,000 sorties and dropped some 59,000 tons of bombs against V-weapon targets. In the course of this it lost 131 aircraft – less than 1 per cent of the sorties – and learned valuable new operational techniques, particularly of daylight-raiding under fighter cover. Among these it discovered that although bombing by day on ground-markers laid by OBOE Mosquitoes usually worked well, there was an equally effective technique for the smaller raids, and one that was certainly simpler. An OBOE-equipped Lancaster led the way. When it dropped its bombs, the aircraft behind followed suit.

The last V-1 launched from France reached England on 2 September. The guns, the fighters and the balloon defences in Britain had performed magnificently, and Bomber Command and the other air forces had greatly helped to reduce the scale of attack. What ended, as opposed to reducing, the V-1 menace, however – except in its very attenuated form of flying bombs launched from aircraft – was none of these, but the overrunning of the launching sites by the Allied armies.

With so much of its effort devoted to CROSSBOW attacks and direct support of the armies, Bomber Command had made no major raids on Germany from 21/22 June, when it had attacked the synthetic oil plants at Wesseling and Scholven-Buer. Now, on 18/19 July, it operated against the same targets. These new attacks were extremely successful, with hundreds of bombs hitting the target areas, great subsequent loss of production, and only five aircraft missing out of the 364 which set forth. Two nights later, however, the German night-fighters showed that they were still very much to be reckoned with. A raid which did great damage to the oil plant at Bottrop lost eight of its 166 heavy bombers, and a similar raid at Homberg, also extremely effective, suffered even worse. Twenty of the 147 heavy bombers – 13.6 per cent – failed to return. No. 75 (New Zealand) Squadron, which had suffered heavily before, lost seven of its 25 Lancasters.

Partly to keep the enemy defences dispersed and avoid such heavy losses, towards the end of July Bomber Command slackened its efforts against oil and reverted to major attacks on German cities. On 23/24 July 612 aircraft, with the help of a MANDREL jamming screen, took the defences of Kiel by surprise and in the space of 25 minutes cascaded nearly 3000 tons of bombs into the town and port. They did enormous damage, to the U-boat yards and to many other areas, and lost only four of their number – 0.6 per cent. Hard on top of this came three devastating blows in five nights by a total of 1660 aircraft against the unfortunate city of Stuttgart. On the third occasion the success of the bombing was marred for Bomber Command by the loss, to German fighters over France, of 39 of the raiders – nearly 8 per cent.

That same night, 28/29 July, 307 Bomber Command aircraft delivered the first major attack on Hamburg since the 'battle' a year earlier. They did further damage and 'bombed out' some 17,000 of the inhabitants, but lost over 7 per cent of their number, again mainly to night-fighters. Thereafter Bomber Command, obeying the needs of the CROSSBOW campaign and of support for the armies in France, made no further major attacks on Germany until 12/13 August, when 379 aircraft set out to bomb Brunswick, a centre of Me 110 night-fighter production. The aircraft were all equipped with H2S, and acted as their own pathfinders, but the bombing achieved little concentration and the 'missing rate' was over 7 per cent.

Brunswick was not the only target in Germany that night. A force of 297 aircraft raided Rüsselsheim and its Opel motor factories, where components were being made for flying bombs. The attack was only partly successful, and nearly 7 per cent of the bombers failed to return. Much more profitable, both in the damage inflicted and in the lighter losses incurred, was another visit by a larger force a fortnight later.

By then, Bomber Command was becoming free of its CROSSBOW commitment, and it seemed that Harris could look forward to dropping a greatly increased weight of bombs on Germany itself. As so often, however, other tasks emerged to compete. The Allied armies were sweeping through France and Belgium, but the Germans were clinging on to much of Holland and had left behind strong garrisons in the ports of Brest, Le Havre, Boulogne and Calais, as well as on Walcheren Island. Until these were reduced, Germany would not suffer the full impact of Harris's increasingly formidable force.

2I

The Last Autumn

Two months after D-Day the Germans still held all the major ports of north and north-west France except Cherbourg. Until these could be freed, the Allies would face increasing difficulties of supply as they streamed eastwards. So it became one of Bomber Command's tasks to join AEAF and the Eighth Air Force in 'softening up' the defences of these places – and the defenders.

Early on the list for liberation was Brest, which General Patton mistakenly declared captured in mid-August. Bomber Command's main contribution was a successful attack on 25/26 August against eight batteries; delivered by 284 Halifaxes and 32 Lancasters, led by 12 Pathfinder Mosquitoes, it occupied only a quarter of the Command's sorties for that night, which reached the record total of 1511. Much other Allied air action against Brest then followed, including an attack on batteries by 60 Bomber Command Lancasters and Mosquitoes on 3 September, but it was not until 19 September that the garrison surrendered. It had detained about a third of Patton's army for a full five weeks.

On the eastern side of the Brittany peninsula American forces had liberated St Malo on 9 August, but its seaward approaches were still dominated by German batteries on the neighbouring Ile de Cézembre. On 31 August Bomber Command joined the artillery and air attack on the island, 165 Halifaxes from No. 6 (Canadian) Group bombing from low level. Other air formations kept up the pressure, and the garrison gave in two days later. Their deep concrete dugouts had protected them well, despite the quantities of high explosive and the

The Chief Targets
in Germany

0   50   100 miles

- - - Canals

S E A

Sassnitz
Peenemünde
Swinemünde
Pölitz
Stettin

Königsberg

ODER

Ruhland

Dresden

700 miles   800 miles   900 miles

Kleve
Wesel
Recklinghausen
Castrop
Rauxel
Bottrop   Wanne
Sterkrade
Osterfeld
Duisburg
Mülheim   Oberhausen
Gelsenkirchen
Essen
Bochum
Langendreer
Dortmund
Hamm
Kamen
LIPPE
RUHR
Hagen
Krefeld
M. Gladbach
Neuss
Düsseldorf   Wuppertal
Elberfeld Barmen
Solingen Remscheid
MAAS
RHINE
Leverkusen
Jülich
Cologne

0   10   20 miles

new American weapon, napalm, directed against them. But, they explained, their distilling plant had been destroyed, and they were suffering from a water shortage.

The main action then shifted to Le Havre, which for a week occupied much of Bomber Command's attention. Every day except one from 5 to 11 September Harris sent out 300 aircraft or more against the German positions in and around the port. On 10 September the sorties totalled 992, all of which returned safely. Unquestionably the week's work, involving nearly 2500 sorties and the dropping of 9750 tons of bombs, fulfilled its purpose. The ground assault after the last air attack on 11 September succeeded with no more than 50 fatal casualties.

Meanwhile on 1 September Dieppe had surrendered to the Canadian First Army and Boulogne had become the next objective. A massive raid by 762 aircraft of Bomber Command on 17 September opened the way for an attack by the Canadians and five days later the garrison gave in. The diary of a captured German officer gave eloquent testimony to the effect of the air action: 'Sometimes one could despair of everything if one is at the mercy of the RAF without any protection. It seems as if all fighting is useless and all sacrifices are in vain.'[1]

The Germans in Calais held out longer. In the eight days 20–28 September, Bomber Command flew over 3000 sorties and dropped some 8000 tons of bombs against the gun positions, including those on Cap Gris Nez. Despite much cloud the bombing was generally effective. The other air forces added their weight of attack, and on 30 September, after only two days of ground fighting, Calais, too, surrendered to the Canadians.

The Germans having comprehensively wrecked the shipping facilities at all these places before they gave in, time was needed to bring them back to working order. With Dunkirk and Ostend still in German hands, the forward Allied troops became increasingly short of vital supplies. By 25 September the point was reached where 70 Halifaxes of Bomber Command had to spend eight days flying jerricans of petrol over from England. More and more it became clear that the key to faster supply was the opening of the great inland port of Antwerp, some forty miles up the River Scheldt. It had been in Allied hands since 4 September, and the hurried departure of the Germans had left it less damaged than the other ports. But it was of little use while German forces still held South Beveland and the island of Walcheren dominating its approaches from the sea.

Walcheren would be a hard nut to crack, and rather than attempt it the Allies first essayed a 'quick victory'. Operation MARKET GARDEN involved using airborne troops to capture bridges over the Maas, the

Waal and the lower Rhine. The result was disaster at 'the bridge too far': the epic resistance and final capture of most of the British 1st Airborne Division at Arnhem. After that, Eisenhower had to settle for longer-term strategies including, for a start, the opening of the Scheldt.

Bomber Command's attacks on Walcheren had begun in the third week of September, with the idea of helping MARKET GARDEN. Hitting the batteries had proved difficult, and on 23 September, after the Canadians had been instructed to capture the island, their commander suggested that bombing might breach its massive sea walls. Much of the land within these was low-lying, and the inrush of the sea would flood some of the batteries. SHAEF approved the plan, and called on Bomber Command as well as AEAF.

On 2 October leaflets and broadcasts informed the local population that flooding was imminent, and the following day 252 Lancasters, with some Pathfinder OBOE Mosquitoes, took off to bomb the dyke at Westkapelle on the west of the island. Attacking in waves of 30 under the control of a Master Bomber they did their job so well that Lancasters of 617 Squadron, standing off with Tallboy bombs, had no need to follow on: they brought their precious stores back home. The attack had created a large gap in a wall 60 feet thick at the top and 204 feet thick at the bottom.

Many parts of the island were now flooded, but the defenders showed no signs of surrender. On 7, 11 and 17 October smaller Bomber Command forces made further attacks on the walls. They scored hits, but not decisive ones, which led Harris to conclude that the heavy bombers could be more profitably employed on other tasks. Nevertheless, in preparation for the end, forces of between 75 and 358 Bomber Command aircraft continued to attack batteries profitably on either side of Flushing and near Breskens, on the mainland at the mouth of the west Scheldt.

The plan now was to take Walcheren by amphibious assault, and as a preliminary 277 aircraft of Bomber Command attacked gun and troop positions on 28 October. The following day another 358 followed suit, to be succeeded by 110 on the day afterwards. On 1 November the Canadian and Scottish troops began their assault, to initiate a week of hard fighting, during which Royal Marine commandos sailed their landing craft through the breaches at Westkapelle made earlier by Bomber Command. All told, Harris's crews had made 14 raids on Walcheren and the adjoining mainland, flying over 2000 sorties and dropping over 9000 tons of bombs. Their casualties had been mercifully light – only 11 missing, less than 0.4 per cent, from the whole series of attacks. But the ultimate aim, the opening of Antwerp, was achieved only after another nineteen days. The Scheldt and its extensive estuary had first to be cleared of mines.

Meanwhile, despite Arnhem, the Allies still entertained some hopes of victory in 1944. In the southern sector of their advance, 20 miles in front of Patton's Third Army, stood the important communications centre of Saarbrücken. On 5/6 October, in response to a request from the Americans, 551 aircraft of Bomber Command set out to attack the town and its railways. The second half of this force inflicted heavy damage, as did the US Eighth Air Force later, but no great military movement ensued, and only in the extreme south did the Americans reach the Rhine. Similarly in the northern sector, on 7 October, Bomber Command met the British 21st Army Group's request to bomb Kleve and Emmerich, two Rhineland towns just within Germany. About 350 aircraft attacked each target with success. No significant advance followed, but at least the bombing helped to prevent any possible German counteroffensive.

There was also some notable precision-bombing by 617 Squadron that same day. The Americans in the south feared that the Germans might release waters restrained by the dam at Kembs, on the upper Rhine below Basle, and so impede a future advance. They preferred to have the waters released well beforehand. At the cost of two Lancasters, 617 Squadron did the job. In pursuit of the same idea, but on behalf of the British, over 200 Lancasters on 8 and 11 December bombed the Urft dam on the River Roer. They scored hits, but made no breach.[2]

The operations mentioned above show how army support remained an important part of Bomber Command's commitment for months after D-Day at a time when it was also trying to develop a more powerful air offensive against Germany itself. In the same way, and at the same time, the Command had also to meet the equally necessary demands of the war at sea.

In the autumn of 1944 Bomber Command continued as before with its productive minelaying. But its maritime activities went far beyond this. Twice in October and once again in January 1945, for instance, it attacked U-boats and U-boat pens at Bergen, inflicting damage though unhappily on the first two occasions also causing many civilian casualties. In the Reich itself, during the last five months of 1944, massive raids hit the ports of Königsberg, Stettin, Bremen, Emden, Kiel, Wilhelmshaven and the former Polish Gdynia. But undoubtedly

Bomber Command's most spectacular feat in the war at sea during the autumn of 1944 was the crippling, and later sinking, of the battleship *Tirpitz*.

The existence of this powerful sister ship of the *Bismarck*, with its potential ability to wreak havoc among the Allied northern convoys, had long galled the Admiralty. During 1940–41 small numbers of Bomber Command aircraft had made six attempts to attack her in harbour at Wilhelmshaven or Kiel; and in the early months of 1942, after she moved to fiords near Trondheim, there had been four further efforts by Bomber Command and one by the Fleet Air Arm. None succeeded, and it was not until September 1943, when two midget submarines penetrated her anchorage, that she received significant damage.

Though the *Tirpitz* had only once fired her main guns in earnest, off Spitzbergen in September 1943, the Admiralty's eagerness to see the end of her had in no way diminished by 1944. Northern convoys carrying aid to Russia, which had been suspended from March to October 1943 and again in March 1944, were due to resume in June, and the refitted *Tirpitz* might still exact a heavy toll. Moreover the War Cabinet was anxious to send warships to the Far East for the struggle against Japan, and the Admiralty was reluctant to withdraw them from European waters while the *Tirpitz* still menaced the northern routes.

In the spring of 1944 the Fleet Air Arm waged a determined campaign to get rid of the offending battleship while she was in Altenfiord, at the extreme north of Norway. Between 3 April and 29 August its aircraft made no fewer than nine attempts. The first of these scored 14 hits and that on 24 August two, but the largest bomb used was the armour-piercing 1400 lb, and the one that penetrated amidships on 24 August failed to explode. Then the task passed to Bomber Command, to its two most highly trained squadrons, Nos. 9 and 617, with the devastating 12,000-lb Tallboy bombs that they could carry.

The first attempt came in mid-September. *Tirpitz* was still in Kaafiord, off Altenfiord, out of Lancaster range from Britain, so it was decided to attack her from Russia. On 11 September 38 Lancasters of the two squadrons under Group Captain C. C. McMullen, together with a weather Mosquito and a film unit aircraft, set off for Yagodnik, an airfield near Archangel. In appalling weather six crash-landed on arrival, putting down on fields or primitive landing grounds. Eventually after frantic maintenance work – and a football match against the local Russians – the two squadrons, now only 28 strong, took off on

15 September for the attack. They approached promisingly, but soon a dense smoke screen hid the ship. Between them they scored one direct hit with a 12,000-lb bomb, and two very near misses, inflicting damage that could not be repaired on the spot. All the attackers regained their temporary Russian base safely, but one was lost on the flight home.

The damage to *Tirpitz* was, in fact, greater than the raiders knew. The Germans gave up hope of a quick refit, and she moved 200 miles south, to a mooring near Tromsö, to act as a floating battery. In this new position she was just within bombing range from Scotland, and on 29 October the two squadrons, accompanied by a film unit aircraft from 463 Squadron, tried again. They had extra fuel tanks, more powerful engines, paddle-bladed propellers to assist take-off, and – to compensate for this additional weight – no mid-upper turrets. They faced a flight, assuming they landed back safely, of some 2250 miles. Almost to the last moment, as the Lancasters approached the fiord, the operation promised well. Then clouds suddenly appeared, to obscure the target. The bombs scored only some near misses. The *Tirpitz* suffered further damage, but still survived.

The next attempt was the satisfactory last. On 12 November, 31 Lancasters of the two squadrons took off from Lossiemouth, with Wing Commander J. B. (Willie) Tait in the lead. They scored three hits and two near misses. German fighters based nearby failed to intervene, and all the raiders returned safely – apart from one which had to land in Sweden. After the second hit there was a violent explosion amidships and the *Tirpitz* rolled over, to finish bottom upwards, with the loss of half her crew.*

With the *Tirpitz* gone, and the *Scharnhorst* sunk by naval action at the end of 1943, the Admiralty now felt free to reinforce the Far East. Sir Arthur Harris, in conversation with the author of this volume many years later, gave a characteristic account of the final episode. He recalled the following conversation with the Prime Minister:

Churchill: Harris, I want you to sink the *Tirpitz*.
Harris: Why bother, Prime Minister? She's not doing any harm where she is.
Churchill: Harris, I want you to sink the *Tirpitz*.

'So', added Sir Arthur, 'I sent the boys out and they sank the *Tirpitz*.'

---

* Among the awards Tait, who already had a DSO and two bars and a DFC and two bars, received a third bar to his DSO. Subsequently he did two more operations to bring his total to 100 before taking a staff position.

It was not really as simple as that, but the boys certainly sank the *Tirpitz*.[3]

In mid-September 1944 the strategic bombers reverted from Eisenhower's control to that of the Combined Chiefs of Staff. Portal had made the point that the Allies were now firmly established on the Continent and that Eisenhower's headquarters, being inevitably mainly concerned with the immediate military situation, might not be able to give due weight to wider possibilities, such as might arise from a sustained attack on Hitler's increasingly precarious supplies of oil.

Before Eisenhower's period of higher control, Portal had exercised this on behalf of the Combined Chiefs. Now, from 14 September, he and his American counterpart, General Arnold, were to hold this power jointly. By agreement, however, they delegated it to deputies – on the RAF side to Air Marshal Sir Norman Bottomley, Deputy Chief of the Air Staff, and on the USAAF side to General Spaatz. This was a lopsided arrangement since one was a staff officer in the Air Ministry and the other an overall air commander in the field, but at least both men were in Europe.

One person displeased by the change was Harris. He had got on well with Eisenhower and Tedder, and even – which was far more difficult – with Montgomery. While collaborating whole-heartedly in military operations when required, he had also enjoyed much freedom in choosing targets within the current bombing directives. He now feared that the exercise of higher control in part by the Air Staff would tie him down more strictly. In particular he feared that the influence of the Director of Bomber Operations at the Air Ministry, Air Commodore Bufton, would impose on him 'panacea' targets, such as ball bearings, in the validity of which he had not the slightest faith.

On 14 September Portal and Arnold sent a directive in broad terms to Bottomley and Spaatz. After these two had conferred with Tedder, Bottomley on 25 September then issued a more detailed directive to Harris. It has been described in the British official history as marking 'the beginning of the final air offensive'. It placed the German oil industry alone in the first category for attack, with German rail and waterborne communications as leading objectives in the second category. (Oil reflected the views of Portal and Spaatz, communications those of Tedder.) After these, but also in the second category, came tanks, ordnance and motor transport plants and depots, and after them – but in no stated category – 'policing attacks' against the German Air Force. (This low priority showed how far the once-mighty Luftwaffe had fallen.) There was, of course, also to be a continuing commitment to the direct support of military and naval operations, and to helping the Special Operations Executive and the Secret Intelligence Service.

With regard to 'important industrial areas', Harris's own preferred objectives, which in practice meant major towns generally, these were to be attacked, using blind-bombing as necessary, when 'weather or tactical conditions' were 'unsuitable for operations against specific primary objectives'.[4] Harris was thus quite clearly briefed that oil and transportation were to be numbers one and two on his target-list; but it remained up to him to decide whether meteorological or tactical conditions made it more advisable on any given occasion to go for 'important industrial areas' instead.

The force at Harris's disposal for these tasks had grown dramatically in the past eighteen months. In February 1943, when by his reckoning he 'began the full offensive', he had on an average night about 500 aircraft with crews available for operations. (This excludes the light bombers of No. 2 Group, soon to be transferred to AEAF.) By September 1944 this number had grown to nearer 1200.[5] Moreover, most of these aircraft were an improvement on their predecessors, alike in speed, ceiling and bomb-load. The Wellingtons and Stirlings had given way to Lancasters and the improved marks of Halifaxes, and the miscellaneous light bombers of 2 Group had been replaced by Mosquitoes which could fly 100 mph faster and 10,000 feet higher.

In the autumn of 1944 many other factors, too, favoured a renewed strategic offensive by Bomber Command. The expulsion of the Germans from France and Belgium, if not yet from all of Holland, provided safer approach routes to the Ruhr, and robbed the German air defence system of early-warning stations. It also enabled Allied GEE and OBOE ground stations to be installed near the German frontiers, and so greatly increased their range over Germany. Further, with the advent of the Allies' long-range escort fighters and the subjugation of the German day-fighters, the Lancasters and Halifaxes could now bomb by day as well as by night, so giving a new and infinitely valuable flexibility to their operations.

On top of this there was the improvement in accuracy for a whole Group of the bombing force – No. 3 – by the extended use of the new radar aid GH. This was a system which had been suggested at the same time as GEE, in 1940. With GEE, pulse transmissions from a 'master' and two 'slave' ground stations, each separated from the others by 100 miles or so, enabled the navigator to determine his position by noting the time-lag between the receipt of the signals. With

H systems, a radar set in the aircraft originated the emissions, alerting two receiving ground stations, which after a given interval responded with distinctive signals. By measuring the time-interval between his originating signal and the two answering signals, the navigator could determine his distance from the two stations and so fix his position. GH was in fact a combination of two principles, the GEE part of the equipment providing the general navigation and the H part the exact determination of position.

Serious work on GH had begun at the Telecommunications Research Establishment in 1942, and by the autumn of 1943 about a dozen individual GH aircraft had made flights over Germany. On 3/4 November 1943, in a full operational trial, 38 GH aircraft had set out to attack a tubular steel factory on the outskirts of Düsseldorf while the main force bombed the city. Largely owing to failures of the equipment only about 15 finally bombed, but these obtained several hits and the general bomb plot was judged to be encouraging. To preserve the secrecy of the equipment, the aircraft were then stripped of their sets, until a powerful GH force could be built up for use in the following spring.

From April 1944 GH aircraft of Bomber Command, AEAF and the US Eighth Air Force – there was keen competition for the sets – operated over France, where the danger of loss was much less. They had considerable success in bombing small targets like dumps and flying-bomb sites, and for daylight attacks they developed formation-bombing. By the beginning of October 1944 Bomber Command had about 60 GH aircraft concentrated in 3 Group, which was given authority, when the weather precluded ground-marking and visual-bombing, and when there was no other urgent requirement, to operate this force independently. It could be used for blind-bombing of precise targets in Germany, either at night or through cloud by day, within the 250 or so miles from the ground beacons by that time installed in France and Belgium. This was a valuable addition to Bomber Command's armoury, and one that would soon prove its worth in the forthcoming 'Second Battle of the Ruhr'.[6]

Despite its continuing commitments to the armies, the war at sea, and action against the flying bomb, Bomber Command's renewed assault on Germany soon gathered momentum. The raid against Brunswick on 12/13 August was quickly followed by others against major cities, and particularly the seaports. On 16/17 August one great force of Lancasters – 461 set out – inflicted huge damage on Stettin while another, 348 aircraft strong, attacked less successfully at Kiel. Two nights later 288 aircraft devastated the centre and port area of Bremen, while on 27/28 August 378 aircraft made a further and more profitable raid on Kiel.

Before the month was out, Bomber Command's reach had also extended, twice, to Königsberg, in East Prussia. This was a supply port for Germany's eastern front, so the raid was particularly intended to help the Russians.

During September 1944 heavy and successful Bomber Command raids repeatedly fell on German ports and other cities. Against the ports, the severest was probably that on Bremen on 16/17 September, which rendered 30,000 people homeless. Among other cities, Frankfurt and Stuttgart, already badly hit, were struck again, and the damage also extended to smaller towns like Munster, Neuss and München-Gladbach. In a raid against Kaiserslautern on 26/27 September 227 Bomber Command aircraft destroyed over a third of the town. The greatest devastation, however, was probably that inflicted a fortnight earlier by 240 bombers on Darmstadt, attacked primarily as a communications centre. The raid left 10,000 of the inhabitants dead and possibly as many as 70,000 homeless.

Meanwhile the offensive against oil also continued, mainly against installations in the Ruhr. At that range strong fighter escort was now possible, and in September Bomber Command made 14 attacks, seven of them by forces of over 100 aircraft. On communications east of the Rhine Bomber Command made few attacks during September, but one was of high importance. The target was once again the vital Dortmund–Ems Canal, a main link between the Ruhr and the North Sea, and the aiming-point was the most vulnerable section – where the canal was carried in twin aqueducts over the River Grane. As these were above the level of the surrounding countryside the opportunity for flooding was an additional bonus. On 24/25 September, with Pathfinder Mosquitoes marking and 617 Squadron carrying the still scarce Tallboy bombs, 156 Lancasters of 5 Group made the attack. Despite much cloud at around 8000 feet, which was the minimum height for dropping Tallboys effectively, the aircraft scored hits on both branches of the canal. The water flooded out, draining the canal for several miles and leaving scores of barges stranded. And this was not simply a one-off piece of temporary damage. As soon as, by the effort of four thousand labourers, the canal was once more fully working, Bomber Command breached it again – and went on doing so as required until the end of the war.[7]

Before the end of September Harris had received Bottomley's

directive giving oil as a clear-cut target priority, with communications in second place. His operations in October reflected this, though much effort had also to be devoted to the siege of Walcheren. With regard to oil, attacks on five days of the month by forces of over 100 aircraft – on one occasion by over 200 – hit six of the main plants and did enormous damage. In the last two attacks at the end of the month, on the synthetic oil plants at Weserling near Cologne and at Bottrop near Essen, around 100 Lancasters of 3 Group bombed successfully from above cloud on GH indications alone.

The most telling verbal testimony to the effectiveness of these attacks, combined, of course, with those of the US Eighth and Fifteenth Air Forces, is to be found in Speer's oil reports to Hitler. In the vital category of aviation spirit, these indicate that in April 1944, when serious US attacks began, the requirement was for 198,000 tons for the month, and the actual production 175,000 tons. In May the production was 20,000 tons less, and in June it was only 53,000 tons. For July, despite the Allies' concentration on OVERLORD, it was a mere 29,000 tons. In August, when repairs were disrupted by further bombing, it was still less – a trickle of 12,000 tons, equivalent to only two days' full production. In September it became a pitiful 9400 tons. Spelling it all out to the Führer on 5 October, Speer estimated that although uninterrupted repair could restore the monthly production to around 65,000 tons, further attacks were in fact likely to keep monthly production down to 9000–12,000 tons. Bad weather in the autumn and intense concentration of fighter and anti-aircraft defences might, Speer concluded hopefully, lead to higher production than his worst estimates.[8]

The fact, then, was that by the autumn of 1944 Germany was in the midst of a serious oil crisis, made all the more acute in that by then the Russians were in control of Romania and the natural oil output of Ploesti. The Allies did not know the full extent of the German shortage – that by the end of October, for instance, output of aviation spirit was meeting only a fifteenth of the Luftwaffe's normal requirements. But they had plenty of indication from ULTRA that there was indeed a serious shortage, and that oil supplies were the most vulnerable point in Germany's war economy.

In terms of tonnage dropped, however, oil targets attracted only 6 per cent of Bomber Command's efforts during October.[9] Such precision objectives, Harris judged, were more suited for attack on one of the rare clear days by crews with the latest navigational and bombing aids than by a large main force still chiefly accustomed to area-bombing by night. Also, it was difficult, he felt, to operate large numbers of aircraft effectively over a small target.

In the last quarter of 1944 nearly half of the tonnage dropped by Bomber Command was aimed at urban areas in general rather than more specific targets.[10] In October many attacks in great strength took place on German towns. Some – on Saarbrücken, Kleve and Emmerich – were undertaken in connection with military operations, while others – on Wilhelmshaven and Bremen – primarily helped the war at sea. The majority, however – 13 in number – were part of the 'progressive weakening' of Germany. Two of these successfully bombed distant targets in the south – Nuremberg and Stuttgart. Nearly all the rest hit the much-bombed Ruhr–Rhineland.

In initiating this 'Second Battle of the Ruhr' on 6/7 October, Harris sent 523 aircraft against Dortmund, with the Canadian Group, No. 6, contributing no fewer than 293 – its biggest effort on any night of the war. The devastation was great, the 'missing rate' less than 1 per cent. On 9/10 October an attack by 435 aircraft on Bochum followed, and then on 14 October came a truly massive effort. On a day during which 1000 American B-17s and B-24s attacked targets in and around Cologne, 957 of Harris's bombers, out of 1013 despatched, aimed 3594 tons of high explosive and 820 tons of incendiaries against Duisburg, the great inland port at the junction of Rhine and Ruhr which was one of the most important industrial and communications targets in all Germany. In case this weight of attack was insufficient, another 1000 Bomber Command aircraft added their bombs during the following hours of darkness, virtually finishing off Duisburg as a great wartime producer of coal and steel. Such by now was the strength of Bomber Command that Harris could spare another 240 aircraft that same evening to obliterate the centre of Brunswick.

The area attacks on the Ruhr–Rhineland continued on 15 October, when 128 Lancasters of 3 Group operated against Bonn. In small formations, under escort, they followed GH-equipped leaders, and bombed when they saw their leader bomb. For the loss of one aircraft they destroyed much of the town centre. Then, on 23/24 and 26 October came two crushing blows on Essen, 1055 aircraft taking off for the night raid, and 711 plus escort for the daylight attack thirty-six hours later. At the cost of 12 aircraft missing – less than 1 per cent – they ensured that Essen, and particularly Krupps, ceased to be an important centre of war production.

Bomber Command's month's work, however, was not yet finished.

On 28 October by day and on 30/31 October and 31 October/1 November by night, huge raids – by 733, 905 and 493 aircraft – struck Cologne. Damage to housing and factories, roads and railways, was again vast, and the attackers' losses again gratifyingly light – 0.4 per cent.

Bomber Command unquestionably won 'the Second Battle of the Ruhr'. But with half the tonnage in October directed against urban areas, had Harris done as much against oil as he might have done? Some of the Air Staff in Whitehall, and not only Bufton, had their doubts. On 1 November Bottomley issued a new directive to Harris emphasising the importance of oil, which remained clear first priority for attack, and placing communications alone in the second priority – i.e. by deleting tank and motor transport factory targets. Attacks on 'important industrial areas', as before, were to be restricted to occasions when 'weather or tactical conditions' were unsuitable for attacks on oil and communications; but there was now also a new restriction, or rather, half-restriction. Attacks on these areas were to be made 'so as to contribute to the maximum destruction of the petroleum industry' and of the German lines of communication, particularly in the Ruhr. This restriction, however, was far from absolute – Harris was to attack oil and communications, and urban areas affecting oil and communications, 'as far as operational and other conditions allow'.[11] The Air Staff, in other words, made the priorities even more clear: but it was still up to Harris to decide whether on any given day or night he could observe them.

In passing this directive to Saundby, Harris scribbled on top of Bottomley's covering letter: 'Here we go round the mulberry bush.'[12] The Air Ministry, he obviously felt, was at him again, prescribing panaceas in which he could never fully believe. Nevertheless as a military man he prided himself on obeying legitimate orders, however much he disagreed with them, and during November he certainly stepped up attacks on oil – his explanation being that the weather was unexpectedly favourable (as in fact it was).

All told, during November 1944 Bomber Command made 22 attacks, of which 14 were major and were by day under fighter escort, against oil targets in western Germany. This took in all the main synthetic oil production plants and two of the refineries. And early in the following month, on 6/7 December, there was even a successful attack by 475 Lancasters and 12 Mosquitoes against the great plant at Leuna, not far short of Leipzig. From all these attacks in November and early December, involving over 4000 sorties, less than 1 per cent of the aircraft did not return. Cumulatively they did vast damage, nullifying all the efforts of Speer's army of repairers, and ensuring that his hopes for the winter months, like the oil plants themselves, were shattered. During October frantic efforts had raised German aviation spirit production from the September nadir of 9400 tons to 18,000 tons, and during November to 41,000 tons – still more than 100,000 tons short of a normal Luftwaffe monthly requirement. But during December, when the full effects of the November raids were felt, the production figure sank disastrously again, to 25,000 tons.[13] If it stayed at that sort of level, or anywhere near it, short of a miracle Germany's fate was sealed.

Meanwhile the area attacks still continued, Harris by now gratified that in attacking towns in western Germany he could take railways as the aiming-points and so powerfully contribute to the offensive against communications. In the first half of December Bomber Command struck by day against such area-cum-railway targets as Oberhausen, Hamm, Giessen, Duisburg, Osterfeld and Heilbronn: the last of these, primarily a railway target, suffered 7000 dead and four-fifths of the town destroyed by fire. By night the attacks fell on Hagen (where local firms suffered three months' loss of production), on Karlsruhe, Soest, Osnabrück and – in its last major night raid – Essen. From all these area attacks and others in Germany during the first half of December, involving some 2500 sorties, only 29 aircraft – little over 1 per cent – failed to return.

On 15/16 December 341 aircraft of Bomber Command set out to bomb Ludwigshafen. At very little cost they did great damage to, among many other industrial concerns, the chemicals giant I.G. Farben – whose production included synthetic oil.

The following morning, in misty weather, German troops, unheralded by any warnings from the code-breakers at Bletchley Park, opened their offensive in the Ardennes. They had carefully husbanded reserves of petrol for the initial attacks, and they calculated on capturing Allied stocks as they advanced.

22

The Ardennes: Oil: Dresden

T
he Ardennes offensive – the Führer's personal brainchild
– caught the Allies unawares. Engrossed in preparing for
their own moves forward, they scarcely heeded signs of
an impending German attack. But after ten days and a 50-mile
penetration the thrust petered out in face of stout American resistance,
Eisenhower's remedial measures, and Allied air action. Nearly three
weeks then passed before the Allies could regain all their lost ground,
but once the initial impact faded and the skies cleared for the Allied
air forces, the issue could hardly be in doubt. Hitler had hoped to
split the Allies apart as in 1940 and capture Brussels and Antwerp
– possibly even to force the British into another of their evacuations.
The gamble was to cost him, and Germany, dear.

At the time when most of the air forces were unable to operate
because of fog, Bomber Command contributed powerfully to the Allied
response. On 19 December 32 of a scheduled 150 Lancasters managed
to take off and attack the rail centre in Germany nearest to the front –
Trier. Two days later, with the Eighth Air Force completely grounded,
94 GH-led Lancasters bombed the same target. That night, and the
following one, Bomber Command raids of 100 or more aircraft also
struck at other railway yards – Cologne-Nippes and Bonn on 21/22
December, Coblenz and Bingen on 22/23 December. A repeat raid by
153 Lancasters on Trier followed the next day.

By this time there were hints of the resurgence of the German Air
Force and on 24 and 24/25 December Bomber Command joined in
attacks on airfields in west Germany. These did considerable damage,

but did not prevent the Luftwaffe scoring a sensational, if suicidally costly, success against Allied airfields in Belgium a week later. On 26 December, as the German advance faltered, clearer weather allowed Bomber Command to intervene nearer the battlefield; a force of 294 Lancasters, Halifaxes and Mosquitoes attacked German troop concentrations and smashed up the roads at St Vith, effectively ending the possibility of any further German advance. All told, in the vital period from 19 to 27 December Bomber Command had flown over 1600 sorties and dropped nearly 6000 tons of bombs in direct response to the German offensive.[1]

The immediate crisis was over, but the Germans had still to be driven from the bulge they had made in the Allied front. To help the ground action Bomber Command between 28 December and 6/7 January put in 15 major attacks on railway centres, including those at Cologne, Bonn and Coblenz, in the course of which its aircraft flew over 3000 sorties and dropped more than 11,000 tons of bombs.[2] It also made two heavy attacks on troop concentrations at a focal point of the struggle, Houffalize. Its final contributions came on 13 and 14 January, after the Germans, to divert attention from their withdrawal from the bulge, had launched an attack in Alsace. In the space of twenty-four hours Bomber Command made three raids on railway targets at Saarbrücken, flying 568 sorties and dropping 1660 tons of bombs for the loss of only one aircraft.

All this, taken in conjunction with the work of the Eighth Air Force and the tactical air forces, was a most powerful factor in the German defeat. Good roads were sparse in the Ardennes, the attackers were short of petrol, and their inadequately run-in new tanks broke down in large numbers. Their forward troops depended heavily on a good railway service at the rear for a smooth flow of supplies, and this the Allied air attacks denied them. With troop trains stopping a hundred miles short of their proper destinations, the strain became too much for German road transport already short of petrol and likewise exposed to air attack. The unanimous view of Speer and two of the leading German commanders, Manteuffel and Dietrich, was that lack of supplies to the front proved fatal to the German plans. Speer himself emphasised that this shortage stemmed directly from the Allied air attacks on oil beforehand as well as on transportation during the actual campaign.[3]

Nearly all these raids by Bomber Command were carried out with very light losses, but there were two exceptions in the strongly defended Cologne area. Especially grievous was the second episode, when six aircraft of the Pathfinders group failed to return on 24

December from attacking the Cologne-Gremberg railway yards. The number of aircraft scheduled for this raid was 39, but only 24 finally attacked. Two of the Lancasters had collided over France, and with no sign of the forecast cloud the bombing orders had been changed *en route*: instead of bombing on OBOE leaders, each aircraft was to bomb visually. This was because OBOE bombing accuracy depended on the pilot holding a straight and level course on the final approach, and in clear weather the Cologne guns were notoriously effective. Unfortunately the first OBOE leader, Squadron Leader R. A. M. Palmer DFC, of No. 109 Squadron but on loan to No. 582, failed to receive the message in the air. As he approached the target on his straight and level course, flak hit his aircraft in several places and set two engines on fire. Believing that he was setting the bomb pattern for others to follow he still pressed on, despite also coming under attack from fighters. He scored direct hits on the target, then spiralled down in flames.

Statistically, Palmer was a dead man long before he perished: he was on his 110th operation. The citation for his posthumous Victoria Cross referred with justice to 'his record of prolonged and heroic endeavour'.[4]

On 1 November 1944, the date of the strengthened 'oil and communications' bombing directive, Harris indited an extremely long letter to Portal. In it he complained about the multiplicity of sources making demands on Bomber Command – 'the number of cooks now stirring the broth' – and pleaded for a renewed concentration on the bombing of urban areas. He maintained that the 'completing' of the area-bombing campaign by the devastation of twelve more German cities, including some in eastern Germany such as Leipzig and Dresden, would do more than anything else – including what the armies might do – to hasten the surrender of Germany.[5]

Twenty-odd letters, half of which were at least a thousand words long and two of which ran to four thousand words, passed between the two men during the next eleven weeks. They could easily have met for a discussion, or spoken on the 'scrambler' telephone, but evidently both wished to record their views in the most unmistakable and durable way.

The central theme of Harris's letters was that trying to take short cuts and bomb 'panacea' targets like ball bearings, molybdenum or oil would not work. Ministry of Economic Warfare forecasts about Germany's shortages had invariably turned out to be wrong: the

Germans always, it seemed, had resources unknown to the British experts. Moreover, small targets like individual factories or oil plants were difficult to hit, or to attack with a large force; and once they became obvious objectives in a sustained campaign they would be so heavily defended that Bomber Command would inevitably suffer heavy casualties in attacking them.

Portal's replies were to the effect that the area-bombing offensive had been essentially a long-term strategy to wear down Germany and assist the return to the Continent. The point now was to help the armies to the quickest possible victory. Apart from giving direct support in special circumstances, the best service the strategical air forces could render the armies at this time was to deprive the German forces of their dwindling resources of oil and shatter their communications. To achieve these ends it might be necessary on occasion – but not consistently – for Bomber Command to suffer a higher rate of casualty, perhaps 3 or 4 per cent, than it had recently incurred. And since Harris was so obviously unconvinced of the merits of the oil plan, Portal queried whether he was seizing all possible opportunities to hit the oil plants, the official 'first-priority' targets. 'Naturally,' Portal wrote, 'while you hold this view you will be unable to put your heart into the attack on oil.'

This nettled Harris, who while continuing to assert that the pursuit of the oil plan was 'chimerical', drew a sharp distinction between views and action. 'It has always been my custom,' Harris wrote, 'to leave no stone unturned to get my views across, but when the decision is made I carry it out to . . . the utmost of my ability . . . I am sorry that you also imagine my staff cannot be devoting the maximum thought and energy to the oil plan because of my views. I do not give my staff views. I give them orders. They do and always have done exactly what I tell them to do. I have told them to miss no opportunity of promoting the oil plan, and they have missed no worthwhile opportunity.'

In reply Portal still strove to arouse some enthusiasm in Harris for the oil plan: '*Your* determination matters more than that of all the rest of us put together.' But Harris declined to be enthused. 'You intimate,' he wrote, 'that I have been disloyal in the past in carrying out to the best of my ability . . . policies which have been laid down. That I absolutely and flatly deny.' He went on to offer his resignation: 'I therefore ask you to consider whether it is best for the prosecution of the war and the success of our arms, which alone matters, that I should remain in this situation.'

At this Portal gave up any attempt at conversion, brushed aside the suggestion of resignation, and concentrated on future action. 'I willingly accept,' he wrote, 'your assurance that you will continue to do the utmost to ensure the successful execution of the plan laid down.' Having probed deeply, Portal was satisfied that even if Harris had neglected opportunities of bombing oil and communications in October in favour of heavy urban area attacks, he was not doing so any more, and would not do so in the future.

The official history, *The Strategic Air Offensive Against Germany*, attaches very great significance to this episode. It regards it as exposing a fundamental difference in view which really did affect action. 'What had previously been a difference of opinion,' the authors wrote, 'became a serious dispute. Nor was the dispute ever resolved, and there can be no doubt that it diminished the effectiveness of Bomber Command in the final stages of the war.'[6] 'In the final phase of the war ... the potentialities of the strategic air offensive were greater than its achievement. This was primarily due to the difficulty of obtaining a united and concentrated policy through the channels of divided command and in the condition of divided opinion. The striking power was stronger and more precise than the organisation which directed it.'[7]

The official history, while always expressing its views with moderation and due qualification, is inclined to blame Portal, as far as the British side of the strategic offensive was concerned, for what it sees as an unnecessary degree of ineffectiveness. 'Sir Charles Portal ... it may be judged, should either have changed or imposed his view.'[8] It considered that divided, unresolved, conflicts of bombing policy, as exemplified in this correspondence, were one of the factors which prolonged the war beyond the point where it could otherwise have ended.*

Should Portal, then, have 'changed his opinion or enforced it'? Clearly he could not have been expected to change it; he was in possession of the latest information from ULTRA and the Joint Intelligence Committee about the critical state of German oil production, and he impressed on Harris that this was not information derived from Harris's bogeymen, the 'experts' of the Ministry of Economic Warfare. If Portal could not change his opinion, why then did he not enforce it? The short answer is that he did, and that he did not need to accept Harris's only half-meant offer of resignation in order to do so.

A brief summary will show the increasing weight of attack that

---

* The draft of the official history in this context wrote that Portal, by not removing Harris in January 1945, had 'virtually abdicated' his responsibilities as Chief of the Air Staff. When the Air Ministry drew Portal's attention to this passage he threatened to sue for libel if it was not withdrawn.[9] The offending phrase did not appear in the published work.

Harris made on oil. From June to September 1944 Bomber Command was much concerned with OVERLORD, the French ports and the flying bomb, and it averaged no more than 1000 sorties a month against German oil. In October, when there were still attacks to make on Walcheren, the number of sorties against German oil declined to 935, but they did great damage. They constituted, however, only about 6 per cent of Bomber Command's operational effort for the month. Portal felt that the attacks should have been made more often, or in greater strength. His probing began.

Doubtless in response to this, but partly also because the Walcheren commitment was over, November then saw Harris striking far more heavily against oil. The number of raids rose to 22, of which 14 were major, and in the course of them Bomber Command flew 3114 sorties and dropped over 16,000 tons of bombs – more than three times the previous month's effort.[10] The attacks, concentrated on the synthetic oil plants in the Ruhr, inflicted immense damage. On 6 November no fewer than 731 aircraft operated against the Nordstern plant near Gelsenkirchen. On 21 November an attack by 160 aircraft virtually ended production at Homberg-Meerbeck and during the ensuing night 273 aircraft were similarly successful against Castrop Rauxel.

Harris could not keep this up in December. The weather was less favourable, and from 16 December there were the demands of the struggle in the Ardennes. During the month Bomber Command made 17 attacks, only four of them major, against oil targets, in the course of which it flew some 1300 sorties and dropped around 5700 tons of bombs – more than in October but far less than in November.[11] But if the raids were fewer, they reached out much farther. In Harris's phrase, the air defences of the Reich 'crumbled' during the autumn of 1944 – as it became possible to establish radar ground stations near the German borders – and Bomber Command was able to operate effectively much deeper into German territory. A new navigational aid, LORAN, obtained from the Americans, like GEE but with much longer range, helped for some of the aircraft, and a new improved Mark III ASV for others. On 6/7 December the Command hit heavily at the great Leuna plant near Merseburg, 500 miles from the British bases, and on 21/22 December it struck with equal effectiveness against another huge plant, at Pölitz, near Stettin. Nevertheless after this last raid Portal complained that more than 207 aircraft might have been used – to which Harris replied that no Group other than the one involved (No. 5) could have achieved comparable results, and that over small targets mere numbers added to the confusion. Portal in turn came back with examples of how twice that number of aircraft had been employed successfully over similar targets.[12]

With better weather and the end of the fighting in the Ardennes Harris could pursue the oil offensive more vigorously again. From mid-January 1945 Bomber Command's attacks against oil increased sharply, and by the end of the month it had doubled its December effort. Its aircraft had made 24 attacks, of which seven were major, and in the course of these had flown nearly 2500 sorties and dropped over 10,000 tons of bombs.[13] Again, several of the raids were against very distant targets: 587 aircraft operated against Leuna on 14/15 January, and two nights later 328 aircraft attacked the plant at Zeitz, near Leipzig, while another 237 headed for that at Brüx, in Czechoslovakia. Evidently Harris was finding that, in the declining state of the German air defences, he could in fact operate large numbers against relatively small targets.

While the oil offensive was going well, at this stage the Allied armies in the west were making disappointingly slow progress. During January 1945 they did little more than force back the Germans from the Ardennes, check a German thrust against liberated Strasbourg, and consolidate positions west of the Rhine. For this they needed no close support from Bomber Command. Elsewhere, however, in the west of France, there was an unhappy episode in Allied army–air cooperation.

Rohan, a town at the mouth of the Gironde, was still held by the Germans. Aware that the German commander there had allowed the civilian population to withdraw, SHAEF arranged for a raid on the town and its defending gun-posts by Bomber Command. On 4/5 January, the weather being unsuitable for operations over Germany, Harris complied, sending an unexpectedly large force of over 350 aircraft. The outcome was tragic: the destruction of most of the town, the death of some hundreds of the inhabitants who had stayed behind, and still no surrender of the garrison. Thereafter it was agreed that any bombardment of French towns must have the personal authorisation of General Juin, the French Army Chief of Staff.[14]

In the same month Harris struck crushing blows against urban areas in Germany. On 2/3 January over 500 Lancasters with path-finding Mosquitoes bombed Nuremberg, previously much attacked but with disappointing results and twice with disastrous losses. On this occasion the raiders wrecked most of the centre of the old city and, more importantly, did great damage to the extensive industrial quarters. Meanwhile another 381 aircraft, mainly Halifaxes, bombed the industrial areas of Ludwigshafen, scoring hits with some 500 High Explosive bombs and 10,000 incendiaries on the I. G. Farben factories. From these two massive and highly successful raids only seven aircraft failed to return.

Three nights later a huge effort against Hanover proved more costly. All but five of the 664 aircraft involved managed to attack, and between them inflicted great damage, but 31 – not far short of 5 per cent – failed to return. However, losses were lighter again on 7/8 January, when some 600 aircraft out of 653 despatched, nearly all Lancasters, attacked Munich. They left a trail of devastation in the centre and the industrial areas of the city, and no more than 15 failed to regain their bases.*

Most of Bomber Command's other attacks in January 1945, apart from those on oil, were directed against the second target priority, communications. In the main this meant bombing railway centres, such as those at Neuss, Krefeld and Saarbrücken, but two highly successful attacks also took place against inland waterways – the Dortmund–Ems Canal, once again, and the Mittelland Canal. The Dortmund–Ems Canal operation, a 'daylight' on 1 January, provided yet one more example of the courage and determination, in this case amounting to heroism, which so generally inspired the crews. Flight Sergeant George Thompson was a wireless operator in a Lancaster of 9 Squadron. Just after his aircraft had bombed, flak tore holes in the fuselage and started several fires. Thompson saw that the mid-upper turret was ablaze, and that the gunner inside was unconscious. At the cost of severe burns to his hands and face he managed to reach the gunner and carry him clear. By this time he was aware that the rear turret too was on fire, and that the gunner there was likewise overcome by fumes. With his already burnt hands Thompson beat out the flames on the rear gunner's clothing and pulled him clear, then he made his way forward, edging round a hole in the flooring, to tell his captain what was happening. Despite much damage to the aircraft and a fire in one engine, the pilot managed to reach Belgium and successfully crash-land, only for Thompson and one of the gunners to die later from their injuries. The citation for the posthumous award of the Victoria Cross to Thompson rightly referred to his 'superb gallantry and self-sacrifice'.[15]

The offensive against oil and communications continued, in the

---

* This night also saw the last operation by a Wellington under Bomber Command – a radio countermeasures sortie by an aircraft of 192 Squadron.

Entrance to underground ops room at HQ Bomber Command.

'FIDO'

The petrol flames on either side of the runway have dispersed the fog, and a Lancaster is taking off, 1945.

Interrogation of Lancaster crews after raid on Berlin, 22/23 November 1943.

Engineer sergeant questioning crew about the performance of their Lancaster on their return from Berlin, 23 November 1943.

Airwoman cleaning and testing a
Lancaster's 96 sparking plugs.

Factory worker producing WINDOW.

Airwomen inspecting flotation jackets
('Mae Wests'). On left, inspected
parachutes hanging up to air.

Airwoman belting up ammunition for a
Lancaster.

Locomotive shop at
Krupps, gutted in 1943
and further damaged
in 1945.

The Arnsberg viaduct
wrecked by a 'Grand
Slam'.

The *Tirpitz* capsized
after bombing,
12 November 1944.

Railway centre at Chambly, France, after attack on 1/2 May 1944.

Gnome et Rhône aero-engine works at Limoges after attack on 8/9 February 1944.

Grusonwerk (subsidiary of Krupps) factory at Magdeburg for manufacture of
telescopes and torpedoes, 1945.

Railway viaduct at Bielefeld after attack on 14 March 1945.

Bomb damage in Krefeld, 1945.

Bomb damage in central Berlin, photographed during a reconnaissance on 8 March 1945.

The Wilhelmstrasse, Berlin, 1945, taken from the bombed Air Ministry.

Ju 88 night-fighters, mostly from NJG3, abandoned at the end of hostilities. Lack of petrol had immobilised many in the last weeks of the war.

latter case often by way of area attack. On 2/3 February over 500 aircraft hit Wiesbaden, the first and the last heavy raid directed against this Rhineland town with British associations.* The railway, industrial and residential quarters all suffered severely. Then, on 7/8 February, came two massive raids in direct military support. The British XXX Corps, planning an attack into Germany in the Reichwold area, requested the bombing of Goch and Kleve, two fortified towns in the German defences. No fewer than 464 aircraft were briefed for Goch, but after 155 had bombed, smoke so obscured the town that the Master Bomber called off the raid. At Kleve another 300-odd aircraft also did great damage, but the resulting rubble in the streets slowed down the British advance, which soon came to a halt.[16]

Meanwhile, events were moving towards the operation which, more than any other, has fuelled controversy about the work of Bomber Command.

There is no mystery, though there has been a certain amount of mystification, about the decision to bomb Dresden.

As a centre of administration, communications and industry – and as a major German city generally – Dresden had long been on Bomber Command's non-immediate target-list. It had been left alone because to attack it would require a very deep, and therefore probably expensive, penetration of Germany, and because Bomber Command had had many more urgent tasks. By February of 1945, however, half-a-dozen raids against oil targets in eastern Germany had been made without crippling losses, and the successful Russian offensive which began in mid-January had created a new military situation. As the Russians advanced through Silesia it became obvious that air attacks on the east German cities confronting them might be of powerful assistance to the Soviet drive. And the disorganisation created in these cities by such air attacks would be all the greater because their populations were swollen by many thousands of refugees – some from bombed cities elsewhere in Germany, but most from the path of the Russian advance.

The immediate, as opposed to the general, chain of events which brought about the Dresden raids began on 25 January 1945, when because of the Russian advance the British Joint Intelligence Committee recommended air attacks on Berlin and other east German towns,

* It had been the headquarters of the British occupying forces after the First World War.

and when Churchill enquired of Sir Archibald Sinclair, the Secretary of State for Air, what plans there were for – as Sinclair remembered the phrase – 'basting the Germans in their retreat from Breslau'. In reply Sinclair pointed out that this was work for the Russian tactical air forces, but that, subject to the overriding priority of the offensive against oil, the possibility of area attacks on Berlin, Dresden, Leipzig and Chemnitz was under examination. To this Churchill announced peremptorily on 26 January: 'I did not ask you last night about plans for harrying the German retreat from Breslau. On the contrary I asked whether Berlin and no doubt other large cities in East Germany should not now be considered especially attractive targets. I am glad that this is "under examination". Pray report to me to-morrow what is going to be done.'[17]

With the Prime Minister obviously on the warpath, events moved quickly. That same day Portal instructed Bottomley to seek the approval of the Chiefs of Staff, SHAEF and General Spaatz for 'one big attack on Berlin, Dresden, Leipzig, Chemnitz or any other cities where *a severe blitz will not only cause confusion in the evacuation from the East but also hamper the movement of troops from the West.*'*[18]

This expressed the essence of the matter, and having secured the necessary approvals Bottomley instructed Harris the following day to carry out such attacks, subject always to priority for oil targets if circumstances permitted. The attacks were to be made 'with the particular object of exploiting the confused conditions which are likely to exist in the above-mentioned cities during the Russian advance'.[19] On grounds of preparedness, this order was not entirely welcome to Harris: Bomber Command was short on data about, for instance, the current defences of Dresden and the best aiming-points for inflicting industrial damage;[20] but on other grounds he can only have welcomed it. On 1 November, as already observed, he had pleaded for permission to attack Dresden, Leipzig and Chemnitz in preference to oil plants.†

At the inter-Allied conference at Yalta the following week the Russians requested the bombing of communications in Germany to prevent reinforcement of the German eastern front. They asked in particular for attacks on Berlin and Leipzig, but made no such request about Dresden. In general they clearly preferred to keep the RAF and the USAAF away from any territory they might soon be occupying. But the 'bomb-line' that was agreed with them placed the

* Author's italics.
† See page 263.

city of Dresden within the zone of Anglo-American air operations.[21]

Meanwhile plans had been concerted with General Spaatz and on 3 February nearly 1000 B-17s of the US Eighth Air Force made a massive raid on railway and governmental targets in Berlin, while another 400 attacked railways and oil in Magdeburg. They did great damage and, incidentally, appear to have killed a large number of Berlin civilians – 25,000, the Germans asserted.[22] Several days of unsuitable weather then followed, during which the Allied air forces awaited their chance to attack Dresden. The Eighth Air Force, which had already twice bombed objectives in Dresden in earlier months, was then scheduled to begin the assault on 13 February, only for bad weather in the early morning to cause a cancellation. So it came about that when, around 9 a.m. that day, the Met. officers at High Wycombe forecast a period of five hours that night during which Dresden would be free of cloud, Harris with characteristic boldness seized the opportunity and struck first.

No lack of thought had gone into the plan of attack. Its main features were to be an initial raid by No. 5 Group, which was to mark the target area and set it well ablaze, followed by a further and heavier raid three hours later by Nos. 1, 3, 6 and 8 Groups. The interval of three hours would allow, it was reckoned, for any night-fighters sent up against the initial raid to have exhausted their fuel, and for the fire-fighters and rescue workers to be fully active on the scene – so that they could be caught in the open by the second attack. Since Dresden was virtually undamaged, the raiders were to carry a very high proportion of incendiaries – 75 per cent of the bomb-load – as had often been done in 1942 and 1943, before such gaps had been created in German towns that fires no longer spread readily. The terrible firestorms at Hamburg and Kassel had sprung up unplanned. This time a firestorm would be no accident.[23]

There were also elaborate plans for diversionary operations. Mosquitoes of the Pathfinders' Light Night Striking Force, in numbers ranging from 6 to 71, were to attack among other places Magdeburg, Bonn, Dortmund and Nuremberg; No. 100 Group was to fly radio countermeasure and INTRUDER patrols; and, to cap all, 368 aircraft, mainly Halifaxes, were to attack the synthetic oil plant at Böhlen, near Leipzig, fifteen minutes before the first bombs fell on Dresden. All this in fact worked well, and distracted German attention from the approaching assault on the Saxon capital.

The first Lancasters of 5 Group, equipped with the new long-range navigational aid LORAN and with H2S Mark III, arrived over Dresden after their ten-hour flight a few minutes before the zero hour of 10.15

p.m. Working from the pictures on their H2S, they dropped white flares and green target indicators to show up the approximate target area. Then came nine Mosquitoes led by the Master Bomber, diving down to 3,000 feet or less to pinpoint, by the light of the flares, the actual aiming-point, a stadium near the centre of the city. This they marked with red target indicators. Only at this point did the citizens of Dresden receive warning of their impending ordeal. Punctually at 10.15 p.m. the main force of 244 Lancasters then began to arrive, running over the city on many different headings and aiming their bombs at the red target indicators. Very little flak came up, and soon the Master Bomber was directing the raiders down lower for greater accuracy. Within fifteen minutes the whole attack was over.

A few minutes before zero for the second raid, timed for 1.30 a.m., the Blind Illuminator Lancasters of the Pathfinder Group arrived to release their flares. Their presence was scarcely necessary. They had seen the fires of Dresden from 50 miles away, and the Master Bomber was perturbed to find the area around the aiming-point completely obscured by smoke and flame. When the huge force of Lancasters, 529 strong, began to arrive, he directed them to extend the area of fire by bombing around its edges. The bombs, a greater proportion now of high explosives, crashed down, but still few anti-aircraft guns fired and no fighters intervened. Flying home, the crews could see the glare in the sky above Dresden from 200 miles away. Plenty of them felt, not perhaps for the first time, an uneasy mixture of exhilaration from a successful mission, relief at a safe return, and sorrow for those they had bombed.

But the ordeal of Dresden was by no means over. The following day, 14 February, 311 escorted B-17s, hampered by smoke from the earlier work of Bomber Command, found and attacked the marshalling yards. There was the inevitable overspill from high-level blind-bombing, but such errors were not as far astray as those of one group of 40 which by mistake bombed Prague.[24]

To extend the attack on east German communications another force of Fortresses, 294 strong, attacked railway targets at Chemnitz at much the same time. The next night, 14/15 February, Bomber Command followed on with two raids of a more general kind, by 329 and 388 aircraft, against the same city. The weather forecast, however, proved to have none of the accuracy of that of the previous night: in ten-tenths cloud recourse was had to sky-markers, and the bombing was very scattered. The raiders dropped some 750,000 incendiaries – 100,000 more than against Dresden – but Chemnitz suffered no firestorm.

To conclude the immediate series of raids, a further 210 B-17s, baulked of attacking oil plants, attacked the Dresden marshalling yards 'blind' as a secondary target on the following day, 15 February, while another much larger force attacked similar objectives at Kottbus, twenty miles from Dresden. US aircraft were to attack Dresden targets again on 2 March (when they also bombed Chemnitz) and on 17 April.

Though the American raids caused widespread damage it was Bomber Command's double blow on 13/14 February, directed at the centre of the old town, which devastated Dresden. It destroyed not only famed cultural monuments in one of Europe's most lovely cities but also, according to an aerial survey made by the British Bombing Survey Unit, 1681 acres of the fully built-up area – a figure which the Dresden authorities nearly double.[25] On the Dresden calculation, this would be about three-quarters of the central nine square miles or so. Out of a total of some 220,000 houses in the whole town, Dresden records 75,338 as completely destroyed and another 11,500 as badly damaged.[26]

Much of this destruction arose from the firestorm caused by 5 Group's initial raid, as did most of the casualties. As a city which had not been seriously attacked before, Dresden lacked the extensive public air-raid shelters common in the west German towns, and many people suffered asphyxiation in their cellars. The precise total of fatal casualties is unknown, but the most authentic figure seems to be around 25,000, with many more thousands of people unaccounted for.*[27] The disposal of such huge numbers of corpses before disease could spread naturally presented an acute problem to the city authorities. Mass burial outside the city finally proving too slow, mass incineration completed the task.

The strategic effects of the attacks are more difficult to assess. The Russians did not capture Dresden until 8 May, so the raids can hardly have prevented adequate German reinforcement reaching that section of the front. It does not appear that the marshalling yards suffered great harm in the American attacks of 14 and 15 February, and though the Bomber Command raids gutted the main railway station, limited traffic was again possible after three days. Among the industrial

---

* Nazi propaganda put forth figures of up to 300,000. David Irving, when he first published *The Destruction of Dresden* in 1963, quoted estimates varying between 35,000 and 200,000. But later, in 1966, he came into possession of the Dresden area police chief's final report (of March 1945). This gave a total of 18,375 dead, and estimated that the final figure would be about 25,000 – apart from persons unaccounted for. Mr Irving accepted this as the authentic total, and stated so in a letter to *The Times* published on 7 July 1966.

premises destroyed, one was certainly important – the Zeiss-Ikon optical works – and much of industrial Dresden was 'out' for the rest of the war, though electricity supplies were generally restored within a week. An important effect – one of the purposes of the raid – was to stop any possibility of Dresden becoming a main administrative and control centre for the German armies fighting farther forward. Shortly after the raid Harris wrote: 'Dresden was a mass of munitions works, an intact Government centre, and a key transportation centre to the East. It is now none of those things.'[28] Of this claim, one can only agree with certainty that Dresden had indeed ceased to be an intact Government centre.

The repercussions from the Dresden raids were immediate, and have scarcely died down yet. On the German side, the leadership naturally denounced Allied inhumanity and terror-bombing, and eventually put forth grossly exaggerated figures of the casualties. Lower down the scale, increasing numbers of Germans were gripped by depression, feeling that the struggle had become hopeless and that no secret weapon of Hitler's, their last hope, could now prevent the utter ruin of their land. But the Germans being still a patriotic, disciplined and regimented people, a lowering of morale did not translate itself into – what would really have helped the Allies – resistance to the Nazi regime.

On the Allied side, the reverberations were particularly strong in the United States, following a despatch from an Associated Press correspondent at SHAEF. An RAF Intelligence officer there, at a press briefing on 16 February, had referred to bombing large population centres and preventing supplies reaching them, or refugees leaving. This, the correspondent enlarged into a statement that 'the Allied Air Chiefs have made the long-awaited decision to adopt deliberate terror-bombing of German population centres as a ruthless expedient of hastening Hitler's doom'.[29] This became front-page news in America, but in Britain there was no comparable furore, for the authorities made sure the despatch did not appear in the press. It was left largely to Richard Stokes MP to probe the Government later in the House of Commons.

The most remarkable comment was that of Churchill six weeks later. On 28 March he minuted Portal and the other Chiefs of Staff: 'It seems to me that the moment has come when the question of bombing German cities for the sake of increasing the terror, though under other pretexts, should be reviewed. Otherwise we shall come into control of an utterly ruined land. The destruction of Dresden remains a serious query against the conduct of Allied bombing . . .'[30]

Coming from one whose eagerness to bomb cities in eastern Germany to help the Russians had recently precipitated the whole series of attacks, this startled and shocked the Chiefs of Staff, who took the view that the Prime Minister had written thoughtlessly under strain. Not only had he ignored his own share of responsibility in the matter, but by bringing in Dresden he had failed to differentiate between the situation in mid-February, when the war seemed far from over, and that at the time of his minute, at the end of March, when the Allies were across the Rhine in force and Germany was nearing the point of surrender. With his fellow Chiefs' approval, Portal quietly persuaded Churchill to withdraw the offending minute – no mean achievement – and substitute one which made the same point of substance in unexceptionable terms. Omitting all mention of Dresden and terrorisation, the new minute concluded: 'We must see to it that air attacks do not do more harm to ourselves in the long run than they do to the enemy's immediate war effort. Pray let me have your views.'[31] With this revised expression of opinion the Chiefs of Staff were in full accord.

This initiated – for by then the time was fully ripe – a reappraisal of the need for Bomber Command to make, even on low priority, any further area attacks on German cities.

23

Victory

U nlike post-war commentators, the Allies in February 1945 had no means of knowing that the war in Europe would end within three months. Until the Russians were in strength across the Oder, and the Western Allies likewise across the Rhine, the final defeat of Germany, though predictable, seemed likely to be less than immediate. Churchill's minute of 28 March about reviewing area-bombing came at a time when Germany was perceptibly on the point of collapse. Before that there were six weeks during which the outcome was less clear, and during which Bomber Command's area attacks continued with undiminished force.

Most of these raids, however, now also served the needs of imminent military operations. Destroying Ruhr and Rhineland towns was no longer only a long-term strategy designed to weaken German industry and morale: it was also an immediate impediment to German resistance and reinforcement along the Rhine. In most, though not all, of the area attacks of this period there were two aiming-points – the local railway yards and the town centre. Between mid-February and the end of March Bomber Command made at least 20 area attacks. A few ranged far afield, but, in accordance with the current directive, most were concentrated on the Rhineland–Ruhr zones facing the armies of the Western Allies.

In the second half of February, after the raids on Dresden and Chemnitz, the towns which Bomber Command hit most heavily were Dortmund, Duisburg, Essen, Worms and Mainz. Forces varying between 342 and 528 bombers carried out the attacks, with an average 'missing rate' of no more than 1.5 per cent. At Essen, according to a German report, 300 high explosives and 11,000 incendiaries fell on Krupps. At Worms and Mainz the historic buildings inevitably suffered as well as the factories and communications, particularly at Mainz where the bombs were aimed on sky-markers. At Worms some 35,000 people became temporarily homeless, and at Mainz about 1200 lost their lives, including 41 nuns in a convent.[1]

Most destructive of all these raids during the latter half of February, and the last predominantly area attack to be delivered by night, was that on distant Pforzheim, in south Germany. All but ten of the 388 aircraft despatched bombed the town, and mostly from only about 8000 feet. They created a firestorm which engulfed much of the built-up area, gutting the railway station and several factories and incidentally causing the deaths of 17,000 people.[2]

It was on this raid, on 23/24 February, that Bomber Command's last Victoria Cross of the war was won – a posthumous award, as so often. Captain Edwin Swales DFC, a South African with 582 Squadron, was acting as Master Bomber. In the target area shots from a fighter put one of his engines and the rear turret out of action. Still Swales persisted, giving instructions to his fellow raiders while the fighter closed in again and scored hits on another engine. Having remained until he could see that the attack was thoroughly successful, Swales then tried to fly his battered Lancaster home on two engines, though the blind-flying instruments were useless and he was running into heavy cloud and increasing turbulence. Knowing that he could not hold the plane aloft much longer, over Belgium he ordered the crew to bale out. He kept the aircraft steady until the last of his crew had jumped. Then the Lancaster plunged to earth, Swales still at the controls.[3]

In the following month Bomber Command made three major, and very effective, area attacks on distant targets. Some 750 aircraft operated against Chemnitz on 5/6 March, over 500 against Dessau, centre of the Junkers industrial empire, on 7/8 March, and nearly 300 against Nuremberg on 16/17 March. Once more, casualties were heavy against this south German town – 8.7 per cent missing. Most of the attacks, however, were still against towns, or towns-and-railways, in the Ruhr–Rhineland. In particular, crushing blows fell during three consecutive days – on Essen (11 March), Dortmund (12 March) and Wuppertal-Barmen (13 March). The number of sorties flown in these three operations, which were under heavy Mustang escort, was no fewer than 2541, and only five (0.2 per cent) failed to return. Alike in Dortmund and in Essen (where Krupps had in fact been virtually out of action since the previous October) significant production ceased for the rest of the war. Both had been attacked by record numbers of aircraft for a single target – over 1050 in each case – and both had suffered from record weights of bombs (4662 and 4851 tons).[4]

Other extremely destructive raids during the month were those by 703 aircraft in clear weather on 2 March against Cologne – which fell to American troops four days later – and by 267 aircraft on 15/16 March against Hagen, in the Ruhr. The attack on Cologne, the last in a long, long series, inflicted heavy damage on the city and the main railway station, and lesser damage on one of the Rhine bridges. At Hagen, in addition to considerable industrial damage, some 30,000 people were 'bombed out'.[5]

All the operations mentioned above, even when the targets included railways, were essentially area attacks, as also were two heavy blows on 17/18 March against Witten, in the Ruhr, and Hanau, east of Frankfurt. But in many other cases the 'transportation' objective was clearly primary and industrial and residential damage secondary. The two, however, were intimately connected. Even when they missed any major transportation target, area attacks usually disrupted local transport and a wide range of telephone, telegraph and postal services, as well as electricity supplies, on which communications in their wider aspects depended.

Largely owing to pressure from Tedder, with Zuckerman as his chief adviser, transportation in Germany had become one of the 'second priorities' for attack, after oil, and had been listed as such in the directive of 25 September 1944.* On 1 November, in the next main directive, this target system, in the wider form of 'the German lines of communication – with particular emphasis upon the Ruhr' – had been elevated into the sole 'second priority' after oil.[6] In connection with these two directives plans were produced for attack on the German railway system in which Bomber Command, the two American strategic air forces, and the tactical air forces would all take part. The first such plan had been a wide-ranging affair which by attacks in Germany visualised also helping the Allied armies in Italy and the Russians. The second plan, produced during November, had been more concentrated but still contemplated operations over very large areas of Germany. The function of the strategic air forces in this plan, broadly speaking, had been 'attrition' – i.e. wearing down the

* See page 253.

German railway system by attacks on marshalling yards, locomotive depots, repair shops and the like. To complement this, the function of the tactical air forces was 'interdiction', or the denying of passage by attacks on moving traffic and sensitive points such as bridges.

By mid-December the strategic air forces had between them made about 130 distinctively 'transportation' attacks when the German offensive in the Ardennes interrupted the sequence and called for the bombing to be applied to transportation nearer the battlefront. Bomber Command's objectives thus far had included not only marshalling yards adjacent to urban areas but also some precision targets such as the Dortmund–Ems Canal. The attacks, however, with the Americans ranging far and wide over Germany, had not greatly impressed the Combined Strategic Targets Committee, which predominantly favoured concentrating against oil. Many on the Committee considered that the transportation campaign had been too diffuse, and the bombing in general too remote from the immediate battle areas, to produce the best possible results.

After the repulse of the Ardennes offensive had shown the great effect of air attacks on communications nearer the front, SHAEF had accordingly produced a new plan of a much more concentrated kind, which, as finally accepted in February 1945, aimed at isolating the Ruhr from the rest of Germany.[7] A central feature of the plan was that the main railway bridges and viaducts from Bremen down to Coblenz should be destroyed, together with all the 25 main marshalling yards between that line and the Rhine. This had the great advantage that by then the isolation of the Ruhr, an area which would be one of the Allies' immediate objectives after they had crossed the Rhine, would serve tactical purposes as well as the strategical ends of depriving the rest of Germany of Ruhr coal and preventing reinforcement of the Ruhr defences.

In connection with this new 'Ruhr Transportation Plan', as it was called, Bomber Command made some highly effective attacks during the latter part of February. Those which set out to destroy urban areas as well as railways have already been mentioned. Among the more precise targets were railways at Wesel, just east of the Rhine, to make it difficult for the Germans either to retreat or to reinforce the area they still held across the river. These railways were attacked every day from 16 to 19 February. Another precise objective was the Mittelland Canal. An operation against this vitally important waterway, carried out on 21/22 February by 125 Lancasters and 12 Mosquitoes of 5 Group, cost nearly 8 per cent of the attacking force but made a substantial breach in the canal.[8]

Such precision raids became even more effective in the following month. On 2/3 March 213 Lancasters and ten Mosquitoes breached the Landberger aqueduct of the Dortmund–Ems Canal in two places and again put a stop to all traffic. Three nights later 138 Lancasters and Mosquitoes continued the assault on railways at Wesel, and on 14 March a small force of 38 Lancasters and five Mosquitoes from the highly trained and well-equipped 9 and 617 Squadrons struck at two of the vital railway viaducts linking the Ruhr with other parts of Germany. On this occasion the Arnsberg viaduct just outside the Ruhr, part of one of the main east–west routes, escaped undamaged, but a huge section of the Bielefeld viaduct, on the main Ruhr–Bremen line, collapsed. Barnes Wallis's new 22,000-lb 'Grand Slam' bomb, on its first operational use, had scored a near miss, exploded deep beneath the marsh, and, with the assistance of a few Tallboys, generated shock waves which brought down seven spans – a full hundred yards – of the viaduct.[9] Five days later, on 19 March, the same squadron took on the intact Arnsberg viaduct. This time, five of the Lancasters, their bomb-bay doors having been removed, could carry Grand Slams, while the other 14 carried Tallboys. Between them, they shattered the centre of the viaduct.[10]

Strategical operations were by now merging with tactical. As the Allies prepared to cross the Rhine in force, Bomber Command attacked the railway yards at Hamm on 20 March, and those at Rheine the following day. Farther afield, 160 Lancasters bombed railway yards at Münster on 21 March and at Hildesheim, a key point on the route across central Germany, the next day. The Hildesheim operation, Bomber Command's first major blow against objectives in this historic city, spilled over into a general area attack. In addition to wrecking railway yards it devastated about 70 per cent of the town, destroyed the cathedral, and killed 1645 people.[11]

Among other operations distant from the Ruhr, Bomber Command during this fortnight also wrecked Zweibrücken, in the southern sector, to block the passage of German troops. A week later, on 22 and 23 March, forces of over 100 Lancasters broke railway bridges at Bremen, Nienburg, and Bad Oeynhausen on the east–west route near Minden.[12]

Meanwhile the American ground forces had been fast advancing towards, and then along, the Rhine. On 7 March some of General Hodges's US First Army had actually seized an intact bridge at Remagen, near Bonn, and established a bridgehead on the east bank. Farther to the south another part of Bradley's US 12th Army Group, General Patton's US Third Army, had cleared the Germans from the

Eifel, reached Coblenz, and swept south along the Rhine. On 22 March this thrusting commander forced his way across the river at a small town well esteemed by wine-lovers, Oppenheim.

Both Hodges and Patton then waited impatiently for Montgomery, who had been many days preparing his set-piece assault, to launch his considerable forces across the river farther north near Wesel.* To assist this, 228 Bomber Command Lancasters and Mosquitoes made a crushing raid on this much bombed town soon after 10 p.m. on 23 March. Before midnight British commandos had successfully dealt with the bomb-shocked and shell-shocked defenders, and soon Montgomery's forces too were across the Rhine. In a generous message to Harris he expressed appreciation for 'magnificent co-operation' and praised a 'masterpiece' of bombing.[13]

The next day, 24 March, other forces of Bomber Command completely destroyed a marshalling yard at Sterkrade, in the Ruhr. The day afterwards, their blows fell heavily on railways (and adjacent buildings) at three key points on the main route between the Ruhr and central Germany – Osnabrück, Münster and Hanover.

By this time the tactical air forces had also done their work brilliantly. Besides attacking moving traffic and marshalling yards they had played the major part in severing the 16 main bridges connecting the Ruhr with the rest of Germany. 'Interdiction' had combined with 'attrition' to produce during the last week in March the complete isolation of the Ruhr. A few days later, on 1 April, Hodges's and Patton's troops, converging from north and south, completed its physical encirclement. Some 350,000 German troops in consequence soon laid down their arms. As Speer had said in a speech in November: 'The Battle of the Ruhr is a battle for the existence of the Reich.'[14] The Allies had won that battle, and soon the Reich would no longer exist.

Throughout all its attacks on cities, marshalling yards, bridges and canals, Bomber Command had continued to play its part in the strategic offensive against oil. February 1945 saw its previous efforts in this direction far surpassed, with 25 attacks – 19 of them by around 200 aircraft – against oil targets. The heaviest raid, on 8/9 February by 475 Lancasters and 12 Mosquitoes, virtually finished off production at Pölitz for the rest of the war.[15] During the month the number of sorties flown against oil, 4346, was nearly 2000 more than in January.

* Montgomery's 21st Army Group comprised at this time the US Ninth Army, the British Second Army, and the First Canadian Army.

All this was to be surpassed again in March, when Bomber Command made 33 attacks, of which 18 were major, against German oil plants. In the course of these its aircraft flew 4524 sorties and dropped over 21,000 tons of bombs. Among other achievements of the month was a particularly successful raid by 224 Lancasters and 11 Mosquitoes of 5 Group on 20/21 March against the synthetic oil plant at Böhlen. Following several earlier raids by the Eighth Air Force and one on 5/6 March by Bomber Command, it eliminated for the rest of hostilities one of Germany's main sources of aviation spirit.[16]

There was no need to maintain this scale of attack throughout April. The combined efforts of Bomber Command, the Eighth Air Force, and the Fifteenth Air Force – which did magnificent work from Italy, in particular against targets in Austria and southern Germany, as it had earlier done against oil in Hungary, Romania and Yugoslavia – had brought production in Germany almost to a standstill. The story may be read in the figures, found in Speer's papers, relating to five of the main oil plants – Leuna, Böhlen, Magdeburg, Zeitz and Pölitz. In January 1945 their combined output of finished oils was 46,750 tons, which was far less than any month's output in the previous autumn. In March they produced only 11,260 tons, and in April a mere 730.[17]

Over the whole period of the oil offensive a similar story appears in the combined output of finished oil products from all the hydrogenation and Fischer-Tropsch plants. In April 1944, before the Allied attacks began, it was 348,000 tons. For March 1945 it was 12,000 tons.[18] In this outstanding achievement the Americans, beginning earlier and with an air force attacking from the south as well as from the north-west, played the greater part. In the raids up to the end of January 1945 the Eighth and Fifteenth air forces together aimed about 80,000 metric tons of bombs against the German oil plants, Bomber Command about 50,000 tons. It seems, however, that some of the British attacks may have caused the most damage: Speer during interrogation stated that 'the last series of night attacks on Pölitz, Brüx and Leuna were more effective than the day [i.e. American] attacks by reason of the fact that the super-heavy bombs caused shattering damage to these plants'.[19] But it is fundamentally unprofitable to try to determine exact shares in the credit. It was the combination of escorted day attacks and night attacks, together with the combined weight of the three air forces, that made adequate defence impossible.

Speer also gave his opinion that the attacks on Germany's synthetic oil industry were 'the most decisive in hastening the end of the war'.[20] Whether that, or some other factor, was the 'most decisive' is a matter for infinite discussion; but it is clear that in waging, with the

Americans, the oil offensive, Harris and Bomber Command made a powerful contribution to victory. Initially Harris had little faith in it, and his pessimism was confirmed by a 'missing rate' of 10 per cent in the attacks of June 1944. But under pressure from Portal and having discovered that GH and the 'crumbling' of the German defences had made accurate attack possible without heavy losses, he later maintained a strong and steady offensive. What surprised, and relieved, him most was that over Bomber Command's whole series of attacks on oil from June 1944 to May 1945, involving some 22,000 sorties, less than 2 per cent failed to return.[21]

To the end of his days Harris maintained that at the outset of the offensive the success was not predictable, and that concentration on area-bombing was a safer bid. In *Bomber Offensive* he wrote: 'I still do not think that it was reasonable, at that time, to expect that the campaign would succeed: what the Allied strategists did was to bet on an outsider and the outsider won.'[22]

That, almost needless to say, is hardly an adequate comment. There was much information available to Harris, as well as to Portal and Spaatz, that – once OVERLORD was successfully launched – fully justified making oil the favourite.

By the beginning of April there was certainly a case, as Churchill had urged, for giving up area-bombing. The policy that emerged after the Churchill–Portal exchanges was not, however, one of complete abandonment: it was that area-bombing would be employed only in situations where the armies were needing direct support. It was in such a context that, to help the Russians, 500 Lancasters and a few Mosquitoes on 14/15 April shattered the town of Potsdam as well as its barracks and its railways. Similarly on 22 April, to help the British XXX Corps, Bomber Command mounted a heavy area attack on Bremen – which fell to the troops five days later.

While forward American forces were waiting at the Elbe for the Russians, and other American groups were streaming south and south-east, the British and Canadians under Montgomery were heading north and north-east for the German ports. The Russians, having meanwhile invested Berlin, did not arrive at the Elbe until 27 April. During this period Bomber Command was helping to remove any remaining threat from the German Navy.

The main danger from the *Kriegsmarine*, though the Admiralty had not at first thought so, was always from U-boats. In 1944 the Admiralty's great concern was that the Germans were building new boats – Types XXI and XXIII – much larger and faster than their predecessors, and equipped with the *Schnorkel* device which enabled them to travel submerged for very long periods. As the concrete pens at the Atlantic operating bases in France had proved so resistant to bombing, Bomber Command had found it more profitable to attack the centres of U-boat production. By the autumn of 1944 its attacks, combined with those of the USAAF, on Hamburg, Bremen and other north German ports had forced the Germans into constructing U-boat parts elsewhere, and then assembling these at the shipyards. It followed that the success of the Allies' bombing campaign against transportation would affect the production of U-boats.

On 8/9 March, 31 March and 8/9 April Bomber Command made heavy attacks, by forces averaging over 400 aircraft, on the Blohm and Voss U-boat yards at Hamburg. There was much cloud, and results were uncertain. It appears that though the yards were greatly damaged, not much harm was done to the U-boats under assembly. Earlier raids, however, had already had their effect. Many of the U-boat parts fabricated elsewhere were too big to be transported by rail or road, and had to be brought to the ports by inland waterways. During November Bomber Command had breached both the Dortmund–Ems and the Mittelland canals, and many U-boat parts had failed to reach the ports. The result appears in the figures of U-boat construction: 14 in October 1944, five in November.[23]

Ordinary U-boat construction recovered considerably in January 1945, but the XXIs and XXIIIs never became the danger that had been feared. By February, according to German plans, there should have been 40 in commission. There were only two. The disruption caused by the Allied air attacks on Hamburg and Bremen helped to make faster progress impossible, as did the loss of the U-boats' best training grounds through Bomber Command's mining of Danzig Bay. By the end of the war the number of Type XXI and XXIII U-boats actually in service was still only in single figures. Of the various causes which accounted for this, the British official historian of the war at sea has stated that the decisive factor was not the destruction at the ports but Bomber Command's breaching of the two canals.[24] However, the destruction at the ports, to which the Americans fully contributed, undoubtedly played its part – or the Germans would not have planned to replace the excellent facilities at Hamburg and Bremen with a vast structure under a concrete roof 23 feet thick at the small port of Farge, on the Weser.*

---

* This was never brought into operation. On 27 March 617 Squadron put two Grand Slams into the roof.

Another, though much lesser, source of vexation to the Allies had been the Germans' small E-boats. After some earlier attempts largely frustrated by the weather, during February two attacks by 617 Squadron smashed in the massive concrete roofs of their shelters at Ijmuiden, which also harboured U-boats. The E-boats themselves were not greatly harmed, but they had to take to the sea, to be rounded up later by the Royal Navy.

The most spectacularly successful of Bomber Command's operations against the German Navy in the last weeks of the war, however, were against capital ships. The Command had already sunk the *Tirpitz* in November and the old battleship *Schleswig-Holstein* at Gdynia on 18/19 December, to add to its earlier success against the *Gneisenau* in 1942. Now, on 9/10 April 1945, a remarkable raid by 591 aircraft on Kiel hit all three shipyards – including the Deutsche Werke U-boat yard – and ended the career of three major warships. It sank the pocket battleship *Admiral von Scheer*, and so severely damaged the light cruiser *Emden* and the heavy cruiser *Hipper* that their crews could not put to sea and afterwards scuttled them. This was not all. A week later No. 617 Squadron, in an attack at Swinemünde that saw one of the Lancasters shot down and nearly all the others damaged, effectively disposed of Germany's last pocket battleship, the *Lützow*.[25]

To add to the destruction of the German capital fleet came the devastation of Heligoland, the highly fortified base which, with its 12-inch guns, commanded the approaches to the estuaries of the Weser and the Elbe. As the island also bristled with anti-aircraft guns an operation by fighter-bombers seemed likely to be too expensive, so Bomber Command was required to make an initial high-level attack, dropping heavy bombs. This it did on 18 April, using a huge force of 969 aircraft, at a cost of three Halifaxes, to wreck the naval base, the town (the civilian population of which had long since departed) and the airfield on the neighbouring island of Dun. The raid destroyed every building together with most of the radar and flak defences. The next day Nos. 9 and 617 Squadrons completed the task by precision-bombing the big guns. Five days later another massive raid hit Wangerooge, the most easterly of the East Frisian islands, the batteries of which had also protected the approaches to the Weser.[26]

On 2/3 May strong forces of No. 8 Group's Mosquitoes – 138 of them – attacked Kiel and the neighbouring airfields. No. 100 Group gave strong support with radio countermeasures and no fewer than 72 'intruders'. This was Bomber Command's last offensive operation of the war. Shortly afterwards Kiel was declared an open city, and thirty-six hours later British and Canadian troops took possession.

*　　*　　*

The last raid by four-engined bombers had taken place a week earlier, on 25/26 April, when 107 Lancasters and 12 Mosquitoes blasted an oil refinery at Tonsberg in Norway. In daylight some hours beforehand, a much larger force had set forth on a much less conventional operation. It was apparently Harris's idea, approved by SHAEF and higher authorities, that an attack should be made on Hitler's villa and the adjacent buildings, including an SS barracks, at Berchtesgaden. No fewer than 375 Lancasters and Mosquitoes took off, escorted by 98 Mustangs of the Eighth Air Force and 13 Mustang squadrons of Fighter Command. To reach the Bavarian Alps they had to fly for the last 250 miles over territory which the Germans still held, but such was the crushing degree of Allied air superiority that no fighters rose to challenge them. There was mist on the Obersalzburg sufficient to prevent visual-bombing, and OBOE was impeded by the height of the mountains. Nevertheless the main force, at the cost of two Lancasters hit by flak, destroyed two barrack blocks and the SS chief's residence, while 50 aircraft including 9 and 617 Squadrons planted bombs on Hitler's villa. The 'Eagle's Nest' near the top of the mountain, which he had visited a mere half-a-dozen times, escaped unscathed.[27]

The crews had hoped to bury Hitler in the rubble of his own residence, but – fortunately for any future myth-making about a German Führer martyred by British bombing – this was rendered impossible by his absence. Instead Hitler was ingloriously in his bombproof bunker underneath the Chancellery in Berlin, with the Russian guns less than a mile distant.

There the last lurid scenes quickly followed: the suicide on 30 April of Hitler and his wife of twenty-four hours, Eva Braun, the poisoning of the Goebbels' six children, the shots in the back of the head for Goebbels and his wife from an obliging SS guard, the cremations and the reek of burning flesh in the garden. By then, a single operation excepted, Bomber Command's offensive work was done. A week later came Germany's unconditional surrender.

There were still tasks of a gentler kind for the Command to fulfil. On 26 April it began Operation EXODUS, the flying home, at first mainly from Brussels, of released prisoners of war. Between then and 4 June Bomber Command's aircraft brought back some 75,000 men.[28] In the prison camps, very few of them had lost the spirit which had earlier inspired them to fight Nazi Germany. Now their ordeal was at last over. 'We collected 24 from an airfield near Reims,' wrote Flight Lieutenant

H. G. Davies of 195 Squadron in a letter to his father on the third day of the operation: 'Some had been captured at Dieppe and others had failed to get away from Dunkirk five years ago. None had ever flown before and several had lost families and friends in that time. It was one of my life's most satisfying experiences and it was the first time that I had seen men cry with happiness as, on a beautiful clear, blue-sky afternoon the white cliffs, the south downs, the green fields, the English villages and church spires were seen from only 1000 ft. as I brought them "home".'

From 29 April, until the general German capitulation on 8 May, Lancasters were also engaged on Operation MANNA – the dropping of food in western Holland. Many of the Dutch were on the point of starvation and the local German commander, aware that the war was in its last stages, agreed that food might be dropped for them on certain airfields and on the racecourse at The Hague. The Eighth Air Force joined in, dropping in more easterly areas (Operation CHOWHOUND). Since there were not enough parachutes, the food was placed in double sacks and dropped from a height of 300–500 feet: the inner sack burst, but the outer remained intact. All told, Bomber Command flew 3156 effective Lancaster sorties (and 156 by Mosquitoes for marking) before the roads and ports were opened at the end of hostilities.[29]

This, too, was deeply satisfying work. 'We flew low over the waterlogged countryside towards Rotterdam,' wrote Flight Lieutenant Davies in another letter home, 'and as we neared the city I took the big plane down so that we were just above the rooftops. Everywhere crowds of people were in the streets or at their windows, waving anything they could – handkerchiefs, flags and tablecloths – and every time I rocked the wings in return we could see them laughing and dancing with joy . . . As a crew we shared the happiness of the Dutch people . . . we knew that they would know that the years of privation, occupation and starvation were nearly at an end . . . That afternoon I experienced the most emotional moment of my life. We flew back to Wratting Common in almost complete silence, each deep in our own thoughts. We grieved that many of our friends and contemporaries in Bomber Command lie silent in graves all over Germany or in deep waters of the North Sea; they have paid the price of a victory they will never see, nor share the joy of the liberation of the Dutch people . . .'

Some squadrons of Bomber Command, equipped with the latest Lancasters or their 'stretched' derivative, the Lincoln, now prepared themselves for their next wartime role – as TIGER FORCE, to join the Americans in bombing Japan. The dropping of the two atom bombs in August fortunately rendered their help in the Far East unnecessary.

Meanwhile, throughout the summer, on an informal basis, Bomber Command aircrew were engaged in the much less exacting task of giving their ground crew 'COOK'S TOURS' of bombed Germany. One who put his name down for the trip was Leading Aircraftman Ian Curtis, an armourer. Fifty years later it was still vivid in his memory:

> I was smart enough to appropriate the rear turret which, being a .5 gun type, provided an excellent viewing point. The flight lasted about four hours and our route took us over Rotterdam and Arnhem, where the countryside was pockmarked with craters and littered with the wrecks of gliders. On over the Dutch/German borders and into the Ruhr, where we passed over Wesel, Düsseldorf, Gelsenkirchen, Essen and Cologne. The damage suffered by these towns was unbelievable – rubble and roofless houses and buildings everywhere. I thought we had had it bad in London in 1940, but there was no comparison with what these places had gone through. In Essen, the streets looked as if they had been bulldozed . . . Krupps' works was smashed, and looking down through the roofs one could see the remains of machinery . . . It was a sobering experience.

Flight Lieutenant Davies was one of those who took his squadron and station ground crew on what was also called Operation BAEDEKER. He flew them at low level over Bonn, Mainz, Hamburg and Hanover, as well as over the Ruhr. Later he wrote: 'They were trips made mostly in silence: the true extent of the terrible destruction from area-bombing and firestorms was vividly evident, to all of us, for the first time. At 20,000 feet we had been remote: bombing was an impersonal, war-winning technique. At 500 feet the true horror became real and we saw the price the German people had paid for their mesmerization by Hitler and the Nazi party.'

There are many similar accounts, nearly all of which mention the awed silence of the ground crews as they gazed at the devastation below. And when they landed, and did speak, it was often to frame the same question about the German people: 'How on earth did they stand it for so long?'

24

Retrospect

Bomber Command began the war as a force seriously inadequate for the many tasks that lay before it. It developed into one of immense power and effectiveness. A glance back at the main stages of the operations over Germany will illustrate this progression.

Very early in the war Bomber Command realised, from its attempts to attack naval vessels in German waters, that it would be unable to make unescorted daylight raids into Germany without heavy losses. In common with other air forces the RAF had not managed to develop long-range fighters capable of holding their own with good short-range fighters, so fighter escort was out of the question. For the strategic attacks it began in May 1940 the Command accordingly adopted a general policy of night-bombing. Its intention was still, as in the pre-war plans, to destroy precise targets such as individual factories. But in this it had little success; and being released from earlier restrictions by the German bombing of Warsaw, Rotterdam, London and Coventry, it consequently sought objectives which were less difficult to find and hit. From mid-1941 it consistently attacked industrial areas, which in effect meant major towns.

Even large towns, however, at this stage often proved beyond Bomber Command's powers to find in the general blackout, especially when the growth of the German night-fighter force made operations in moonlight inadvisable. To this problem the scientists at TRE supplied the main answers in a succession of radio and radar navigational aids – GEE was widely fitted by the spring of 1942, OBOE and H2S came in from early 1943. The formation of the Pathfinder Force and the development of target-indicator bombs also greatly helped. During 1942 the Command at length began to inflict serious damage, notably in its incendiary attacks on Rostock and Lübeck and in the 'Thousand-Bomber' raid on Cologne. In 1943 it went on to inflict far more, devastating the Ruhr and Hamburg, and beginning, at heavier cost, the systematic devastation of Berlin.

It was in 1943, too, that the USAAF joined in the assault on the Reich. This confronted the Germans with the formidable task of repelling mass attacks by day as well as Bomber Command's by night. But despite the impressive fire power of their formations the Americans suffered heavy casualties in their daylight-raiding – until they developed long-range escort fighters. By April 1944, with the help of these, they had won sufficient air superiority by day over Germany to strike the first heavy blows in the ultimately triumphant Allied air offensive against German oil.

At this stage, in accordance with Allied grand strategy, Bomber Command had to transfer its main weight of attack from Germany to tasks connected with OVERLORD and the liberation of western Europe. This it did, with great success. After five months the expulsion of Hitler's forces from France, Belgium and part of Holland then allowed it to concentrate once more on Germany.

By that time the powerful German air defences were breaking down. They had already, in 1943, suffered grave setbacks when WINDOW began to confuse their short-range radar and when Bomber Command's tactics of heavy concentration proved too much for the Kammhuber line of fighter 'boxes'. Now, with the Allied armies closing in towards the Rhine, the Germans lost most of the early-warning system they had established in occupied territory. In September 1944 the air defences of the Reich, in Harris's phrase, 'crumbled'.

This meant that Bomber Command could soon not only strike still more devastatingly by night but could also, especially when escorted by the new long-range fighters, operate over Germany by day. In either case, by radar or visually, it could attack precise targets with good chances of success, and take its full part in the joint air offensive against oil and communications. This spelled doom for the Luftwaffe, despite the Germans' huge production of fighters from dispersed factories. Though their night-fighter force was never overcome in combat as their day-fighter force had been, it became equally impotent: a collection of aircraft grounded for lack of petrol and other supplies.

In the last four months of the war Bomber Command rode the skies of Germany, if not with impunity, at least with losses of not much more than 1 per cent.

Though the progression outlined above depended on technical developments, it also of course depended on the increased size of the bomber force. On 27 September 1939, after 19 of the squadrons had been designated for reserve and/or training, and another ten had gone to France as the AASF, Bomber Command possessed only 23 operational squadrons. The average number of serviceable aircraft available for operations, with crews, was only 280.[1]

For two years the build-up of this force proceeded extremely slowly. About half of the AASF aircraft did not return from France; the delivery of new aircraft often fell behind schedule; new squadrons trained within Bomber Command had to be allocated or 'lent' to Coastal Command or the Middle East; squadrons became non-operational for considerable periods while they were re-equipped with the new heavy aircraft. By November 1941, after over two years, the average number of serviceable aircraft available with crews had risen only to 506.[2]

In the following year, 1942, the growth in numbers of aircraft normally available was almost nil; in January 1943 there were only nine more than in November 1941.[3] But the growth in the weight of bombs the force could carry, as the four-engined bombers replaced the two-engined, was considerable. On a trip to the Ruhr a Hampden carried its maximum bomb-load – under two tons. A Wellington normally carried a little over two tons, a Whitley about three. On the same trip the early Stirlings and Halifaxes could carry nearer six tons, and soon the Lancasters would carry more still.

From 1943 the growth was much faster, until at the peak point in April 1945 Harris had 98 squadrons and an average availability of 1609 serviceable aircraft with crews.[4] Moreover, these serviceable aircraft were of the types which had proved to be the best. Among the 1440 heavy bombers, 1087 were Lancasters, with the later Halifaxes making up the difference. The 203 light bombers were all Mosquitoes.[5]

This expansion was of course reflected in the tonnage of bombs dropped – though other factors, such as the average distance of the flights and the proportion of incendiaries, also had their effect. Up to the end of 1940 Bomber Command dropped against all targets 13,045 tons of bombs. In 1941 it dropped 31,704 tons. In 1942, with the same number of aircraft but including some of the new heavy bombers, it dropped 45,561 tons, or half as much again. In 1943 it dropped 157,257 tons; in 1944 (with many short cross-Channel flights) 535,308. In the first four months of 1945 it dropped 181,403 tons.[6] This means that in 1944–5 Bomber Command dropped more than twice the tonnage that it did between 1939 and 1943. In fact the bomb tonnage dropped in the final seven months, from 1 October 1944 to 30 April 1945, was rather more than that dropped in all the previous 61 months of the war put together.

Except among the crews, there has been general agreement about the performance of Bomber Command's aircraft. (Perhaps to sustain their morale, crews tended to champion the merits of whatever aircraft they had to fly.) Of the dozen or more types employed in the course of the war, only the Battle was seriously out of date by the time it operated. Nearly all the rest were reasonably efficient for their period, and three, the Wellington, the Lancaster and the Mosquito, turned out to be among the great aircraft of aviation history.

Among the early machines the fastest, the Blenheim IV, had the misfortune to be sent on daylight operations long after the rest of the force had gone over to night-bombing. As it also had the highly dangerous task of attacking shipping, its casualties were among the worst. Its contemporaries, the slow-moving Whitley and the faster Hampden, also did much good work. But undoubtedly the best of the early bombers proved to be Barnes Wallis's Wellington, with its sturdy geodetic construction. Operating continuously in Bomber Command from 1939 until November 1944 (in the final stages as a radio countermeasures aircraft), Wellingtons made over 47,000 operational sorties – more than any other type except Lancasters and Halifaxes.

When the four-engined bombers began to come into service, from the spring of 1941 onwards, it soon became evident that the Stirling had far too low a ceiling. Crews liked it because it was roomy and handled well at low altitudes, but they tended to lose their enthusiasm if, on a raid, bombs from higher-flying Lancasters and Halifaxes came screaming down past them. The early Halifaxes also disappointed, and Harris was known to say harsh things to, and about, their parent manufacturer, Sir Frederick Handley Page. But the Halifax Mark III with new Hercules engines and longer wings was a vast improvement on the earlier models, and played a large and successful part in the offensive against Germany until the end. In Harris's opinion, however, it still remained much inferior to the Lancaster. In *Bomber Offensive* he was later to write: 'The Lancaster was so far the best aircraft we had that I continually pressed for its production at the expense of other types. I was even willing to lose nearly a year's industrial production from the Halifax factories while these were being converted to produce Lancasters. I did not get my way . . .'[7]

Among the features of the Lancaster which appealed to Harris were its comparative ease of handling, its good safety record, and the combination of long-range with great bomb-carrying capacity. It was the only aircraft which could take six tons of bombs to Berlin. It was the only aircraft which could carry Barnes Wallis's 12,000-lb Tallboy. And it was of course the only aircraft which – with bomb doors and various other items removed – could carry Wallis's 22,000-lb Grand Slam. The part Lancasters played both in the general devastation of German industrial towns and in the attacks on more precise targets can hardly be exaggerated, for in addition to carrying the greatest bomb-load for the greatest distances they also, by reason of their constantly increasing numbers, flew far more sorties than the other types. By the end of hostilities Lancasters had flown twice as many sorties as Halifaxes, and more than the Blenheims, Wellingtons, Whitleys, Hampdens, Stirlings and Mosquitoes put together.[8]

The Lancaster did much the most of all the British bombers to wreck industrial Germany, but its general success was rivalled by that of the Mosquito. The 'wooden wonder' certainly vindicated the concept of the 'speed' bomber unhindered by the weight of armament. It is worth while recalling how this extremely versatile aircraft, which was also in much demand for fighter and reconnaissance work, contributed to the operations of Bomber Command.

When No. 2 Group left Bomber Command in June 1943, and Harris managed to retain its two Mosquito squadrons, he assigned them to Bennett's No. 8 Group. There they acted as Pathfinders and in addition formed the nucleus of what became the Light Night Striking Force. This steadily expanded until by March 1945 it consisted of 11 Mosquito squadrons with a normal availability of over 200 aircraft. But these were not the only Mosquitoes in Bomber Command. In addition, No. 100 Group had seven squadrons for Bomber Support work – such as disrupting the Germans' radio and radar, and intruding over their airfields.

When there were still only a few of them, Mosquitoes specialised in 'spoof' raids, with much use of WINDOW, to mislead the German fighters while the main force headed for the true target elsewhere. They also carried out widespread 'nuisance' raids at night to keep the defences stretched and the German population out of bed. Later, as their numbers increased, they became a formidably destructive force. A Stirling could take no bomb bigger than 2,000 lb, but a modified

Mosquito could carry a 4000-lb 'cookie', as well as a 500-pounder under each wing.

Mosquitoes proved particularly useful against the smaller special targets, like some of the railway objectives in occupied France before OVERLORD, but their most concentrated work was against Berlin, their so-called 'Milk Run'.* In the first four months of 1945 they made almost 4000 bombing sorties against the German capital, at one time attacking with forces averaging 60 aircraft on 36 consecutive nights. For the biggest raid of this spell, by 142 aircraft on 21/22 March, several of the Mosquitoes made two sorties during the night, picking up a fresh crew for the return trip. Capable of 400 mph, and with a ceiling of over 35,000 feet, they met little opposition from the German fighters; only the new jet Me 262 and the rocket-propelled Me 163 stood much chance of catching them, and there were not enough of these to affect the issue.

The overall 'missing rate' of Bomber Command Mosquitoes during the war was only 0.63 per cent of sorties. In view of the damage, physical and 'moral' that they did, this must be accounted one of the great successes of the bomber offensive. Should the Air Ministry, then, in 1936, have opted for fast unarmed light bombers instead of heavy bombers slowed down by gun turrets? Harris, writing his memoirs, was in no doubt that, though a force of 1000 good light bombers would always have been a welcome asset in his Command, the planners in 1936 made the right decision: 'The decisive factor was the supply of pilots: the heavy bomber carries about three times the load of the medium type; but both aircraft need only one pilot. It is certain that even with the whole resources of the Empire Training Scheme we should never have got enough pilots to fly enough medium and light bombers to drop the bomb-load that was dropped by the heavies. And of course the problem of concentrating the bomb-load, if it had been carried by many light bombers instead of a comparatively few heavies, would have been insoluble.'9

This seems fair enough as a general verdict, though it does not address itself to the question of relative accuracy, as opposed to bomb-load. Bombers unharassed by fighters tend to bomb more accurately than those under attack. And lest we endow the pre-war planners with too much prescience, we should perhaps remember that from their conception in 1936 until the size of the pilot-training problem became realised in the spring of 1942, the new heavy

* A name earlier given in the Middle East to the Wellington attacks on Benghazi from the Canal Zone.

bombers – like the old Wellingtons – were scheduled to carry two pilots.

Looking back on the whole series of Bomber Command's aircraft, and remembering that years must normally elapse between the design and the entry into service, it seems clear that the Air Ministry, the Ministry of Aircraft Production and the aircraft industry served Bomber Command well. It also appears, however, having regard only to improvements that were strictly practicable at the time, that in two respects they might have done better. The first was that the heating systems in several of the aircraft, and particularly in the earlier ones, were far too patchy, and caused unnecessary hardship to many of the crews. The second was that the bombers' .3-inch machine guns gave no adequate defence against the heavier weapons of the German fighters.

In *Bomber Offensive*, Harris described how it took him 'more than three years of bitter dispute and argument to fail to get a serviceable and useful .5-inch gun turret through the official channels'.[10] Towards the end of the war he did in fact get a very effective one for a limited number of aircraft, mainly through the efforts of the later 1 Group commander, Air Vice-Marshal E. A. B. Rice, and the Rose Bros. firm in Gainsborough. There was always of course the production time factor and the additional weight of heavier weapons and larger turrets to consider, but on balance it seems that in this matter Harris was quite justified in awarding the authorities less than full marks.

A vital element in Bomber Command's strength was the participation of so many squadrons and individual airmen from the Commonwealth and from Allied countries overrun in the early stages of the war.

The Allied squadrons were fewer than in some other RAF Commands, but their presence was a general inspiration. In all, seven operated: four Polish, one Czech, and two French. The four Polish squadrons all formed in 1940; two began operations that autumn, the other two the following spring. But from May 1942, when Harris had reluctantly to hand over No. 304 to Coastal Command, their paths began to diverge. In April 1943 the lack of further Polish aircrew forced the disbandment of No. 301, and a few months later No. 305, exchanging its Wellingtons for light bombers, transferred to the 2nd Tactical Air Force. So only No. 300, with some British aircrew reinforcement, went on in Bomber Command to the end. Its record was both a proud and a sad one. It flew more sorties, and suffered heavier casualties, than any other Allied squadron.[11]

The Czechoslovak squadron, No. 311, formed as early as July 1940 and was the first of Bomber Command's Allied squadrons to operate. Like the Polish 304, it found itself transferred to Coastal Command in the spring of 1942, during the crisis in the Battle of the Atlantic. The two French squadrons, Nos. 346 and 347, formed later, in May–June 1944. They operated successfully on Halifaxes until the end of the war.

The Commonwealth squadrons serving with Bomber Command at various times numbered 25, of which 22 were in the line of battle during the final stages. This represented between a fourth and a fifth of the Command's entire strength – a massive contribution. Among the squadrons No. 44 (Rhodesia) – an RAF squadron but with strong Commonwealth connections – operated throughout the war from the first day onwards, while another with exceptionally long, arduous and honourable service was the first of the two New Zealand squadrons, No. 75. The powerful Australian contingent extended to eight squadrons, of which the first two began operations in 1941. At various times in 1942–3 three squadrons were posted away to other commands, but the other five remained and three of them – Nos. 460, 466 and 467 – operated continuously from 1942 to the end.

Reflecting its greater population, wealth and industrial resources, and less directly concerned than the other Commonwealth countries with the Middle East, Canada made an exceptionally large contribution. With its own individual Bomber Command Group, No. 6, from January 1943, the Royal Canadian Air Force provided no fewer than 15 squadrons. Most of these operated continuously from 1943 onwards, and four of them – Nos. 405, 408, 419 and 420 – began as far back as 1941.

But it was not only in the field of operations that the Commonwealth helped Bomber Command so greatly. Of prime importance, too, were the flying training facilities provided under the Commonwealth Air Training Plan. The scope of this Plan was finally enormous – and needed to be. At the peak point, in September 1943, the full tally of Flying Training Schools amounted to 333, of which 153 were in the United Kingdom. Of the other 180, 92 were in Canada, 26 in Australia, 25 in South Africa, 10 in Southern Rhodesia, 9 in India, 6 each in New Zealand and the Middle East, and 1 in the Bahamas. The remaining 5 were in the USA. These schools of course produced aircrew for the entire RAF and the individual Commonwealth air forces and in no sense only for Bomber Command, but without their output Bomber Command could never have grown into the formidable force it became.

All told, Commonwealth nationals, whether in Commonwealth or RAF squadrons, provided a surprising proportion of Bomber Command's aircrew. At the peak in April 1944 over 30,000 of the 226,000 aircrew in Bomber Command – a total which includes those in administration and training – came from Canada, Australia and New Zealand.[12] That figure defines the quantity. The quality is perhaps indicated by the fact that more than a third of the Victoria Crosses awarded to Bomber Command went to Commonwealth airmen.

Just as the Commonwealth squadrons normally included, particularly among the ground staff, men from the general body of the RAF, so many Commonwealth nationals, even after the formation of their own units, served in ordinary RAF squadrons. Whether from service in the same squadron, or from the presence of a Commonwealth squadron nearby, many on both sides found this closeness educational, agreeable, and a source of strength. Fifty years later Wing Commander E. G. Jones DFC, AFC, a pilot with 115 and 139 Squadrons, could write: 'The quality of the Bomber spirit was second to none. What to my mind made it so special was the mix. The Aussies, Kiwis, Canadians, South Africans etc. struck sparks from each other. In my experience, the mixed crews were the best. It was not that we were trying to outdo each other, but that we brought out the best in each other. The bonds that developed between us are as strong as ever.'[13]

In considering Bomber Command's overall achievement it is important to remember the obvious: that victories usually depend on many others besides the combatants on the spot. Thus Bomber Command could not have existed without the men and women who made planes, the scientists in industry and the research establishments, or the seamen who brought in petrol. Nor could it have ranged over Germany with relative impunity in 1945 without the parallel activity of the USAAF and the overrunning of the German air defence system in France and Belgium by the Allied armies. Equally the Allied armies in 1944–5 could never have established themselves in France and advanced so rapidly to the German frontiers without the overwhelming air superiority attained by the Allied tactical air forces. In modern war such interrelationships are ubiquitous, and too important not to be constantly borne in mind.

Nevertheless it is still possible to point to a number of achievements for which Bomber Command was either jointly or solely responsible at the sharp end. The first was in handling its own approved expansion from a small and doubtfully effectual force into one of massive power.

Bomber Command did not of course supply the equipment or construct the airfields, but it did manage with exemplary efficiency the whole system of Groups, stations, satellites, bases, squadrons, Operational Training Units, Heavy Conversion Units and the rest, so that the Command was even better run in 1945 with nearly 100 operational squadrons than it had been in 1939 with 23.

Operationally, the Command's first significant achievement was in connection with the Dunkirk evacuation, where its Blenheims helped to impose slight but crucial delays on the advancing German armies. Following this, it soon had two more successes. The first was almost accidental. Its 'revenge' bombing of Berlin at the end of August 1940, prompted by Churchill, stung Hitler into the desire to bomb London instead of Fighter Command's airfields, and so helped to turn the tide in the Battle of Britain. The second success had nothing accidental about it. Bomber Command's attacks in September 1940 on the French and Belgian Channel ports and the barges mustered there compelled the Germans to disperse their craft, and warned them that any expedition attempting to cross the Channel would be roughly treated from the air. These attacks on the cross-Channel ports should be ranked third only to the heroic victories of Fighter Command and the existence of the Royal Navy in having saved Britain from invasion.

In the long months that followed, and throughout 1941, Bomber Command's achievement was mainly moral. The force was too small, its night-bombing too inaccurate, to do much physical damage to Germany. But on the moral side its achievement was considerable. It was quite literally the only force which could damage the German homeland, and as such its operations – which were proclaimed and generally understood in Britain to be much more effective than at first they actually were – heartened British citizens with the thought that the Germans were getting something unpleasant back in return for the bombing of London and the provincial towns. Moreover it was not only British citizens who were heartened. The United States took notice that Britain, whatever the odds, had no thoughts of surrender. The Soviet Union, when Hitler was mad enough to invade it, regarded the British bombing of Germany as some compensation, if an inadequate one, for the 'Second Front in Europe' it was soon strenuously and for over two years vainly demanding.

In the incessant war at sea, Bomber Command's achievement was both continuous and rewarding. The operations took four main forms, of which the first to show good dividends was minelaying. In the end, including the small initial contribution by Coastal Command, the air mining offensive sank 717 merchant vessels and damaged another

665 – a success for every 16 sorties flown. In addition, mines laid by Bomber Command – which totalled over 47,000 during the war – had important strategic effects at critical times. They delayed the emergence of U-boats from their Biscay bases during the TORCH and OVERLORD operations; and in 1944 they drove the new large U-boats from their Bay of Danzig training waters, and so helped to ruin Admiral Dönitz's chances of operating them in significant numbers before the end of the war. Mines laid in the Baltic also induced Sweden to withdraw ships which had been working under German control.

Direct air attacks on merchant shipping by Bomber Command aircraft proved to be costly, but they undoubtedly deterred many neutral vessels from trading freely with Germany and its occupied territories. Much more completely successful in the end was the offensive against the U-boats. Though the attacks on the Biscay bases in 1942 achieved little, the later bombing of Hamburg, Bremen, Kiel, Emden and other north German ports, as well as of the Dortmund–Ems Canal, achieved a great deal. In this the USAAF was fully associated, as it also was in attacks on inland towns manufacturing U-boat components. According to the British Bombing Survey Unit's report after the war, Bomber Command and the USAAF between them destroyed 111 U-boats in production and sank 54 which had been delivered to the German navy.[14] In addition their destruction of communications and U-boat components by both area and selective attacks prevented the assembly of perhaps as many more U-boats again. In all, the loss of U-boats from these raids exceeded the total number of U-boats normally operating.

A final achievement of Bomber Command in the war at sea remains to be recalled. Aircraft of the Command sank or rendered useless for further action six of Germany's twelve major warships.[15]

A significant achievement of another kind was that Bomber Command in 1942–3 sharply brought home to the Italian people the realities of the war into which their dictator had plunged them. A few heavy raids against Milan, Turin and Genoa, coupled with the free-ranging activity of the Mediterranean Allied Air Forces in the south and the knowledge that invasion forces were at hand, sufficed to bring about a change of allegiance.

Another of Bomber Command's achievements – by means of the raid on Peenemünde and the attacks on the original launching sites – was to delay and reduce Hitler's V-weapon assault on Britain. And of paramount importance was the Command's contribution to the success of OVERLORD – notably by the attacks on railway centres beforehand, the D-Day 'spoof' invasion and the elimination of coastal batteries and radar stations, and the subsequent operations against the German armies' points of resistance.

This still leaves for consideration Bomber Command's biggest activity of all – the bombing of Germany's major towns. Here controversy has developed about both its morality and its effectiveness. The moral objection is that it involved the wholesale slaughter of German civilians – about 300,000 were killed, and another 700,000 injured, by all types of bombing, British, American and Russian, but predominantly by the British area offensive. The objection is a strong one, but there have been plenty of arguments put forward on the other side. Among them are that 'Germany began it first', with Warsaw and Rotterdam; that the British intention was not to kill civilians but to destroy their homes and drive them from the centres of industry; that civilians are so important for war production that they are a legitimate objective; that, in the words of Admiral Lord ('Jackie') Fisher, 'the essence of war is violence: moderation in war is imbecility'; and that the supreme need was to win the war, as these attacks would help to do, against an opponent capable – as was afterwards shown – of despatching some six million men, women and children to their deaths merely for their race or religion. There was also the basic fact that for a long period only by bombing urban areas at night could the RAF inflict any damage at all on Germany without suffering disastrous losses.

To those who point to the moral superiority of the unvarying American policy of attacking only precise targets in Germany there are two answers that can be given. The first is that, in adverse circumstances of weather or opposition, American precision-bombing was often little different in its effects from British area-bombing. The second is that the Americans displayed no such moral scruples against the Japanese. No area-bombing of Germany was more horrific, or more effective, than the fire-bombing of Tokyo, and the atom-bombing of Hiroshima and Nagasaki.

The actual results of the area-bombing have aroused controversy of a more academic kind. It stems partly from the difficulty of assessing effects which were wide-spread and of the utmost complexity, and which were often impossible to untangle from the effects of other raids on the same or neighbouring districts. It also stems from the nature of the post-war investigations, in which the organisation of a large American team of over a thousand, not particularly interested in the effects of British area-bombing, preceded by more than a year the organisation of its small British official counterpart, which Churchill in a fit of economy or wrong-headedness had initially tried to limit to 'some 20 or 30 persons'.[16] The Americans had been strongly in favour of the offensive against oil in the final year of the war, and in their survey 'oil' emerged as the big winner. Tedder's scientific adviser at SHAEF, Professor Zuckerman, had, during the same period, been an equally ardent advocate of attacks on communications. In the report of the British team, of which Zuckerman was the scientific head, communications emerged as the big winner. The British throughout inevitably used a large number of the American-gathered statistics and documents. Neither survey indicated any decisive or even very substantial decline in German productivity from area-bombing. One set of figures did indeed suggest the contrary: a decline in the war-purposes production of the metal-processing industry of 46.5 per cent in the second half of 1943 and 39 per cent in the second half of 1944. But this was dismissed by the British survey as 'spurious'.[17]

The American survey, which investigated only a few area attacks, came out with a figure which suggested that area attacks had caused a loss of 9 per cent in all production in 1943 and 17 per cent in 1944. The British survey figures did not suggest even this, but maximum losses of 8.2 per cent in the second half of 1943, 7.2 per cent in the second half of 1944, and 9.7 per cent during 1945. Its estimates for loss of specific war production such as armaments were lower still: they averaged less than 3 per cent for 1943 and barely 1 per cent for 1944.[18] Considering that urban bombing had taken up about 45 per cent of Bomber Command's efforts in terms of tonnage dropped, these estimates seemed to show that the area offensive had profoundly disappointing results.

Disregarding any possibility of bias, and accepting the estimates – which are the only official ones – at their face value, it is nevertheless evident that a very different impression is received if emphasis is put upon what the Germans produced in relation to what they actually planned to produce before the major attacks occurred. In the first half of the war the German economy was far from tightly stretched and for most of the conflict it had the benefit of plunder and slave labour from the occupied countries, as well as substantial collaboration from some. Once a planner of the calibre of Speer got to work on armament production, it was quite possible for very large increases to be achieved, particularly in certain categories.

The increases in most cases, however, were nothing like as big as Speer had intended. On 27 January 1945 he informed Guderian that, because of bombing and the loss of territories, production in the last quarter of 1944 had been below expectations. Output of coal, steel and oil had declined sharply.[19] In the case of the aircraft industry, there was a particularly striking shortfall. The Germans had planned to produce over 12,000 fighters in the last three months of 1944. They actually produced about 8,600.[20] Undoubtedly bombing, area as well as precision, was the main factor contributing to this failure. Very obviously it was bombing that enforced the dispersal of aircraft manufacture. This enabled the industry to survive, and even to make substantial increases in production – but at nothing like the rate it would have achieved had it not been compelled to disperse. And in the final year the effects of the offensive against oil and communications were of course all the greater on any industry that was widely dispersed.

It is also important to observe that much of the increase in German war production in 1943 and 1944 – it declined sharply in 1945 – was devoted to defensive purposes. The number of bombers produced, nearly 4,000 in 1940, was not much more than half as much again in 1944.[21] The great increase occurred, ninefold over the same period, in the easier-to-produce defensive category – fighters. Similarly there was a big increase in the production of 88-mm guns, all of which might have been used against the Allied armies if nearly 20,000 had not been required for home defence against the bombers. Moreover about a million men were involved in this defence, and another million in the air-raid precautions, fire and rescue services.[22] All this defensive apparatus, built up at the expense of Germany's offensive capacity, was a consequence of the bombing – British area-bombing quite as much as British and American precision-bombing.

Intervention at Dunkirk, the bombing of the invasion barges, the bolstering of British morale, the mining campaign, the substantial part in defeating the U-boats and in finishing off the German fleet, the share in knocking out Italy, the help in mastering the V-weapon menace, the assistance to the Allied armies at critical moments from the Normandy landings onwards, the tying-down of vast German resources to anti-aircraft defence, the final deadly offensive against oil and communications – the list of achievements is impressive enough, whatever view is taken of the losses in production caused by area-bombing.

The controversy that has surrounded the area offensive has certainly not escaped its chief executant and protagonist. Harris ('Bomber' or 'Butch' to his crews, 'Bert' to his intimates) now has his statue near that of Sir Hugh Dowding outside the Church of St Clement Danes in the Strand. The juxtaposition rightly reminds passers-by that the RAF was as successful in attacking the enemy's homeland as it was in defending our own. But Harris's statue is much more likely than Dowding's to attract 'protest' in the form of red paint. In death, as he did in life, Harris arouses strong feelings among people who never remotely encountered him.

Some part of this stems from a double misconception. Harris in no way initiated area-bombing, which began regularly on moonless nights months before his appointment to Bomber Command in February 1942. Nor was he responsible for continuing it as a policy: strategic decisions of that kind emanated from Whitehall, not High Wycombe. But the popular identification of Harris with the area offensive is in other ways not mistaken. As already indicated, he became not only its chief executant but also – though always within the official channels – its most ardent, eloquent and obdurate champion.

This public perception of Harris simply as a wrecker of German towns tends to obscure his general qualities as a commander. Among these were his intelligence, courage, decisiveness, technical competence, and dominant but not unfriendly personality. He was also very cooperative in action with senior officers of the other Services, however much in private he might inveigh against some of their fixed convictions. Above all, through his clarity, firmness, competence, humour, and obvious determination to give the enemy a hard time, he enjoyed the awed respect and obedience of his entire Command – something the more remarkable in that he rarely visited stations, having neither the time nor a great deal of inclination to do so. (He felt some embarrassment at joking with crews he might be sending within a few hours to their death.) As the head of Bomber Command, Harris had in fact only two significant weaknesses. One was his habit of exaggerating in order to press his points. The other was an undue readiness to brush aside the views of any, whether in the Ministry of Economic Warfare or the Directorate of Bomber Operations at the Air Ministry, who sought to have bombing targets prescribed that he thought impractical.

Like the efficient commander he was, Harris was a good delegator and chose his chief lieutenants well. His Deputy, 'Sandy' Saundby, by his great friendliness made up for any gruffness on the part of his chief, and was throughout a most able, understanding and unselfish source of support. Equally the Senior Air Staff Officer of the final year, Air Vice-Marshal Hugh Walmesley, was another most efficient helper and attractive personality. Out at the Groups there was talent in abundance as well. Two officers whose appointments Harris had personally pressed, Bennett at No. 8 Group and Cochrane at No. 5, were perhaps outstanding in their abilities, but there were also earlier stalwarts like Air Vice-Marshal C. R. Carr, who ran No. 4 Group effectively from July 1941 until February 1945. In general, the quality of the Group commanders, which had been set so high in the early months of the war, was maintained to the end.

The high standard of the principal officers in Bomber Command was fully matched by that of the officers in the Air Ministry who had to deal with the bomber offensive. In Portal, Harris was fortunate to have as his superior a Chief of the Air Staff with an exceptional combination of intelligence, tact, balance and determination – an officer of whom General Ismay, Churchill's right-hand man, could say: 'he was the best of all the war leaders – *quite easily*.' ('Without Portal,' Harris was to say later, 'there would have been no bomber offensive.') But there were others in the Air Ministry who served the bomber offensive well, including the Deputy Chief of the Air Staff Sir Norman Bottomley and the Director of Bomber Operations, Air Commodore Bufton, whose influence on policy in the direction of selective bombing against oil Harris resented.

No amount of ability and determination at the top, however, could have availed without the remarkable quality of the crews, in whom skill and courage could be taken for granted. The ground crew and ground staff rarely had call to show courage equal to that of the aircrew, but it was there when needed in the emergencies of crashes or enemy bombs, and their devotion to the men who flew was complete. Some had jobs without hardship in offices, others jobs without too much hardship in hangars, but those out at the flights had to service their aircraft for months on end in foul or bitter weather. In any case, whether the job was a tough one or not, and whether it fell to a hard-bitten regular or a new WAAF ACW2, the determination was the same: never to let the aircrew, and especially *your* aircrew, down.

About the aircrew, perhaps the most remarkable fact is that despite the cold, the dark, the navigational difficulties, the flak, the fighters, the blinding searchlights, the loss of comrades, the constant strain and the recurrent fear, the general morale never weakened, nor was there ever any lack of eager newcomers to fill the places of those who did not return. The number of aircrew who from loss of nerve were unable to continue operating and who 'forfeited the confidence of their Commanding Officer' (i.e. found themselves liable to be categorized 'LMF') was small indeed – less than one in 200.[23] Yet to undertake a tour of 30 operations with Bomber Command in the central period of the war, before the Germans were expelled from France, was to have only about a one-in-two chance of surviving, and to undertake a second tour of 20 operations – which was the official requirement except for the Pathfinders, though frequently not exacted – was at some periods statistically almost a death sentence.

Broad statistics in this matter, however, tend to disguise as well as illuminate. It was generally reckoned, for instance, that the chances of a crew's surviving a first tour were altogether better if it could survive the first five operations. And there was a whole world of disparity according to when, and in what, the crew was flying. The chances of coming back from Germany were about five times better in a Mosquito than in a Stirling. The chances of coming back from anywhere were several times better if the year was 1945 and not 1941, 1942, or 1943. If the year was 1944, the odds were greatly superior in the second half.

The fatal casualties to Bomber Command aircrew, including those who died while prisoners of war and a few killed by German bombing, totalled 55,500. Of these, 8195 lost their lives in crashes or other accidents. If, to the 55,500, are added the prisoners of war – 9838, including many wounded – and the 8403 wounded on operations or in accidents, the aircrew casualties in Bomber Command amounted to 73,741.[24] Harris has recorded the number of aircrew who flew in Bomber Command as 125,000.[25] Assuming that figure is correct and relates to operations, it means that more than one in every two Bomber Command operational aircrew suffered wounds, imprisonment or death.

The price that the aircrew of Bomber Command paid for helping to preserve freedom in Britain and restore it to western Europe was an extremely heavy one. It is unlikely that any heavier, or equally heavy, price was paid by any other major branch of the British armed services. To make a comparison within the Royal Air Force, Bomber Command lost more than twice as many aircrew on operations as did all the other Commands put together. That is one reason why this book is called *The Hardest Victory*. But perhaps there is little point in making comparisons. What Bomber Command achieved, and helped to achieve, was unquestionably hard-won. And, with equal certainty, it was victory.

25

Fifty Years On:
The Crews Remember . . .

Ranks are those held in 1945. Decorations include those awarded subsequently.

TRAINING

Sergeant W. E. Wilkinson, fitter II (engines), 142 Squadron
Ground-crew training before the war was unequalled. I feel I had the finest training possible. No notes were given. Rough notes had to be taken, and fair notebooks made up in your own time, and in your own words. Fair notebooks were collected Fridays, and returned marked on Mondays. This way both instructor and pupil could monitor progress. The course from March 1938 to March 1939 was split into 12 sections, with an examination once a month at the end of each. The final trade test took place in April 1939 by a Board appointed by the Group Engineer. Facilities were available to improve your general education, and sports and pastimes were organised. You were encouraged (almost ordered) to compete.

Flying Officer M. C. Wright DFM, navigator, 9, 4, 142 Squadrons
The Empire Air Training Scheme was a brilliant conception. It ensured a constant supply of replacements even when losses were extremely

high. On occasion I believe the training was sluggish in keeping pace with new developments. For example, we spent a great deal of our navigation training on visual methods, including astro-navigation, in Canada. On arrival in England we had to learn from scratch all about radar, which was the only really effective way to navigate in Europe at night given the usual weather conditions.

From an enjoyment point of view, what greater adventure could a teenager wish for than going to Canada? Away from the dreariness of 1942 wartime Britain into a vast, beautiful land of plenty. Added to this was the fantastic generosity of the Canadian people, who opened their homes and their hearts to us.

Sergeant J. W. Grimstone, radio mechanic, 102 Squadron
We were very well schooled in the theory and practice of blind-flying equipment, using the Lorenz (German) system built by Standard Radio. We had to fly in Avro Ansons in very foggy conditions to gain first-hand experience of flying and landing with this BA equipment. We also had very extensive instruction in the maintenance of the Link Trainer. Both courses were excellent, and we were most competent in the installation, setting-up, air-testing and maintenance of the BA equipment. Sad to relate, though, that many of the Whitley pilots at that time ('40/'41) did not share our confidence in the Beam-Approach system of blind landing. Used correctly it was as near perfect as possible.

Leading Aircraftman I. Curtis, armourer, 101 Squadron
On our first day of training, we were given a rough cast-iron block about four inches square and three-quarters of an inch thick. This had to have the rough scale chiselled off, and then using files of different cuts, reduced to a smooth dead-flat square block, the measurements of which had to be within a tolerance of two-thousands of an inch. Not being particularly dextrous with my hands, I sweated blood the whole time I was on this exercise, especially when the tolerance limits were being reached. Further exercises involving the block occupied the succeeding weeks, followed by the manufacture of a spanner (badly done), chisel, a P14 extractor spring and a cartridge stop. One of my test pieces was the splined disc, a frightening job! It involved making a male key in the shape of the old London Underground sign – a circle with a rectangle superimposed across it. This had to fit into a similar shape cut out of the cast-iron block, once again within the inevitable two thou.

307

Flight Lieutenant H. Yeoman, pilot, 12 Squadron
As I had no yardstick to judge it by, I naturally assumed it was the best possible training. In retrospect, I suppose that to arrive on a squadron with 184 hours in one's logbook wasn't all that much, but there it was, and there I was. I enjoyed it thoroughly, or rather, 99 per cent of it. At 19 I'd never driven a car, and to fly any sort of aircraft was beyond my wildest dreams. It was both challenging and exhilarating to a degree. The other 1 per cent of the time I was scared stiff, doing something stupid and making some elementary blunder!

Squadron Leader W. B. Mackley DFC and bar, pilot, 58 Squadron
I commenced operations with 58 Squadron with 259 hours. Training was good in the light of experience at that time but in hindsight was quite inadequate for the job we were expected to do. My conversion time on to Whitleys was just *one hour* before going on ops as second pilot. I don't recall that at that time single-motor flying was ever practised. There were no emergency drills and we knew little or nothing of aircraft performance except what was in the aircraft manual – and that didn't tell us much!

Wing Commander R. M. Pinkham DFC, pilot, 77 and 150 Squadrons
There were many occasions when I was faced with extremely hazardous conditions, such as icing, fog, low cloud, and other severe weather conditions, which thanks to training, I was able to cope with. We had every opportunity to get in as much training as we were prepared to do. Getting as much time in on the 'Link' trainer as possible, carrying out emergency landing procedures, doing 'Beam Approach' practice at every opportunity, and all the other essential elements of 'safe' flying, all added up to one thing – survival.

Flight Sergeant R. Palmer, flight engineer, 578 and 10 Squadrons
At the end of one year's technical training I was promoted to Sergeant Flight Engineer without ever having flown, or in fact even placing a foot in a 'real' aircraft. I then went straight to HCU, met the rest of my crew, and flew for the first time.

Leading Aircraftwoman M. West (née Allcock), driver, Waddington
The driving training at Pwllheli was excellent. The finest training anywhere other than the police force perhaps, and it was so varied. I drove everything from the Group Captain's car through crew buses, every type of van or lorry and finished up towing the Lancs on an operational Australian squadron, 467. The male tractor drivers had

had a few prangs knocking wingtips off the aircraft so we women had to prove that we could do better.

Flight Lieutenant E. Appleton DFC, flight engineer, 429 (RCAF) Squadron

I soon detested the sight of a Hurricane coming in fast to the rear to engage in fighter affiliation training for the pilots. I was able to complete only one flight in relative comfort without being physically sick. No one liked to make a fuss on this score, LMF was a stigma that was undesirable for anyone to face. Fortunately, I never got nauseous on operations!

The training covered numerous subjects that would never be seen or heard of again, at least in our field of endeavour. For example, how to make splices, fabric work, rigging of biplanes, etc. All these irrelevant items were covered in detail, and every phase of the course had to be passed before advancing to the next subject. Additionally, guard duties were a steady diet, when we could have been devoting the time to further study.

Warrant Officer N. A. Tranter, bomb-aimer, 106 Squadron

Ab initio Bombing and Gunnery training in Canada were, quite frankly, boring. On return to the UK the training at OTU, HCU and LFS was very effective and interesting. The instructors were all 'tour expired' aircrew who had 'been and seen and done'; they taught not by the book but by life as they had experienced it over Germany and we LISTENED and LEARNT!!

Training in 1941, at least in the technical schools, was very hurriedly put together to accommodate the enormous increase in numbers to be trained. However my experience was that the mainly regular NCOs doing the work were bending over backwards to make good mechanics and fitters of us. With very few exceptions both trainers and trained were keen to get good results, and did.

Flying Officer H. R. Oldland DFC, MBE, flight engineer, 455 (RAAF) and 405 (RCAF) Squadrons

Fl. Eng. was the one branch of aircrew for which there was no air experience during initial training. First flights were at HCU and first operational sorties were undertaken with no more than five or six hours in the logbook. In my own case my logbook shows 2 hrs 45 mins before the first operational flight to Stuttgart. But by and large training was certainly interesting, varied and more than adequate to equip one to join a crew and a squadron.

Sergeant H. C. Towler, air-gunner, 100 Squadron
After elementary flying training solo, waiting at Manchester for ship to Canada to partake in the Commonwealth Air Training programme, 'D-Day' occurred, and we were returned to London for three days of intense aptitude tests. These proved that of the 250 pilot-navigator-bomb-aimer trainees, 200 of us had the aptitude to become air-gunners – the exact number required.

EQUIPMENT

Squadron Leader W. B. Mackley DFC and bar, pilot, 58 Squadron
The Whitley was a horrible-looking aircraft, but it was rugged. While the Wellington was the glamour aircraft, I will always maintain that the Whitley was superior. At least you could get it up above 20,000 feet. The Whitley's lack of cockpit heat in the early models was a major disadvantage – battling the cold was worse than battling the enemy in the early days of the war. The Whitley's one front gun – a Vickers G.O. – was a major defect in the armament, but we never had occasion to use it. The old Whitley was reasonably reliable and we had confidence in it. The Merlin motors suffered the grave disadvantage of being liquid-cooled. This was the major problem with the Merlin and at that time (1939–41) probably more crews were lost due to coolant problems than were lost to the enemy.

Squadron Leader C. G. Rawlins OBE, DFC, pilot, 144 Squadron
The Hampden, as everyone knew, was aerodynamically good: it carried a good load, had a reasonable range (considerably increased with wing tanks) and was relatively fast but it had the operational disadvantage of being, in effect, a one-pilot aircraft, so that the pilot was fixed to his seat for anything up to nine hours. In practice this was not a problem, except in so far as bodily functions were concerned.

The aeroplane's equipment, while mainly of pre-war vintage, generally worked well. The heating did not work properly on some occasions, resulting in frozen fingers. Perhaps the radio equipment was the most likely source of complaint, though one never knew whether it was the set or the operator which was really at fault. More often than not, we got little radio help but when one considers that the sets had first to be tuned and then messages (except at relatively short range from base) to be transmitted by Morse, it was perhaps not surprising. At the time we accepted it all as normal. In effect, if the engines ran properly, we did not worry too much about other equipment.

Warrant Officer H. R. Moyle, observer, 44 Squadron
Equipment on Hampdens was pretty basic; no fancy navigational aids, and wireless communication was by Morse code. The only nav. aid was the loop aerial, by means of which the W/T operator tried to obtain bearings of ground stations . . . these were not often to be relied upon. We had the Mk IX bombsight on the Hampdens until just after the war broke out, when we were re-equipped with an automatic bombsight which operated through a gyro-compass and was, in my tender hands at least, pretty bloody useless. The gyro had a habit of putting in jerky alterations of course on the bombing run and seemed to release the bomb when it felt like it.

Warrant Officer W. Wescomb, flight engineer, 75 (NZ) Squadron
As aircrew I regretted changing from the Stirling to the Lancaster. The old Stirling could not make a decent operational height, it was a pig on the ground and when taking off and landing, but in the air it was a darling – it could turn inside a Spitfire, as we discovered on fighter affiliation exercises. It was built like a battleship but flew like a bird. We could keep it up on one engine, and when stalling, it went gracefully nose down, not sliding all over the place like most heavies. The Lancaster was undoubtedly a better tool from the Air Ministry point of view, and we did get to like it after a while, but the Stirling was for me the best.

Squadron Leader R. A. Read DFC, pilot, 78 Squadron
Our aircraft (Halifaxes) changed, in recognition of new German tactics. Some time in January '43 the front turrets were removed and a new nose-section fitted. There wasn't much point in carrying a front gun – nothing was slower than we were. In early February our mid-upper turrets were also taken out and faired over. Again there was little use for them. Almost all fighter attacks were now being made from below. It was decided that the reduction of weight would give more speed and height. Aircraft so modified were recoded from a Halifax 2 to a Halifax 2, Series 1. Whatever they called it, it remained a lumbering, underpowered, sitting target for enemy night-fighters.

Now we had only the rear turret to fight back with. Fitted with four puny .303-inch Browning machine guns of limited range, we were at a great disadvantage against the Ju 88 night fighters, who now carried three 20-mm cannon and three 7.9-mm machine guns in the nose, as well as a 13-mm machine gun facing the rear.

We were slowly becoming aware that most of the attacks were being made from the blind area beneath us. With the withdrawal of the mid-upper turret, we had a spare gunner. To help to improve the total blind spot that existed below, a small blister window was fitted in the floor of the fuselage. Here, the poor mid-upper had to be on his belly, with his head poked into the blister, to try to spot a climbing fighter. Someone could do this for a short period, but it was absurd to expect him to stay alert for the three to six hours we spent over enemy territory.

Another change was the removal of the shrouds covering the glowing exhaust pipes. Their effect on the airflow over the wings reduced performance. With their removal, we gained a hundred feet or two in height, but were left with eight red-hot glowing exhausts displayed to the world. A British Beaufighter, flying in bad visibility, thought the exhausts he saw from a Halifax marked a flarepath, and tried to land along it . . .

The Halifax seemed a dangerous aircraft, even before the Germans got at it. We found at first it was hard to taxi. The heavy undercarriage needed lots of outer throttle, to change direction on the ground. Another frightening problem was that with four powerful engines turning four large props in the same direction, the Halifax swung violently to the right on take-off. In the way of our kind, we soon got to grips with things, and for all its faults, eventually got to like the old Halifax. That we did so, was really a state of mind that every successful pilot had to adopt. Since you were stuck with the type of aircraft you were given, you soon convinced yourself that it was a jolly good one.

Flying Officer O. C. Cronshaw DFC, pilot, 102 Squadron
The Halifax Mk 2 was not a great aircraft but the Mk 3 was second to none and could easily outclimb the great Lancaster. The Halifax was a very robust aircraft, more so than the Lanc. The Lanc., of course, was the all-time great because of its tremendous bomb-carrying capacity. The Halifax was more difficult to fly than the Lanc., which was a beauty to fly and had a very easy rudder pedal action which for a small person was a great help on take-off and on two- and three-engine flying. When all is said and done, the Halifax never got the praise it deserved from the press.

Flying Officer G. Cairns OBE, flight engineer, 460 (RAAF) Squadron
Due to the dedication of the ground crew, we never experienced any technical failure which led to an abortive sortie. The Lancaster was a reliable piece of equipment and could absorb a fair amount of battle damage and still get you back to base. Our only complaint was the heating system; the blackout curtain which shut off the navigator's

compartment also blocked off the heat to the pilot, flight engineer and bomb-aimer. We froze whilst the navigator and wireless operator sat back in comfort.

Flight Lieutenant D. J. Furner CBE, DFC, AFC, pilot, 214 Squadron
In the early days we were doing our best with rudimentary devices in somewhat difficult circumstances. But one was vaguely aware that considerable effort was going on behind the scenes to improve our navigational tools. GEE was a sensation: line up the blips, read off the hyperbolic lattices and there you are! And when we reached HCU, we asked ourselves what that strange bulge was under one of a visiting aircraft; mysteriously, it was said, you could see through cloud. Of course, later on the squadron, H2S was fitted one by one to our aircraft and initially it was thrilling stuff; but it was of poor quality and unreliable. And the GEE began to disappear with jamming soon after crossing the enemy coast. So one never forgot the basics of DR navigation, the old faithful Dalton 'computer'(!), and, when allowed by comparatively quiet conditions such as return over the sea, the fascinating combination of the sextant and the astrograph.

Flying Officer M. C. Wright DFM, navigator, 9, 44, 142 Squadrons
I used GEE, LORAN and H2S, all of which were marvellous aids to navigation. The only real complaint was in respect of GEE. When on Mosquitoes in order to combat jamming it was necessary to change frequency and at one stage this was achieved by changing small boxes in the main component. Unfortunately the boxes were poorly designed in that in order to make contact one had to secure four tiny butterfly screws into threaded holes. I often found this impossible as in a Mosquito the main component into which the frequency box had to be fitted was under the navigator's seat. Visualise the antics. First to remove the navigation table, complete with maps, navigation instruments, log, etc. Then to feel between your feet in the dark. Use of a torch could bring down the wrath of the pilot whose night vision could be ruined. Removing the box was not too difficult but the crunch came when trying to fit the screws into the elusive holes, as it seemed that unless all four lined up and were screwed home contact could not be made. Fortunately this method was succeeded in due course by a dial on the main box to change frequency. Now it was simple: just put your head between your legs and read the dial upside down in the dark.

Leading Aircraftman I. Curtis, armourer, 101 Squadron
The bombs were loaded by means of a hand-operated winch, the cable

of which was fed through the floor of the bomb bay and attached to the bomb carrier. Then the winch handle was turned and the carrier and its attached bomb would slowly rise up into its station in the bomb bay. I forget how many revolutions of the handle it took to raise the load one inch – something like twenty, I think. Loading bombs into the forward positions seemed a never-ending task, as they had to be raised so much higher than those in the rear position. Furthermore, with some of the positions, the loader had to contort himself around fixtures in order to operate the winch, all of which was heartbreaking if the load had to be changed or the aircraft debombed. Eventually, power-operated winches were brought into use.

The 4-lb incendiary was nothing more than a stick of magnesium some 18 inches long and weighted at one end. It had no ballistic properties at all, so could not be aimed accurately. This did not matter very much as its main purpose was to set alight the debris scattered by bomb blasts. From our point of view, 4-lb incendiaries involved a lot of back-breaking work. They came in metal boxes containing 30 bombs, and the SBCs took three boxes to a container. The boxes had to be lifted into and clamped on to the container, and then the loaded SBC manhandled on to the bomb trolleys. On the other hand, high-explosive bombs, although intrinsically heavier than the incendiaries, were much easier to handle as these involved the use of mechanical aids such as gantries instead of sheer physical labour alone.

The 4-lb incendiary could be set alight merely by tossing it up into the air, which shows that it did not have much safety margin built into it. However, if one was set off accidentally, it could be kicked or thrown clear without any trouble, but some of the American-made 4-lb incendiaries contained an explosive charge to scatter the burning bomb particles. Naturally, these were treated warily.

Squadron Leader J. C. Cazes DFC, navigator, 158 Squadron
I would sum up operational flying as 90 per cent of the time bloody cold and 10 per cent of the time bloody cold and bloody frightening. Efficiency was considerably reduced by cold and fatigue, particularly on the return flight. Naturally, one could not expect the comfort of a passenger aircraft, but slightly more comfort and slightly better heating, even at the cost of a small reduction in the payload, would have meant quite a few more aircraft returning safely.

Flight Sergeant R. F. Pritchard, RAAF air-gunner, 550 Squadron
Most of the equipment used in training was clapped out. The efforts

of maintenance crews to keep everything operating were on a scale reaching the heroic. They were short of everything necessary to enable them to function efficiently. On some units the cornflake packets and waxed inners were used as gaskets!! I personally know of pilots who stayed on at squadron for additional ops to avoid posting to OTU and HCU to avoid the danger of flying beat-up aircraft with green crews.

STATION LIFE

Warrant Officer N. A. Tranter, bomb-aimer, 106 Squadron
Bomber stations were, perforce, situated a goodly distance from the 'bright lights'. At Metheringham our nearest large city was Lincoln, all of 14 miles away and there was no regular bus service. Our nearest village was Martin, half a mile from our billet; it boasted two pubs, both of which were generally popular. Entertainment on camp was a bit scarce but, on many occasions when ops were not on, there would be a great 'thrash' in the Sergeants' Mess. Contrary to post-war Mess life, these parties were actively encouraged by the 'top brass', as a way of letting off steam. Discipline was pretty relaxed; I cannot recall ever being on a parade in the six months we were on 106 Squadron. It seemed that, as long as we were available and ready to fly on ops, that was all that was required of us!

Flying Officer H. R. Oldland DFC, MBE, flight-engineer, 455 (RAAF) and 405 (RCAF) Squadrons
Squadron life was just about everything a young man could wish for, and for many it opened up a world they could never have dreamed about. Station life was organised in such a way that aircrews had very little to do other than fly. It was exhilarating, and for those lucky enough to get away with it, tremendously exciting. On a PFF station the main preoccupation was to fly, to train whenever not operationally involved, to hone our skills to the greatest degree of perfection we could attain for the special responsibilities we carried as a PFF crew. Work hard, play hard, feed 'em well was the station motto, and the organisation stood up to it well.

Squadron Leader C. G. Rawlins OBE, DFC, pilot, 144 Squadron
I did my training and operations from fully equipped pre-war-built RAF stations (Upper Heyford and Hemswell). They were comfortable and, to my untrained young mind, apparently efficient and well-run.

I had no complaints. We were nearly all very young and behaved sometimes childishly (Mess games), sometimes selfishly (always looking for a good time), probably always arrogantly.

I did feel that there was not enough contact between the operational stations and the world outside, apart from pubs and girls, but it was difficult to pursue other interests. The main aim was to get one's tour over, to survive, then there would be time for other activities.

Life in the Mess itself was materially good but mentally rather narrow. Talk was almost always one of aeroplanes and extramural fun and games. A few did try to keep up sporting activity but this was difficult to organise.

Flight Lieutenant B. Bressloff DFC, navigator, 635 Squadron
Mess life was congenial. The Officers' Mess, particularly, was run like a good club. It was spacious and well furnished; an armchair was always vacant if one wanted to read or doze. It had a games room and a cosy bar which was stocked with plentiful supplies of weak wartime beer, the tipple favoured by most of us, and which provided the lubricant for the carousals which were our way of shrugging off the tensions and stresses of operational flying. We loved a singsong – bibulous and bawdy ditties, sung as loudly as we could. The Padre, no mean pianist, would sometimes accompany us on the battered barroom piano. I always admired the stoical detachment with which he played, seemingly oblivious to the lewdness of the lyrics, although he would wince a bit if they became somewhat blasphemous . . .

After a pint or two, and with hoarse voices, most of us would be ready for bed; but there were some stalwarts, endowed with endless stamina, who would stay on for a bit of schoolboyish horseplay. A favourite prank of these jesters was to plant their footprints on the ceiling. This was done by mixing soot with beer: this disgusting mixture was then liberally applied to the soles of the feet and the imprint achieved by swinging from the rafters until the feet could be firmly planted on the ceiling. Our CO, a man of ample proportions, managed the extraordinary stunt of imprinting his bare buttocks!

Flying Officer O. C. Cronshaw DFC, pilot, 102 Squadron
Below commissioned level things were pretty spartan. At officer level they were much better and even very good at permanent stations, e.g. RAF Swinderby. Food was usually adequate and good on the squadron – but then we got bacon and eggs before ops. Also we had sweets, chocolate and chewing gum for ops. Always rum in coffee after the op during debriefing. We were well looked after. Neighbourhood

relationships were fairly good considering that most aircrew were larger than life and sometimes rowdy – but all in good fun.

Corporal F. L. Warner, armourer, 15 Squadron
We had a very good station commander, G/Cpt Ken Bachelor, and a Squadron commander who treated all as human beings and thus got the best out of everyone. Food at Mildenhall was very good and plentiful. However when I was stationed at Bexwell (Downham Market) for about four months, the NCOs' food was terrible – until one day a meeting was called and it was then decided to take action!! One lunchtime, we all drew our food and sat waiting for the Orderly Officer to make his usual appearance. He duly arrived and a corporal answered his 'Any Complaints' with 'Yes! Sir.' The corporal stated that the food was 'not fit for a dog to eat!!!' The Armourer's Mascot was to hand and the officer said 'We'll see if a dog will eat it.' The corporal's plate was placed in front of the dog. The dog took one sniff and walked away!! The entire cookhouse staff was posted and a new set sent from Marham. The food was then excellent from that day forward. What the Orderly Officer did not know was that a small quantity of paraffin had been placed in the middle of the plate.

Corporal N. E. Lowther (née Older), administration
One experience I found to be quite traumatic in Bomber Command was as the Corporal Admin. having to march a small detachment of WAAF to the local cemetery, just below our campsite, on funeral parades. This was during 1941 at RAF Cottesmore, when the Hampdens ('flying suitcases') were based there. Many of the young airwomen found it difficult not to be overcome by the solemnity of the occasion, especially the firing of the funeral escorts' rifles over the young airmen's graves. Some of the girls could not experience it for a second time. We all learned to be 'brave' very quickly in those war years – and were very proud to wear our uniform – and hoped we were of some assistance (perhaps a lot) to the RAF.

Aircraftwoman S. Duenas (neé Barton) pending flight mechanic training
I was 17 years old. Billeted in the pre-war married quarters at Abingdon, my roommate and I had little sleep the first two nights owing to the subdued laughter and noise in the room above, occupied by two WAAF corporals. We couldn't decide whether they were overhead dancers or PT instructors. The third night, Service Police joined the party and carted off the two corporals and two pilots. All four were put under open arrest awaiting court martial. One girl being put in

317

the cookhouse, served up quips and snatches of song along with the dollops of mash to the tight-lipped WAAF queues. So while I cannot comment on morale in general, I would say some of our happiest pilots were based at Abingdon.

Section Officer A. Tedder (née Harris), clerk at 12 OTU, Abingdon
Highlights were parties in the Sergeants' Mess – if you were lucky enough to be invited. At such parties we WAAF had to be on our guard as far as the Polish and the French Canadians were concerned. They, in particular, lived for the moment. (This also applied to most of us.)

A very sad incident occurred one bitterly cold night at 0200 hours. Night-flying was on, and a particular pilot of a Wimpy was instructed, repeatedly, to land at our satellite as the ground mist was thick. Alas, he decided to land here and pranged the aircraft on the only available spare bit of land on our sleeping site on the hillside. One engine was on fire outside the front door of our Nissen hut, so we all dressed hurriedly (slacks over pyjamas, and greatcoats), rushed out through the back door down the hill to the Ablution Hut and formed a human chain of buckets of water to the aircraft until the fire engines arrived. The entire crew were killed except for the pilot.

Flight Lieutenant H. Yeoman, pilot, 12 Squadron
Mess life was something unique in my experience, the sense of comradeship was unsurpassable. But there were moments of almost unbearable poignancy, as when I came back off sick leave to Binbrook to be told by my roommate that my crew had gone missing two nights previously. (They have never been found.) Or when, much later, at Breighton, as an Intelligence Officer, I started a game of chess with a bomb-aimer, whose name I didn't know. We didn't finish the game before he had to go up to the Flights – he didn't come back from that night's op, so the game was never finished.

Flight Lieutenant E. G. Jones DFC, AFC, pilot, 115 and 139 Squadrons
I remember one night when we had three funeral pyres burning at the same time. Two aircraft had gone in at the 'Six Hills' bombing range and one in the circuit at Wymeswolde. I had two incidents where I sent students solo to see them finish up as burning heaps. And I was supposed to be a good instructor.

Aircraftman A. Turner, navigator under training, 55 Base, East Kirkby
It was a severe winter and, as the frost increased its grip, the ablutions ceased to function one by one. We trekked across the

bleak snow-covered countryside from one site to another in search of establishments that still had flushable toilets. At one stage we were reduced to collecting snow and melting it over the stove in order to wash. Conditions became so unpleasant that I even heard of a desperate plot to leave all the cookhouse windows open at night. The theory was that if the cookhouse froze up the station would have to close and we should all be sent on leave . . . Nothing came of this, unfortunately!

Sergeant R. J. Ball, fitter II (engines), 115 Squadron
Apart from occasional 'blips', 'bull' was fairly nonexistent. Our Squadron F/Sgt Discip. sometimes felt the need to justify his role, but in retrospect he was no martinet, so that we all got on with our jobs. This general attitude common to many Operational Squadrons was demonstrated on my arrival. Fresh from Training School, I watched with amazement each morning as Flight personnel wearing plimsolls and scruffy order ambled off to their kites. I soon found that technical conscientiousness was far more important than sartorial perfection.

Aircraftman A. Turner, navigator under training, 55 Base, East Kirkby
I was thrilled to be issued with a flying suit, but soon found that its purpose was only to keep out some of the bitter cold as I spent the first night on the back of an open lorry cruising up and down the runways and perimeter tracks while we shovelled out grit on to the snow-covered surface. It was a hazardous job, for the vehicle had to lurch off the tarmac prior to each take-off and landing. If we had not been thrown off our feet by that manoeuvre, the next pleasure was the dense blizzard generated by four Merlins rushing past. Then drifting snow covered the electric lights sunk into the surface to mark the runway edges, and we had to set out with a lorryload of gooseneck flares. These were just like watering cans with long spouts fitted with wicks. One or two were kept burning on the lorry, and from them we lit up those we were to place down the runway beside the electric lights glowing faintly through the snow. The lorry drove slowly down the middle of the runway while we dashed to and from it, grabbing a flare, igniting it, and running back to place it in position, with much splashing of paraffin. By the time we had set out several dozen of them our clothes reeked of the stuff, and we were in some danger of ending up in a blaze of glory.

Pilot Officer E. R. Bowden DFC, pilot, 578 Squadron
The idea of an aircrew using the same aircraft whenever possible

created great *esprit de corps* with the ground crew, who always waited up for their aircraft to return.

Leading Aircraftman E. Howell, flight mechanic (engines), 44 Squadron
Just before take-off was a very uneasy time for us ground crew, as we were viewing men who were risking their lives in a most unpleasant manner several times a week, and the ground crews were helping to send them on their way in this endeavour. Some were tense and uncommunicative, others seemed to be at fever pitch and very hyper, but all appeared to be in full control of themselves. There was an air of unbelievability to the whole situation, as if this could not possibly be happening to them.

After a certain time they would board the aircraft and start the engines, which had to be accompanied by one of the ground crew climbing up under the undercarriage and pumping a Kygass priming pump for each engine until each engine was running. At their signal we would pull the chocks away, give them the thumbs-up, and away they would taxi to the top end of the take-off runway. At this time the whole station would be at a high pitch, and if prayers really counted every one of those gallant aircrew would have returned to Waddington. But that was not to be.

Flight Lieutenant J. M. Catford DFC, AE, air-gunner, 635 Squadron, Downham Market
The only problem from which we really suffered was a shortage of fuel, coke and coal, during the exceptionally cold winter of 1944. For us, the initial answer was the purchase of a cross saw from the local ironmongers. Shortly afterwards, small and medium-sized trees, in and around our billet, became a rarity. Eventually, our flight engineer came up with the answer. We adapted the coke stove in our billet to run on waste engine oil, fed from a drum and pipe placed immediately above the stove, and putting an iron catchment plate inside the stove. Also included was another pipe running alongside the oil pipe. This fed a calculated number of drips of water to each very much larger amount of oil going into the stove. This resulted (I know not how) in a roaring fire, with unlimited fuel from oil changes on the Lancasters, and to a lesser extent from cars on Camp.

Local families tended to 'adopt' whole crews. One such family of farmers adopted my crew – the friendship which developed was fantastic. Their home became our home. Any time which became available to us was largely spent with them. The friendship continues to this day, with occasional visits.

Leading Aircraftman D. F. Aris, armourer, 141 Squadron
In general station life was good. Obviously wartime-built Nissen-hutted airfields were primitive and uncomfortable, but the permanent peacetime-built stations were excellent, even if accommodation was at times overcrowded with bunks installed in barrack blocks. Food in general wasn't too bad; young healthy appetites could eat almost anything. In general the social and recreational sides were well catered for, bearing in mind the wartime conditions. For an airman the social life outside the station was usually the pub or an occasional village hall dance and, if near a town, the cinema. I found no bad feeling or resentment from local civilians who had to put up with hundreds and sometimes thousands of Service men and women in their locality.

Flying Officer G. Cairns OBE, flight engineer, 460 (RAAF) Squadron
Relations between the station and Binbrook village were excellent and still exist to this day despite the closure of the station in 1988. 460 Squadron Association in Australia still maintains contact with the Parish Council and the villagers care for the squadron memorial erected in the village. A Book of Remembrance, which lists the names of the 1000 aircrew of 460 squadron who lost their lives, is located in the village church, and a memorial window reflecting the history of the station has been installed. The cost was covered by donations from past members of the station and squadrons based there.

Flying Officer H. R. Oldland DFC, MBE, flight engineer, 455 (RAAF) and 405 (RCAF) Squadrons
A plaque under the memorial window in the church at Great Gransden says:

> The people of these villages cared for the Airmen
> who flew from R.A.F. Gransden Lodge.
> They watched for them and prayed for them.

This just about sums up the relationships between station and locals. What they had, they shared willingly, and gave generously, from the churns of fresh milk in the messes every day, teas in local farmhouses, boiled eggs, home-baked bread, and home-made butter, extra messing that must have broken the rationing laws many times over.

Flying Officer W. D. Parlett, pilot, 115 Squadron
One pay parade, at the last moment two air-gunners, who were not the smartest men on parade, slouched in late and the Station Warrant Officer spoke to them. Where have you been? They looked him up

and down and said 'Berlin – Ever been there?' The answer left him speechless.

OPERATIONS

Squadron Leader C. G. Rawlins OBE, DFC, pilot, 144 Squadron
Take-off on a dark night with a low cloud base in a war-laden aircraft was sometimes a grim affair. Bumping down the flarepath, watching the slow build-up of the extra speed needed for the heavy load; hoping to be airborne before that last flare with still some visual reference to the ground; entering the black void beyond, teetering near the stall, head down on the instruments, checking the speed, keeping straight and climbing to avoid those unseen trees one knew were dead ahead . . . Then undercarriage, flaps, cowling gills, revs, boost, trim, temperatures and pressures, back to the instruments to settle into the climb and turn on to course, then breathe a sigh of relief that one of the most dangerous parts of the op was safely over.

Warrant Officer K. P. Collins AE, observer, 82 Squadron
Although we were proud of our Blenheims, I think that they were unsuited to the ops we had to undertake. Low-level flying *was* dangerous and our last two low-level flights were at night and were particularly 'dicey'. By May 1941 we were the longest surviving crew on the squadron. New crews came and went with alarming rapidity before we even came to know them, and this was not conducive to peace of mind. I had said to my pilot, Ted Inman, that we seemed to be going on for ever but he replied 'We've got to go sometime, it's inevitable.'

We all realised that the end was in sight when we were sent to Malta in May 1941. We came down on our 39th op and I was the only survivor from two Blenheims which were blown up when our bombs exploded on a ship we attacked in the Med.

Flight Lieutenant M. Tomlinson, Intelligence Officer, Coningsby
4/5 April 1941. Coningsby 106 Squadron. *Scharnhorst* and *Gneisenau* (but possibly at that early stage some other German vessel or vessels) were at Brest and presented a shockingly heavily defended target. Volunteers were called to go in low. (Wicked in my opinion.) The CO Wing Commander P. Polglase (a very well-bred quiet man) felt obliged to volunteer. His 2nd Pilot and Navigator was a stocky little Northerner, P/O W. Brown, absolutely new to ops. 'Brownie' had

had a son on 5th March. 'I don't want to volunteer to go in low,' he said to me, 'I've only seen my son once. But what can I do, the CO's volunteered.' They were killed, of course.

Wing Commander J. Partridge DSO, DFC and bar, pilot, 83 Squadron
We were ordered at very short notice to try to find the battleships *Scharnhorst*, *Gneisenau* and *Prince Eugene* as they were escaping up the Channel from Brest. Although daylight, the weather was very foggy with a very low cloud base. Very few aircraft found the ships but when we broke cloud we were right over them at under 100 feet. We encountered intense gunfire and received much damage. Unfortunately our hydraulics were hit and we were unable to open our bomb doors, or later lower flaps or undercarriage. We had to set course for base with only one serviceable engine and our rear-gunner was seriously injured and eventually died. We made for the nearest grass airfield and made a 'belly' landing at Buckland Newton with all our bombs on board. We came to a stop in a hedge on the edge of the airfield. This was my first operation in a Manchester.

Flight Lieutenant E. C. Stocker DSO, DFC, flight engineer, 415 Squadron
Superstition? I did carry a lucky emblem, and was also requested to relieve myself on the tail-wheel prior to take-off by the rest of the crew. I understand now that this was not original.

Flight Lieutenant E. H. Woods, AE, navigator, 106,144,61 Squadrons
The Germans had developed a Master searchlight system whereby some sort of range and direction device enabled them to pick us up. Once this had been achieved, a team of adjacent searchlights would then join the 'master' and form the dreaded cone around us. If you became trapped, it was almost impossible to see out and the pilot had to revert to basic blind-flying instruments, putting the nose down in an attempt to adopt a manoeuvre which would fox the Germans, or in extreme cases put the nose firmly down and head for the deck.

   To see another aircraft trapped in such a cone was an eerie sight for it often looked like a bright silver cigar in the centre of the cone, but when that silver turned to a golden glow it showed immediately that some poor soul had been hit. It was a dreadful sight to see such an aircraft falling slowly like a burning star, and many a silent prayer was offered up in the hope that the crew would have time to bale out.

Flight Lieutenant E. Blanchard DFC, flight engineer, 57 Squadron
I was at the caravan with the CO watching the squadrons depart

when an Australian skipper thundered down the runway fully laden for a long trip. Soon after lift-off he lost power and crashed a short distance from the airfield.

We hurried by car to the hamlet where he had crashed. In the road were 1000-lb bombs looking red hot and there was an armaments officer calmly working on them. The house was on fire, and our ambulance crew were searching for the bodies. There in the ditch was a gunner with his parachute smouldering. One of the ground staff asked me to give him a lift, but the poor chap's legs just flapped about – he was dead. It wasn't my cup of tea. It brought home to me how our ground staff had to cope with these disasters.

Flight Lieutenant L. R. Sidwell, air-gunner, 7 Squadron
Quiet over the North Sea and I think we were running up to the Hamburg target when things happened. A decoy headlight was seen and tracer came up from below – a night-fighter attack. We were hit and put on fire. A fighter came in from astern; I may have hit him with a burst but as I followed him round in my sights, the power went off and guns and turret were U/S. He came in again and shattered my perspex. I heard the captain give the Emergency Baling Out Order, followed immediately by what I thought were his cries at being hit. Then the intercom went completely dead.

I'd been left partly on the beam in my rear turret when the power failed and I set to work on the 'Dead Man's Handle' to centralise my turret so that I could get into the fuselage to grab my parachute from its stowage outside the turret to bale out. I wound away like mad on this hand-winding emergency gear behind me, very conscious that we were losing height and on fire, whilst watching as if in a dream another fighter closing in and still firing. He seemed very close when he broke away to starboard, while I wound away on that painfully slow hand-gear . . .

I finally managed to centralise my turret and fell back through the doors into the fuselage, grabbed my precious parachute from its stowage and snapped it on hurriedly as I feared we might have lost a lot of height. I forced open the nearby rear emergency exit door on the starboard side and jumped into space without thinking or hesitation and immediately pulled the ripcord. As I went out I was conscious of flame and smoke up the fuselage but in my haste to quit the doomed Stirling I partly knocked myself out. However I must have been conscious enough to pull the ripcord properly. The sudden jerk of the harness when the parachute opened brought me to my senses; I was swaying gently in the air and looking

down on the wide R. Elbe with the bright moon gleaming on
the water.

Flight Lieutenant R. Davey, navigator, 218, 514 and 139 Squadrons
One of our aircraft was suffering a very persistent night-fighter attack
and the rear-gunner was screaming very violent evasive tactics to the
pilot. Now the pilot was a very religious man and he shouted to the
gunner, 'Have no fear, the Lord is with us.' The gunner retorted, 'He
might be up the front with you but he ain't down here.' I gather that
when they landed the gunner was transferred to another crew!

Flying Officer C. Cairns, OBE, flight engineer, 460 (RAAF) Squadron
We were just leaving the target area [Kassel on 22 October 1943]
when we were hit by flak and attacked by a fighter simultaneously.
Both gunners were wounded, the mid-upper being blown out of his
turret and receiving serious wounds to his legs. No. 2 starboard wing
fuel tank and its outer engine were on fire. I feathered the engine
and the fire went out. The skipper put the aircraft into a steep dive
which eventually extinguished the fuel tank fire and lost the fighter.
A fire which had developed in the fuselage was put out by the wireless
operator. The wounded rear-gunner remained in his turret and the
mid-upper was placed on the rest bed and given a shot of morphine
to ease his pain. The aircraft was difficult to fly straight and level, so
a rope from my toolkit was attached to the starboard rudder pedal,
and by pulling and slackening the skipper got us home.

Flight Lieutenant E. Blanchard DFC, flight engineer, 57 Squadron
'WINDOW' was used for the first time on Hamburg. On 57 Squadron
the flight engineers were issued with the electrically heated suit
worn by rear-gunners. This meant that we were unusually hot and
uncomfortable whilst performing the normal engineer's duties up in
the cockpit. At a certain time from the target we crossed the main spar
into the area aft of the bomb bay and close to the flare chute. Bundles
of 'WINDOW' had been placed there ready for use. The bomb-aimer
had been issued with a stopwatch, and when we had to commence
dropping he was to say 'window' over the intercom. I then chucked
a packet of 'WINDOW' down the flare chute. It was an awful place
to be – the mid-upper gunner was swivelling above me and I was
plugged into a point to heat the suit and the oxygen economiser.
Nothing much to hang on to and it was dark.

Thankfully someone must have guessed that one couldn't keep
sending the FE down to do the job, and for the next op a slot

had been cut just between the cockpit and the BA compartment. No longer did we natter 'window'. The stopwatch was still around but mostly unused, and both the FE and the BA could chuck out the 'WINDOW'.

Flight Lieutenant W. D. Spence, bomb-aimer, 44 (Rhodesia) Squadron
We were just landing when over the intercom we heard a shout 'Look out!' It was cut off almost as soon as it was uttered. At the same instant there was a huge explosion ahead of us and pieces of aircraft on fire fell to the ground. Two planes had collided in the funnels, one coming in to land, the other – who knows why he was where he was or at the height he was. The ground was littered with the blazing wreckage right across the area just short of the runway, so that we had to fly just above the flames in order to touch down. But the thing which sticks in my mind was the calmness of the WAAFs in the control tower who must have been devastated by the scene. They continued to talk us down, and the rest of the squadron, as if nothing had happened.

Warrant Officer W. Taylor, bomb-aimer, 70 Squadron
After bombing Milan, 13th July 1944, we collided with another Wellington at 9000 feet. Both engines were knocked out and the door jammed. The pilot, Harry Pollard, stayed at the controls, keeping the aircraft in a dive. I handed him his parachute and he threw it away and told me to get out of the emergency hatch. I got out at 1500 feet and saw the aircraft crash into the ground on fire. He sacrificed himself so that the rest of the crew survived.

Flying Officer K. M. Pincott, DFM, navigator, 15 Squadron
On the night of April 22nd 1944 we were detailed to bomb Düsseldorf and because we were by this time a fairly experienced crew we were detailed to be backers-up to PFF. This meant we had to bomb the target one minute before zero hour and start fires. We were on our bombing run when we were hit by a fighter and at the same time a high-explosive shell also hit the aircraft. We were immediately set on fire at the back of the aircraft and also had a fire in the wing. The aircraft plunged from 21,000 feet down to 14,000 when the pilot levelled out but the aircraft dropped to 7000 feet immediately. I thought that I was the only crew member alive and decided I should try to bale out. Just then the pilot shouted over the intercom for a course out of the target, which I gave him. A crew check was carried out and we discovered the bomb-aimer had been killed and the wireless operator was also very seriously

injured, but we had managed to put out the fire. With two engines out of action, the elevators and controls and the flaps were affected whilst the undercarriage was also damaged. The aircraft gradually lost height during the homeward flight and it became necessary to jettison all heavy movable equipment. The wireless operator died from his injuries half an hour before we crashed at Woodbridge.

Pilot Officer R. J. Durran, flight engineer, 576 Squadron
During a daylight raid on Heligoland one engine failed before bombing. With a full bomb-load and maximum fuel the Lancaster, whilst forced down from operational height of 17,000 feet to 10,000 feet, still behaved perfectly. The sight of hundreds of bombs screaming past us from the main force above is still vividly recalled and brings me out in a cold sweat: an excuse to reach for the whisky!

Flight Lieutenant D. Hawker DFC, pilot, 630 Squadron
The most devastating innovation that the enemy evolved was fixed cannons pointing upwards at 60°. Having located a bomber with the aid of radar the fighter pilot could then fly unseen under the bomber and put fifteen incendiary cannon shells into the petrol tanks between the two motors on the starboard side. It usually took only about eight seconds before the bomber exploded.

Flying Officer K. W. Marshall, DFC, flight engineer, 578 Squadron
I remember seeing a crew returning from an operation after a stray bomb had passed clean through their aircraft, demolishing everything in its wake except the crews' morale. Having landed away from base they returned to the squadron on the crew truck, with one member sporting the Elsan seat round his neck, and giving the thumbs-up sign.

Squadron Leader R. A. Read DFC, pilot, 78 Squadron
The next operation was on 10th March to Frankfurt. I was not going again, and just beginning to get used to it. The Group Captain was going though, having managed to get Group's permission. Normally station commanders were not allowed to go on ops. It was considered that they were privy to too many secrets.

Groupy Whitley was different. He'd been an operational pilot with the squadron in 1940–41, and presumably wanted to get an updated view of the problems of his crews. He was that sort of man. He was going with Flt Lt Hull of 78 Squadron, an experienced pilot, who'd started at the same time as me.

With Gerry Warner, I drove out to Hully's aircraft, and we made a special point of saying goodbye and good luck to the Groupy, and the crew. Groupies didn't go on ops very often.

I was OC flying for 78 that night. I remember the long weary wait, as it became apparent that Hully wasn't going to come back. The Group Captain was missing. A little shiver ran through us in the control tower. If they could get old Groupy, we thought, they could get anybody . . .

LEADERSHIP

Squadron Leader C. G. C. Rawlins OBE, DFC, pilot, 144 Squadron
To the young and eager pilots of those days, most brought up and accepting the British system of hierarchical leadership, it all seemed perfectly sound. There was, perhaps, more camaraderie between ranks (both of officers and NCOs) than there would have been in pre-war days and consequently a little less automatic respect for higher ranks. Flight commanders were social friends, squadron commanders rather more distant. It was a man's operational rather than his service record which marked him out as a respected leader in an operational squadron. Some who came into operations with senior rank but no operational experience generally had to show their worth by getting in a few ops; several fine men were lost in this process, probably needlessly since their maturity and wisdom (which were not, in my opinion, common qualities of the average Bomber Command aircrew) might have served the cause better.

Pilot Officer J. Curtiss KCB, KBE, pilot, 178 and 578 Squadrons
When I joined 578 it had a very fine CO on his third tour who really led from the front. So much so that the AOC sent him to Training Command for a rest – where he was killed in an accident. We all felt his death deeply. It was only after the war that I discovered he was only 26!

But leadership at all levels was very good and the squadron had a press-on spirit and great confidence in its abilities.

When my whole crew apart from myself and the signaller were killed in a flying accident we were very well handled, put back in the air quickly, and re-crewed very successfully.

Flight Sergeant R. F. Pritchard RAAF, air-gunner, 550 Squadron
The whole tone of a squadron was created by its commanding officer.

When commanded by a CO who had earned their admiration and respect the squadron performed well and confidently. Morale sank to rock bottom when the commanding officer resorted to high levels of dress, discipline and a regime of petty tyranny. Low levels of maintenance, high levels of sickness and an increase in boomerangs usually followed. I served under both sorts of commanding officer and it was a constant source of surprise to me of the high esteem that the martinet type CO was held by his superiors. The complete opposite applied in the RAAF.

Sergeant R. J. Ball, fitter (engines), 115 Squadron
For ground crews on an operational squadron the Flights were the place to be. Having 'adopted' your kite, you were as close to flying as practicable. Rapport with the intrepid birdmen was always satisfying, more particularly in the Lanc. days. Supportively sharing their problems and fears meant emotional celebrations when they hopefully completed their tour. Squadron and Flight Commanders set the leadership tone which, filtering down through the flying crews, tended to permeate servicing personnel, and produced a conscientiousness beyond, as it were, the call of duty.

Flying Officer M. C. Wright DFM, navigator, 9, 44 and 142 Squadrons
In retrospect I think our leaders should have done more to equate aircrew and ground staff. I think it unfortunate that the distinction in rank in the traditional service manner seemed to prevent a more natural, closer relationship. It is only since the war that I have come to realise this, and I regret not having got to know our ground crew much better than I did at the time.

Bomber Command and Group Headquarters were too remote for me to appreciate leadership qualities from that direction. At squadron level our senior officers were complying strictly with instructions from above, giving little opportunity to exercise such leadership as would have been possible, say, in a daylight fighter squadron. Each aircraft on night operations in Bomber Command was an isolated unit.

Flying Officer J. C. Richardson, bomb-aimer, 102 Squadron
As regards leadership, I was extremely lucky in having Group Captain Cheshire as CO at Conversion Unit, Sir Gus Walker as CO of the clutch at Pocklington, and Squadron Leader Les Ames. They were all marvellous examples and inspired confidence in all who served under them. I knew Gus Walker best. I expect most of the aircrew will remember him: as each aircraft took off on an op he would run

down the runway waving it goodbye with the Crew List in his one good arm . . . and I can still see him now waving us off, and it may well have been for many the last person they saw before they got the chop.

Flying Officer H. R. Oldland DFC, MBE, flight engineer, 455 (RAAF) and 405 (RCAF) Squadrons
The troops are only ever as good as the man out front. The man out front (in No. 8 Group) was AV-M. Bennett and the qualities of his leadership were reflected at station and squadron level, and right down to the crews themselves. Regularly seen in the debriefing room, at all hours, out on the flights talking to both air and ground crews, flying his own Beaufighter round his stations, he was recognised and respected as a leader who had done it himself, whose knowledge of every facet of aircrew duties, and not just that of a pilot, had been proved. He set the example, demanded equally high standards of his crews, and got them.

Leading Aircraftman E. Howell, flight mechanic (engines), 44 Squadron
Leadership at the squadron, flight and dispersal levels was absolutely first class. Ground crews had a good rapport with our officers and NCO aircrews that was easy to understand, and our respect and admiration for them was boundless.

Sergeant G. F. Everett, fitter II (engines), 44 Squadron
The leadership that I thought the most outstanding was that which existed in the aircrew, who were well known for their laughing and joking among themselves, even as they were climbing aboard the aircraft for ops. There was obviously great leadership there; no 'orders' given, no need for them, they all knew their jobs and were following a naturally accepted leader, their pilot, whom they trusted. And they also trusted each other.

To a certain extent, this sort of leadership existed among the ground crews. We knew and trusted each other, with very few exceptions, once we had established a regular crew.

COURAGE, FEAR, MORALE

Flight Lieutenant S. T. Wingham DFC, bomb-aimer, 102 and 76 Squadrons, and navigator, 105 Squadron
Morale was almost an individual matter for each crew, although

obviously what was going on around one did have its effect. Often one saw a new crew come on the squadron who somehow had a smell of death about them. You knew other aircrew who intuitively had also spotted this, and although no word was said surprise was not expressed when the crew failed to return, usually in their first 4/5 ops. When a crew who had passed the middle of their tour failed to return or an experienced Flight Commander didn't make it, then you started to think about the odds. But even this was done on one's own. Publicly or with one's crew it was a matter for jokes about the 'chop rate' going up.

Flight Lieutenant H. Yeoman, pilot, 12 Squadron
At the time I was operating, England's fortunes were about at rock bottom. But, on 12 Squadron, our morale was very high; defeat never entered our minds, we knew we were going to win, nothing could stop us. The thought of defeat never occurred to us at any time.

I was frightened speechless more times than I care to remember, more often that I could even count. The time I was most frightened was on the Lübeck trip, when we were trapped in the Kiel defences completely alone, for what was probably 15 minutes, but seemed like hours. I was scared out of my wits – and then, having decided that I was going to die in the next few seconds, I seemed to go through a barrier, and passed from extreme fear to complete calm, where I had made my mind up that my life was over, and so what? It didn't matter any more. The only thing I then felt was regret that there were so many things I hadn't done which now I would never do.

I never saw any lack of courage in anyone, and certainly not in my own crew. As everyone got well and truly shot at and as everyone went back to get shot at again, I think the average person would say 'They were courageous'. But at the time neither I, nor I think anyone else I knew, went around looking for signs of courage around us. We simply had our jobs to do and we tried to do them as best we could.

Flight Lieutenant R. M. Brookbanks DFC, pilot, 10 Squadron
Bomber crews lived from day to day, and I found the worst time was in the morning, waiting to hear whether a call for ops would come through, and if so, what was the petrol-load called for, so that we could get some idea of the possible target. Once the call came through, you would be kept busy, test-flying your aircraft and checking with your crew that everything was OK. Once briefing was over, there was not much to do, and time could hang heavily on your hands. Once the time came to start up your aircraft and prepare for take-off, you

were fully occupied with flying the plane etc., things were OK. The next period of tension was the bombing run, and getting clear of the target area. Once clear, you could breathe a bit easier, but in no way relax.

Flying Officer H. R. Oldland DFC, MBE, flight engineer, 455 (RAAF) and 405 (RCAF) Squadrons
As a member of a crew, one of seven, the feeling of not letting the side down was greater than might have been felt as individuals. PFF Squadrons were invariably a mixture of nationalities – Canadian, Australian, Kiwis, South Africans and even Americans on exchange served alongside RAF personnel on 405. This mixture gave a tremendous feeling of belonging, of representing your country in your own small way, and no way were you going to be less than the rest.

Warrant Officer A. R. Harris, bomb-aimer, 50 Squadron
Fear came, for me at least, in spells or waves, starting with the appearance of our crew on the 'Order of Battle' notice in the Mess Foyer. It usually subsided during the next hour or so, as I fiddled with my motor-bike, or swam in the quarry. Then it came and went until briefing, and disclosure of the target, rising for some targets and falling for others. In the truck to the aircraft one just felt sorry for the chaps opposite – 'their turn tonight' we fondly believed.

In flight things were different; there was a job to do, and striving to do it properly eased the tension. Furthermore, I was comfortable, stretched out in the nose, lying on the escape hatch, parachute handy (or on me) – what more could one want at such a time? Furthermore, I enjoyed map-reading – still do – and bomb-aiming was always an interesting challenge, though often I felt sorry for what happened below.

Squadron Leader D. J. Knight DFC, air-gunner, 35 Squadron
I think it is generally agreed now – and was at the time – that we were all afflicted by fear. I except the few 'flak happy' characters who seemed to have survived too many ops and were immune to everything including fear! I personally came across a few with over 100 trips to their credit and some of them were burned out physically and mentally.

Fear was given a back seat when one became airborne and there was work to do – incidents on the journey did of course give one the odd stab of fear, the 'this is it feeling', but not the meditated

332

fear before getting airborne (some the result of a sombre warning of what to expect at Briefing!).

For myself it was a case of living in a trauma aggravated by fatigue and slogging on in the hope of finishing the tour.

Flying Officer A. G. Harrison DFC, bomb-aimer, 83 Squadron
Bomber Command aircrew were a self-selected group who had been at school in the '30s, a time when there was a greater stability of values and there was no question that they were fighting a necessary war. Compared with their post-war counterparts some might regard them as naive or unworldly. This could be part of the basis of their morale, which I felt as some undefinable quality when I first met them and which seemed to carry one on.

Flight Sergeant M. C. Bird, bomb-aimer, 192 Squadron
I was very superstitious, carrying two woolly dolls made by a WAAF acquaintance and a lucky horseshoe with my identity discs. I prayed hard when on operations and even harder when attacked by night-fighters. We were one of two crews that joined 192 from 26 OTU in August 1944. Later three aircraft had been lost from 'B' Flight, three had been lost from 'C' Flight and two from our own 'A' Flight. I convinced myself that the next one to go would be one of the two of us that had joined the squadron in August. We operated on alternate nights and it became an obsession – almost a feeling of anger when they returned safely and it became our turn again. I hated myself for my reaction but there it was – a sort of Russian roulette. In the event we both survived, but I have despised myself for the feelings that I had and will do to my dying day.

Leading Aircraftwoman D. Search, cook, Warboys, Feltwell and Syerston
I think we all needed a sense of humour, especially on the bomber station at Warboys, with the tragic happenings of every day – so often seeing most go out and not return, people being killed at the airfield through accidents, or bombs going off, or even crews being killed crash-landing on coming home. But life went on, and you went off to the next dance or pub and put it behind you.

Sergeant R. J. Ball, fitter (engines), 115 Squadron
I recall most vividly the collective courage shown by our operational crews as they prepared for ops take-off.

Chances of tour survival varied during the course of the war but were always slight. As the new 'volunteer' crews arrived – many perhaps seduced by the apparent glamour of flying and the distinctive brevet – they faced the harsh reality of their job. Taking off at night initially with inexperienced companions against the countless perils of weather, terrain, often navigational uncertainty to say nothing of attack in many unpleasant forms over enemy territory – even on return and over their own base. Each time all of them had to conquer fear and therein in my view lies courage of the highest order.

Flight Lieutenant E. H. Woods, AE, navigator, Squadron
I have often been asked how I felt when I released bombs which in all probability would bring death and destruction below, and I must confess, like a lot of my colleagues, that concern at the consequences never entered my head. We had all seen what had happened to London and most of the other large cities and so our attacks seemed fully justified, but that was all. No deep thoughts or feelings of concern, or even of hatred, as far as I can remember.

Many of the crews who had lost relatives or homes in the German raids brought bricks from the debris back to the unit and dropped them over the targets, a wasted but satisfying gesture.

Flight Lieutenant J. M. Catford DFC, AE, air-gunner, 635 Squadron
I feel that morale was largely a question of one's mental make-up and imagination. For myself, I found the whole of life so exciting that I looked forward to each trip with no sense of fear. However, if we experienced a difficult trip, and suffered a number of attacks, particularly over a well-lit target, then under such circumstances I was very much afraid, invariably thinking to myself 'Why the hell did I volunteer for this bloody job!' On such occasions fear affected me to such an extent that I sweated and had to turn off my electrically heated suit, even though on such occasions the temperature was perhaps 50 degrees below zero. As soon as the combat was over, I commenced to freeze and had to turn on the heating again. Upon our safe return from such a trip, I mentally, and sometimes physically, kissed the earth upon getting off the aircraft. Immediately following this, I again looked forward to the next trip. One rarely discussed one's fears, and in our case can only assume that we all felt much the same. This was perhaps borne out by the fact that at the end of our first tour, we all volunteered for a second tour, and later did the same for our third tour. On both occasions we declined the normal six months' 'screening'.

Flying Officer K. M. Pincott DFM, navigator, 15 Squadron

We would think about the statistics of after 20 ops one is living on borrowed time. As far as I can recollect from the period between Oct. '43–June '44 only one crew that arrived on the station when we did, completed its tour with all the crew surviving. We were always upset when we learned that various aircrew members on the squadron refused to fly on operations. They were immediately removed from the station because of the effect on the morale of others. They were rather harshly treated, with a lack of understanding of the effects which caused the chaps to be branded LMF (Lack of Moral Fibre). The effects of operating were very stressful, especially after being attacked and seeing crew members killed and injured. At every briefing for a raid one would look around the room and see crews who you thought vulnerable and would not be returning. Up to the time your crew suffered casualties you felt it would not happen to you, but when it did, every raid became an ordeal from then on.

In spite of the fear you pressed on regardless – there was not any real alternative – and you lived each day with the expectation that it could be your last.

Flight Lieutenant B. Bressloff DFC, navigator, 635 Squadron

There was one particularly harrowing operation when, after being repeatedly hit by enemy ground fire, we had limped home across the North Sea in a badly damaged Lancaster. We were flying on two engines and with most of the flying control surfaces shot to ribbons. Our Skipper, Flt/Lt G. A. Thorne, was trying to land at the emergency airfield at Woodbridge which had a five-mile runway. A third engine failed on the approach and by dint of superb flying he managed to crash-land in a field after smashing through a line of saplings. The aircraft broke its back and caught fire. I was momentarily trapped in the mid-section with the oxygen cylinders blazing around me. I managed to propel myself through the escape hatch knowing that the wing tanks would explode at any moment. We lost our Wireless Operator, whose charred body was later found in the wreckage. A truck was sent out to take us to Woodbridge, where a doctor attended to our injuries. Our Skipper was taken to the RAF hospital at Ely for treatment to a head wound and the rest of us spent the night at Woodbridge waiting for one of our squadron's aircraft to ferry us back to base.

We were badly shaken by our experience, and shattered by the loss of Flight Sergeant Crabtree, our Wireless Operator. Next morning a 635 Squadron Lancaster was waiting to take us back to our Unit.

When I was about to board the aircraft I was overcome by the most dreadful feeling of fear; I was literally paralysed with funk, and couldn't climb into it. This is, I suppose, the nature of phobia, as distinct from normal fear. It was quite irrational; there was no danger – we were simply being flown back the short distance to base, and yet, I was shaking with terror. I'm quite certain now that had I not forced myself to board that aircraft, I would have never again been able to fly. In the event I somehow managed to get a grip on myself and mounted the ladder into the aircraft. I went on to complete the rest of my tour of operations and did not experience such profound terror again.

Squadron Leader R. A. Read DFC, pilot, 78 Squadron
Many more cases of LMF might have surfaced if we hadn't been of the generation we were. Disciplined in ourselves, born to respect authority, and obey orders. Above all, regarding any show of fear as an appalling breach of the code.

Many of us suffered a loss of confidence from time to time, but somehow or other we would find a way to rationalise events, and carry on until we reached the end of our tours.

Or, literally, die in the attempt.

THE SPIRIT OF BOMBER COMMAND

Sergeant W. E. Wilkinson, fitter II (engines), 142 Squadron
As far as my time with 142 Squadron from 1940 to late 1942 was concerned, the comradeship was deeper than I have experienced anywhere else. Everybody did every possible thing to give the aircrews the best possible chance. The aircrews knew and appreciated this. Every aircrew would sooner take their own aircraft than the spare, and the ground crew would sweat blood to see they got their wish.

Leading Aircraftwoman M. West (née Allcock), driver, Waddington
The spirit of Bomber Command will live for ever, the camaraderie, the comradeship, the pulling together, teamwork, the valour, the Aussies working alongside the Poms.

Sergeant S. Fletcher, flight engineer, 420 (RCAF) Squadron
There was no 'gung-ho' attitude. No press on regardless, though my crew would have hated to turn back. My own attitude was I had volunteered for this. I had a good crew I had confidence in, especially

the navigator. Without a good nav. you had no chance. The enemy did not let you wander about the sky. He chopped you.

Sergeant R. J. Ball, fitter II (engines), 115 Squadron
Fine team spirit prevailed, particularly on the Flights where our duties brought daily contact with aircraft and their crews and thus possibly a greater feeling of involvement than any other ground trade. Aircrew reliance on sound maintenance invariably created a common bond strengthening during the 6/12 months (if the fates were kind) of a normal tour. This continuity probably produced on heavy Bomber Squadrons a greater opportunity for mutual fellowship than in any other Command.

Pilot Officer J. Curtiss KCB, KBE, pilot, 178 and 578 Squadrons
Morale was extraordinarily high. By 1944 the period of high losses was over and we all felt we were doing an important and successful job in playing a very big part in defeating Germany. Although seldom if ever seen at squadron level the C in C was held in great reverence and awe.

Flight Lieutenant J. Waterhouse DFM, navigator, 9 Squadron
There was a complete belief throughout all ranks that even in the darkest moments we were superior to the enemy in equipment and skills, and that we could not possibly lose the war.

Flying Officer W. W. Burke, navigator, 207 and 627 Squadrons
Despite the appalling losses the spirit of Bomber Command was fantastically high to the point almost of arrogance. And when one joined Pathfinder Force one really felt that one was a member of the crème de la crème de la crème.

I think that it was partly a consequence of youth (the war was over before I was 21 and I had completed 40 operations), partly the feeling that nothing nasty would ever happen to you (as distinct from other people), and partly a fear of showing fear to one's comrades.

Flight Lieutenant H. F. Le Marchant, navigator, 57, 630 and 97 Squadrons
I will always feel honoured to have had the privilege of serving with such a wonderful team of people and happy that I am still able to be in regular contact with some of us lucky ones who survived. One looks for the same spirit these days in civilian life but regrettably it is not there. It was something very, very special and so very

precious. Old and new friendships flower today just as they did in yesteryear within the Squadron Associations, Caterpillar Club, Bomber Command Association and Aircrew Association.

THE SPIRIT LIVED ON

Courage and comradeship were hallmarks of Bomber Command. Among the survivors they still are. In the last days of his life in 1991 R. H. Robilliard, an Australian who had served as a pilot with 101 Squadron, began an air letter to his former crew mates. He did not live to finish it, but his widow, Joy, adding the details of his death, sent it on from Australia to the bomb-aimer, Neil St Clair L'Amie, in Scotland.

28.8.91.
Hi Chaps!
Since I haven't heard aught from any of you in similar vein I can but presume you're all waiting for me to do a pathfinder job for you. Any messages etc. you want delivered to the 'great beyond', you'd better get them in quick because ETD* is closing rapidly – three – four weeks is about it, apparently. 'The Big C'† of course.

14.9.91.
Dear Neil,
The above is a letter started by Richard on the 28.8.91 (Wednesday). Sadly he died on the following Monday (2.9.91. at 2.40 p.m.). He died as he lived – with quiet dignity. He had gone downhill badly since you were here, but I managed to nurse him right up to the last 3 hours of his life. He was taken to hospital at around 10.30 on that Monday morning – not being able to eat or drink, was in pain at the site of the lung cancer, and had congestive cardiac failure. That morning he said when he woke up, 'I'm stuffed, darling – I just can't go on' and he didn't for long. He had a cardiac arrest at 2.30 and with myself holding one hand and his G.P. holding the other, life went from him very peacefully. Just as he wanted it to happen – he had tidied all the loose ends in his life – seen all the family and close friends and arranged his funeral on the Thursday before his death. We scattered his ashes in the lake he so loved from his yacht, the 'Wendy B'. They draped a flag on his coffin and we placed red poppies on it. It was a lovely

* Estimated Time of Departure.
† Chop.

moving ceremony. PS. I did toss up whether or not to send this letter written by Richard – but decided it was so typical of him, that I should.

The spirit of Richard Robilliard was the spirit of Bomber Command.

Chronology

1936	Bomber Command formed from Air Defence of Great Britain.

1937
September

12	ACM Sir Edgar Ludlow-Hewitt AOC-in-C.

1939
September

1	German invasion of Poland.
2	AASF (10 Battle squadrons) to France.
3	War on Germany declared by Britain and France.
3/4	First night of leaflet-dropping over Germany.
4	First attacks on the German fleet.
29	Poland partitioned between Germany and USSR.

November

4	Neutrality Act (Cash and Carry) enacted in USA.

December

3	Attack on seaplane bases at Hornum and Sylt. Beginning of anti-mining patrols.
17	Empire Air Training agreement signed.
18	Attack on warships at Wilhelmshaven: 12 Wellingtons lost.

1940
March

11	U-boat sunk by a Bomber Command Blenheim.
16	First British civilian killed by a German bomb.
17	Attack on seaplane bases on Sylt by 50 Whitleys and Hampdens.
28	AM C. F. A. Portal AOC-in-C.

April

9	German invasion of Denmark and Norway.
11	Attack on Stavanger airfield – the first on a mainland target.
13/14	First minelaying by Bomber Command: by Hampdens off Denmark.

May

10	German invasion of Holland, Belgium and Luxembourg. Coalition in Britain under Winston Churchill.
10/11	First Bomber Command bombs on the German mainland.
12–14	German breakthrough across the Meuse. Heavy losses by the AASF.
14	German bombing of Rotterdam.
15	Bombing east of the Rhine authorised by the War Cabinet.
15/16	Attempted attack by 96 bombers on oil and railway targets in the Ruhr.
17/18	53 bombers operated against the Meuse crossings, 78 against targets in Hamburg and Bremen.
26 to 4 June	Evacuation from Dunkirk.

June

5	German attack across the Seine.
5/6	Beginning of German night reconnaissance and minor bombing over Britain.
10	Italy entered the war.
11/12	First attack (by Whitleys) on Italian targets.
15–17	Remains of AASF rejoined Bomber Command.
17	Armistice requested by France.
20	Directive to Bomber Command: to reduce scale of German air attack on Britain.

July

1/2	First 2000-lb bomb dropped by Bomber Command – against the *Scharnhorst* at Kiel.
10	Beginning of intensive air-fighting over the English Channel.

August

12	Beginning of intensive air attacks on Britain.
12/13	Dortmund–Ems aqueduct breached by Hampdens.
24/25	First German bombs on central London.
25/26	First Bomber Command bombs on Berlin.

September

7/8	Beginning of heavy air attacks on London.
8	'Invasion Alert No. 1': attacks by Bomber Command on airfields and ports.
13/14	First of Bomber Command's attacks on invasion barges.
23/24	Raid against Berlin by 119 bombers.

October

4	AM Sir Richard Peirse AOC-in-C.
25	ACM Sir Charles Portal Chief of the Air Staff.
30	First directive sanctioning area-bombing.
31	Official Air Ministry date for the end of the Battle of Britain.

November

14/15	Heavy German air raid on Coventry.

16/17   Most concentrated Bomber Command raid to date: 131 aircraft against four Hamburg targets.

December
16/17   First major Bomber Command area attack, without specific targets: 134 bombers against Mannheim.

1941
January
1/2 ⎫
2/3 ⎬   Attacks on Bremen.
3/4 ⎭
15   New bombing directive: oil primary target.

February
10/11   First operation by Stirlings – against oil tanks at Rotterdam. 221 bombers sent against targets at Hanover.
24/25   First operation by Manchesters – against warships at Brest.

March
10/11   First operation by Halifaxes – against targets at Le Havre.
12/13   First attacks by Halifaxes and Manchesters on targets in Germany (Hamburg).
15   'Battle of the Atlantic' directive.
30/31   Beginning of sustained attacks on *Scharnhorst* and *Gneisenau* in Brest.
31/1   First 4000-lb bomb dropped – by a Wellington at Emden.
April

April
6   German invasion of Greece and Yugoslavia.

May
8/9   Biggest Bomber Command operation to date: 359 aircraft against north German (Hamburg–Bremen) targets.
26/27   Minelaying by 112 aircraft outside Brest and St Nazaire.
27/28

June
22   German invasion of USSR.
23   First chain of three GEE stations completed.

July
4   Low-level daylight raid by Blenheims on Cologne targets.
8   First operation by Bomber Command Fortresses – by day against docks at Wilhelmshaven.

August
12   Daylight raid by 53 Blenheims on power stations at Cologne.

September
25   Last daylight raid by Bomber Command Fortress.

342

November
7/8   21 of 169 aircraft lost from raid on Berlin. 'Conservation' order subsequently issued.

December
7   (local time) Japanese attack at Pearl Harbor.
8 and 9   Britain, Commonwealth countries, USA and China – declaration of war against Japan.

1942
February
12   Escape of *Scharnhorst* and *Gneisenau*.
15   Fall of Singapore.
16   Regular operations begun by Bomber Command Bostons.
20   Air Marshal (Sir) Arthur Harris AOC-in-C.

March
3/4   Raid against Renault factories at Billancourt. First Lancaster operations (mining).
8   Daylight raid by Bostons against Matford factories at Poissy.
8/9   First major use of GEE – against Essen.
10/11   First bombing operation by Lancasters – against Essen.
28/29   Very destructive raid by 234 aircraft on Lübeck.

April
10/11   First 8000-lb bomb dropped – on Essen.
17   Daylight raid against MAN works at Augsburg.
20   New aircrew category – Air-bomber (or Bomb-aimer). Observer renamed Navigator.
23/24   First of four heavy raids in five nights on Rostock.
29/30   Last bombing operation by Whitleys (other than by OTU aircraft).

May
30/31   First 'Thousand-Bomber' raid – against Cologne. First bombing-reconnaissance operation by Mosquitoes – against Cologne.

June
1/2   Second 'Thousand-Bomber' raid (956 aircraft) – against Essen.
25/26   Third 'Thousand-Bomber' raid (960 aircraft) – against Bremen. Last operation by Manchesters.

July
5   Cabinet permission for use of magnetron valve in H2S.

August
6   MOONSHINE first used operationally against German early-warning radar.
15   Formation of Pathfinder Force in 3 Group.
17   First USAAF raid – railway yards at Rouen.

17/18	Last operation by Bomber Command Blenheims.
18/19	First Pathfinder Force operation – Flensburg.
19	Dieppe combined operation.

September

10/11	First use of 4000-lb incendiary bomb.
14/15	Last operation by Bomber Command Hampdens.
19	First daylight raid (by Mosquitoes) on Berlin.
28	Daylight raid by Mosquitoes on Gestapo HQ in Oslo.

October

10	First USAAF raid by over 100 bombers (Lille).
16	50-squadron plan introduced.
17	Daylight raid by Lancasters on Le Creusot.
22/23	First raid by over 100 bombers on Italy (Genoa).
24	Daylight attack on Milan by Lancasters.
25	Formation of No. 6 Group.

November

3	First operation by Venturas.
8	Allied landings in North-West Africa.
11	German occupation of 'Vichy' France.

December

| 6 | Daylight raid on Philips' works at Eindhoven. |
| 20/21 | First OBOE operation – against Lutterade power station. |

1943
January

11	Area-bombing of U-boat bases on Biscay coast sanctioned by War Cabinet.
16/17	250-lb target-indicator bombs first used – in first major attack (by 201 aircraft) on Berlin since 7 November 1941.
21	Casablanca bombing directive.
22	First operation by Mitchells (against oil in Belgium).
25	Pathfinder Group formed – No. 8.
27	First USAAF raids on Germany (Emden and Wilhelmshaven).
30	Mosquito daylight attack on Berlin for Nazi Party's tenth anniversary.
30/31	First operational use of H2S (on Hamburg).

February

2	German capitulation at Stalingrad.
4	Directive to Bomber Command: 'top priority' U-boat bases.
13/14	466 aircraft sent against Lorient.
25/26	337 aircraft sent against Nuremberg.
26/27	417 aircraft sent against Cologne.
28 to 1st March	428 aircraft sent against St Nazaire.

March

| 3 | Attack by Mosquitoes on molybdenum mines at Knaben. |

5/6   442 aircraft sent against Essen. Beginning of 'the Battle of the Ruhr' (heavy attacks till 30/31 July).

April
16/17   Attempted attack on Skoda works near Pilsen.
27/28⎱
28/29⎰   Biggest minelaying effort thus far – 367 sorties.

May
13   Final Axis capitulation in Tunisia.
16/17   Attack on Möhne, Eder and Sorpe dams.
23/24   826 aircraft sent against Dortmund – biggest force since 'Thousand-bomber' raids.
31   Last raids by 2 Group before leaving Bomber Command.

June
10   POINTBLANK directive: 'top priority' German Air Force and industry.
18   'RDF' or 'radiolocation' renamed 'radar'.
20   First 'shuttle' operation, with stop at Algiers. Friedrichshafen attacked on outward flight, La Spezia on return.
30   Beginning of SERRATE operations.

July
10   Allied invasion of Sicily.
24/25   Beginning of 'the Battle of Hamburg' – (four nights, over 3100 sorties, ending 2/3 August). First use of WINDOW.

August
7/8   First use of 'Master Bomber' (against Turin).
16/17   Last attack on Italy (Turin).
17/18   Attack on Peenemünde.
31/1   Flares first used by German fighters.

September
3   Allied invasion of Italy.
8   Armistice with Italy announced.
15/16   First 12,000lb-HC bomb dropped – against Dortmund–Ems Canal.
22/23   First 'Spoof' raid (against Oldenburg, main force against Hanover).
23/24   First OBOE marking for main force.

October
4/5   First operational trials of GH.
7/8   First AIRBORNE CIGAR operations (jamming VHF R/T).
8/9   Last bombing operation by Wellingtons in Bomber Command.
22/23   Very heavy raid on Kassel. First CORONA operations ('Spoof' orders to German night-fighters).

November
3/4   First blind-bombing by GH Lancasters (Düsseldorf).

10/11	Raid on Mount Cenis railway tunnel.
15	AEAF activated. Fighter Command to be known as Air Defence of Great Britain.
16	Large emergency runway at Woodbridge opened.
18/19	Beginning of the main 'Battle of Berlin'. Fifteen attacks in the next three months. First night with two major raids (444 aircraft against Berlin, 395 against Mannheim).

December

3	Formation of No. 100 Group.
16/17	Beginning of Mosquito and Beaufighter operations as 'intruders' under Bomber Command control.
20	Beginning of Bomber Command CROSSBOW attacks (against V-weapon sites).
23	General Eaker appointed to MAAF, General Doolittle to Eighth Air Force.
	General Eisenhower appointed Allied C-in-C for OVERLORD, with ACM Sir Arthur Tedder as Deputy.

1944
February

8/9	12,000-lb bomb dropped for first time – in attack by 617 Squadron on Gnome et Rhône factory at Limoges.
15/16	Heaviest attack on Berlin to date: 891 aircraft despatched, 2643 tons dropped.
18	Attack by Mosquitoes on Amiens prison.
23/24	Mosquito first dropped a 4000-lb bomb.
	Beginning of 'Big Week' against German fighter force and industry.
24/25	734 aircraft sent against Schweinfurt.

March

4	First USAAF attack on Berlin.
6	800 USAAF aircraft against Berlin.
6/7	Bomber Command offensive against rail centres begun (Trappes).
24/25	Last major Bomber Command attack on Berlin: 72 aircraft lost.
30/31	The heaviest loss: 94 out of 795 aircraft sent against Nuremberg.

April

14	Control of strategic bombers placed under General Eisenhower.
26/27	Unsuccessful attack on Schweinfurt.
27/28	Very successful attack on Friedrichshafen.

May

3/4	Attacks on German airfields in France begun.
9/10	First major attack on coastal batteries in Pas de Calais.
12/13	Minelaying by Mosquitoes in Kiel Canal.

22/23 Last industrial area attacks (Dortmund and Brunswick) until 24/25 July.

June
4/5 ⎫
5/6 ⎬ Heavy attacks on coastal batteries in France: on 5/6 by over 1000 aircraft.
6   D-Day.
6/7 Communications behind the Normandy battlefront bombed by over 1000 aircraft.
8/9 First 12,000-DP bomb ('Tallboy') dropped at mouth of tunnel near Saumur.
12/13 Attack on German oil plant (Nordstern at Gelsenkirchen).
13/14 First flying bombs (V-1) fell on Britain.
14 234 aircraft sent against harbours and E-boats at Le Havre. First daylight raid by Bomber Command since departure of 2 Group in June 1943.
16/17 Attacks on V-weapon sites – until September.

July
7 Heavy attacks in support of armies near Caen.
18 Bombing by 942 aircraft in support of Operation GOODWOOD.
24/25 Campaign in Normandy officially ended. Area-bombing of German towns resumed (Stuttgart).

August
7/8 Big attacks south of Caen in support of Allied troops.
14 805 aircraft in attacks to support Canadian advance on Falaise.
23 Liberation of Paris.
27 First daylight raid by Bomber Command against oil in Germany (Hamburg). First major daylight raid on Germany since 12 August 1941.
30 Ploesti captured by the Russians.

September
3 Brussels liberated.
8 First V-2s fell on London. Last bombing operation by Stirlings in Bomber Command (Le Havre).
10 ⎫
11 ⎬ US troops reached German frontier near Aachen. Big attacks on Le Havre in military support.
12/13 First operational trials of LORAN (long-range navigational aid).
15 Campaign in France ended. Strategic bombers henceforward under control of Combined Chiefs of Staff.
16/17 Operations to support landings at Arnhem on the 17th.
23/24 Dortmund–Ems Canal breached by 12,000–lb bomb.
25 Bombing directive.

October
3 Seawall at Westkapelle, Walcheren, breached by air attack.
6/7 Beginning of new series of heavy raids on the Ruhr (Dortmund).

347

7	Kembs dam (on Rhine north of Basle) breached by 617 Squadron.
14/15	Bomber Command's biggest night of operations in the war.
15	Air Defence of Great Britain renamed Fighter Command.
18	Combined Strategic Targets Committee formed.
23/24	1055 aircraft sent against Essen.
25	771 aircraft sent against Essen. Effective end of Krupps as major producer.
28, 30/31,	Very heavy raids on Cologne.

November

2/3	992 aircraft sent against Düsseldorf.
4/5	749 aircraft sent against Bochum, 174 aircraft against the Dortmund–Ems Canal. Canal again breached.
9	Walcheren captured.
12	*Tirpitz* sunk in operation by 9 and 617 Squadrons.
16	Kleve, Jülich and Heinsburg bombed in support of US First and Ninth Armies.

December

6/7	487 aircraft sent on Bomber Command's first major attack on oil in eastern Germany (Leuna).
16	German offensive in Ardennes.
19–26	Attacks against German communications and airfields.
26	Attack at St Vith – offensive checked.
31	Attack by Mosquitoes on Gestapo HQ at Oslo.

1945
January

1/2	157 aircraft sent against the Mittelland Canal. Canal breached.
4/5	Attack on Royan. Many French casualties.
5/6	664 aircraft sent against Hanover, 140 successfully against German communications in the Ardennes (Houffalize).
7/8	654 aircraft sent on the last major raid against Munich.
26	All lost ground recovered in the Ardennes.

February

7/8	Attacks on Kleve and Goch in support of British offensive.
13/14	803 aircraft sent against Dresden, 368 against oil at Böhlen.
14/15	717 aircraft sent against Chemnitz.
16–19	Attacks on Wesel in preparation for British offensive.
20/21	First of attacks on 36 consecutive nights by Mosquitoes on Berlin.
21/22	Beginning of intense attacks on communications to isolate the Ruhr. Successful attack on Mittelland Canal.

March

| 7 | Americans captured Rhine bridge at Remagen. |
| 11 | 1079 aircraft sent and 4680 tons of bombs dropped in final raid on Essen. |

12	1108 aircraft sent and 4851 tons of bombs dropped in raid on Dortmund.
14	Bielefeld viaduct broken in attack using the first 'Grand Slam' (22,000-lb) bomb.
23/24	218 aircraft sent against Wesel in preparation for 21st Army Group assault.
24	British crossing of Lower Rhine.
27	Successful attack on new U-boat shelter at Farge, using 'Grand Slam'.
27/28	Last V-weapons landed in Britain.

April

6	Area-bombing to be discontinued, unless in exceptional military situation.
9/10	*Admiral Scheer* sunk at Kiel in attack by 591 aircraft, *Hipper* and *Emden* damaged.
14/15	512 aircraft sent against Potsdam.
16	*Lützow* sunk by 617 Squadron in raid on Swinemünde.
18	969 aircraft sent against Heligoland. Surrender of German troops in the Ruhr.
20/21	Last Mosquito attack on Berlin.
22	767 aircraft sent against Bremen in preparation for ground attack.
25	Attacks by 482 aircraft on Wangerooge and 375 aircraft on Berchtesgaden.
25/26	Last operation by heavy bombers – against oil refinery at Tönsberg (Norway).
26–	Operation EXODUS begun – repatriation of British prisoners of war.
29–	Operation MANNA begun – food for the Dutch.
30	Suicide of Hitler.

May

| 2 | Russian capture of Berlin completed. |
| 7 | Germany's unconditional surrender, effective from midnight on 8 May. |

Bomber Command Orders of Battle

AS AT 27 SEPTEMBER 1939

Advanced Air Striking Force, HQ Reims
Squadrons Nos. 12, 15, 40, 88, 103, 105, 142, 150, 218, 226
Equipment Battles

No. 2 Group, HQ Wyton

Squadron	Location	Equipment
114	Wyton	
139	Wyton	
107	Wattisham	
110	Wattisham	Blenheims
21	Watton	
82	Watton	

No. 101 Squadron non-operational at West Raynham.

No. 3 Group, HQ Mildenhall

Squadron	Location	Equipment
37	Feltwell	
38	Marham	
115	Marham	
99	Mildenhall	Wellingtons
149	Mildenhall	
9	Honington	

No. 4 Group, HQ Linton-on-Ouse

Squadron	Location	Equipment
10	Dishforth	
77	Driffield	
102	Driffield	
51	Linton-on-Ouse	Whitleys
58	Linton-on-Ouse	

No. 78 Squadron non-operational at Dishforth.

No. 5 Group, HQ Grantham

Squadron	Location	Equipment
61	Hemswell	
144	Hemswell	
49	Scampton	
83	Scampton	Hampdens
44	Waddington	
50	Waddington	

Nos. 106 and 185 Squadrons non-operational at Cottesmore.

AS AT 4 FEBRUARY 1943

No. 1 Group, HQ Bawtry

Squadron	Location	Equipment
12	Wickenby	Lancaster
		Wellington II
101	Holme	Lancaster
		Wellington III
103	Elsham Wolds	Lancaster
		Halifax
		Wellington IV
460 (RAAF)	Breighton	Lancaster
166	Kirmington	Wellington III
199	Ingham	Wellington III
399 (Pol.)	Hemswell	Wellington III
301 (Pol.)	Hemswell	Wellington IV
305 (Pol.)	Hemswell	Wellington IV

No. 100 Squadron (Lancasters) non-operational at Grimsby.

No. 2 Group, HQ Huntingdon

Squadron	Location	Equipment
88	Oulton	Boston III (A-20)
107	Gt. Massingham	Boston III (A-20)
226	Swanton Morley	Boston III (A-20)
105	Marham	Mosquito
139	Marham	Mosquito
		Blenheim V
21	Methwold	Ventura (B-34)
464 (RAAF)	Feltwell	Ventura (B-34)
487 (RNZAF)	Feltwell	Ventura (B-34)
98	Foulsham	Mitchell (B-25)
180	Foulsham	Mitchell (B-25)

No. 3 Group, HQ Exning

Squadron	Location	Equipment
15	Bourn	
75 (NZ)	Newmarket	
90	Ridgewell	
149	Lakenheath	Stirling
214	Chedburgh	
218	Downham Market	
115	East Wretham	
		Wellington
138 (Special Duties)	Tempsford	Halifax
161 (Special Duties)	Tempsford	Lysander
		Halifax
		Hudson
		Havoc
		Albermarle/Hudson
192 (RCM)	Gransden Lodge	Halifax
		Wellington X
		Mosquito
		Wellington IC

Nos. 138 and 161 Squadrons (Special Duties) were administered by Bomber Command but were controlled by the Assistant Chief of Air Staff (Intelligence) at the Air Ministry.

No. 4 Group, HQ York

Squadron	Location	Equipment
10	Melbourne	Halifax
51	Snaith	Halifax
		Whitley
76	Linton-on-Ouse	Halifax
77	Elvington	Halifax
		Whitley
78	Linton-on-Ouse	Halifax
102	Pocklington	Halifax
158	Rufforth	Halifax
		Wellington II
196	Leconfield	Wellington X
429 (RCAF)	East Moor	Wellington III / Wellington X
466 (RAAF)	Leconfield	Wellington X

No. 431 (RCAF) Squadron non-operational at Burn.

No. 5 Group, HQ Grantham

Squadron	Location	Equipment
9	Waddington	
44 (Rhod.)	Waddington	
49	Fiskerton	
50	Skellingthorpe	
57	Scampton	
61	Syerston	Lancaster
97	Woodhall Spa	
106	Syerston	
207	Langar	
467 (RAAF)	Bottesford	

No. 6 Group (RCAF), HQ Allerton

Squadron	Location	Equipment
405	Beaulieu	Halifax
408	Leeming	Halifax
419	Middleton St George	Halifax
420	Middleton St George	
424	Topcliffe	
425	Dishforth	Wellington III
426	Dishforth	
427	Croft	
428	Dalton	Wellington X

No. 405 Squadron temporarily detached to Coastal Command.

No. 8 Group, HQ Wyton

Squadron	Location	Equipment
7 (PFF)	Oakington	Stirling
35 (PFF)	Gravely	Halifax
83 (PFF)	Wyton	Lancaster
109 (PFF)	Wyton	Mosquito
		Wellington IC
156 (PFF)	Warboys	Lancaster
		Wellington III

Part of No. 156 Squadron re-equipping.

AS AT 22 MARCH 1945

No. 1 Group, HQ Bawtry

Squadron	Location	Equipment
12	Wickenby	
100	Grimsby	
101	Ludford Magna	
103	Elsham Wolds	
150	Hemswell	
153	Scampton	
166	Kirmington	
170	Hemswell	Lancaster I, III
300 (Pol.)	Faldingworth	
460 (RAAF)	Binbrook	
550	N. Killingholme	
576	Fiskerton	
625	Kelstern	
626	Wickenby	

No. 3 Group, HQ Exning

Squadron	Location	Equipment
15	Mildenhall	
75	Mepal	
90	Tuddenham	
115	Witchford	
	Tuddenham	
149	Methwold	
186 (⅞)	Stradishall	Lancaster I, III
195	Wratting Common	
218	Chedburgh	
514	Waterbeach	
622	Mildenhall	

No. 138 Squadron non-operational at Tuddenham and two flights of No. 186 non-operational at Stradishall.

No. 4 Group, HQ York

Squadron	Location	Equipment
10	Melbourne	Halifax III
51	Snaith	Halifax III
76	Holme	Halifax VI
		Halifax III
78	Breighton	Halifax III
158	Lissett	Halifax III
346 (FAF)	Elvington	Halifax VI
		Halifax III
347 (FAF)	Elvington	Halifax III
		Halifax VI
466 (RAAF)	Driffield	Halifax III
640	Leconfield	Halifax VI
		Halifax III
77	Full Sutton	Halifax VI
		Halifax III
102	Pocklington	Halifax III
		Halifax III

No. 5 Group, HQ Swinderby

Squadron	Location	Equipment
9	Bardney	
44 (Rhod.)	Spilsby	
49	Fulbeck	
50	Skellingthorpe	
57	East Kirkby	
61	Skellingthorpe	
106	Metheringham	
189	Fulbeck	
207	Spilsby	Lancaster I, III
227	Balderton	
463 (RAAF)	Waddington	
467 (RAAF)	Waddington	
619	Strubby	
630	East Kirkby	
617	Woodhall Spa	
83 (PFF)	Coningsby	
97 (PFF)	Coningsby	
627 (PFF)	Woodhall Spa	Mosquito IV, XX, 25

Nos. 83, 97 and 627 Squadrons on loan from No. 8 Group.

No. 6 Group (RCAF), HQ Allerton

Squadron	Location	Equipment
415	East Moor	Halifax III
		Halifax VII
420	Tholthorpe	Halifax III
425	Tholthorpe	Halifax III
408	Linton	Halifax VII
426	Linton	Halifax VII
432	East Moor	Halifax VII
424	Skipton-on-Swale	Lancaster I, III
427	Leeming	Lancaster I, III
		Halifax III
433	Skipton-on-Swale	Lancaster I, III
		Halifax III
419	Middleton St George	Lancaster X
428	Middleton St George	Lancaster X
431	Croft	Lancaster X
434	Croft	Lancaster I, III

No. 429 Squadron non-operational at Leeming.

No. 8 Group (PFF), HQ Huntingdon

Squadron	Location	Equipment
7	Oakington	Lancaster I, III
35	Graveley	Lancaster I, III
83		Lancaster I, III
97		Lancaster I, III
156	Upwood	Lancaster I, III
405 (RCAF)	Gransden Lodge	Lancaster I, III
582	Little Staughton	Lancaster I, III
635	Downham Market	Lancaster I, III
105	Bourn	Mosquito IX, XVI
109	Little Staughton	Mosquito IX, XVI
128	Wyton	Mosquito XVI
139	Upwood	Mosquito IX, XVI
		Mosquito XX, 25
142	Gransden Lodge	Mosquito 25
162	Bourn	Mosquito XX, 25
163	Wyton	Mosquito 25
571	Oakington	Mosquito XVI
608	Downham Market	Mosquito XX, 25
627		Mosquito IV, XX
692	Graveley	Mosquito XVI

No. 578 Squadron non-operational at Graveley.

No. 100 Group, HQ Bylaugh Hall

Squadron	Location	Equipment
23 (BS)	Little Snoring	Mosquito VI
85 (BS)	Swannington	Mosquito 30
141 (BS)	West Raynham	Mosquito 30
157 (BS)	Swannington	Mosquito VI
169 (BS)	Great Massingham	Mosquito XIX
		Mosquito VI
239 (BS)	West Raynham	Mosquito 30
515 (BS)	Little Snoring	Mosquito VI
171 (BS)	North Creake	Halifax III
192 (BS)	Foulsham	Halifax III
		Mosquito XVI
		Anson
199 (BS)	North Creake	Halifax III
		Stirling III
462 (RAAF) (BS)	Foulsham	Halifax III
214 (BS)	Oulton	Fortress III
223 (BS)	Oulton	Liberator
BSDU	Swanton Morley	Mosquito VI
		Mosquito XIX
		Mosquito 30
		Mosquito II

Aircraft Performance

MAIN RAF BOMBERS

Aircraft	Max. speed at height (mph)	(feet)	Service ceiling (feet)	Range (miles)	and Associated bomb-load (pounds)	Armament
Battle	241	13,000	23,000	1050	1000	2 × .303 in.
Blenheim IV	266	11,800	22,000	1460	1000	5 × .303 in.
Hampden	254	13,800	19,000	1885	2000	8 × .303 in.
Whitley V	222	17,000	17,600	1650	3000 (or 470 m.–7000 lbs)	7 × .303 in.
Wellington Ic	235	15,500	18,000	2550	1000 (or 1200 m.–4500 lbs)	6 × .303 in.
Wellington II	247	17,000	20,000	2450	1250 (or 1400 m.–4500 lbs)	6 × .303 in.
Wellington X	255	14,500	19,600	2085	1500 (or 1475 m.–4500 lbs)	6 × .303 in.
Stirling I	260	10,500	16,500	2050	3500 (or 740 m.–14,000 lbs)	8 × .303 in.
Halifax I	273	17,750	18,200	1840	6750 (or 850 m.–13,000 lbs)	9 × .303 in.
Halifax III	281	13,500	20,000	2005	6250 (or 980 m.–13,000 lbs)	9 × .303 in.
Halifax VI	290	10,500	20,000	2160	7400 (or 1260 m.–13,000 lbs)	9 × .303 in.
Lancaster I and III	270	19,000	22,200	2350	5500 (or 1000 m.–14,000 lbs)	9 × .303 in.
Mosquito IV	380	14,000	33,000	1620	2000 (or 1450 m.–4500 lbs)	none
Mosquito IX	408	26,000	36,000	1870	1000 (or 1350 m.–5000 lbs)	none
Mosquito XVI	415	20,000	39,000	1795	2000 (or 1370 m.–5000 lbs)	none
Boston III	304	13,000	24,250	1000	2000	8 × .303 in.
Mitchell II	292	15,000	20,000	1635	4000 (or 950 m.–6000 lbs)	6 × .50 in.
Ventura	274	14,000	25,000	925	2500 (or 1795 m.–2000 lbs)	6 × .303 in. or 4 × .50 in.

MAIN GERMAN FIGHTERS

Aircraft	Max. speed at Height (mph)	(feet)	Service ceiling	Climb-time to Height (minutes)	(feet)	Armament
Junkers 88C6	283	14,765	29,530	10.3	18,500	6 × 7.9 mm 3 × 20 mm
Junkers 88G1	323	19,635	32,000			6 × 20 mm
Messerschmitt 109G	400	22,000	38,500	6	19,000	2 × 7.9 mm 4 × 20 mm
Messerschmitt 110G	365	19,000	34,800	7.3	18,000	6 × 7.9 mm 4 × 20 mm
Focke-Wulf 190A3	385	19,000	36,000	6.5	18,000	1 × 37 mm, 2 × 7.9 mm 4 × 20 mm
Focke-Wulf 190D	435	25,000	39,000	6.5	20,000	1 × 30 mm 2 × 20 mm
Late High-Performance Fighters						
Messerschmitt 262 (jet)	500–550	29,000	39,500	5	32,000	4 × 30 mm and 3 × 20 mm or 6 × 30 mm
Messerschmitt 163 (liquid rocket)	560 ?	40,000				2 × 30 mm
Arado 234B	490	25,000	38,000	8	20,000	4 or 5 × 20 mm

Notes 1 Performance figures vary in different sources. The manufacturers' figures, the Service figures, and the figures experienced by the crews rarely completely coincide.

2 The Me 163 and 262 and the Ar 234 appeared only in small numbers in the closing months. Among the night-fighters, by 1944 the Me 110G and the Ju 88C6 and G1 far outnumbered all the rest.

357

Bombs and Bombsights

BOMBS

The main categories were high-explosive, incendiary, and target-indicator. Disregarding specialised bombs like Barnes Wallis's UPKEEP and the armour-piercing types used against warships, there were three main types of HE bombs employed by Bomber Command.

High-Explosive bombs (HE)

General Purpose (GP) These were made in seven sizes, and the numbers dropped by Bomber Command during the war were as follows: 20-lb 4940 40-lb 42,936 250-lb 149,656 500-lb 551,334 1000-lb 82,164 1900-lb 2141 4000-lb 217.

The GP bombs predominated in the first two years of the war until more effective ones were produced. They suffered from having only a low charge-weight ratio – mostly about 27 per cent charge as compared with about 50 per cent in the corresponding German bombs. Also a higher proportion failed to explode than in the case of German bombs dropped on Britain.

Medium-Capacity (MC) At the end of 1940 a review indicated the limitations of the existing GP bombs and a programme was initiated to produce bombs of at least 40 per cent charge-weight ratio, with better explosives. The first of these MC bombs, the 500-lb, came into use towards the close of 1941, but suffered a high rate of failure – perhaps as much as 30 per cent. Later marks were greatly improved, and more 500-lb MC bombs were dropped than any other kind except the less satisfactory 500-lb GP. From 1943, 1000-lb and 4000-lb MC bombs also came into use, with good results. The Barnes Wallis 12,000-lb 'Tallboy' which became available in very limited numbers in 1944 and the later 22,000-lb 'Grand Slam' were still technically MC bombs, with exceptional penetrative power.

High-Capacity (HC) These bombs, with a relatively thin casing and up to an 80 per cent charge-weight ratio, were designed for maximum blast effect, and were commonly known as 'blockbusters'. Together with the 4-lb incendiaries, they were the most effective weapons of the area offensive, though they had no great ballistic properties – at first they were fitted with parachutes, later with tails. From 1942 they gradually became available in versions of 2000 lb, 4000 lb, 8000 lb and 12,000 lb – the last two of which could be carried only in Lancasters with the bomb doors removed. Improved explosive fillings – RDX/TNT, Torpex and Minatol – progressively used in place of Amatol, greatly added to the destructive power of the HE bombs.

Incendiary bombs (IBs)

The 4-lb incendiary, consisting largely of magnesium, was throughout one of Bomber Command's main weapons. For much of the war carried in the aircraft in boxes known as Small Bomb Containers, they fell individually and haphazardly. To remedy this the bombs were later, in 1944, grouped into clusters of 350-lb, 500-lb and 1000-lb sizes, which could be much more effectively aimed.

Other incendiary bombs were produced in quantity but with little similar success. The 30-lb phosphorus bomb functioned well, but the 40-lb bomb, which contained 35 lb of steel, was abandoned in 1941 on grounds of economy, and the 25-lb bomb was abandoned in 1942 for an even more potent reason – that it consistently broke up without igniting. Liquid incendiary bombs, of which the most widely used was the 30-lb 'J' bomb, were introduced in 1944. In Harris's opinion they were only half as effective as the standard 40-lb bomb in clusters.

Target-Indicator bombs (TIs)

After the failure of so many crews to find their objectives at night, incendiary bombs were developed for marking, or at least illuminating, targets. The largest of these was the '4000-lb' (actually weighing 1200 lb less) 'Pink Pansy'. This had a filling of benzol, rubber and phosphorus. When the Pathfinder Force came into being, something with better ballistics for more accurate aiming was soon demanded, and some forty varieties of target-indicator bomb were used between January 1943 and the end of the war.

The target-indicator bombs had metal cases with good ballistic properties. At a predetermined height the bomb was detonated by a barometric fuse and, according to the setting, candles of selected colours either ignited in the air (sky-marking) or on the ground (ground-marking). For sky-marking the candles carried a small parachute, for ground-marking often a small explosive charge to deter fire-fighters. The most commonly used target indicator weighed 250 lb, though larger ones were developed. For marking in daylight in the last year of the war, indicators emitting coloured smoke or dust were also developed.

In his *Despatch* (unpublished, p. 91), Harris was extremely critical of the general level of official Air Ministry–Ministry of Aircraft Production armament design. He contrasted the efficiency of the Admiralty mines, the Rose turret, the Wallis bombs, and the various Service modifications with the official AM–MAP products issued to his Command, and stated that the latter 'showed throughout a standard of incompetence which had the most serious repercussions on the efficiency and effectiveness of Bomber Command'.

BOMBSIGHTS

Course-Setting bombsights

These had originated in the First World War, and in improved versions they were in general use by Bomber Command until 1942. They were in part manual, in part automatic. The height, course and speed of the aircraft were fed, mostly manually, into an elementary computer, together with the speed and direction of the wind – the latter obtained (with problematical accuracy) from observation of a 'drift wire' outside the aircraft. The aircraft then made a straight and level run towards the target, and the bombsight indicated when the bomb should be released.

The bombsight's main defects arose from the difficulty in measuring the wind and from the fact that it required the aircraft to be held straight and steady, so presenting a good target to the gunners on the ground.

Stabilised Vector Sights, notably the Mark XIV, introduced in 1942, were more fully automatic than the Course-Setting bombsights. They did not demand the same rigidity of approach; the aircraft could manoeuvre moderately until the actual moment of releasing the bomb. The Pathfinders were the first to receive this equipment, which by the beginning of 1944 was virtually standard throughout the heavy-bomber force. Admirably suited for area-bombing, the Stabilised Vector Sights still lacked the precision necessary for the accurate bombing of small targets at night.

Tachometric bombsights were developed by early 1942, when the first Stabilised

Automatic bombsights were fitted experimentally. They proved to be extremely accurate, but difficult for the bomb-aimer to master. Also, as with the Course-Setting bombsight, the aircraft had to be held straight and level on the approach. The use of this bombsight was therefore confined to specialist squadrons, notably No. 617, which were given time for the necessary training and employed on tasks demanding the greatest possible accuracy.

The Bomber Command Operational Groups

1 Group HQ Bawtry, near Doncaster
Re-formed in June 1940 after the return of the AASF.
AOCs

Air Cdre J. J. Breen OBE	27 June 1940
AV-M R. D. Oxland CB, CBE	27 November 1940
AV-M E. A. B. Rice	24 February 1943
AV-M R. S. Blucke CBE, DSO, AFC and bar	5 February 1945

*Aircraft**
Battles, WELLINGTONS, Halifaxes, LANCASTERS

2 Group HQ Huntingdon
Detached from Bomber Command as from 1 June 1943.
AOCs

AV-M C. T. Maclean CB, DSO, MC	16 May 1938
AV-M J. M. Robb CB, DSO, DFC, AFC	17 April 1940
AV-M D. F. Stevenson DSO, OBE	12 February 1941
AV-M A. Lees CBE, DSO, AFC	17 December 1941

Aircraft
BLENHEIMS, Fortresses, Bostons, Mosquitoes, Venturas, Mitchells

3 Group HQ Exning, near Newmarket
AOCs

AV-M J. E. A. Baldwin CB, DSO, OBE	29 August 1939
AV-M The Hon. R. A. Cochrane CBE, AFC	14 September 1942
AV-M R. Harrison CB, CBE, DFC, AFC	27 February 1943

Aircraft
WELLINGTONS, STIRLINGS, LANCASTERS. Other types for Special Duties

4 Group HQ York
AOCs

AV-M A. Coningham DSO, MC, DFC, AFC	3 July 1939
AV-M C. R. Carr CB, CBE, DFC, AFC	26 July 1941
AV-M J. R. Whitley CBE, DSO, AFC	12 February 1945

* Aircraft printed in capitals were the main equipment at the time concerned, and responsible for the greatest number of sorties.

Aircraft
WHITLEYS, Wellingtons, HALIFAXES

5 Group HQ Grantham, then Moreton Hall, near Swinderby
AOCs

AV-M A. T. Harris OBE, AFC	11 September 1939
AV-M N. H. Bottomley CB, CIE, DSO, AFC	22 November 1940
AV-M J. C. Slessor DSO, MC	12 May 1941
AV-M W. A. Coryton CB, MVO, DFC	25 April 1942
AV-M The Hon. R. A. Cochrane CB, CBE, AFC	28 February 1943
AV-M H. A. Constantine CBE, DSO	16 January 1945

Aircraft
HAMPDENS, Manchesters, LANCASTERS, Mosquitoes

6 Group (RCAF) HQ Allerton, near Knaresborough
Formed 1 January 1943
AOCs

AV-M G. E. Brookes CB, OBE	25 October 1942
AV-M C. M. McEwen CB, MC, DFC	29 February 1944

Aircraft
Wellingtons, HALIFAXES, LANCASTERS

8 Group (PFF) HQ Wyton, then Huntingdon
Formed January 1943, following the formation of the Pathfinder Force in August 1942
AOC

AV-M D. C. T. Bennett CB, CBE, DSO	13 January 1943

Aircraft
Stirlings, Wellingtons, HALIFAXES, LANCASTERS, MOSQUITOES

100 (Bomber Support) Group HQ Bylaugh Hall, near East Dereham
Formed in December 1943
AOC

AV-M E. B. Addison CB, CBE

Aircraft
Beaufighters, MOSQUITOES, Wellingtons, STIRLINGS, HALIFAXES, Liberators, FORTRESSES, Lightnings E

APPENDIX VI

Bomber Command Casualties

The following figures were supplied by the Air Ministry to the authors of the official history, *The Strategic Air Offensive Against Germany*. They cover RAF, WAAF, Dominion and Allied personnel serving with Bomber Command between 3 September 1939 and May 1945

AIRCREW

Operational

Killed and presumed dead	47,120
Died prisoners of war	138
Missing now safe	2868
POW now safe	9784
Wounded	4200

Non-operational

Killed	8090
Wounded	4203
Died other causes	215
Missing now safe	83
POW now safe	54

GROUND STAFF

Killed	530
Wounded	759
Died other causes	1040
Missing now safe	26
POW now safe	52

References

PRO: Public Record Office AHB: Air Historical Branch

1: *Small Beginnings*

1 PRO AIR 27/958 (139 Sqdn Operations Record Book), 3 September 1939
2 PRO AIR 24/200 (Bomber Command HQ Operations Record Book), 3 September 1939
3 Sir Charles Webster and Noble Frankland, *The Strategic Air Offensive against Germany* (HMSO, 1961), vol. I, pp. 98 and 105; J. R. M. Butler, *Grand Strategy* (HMSO, 1957), vol. II, pp. 567–8
4 H. Montgomery Hyde, *British Air Policy between the Wars* (Heinemann, 1976), p. 74
5 Viscount Templewood, *Empire of the Air* (Collins, 1957), pp. 69–70
6 H. Montgomery Hyde, *op. cit.*, p. 408

General sources include:
H. Montgomery Hyde, *op. cit.*
AHB Narrative, *The Expansion of the RAF* 1934–39
AHB Narrative, *The RAF in the Bombing Offensive against Germany*, vol. I (hereafter cited as AHB *Narrative*)
N. H. Gibbs, *Grand Strategy*, vol. I (HMSO, 1976)
Asher Lee *et al.*, *The Rise and Fall of the Luftwaffe* (Air Ministry Pamphlet 248)
Andrew Boyle, *Trenchard* (Collins, 1962)

2: *Order of Battle*

1 Performance figures are as officially given by the Air Ministry in 1947. Readily accessible performance figures are in Owen Thetford, *Aircraft of the RAF since 1918* (Putnam, 1979), and Bill Gunston, *Bombers of World War Two* (Salamander, 1980)
2 Webster and Frankland, *op. cit.*, vol. I, p. 79

Bomber Command Orders of Battle pre-war are given in AHB *Narrative*, vol. I. Wartime Orders of Battle are given in BC Operations Record Book, in AHB *Narrative* as above, vols II–III, and in Webster and Frankland, *op. cit.*, vol. IV

3: *Experience Teaches*

1 PRO AIR 27/958, 4 September 1939
2 AHB *Narrative*, vol. II, p. 56
3 Quoted in Denis Richards, *Royal Air Force 1939–45*, vol. I: *The Fight at Odds*, (HMSO, 1953), pp. 38–9
4 S. W. Roskill, *The War at Sea* (HMSO 1954), vol. I, p. 66
5 AHB *Narrative*, vol. II, pp. 56–7
6 Guy Gibson VC, *Enemy Coast Ahead* (Michael Joseph, 1946), pp. 37–40
7 PRO AIR 27/491, 5 September 1939
8 PRO AIR 27/200, Appendix B1
9 AHB *Narrative*, vol. II,

p. 44, War Cabinet, 17th
meeting
10 AHB *Narrative*, vol. II, p. 45
11 AHB *Narrative*, vol. II, pp. 46–8;
PRO AIR 27/200, Appendix D;
PRO AIR 27/491, 27 October 1939
12 Tom Sawyer, *Only Owls and
Bloody Fools Fly by Night* (Goodall
Publications, 1985), pp. 26–7
13 AHB *Narrative*, vol. II, pp. 51–2;
PRO AIR 27/200, Appendix D283
14 Sir Arthur Harris, *Bomber Offensive*
(Collins, 1947; Greenhill Books,
Presidio Press, 1990), p. 36
15 PRO AIR 27/200 Admin.,
November–December 1939
16 AHB *Narrative*, vol. II, p. 58
17 *Ibid.*, p. 59
18 *Ibid.*, p. 60
19 *Ibid.*
20 *Ibid.*, pp. 60–1
21 PRO AIR 27/200 Admin., 8
January 1940
22 AHB *Narrative*, vol. II, pp. 72–3
23 *Ibid.*, p. 68
24 PRO AIR 27/200 Admin., 8
March 1940
25 Denis Richards, *Portal of Hungerford*
(Heinemann, 1978), pp. 64–5
26 *Ibid.*, pp. 120–40

4: *Against the Tide: Norway*

1 PRO AIR 27/ (51 Sqdn ORB,
6/7 April)
2 PRO AIR 27/ (107 Sqdn ORB,
7 April)
3 F. H. Hinsley, *British Intelligence
in the Second World* War, (HMSO,
1979), vol. I, p. 120
4 *Ibid.*, pp. 118, 122
5 S. W. Roskill, *op. cit.*, vol. I, p. 158
6 *Ibid.*, p. 161
7 PRO AIR 27/ (102 Sqdn ORB,
11/12 April)
8 Gibson, *op. cit.*, pp. 60, 62
9 PRO AIR 24/200, 12 April 1940
10 Gibson, *op. cit.*, p. 67
11 Harris, *Bomber Offensive*, pp. 38–9
12 T. K. Derry, *The Campaign in Norway*
(HMSO, 1952), p. 58
13 AHB *Narrative*, vol. II,
p. 78
14 G. L. 'Larry' Donnelly, *The Whitley

Boys* (Air Research Publications,
1991), pp. 89–90
15 Raymond Chance, *The Chance
Papers* (Norwich, 1984), quoted in
Donnelly, *op. cit.*, pp. 91–2, and
in Laddie Lucas, *Out of the Blue*
(Grafton Books, 1987), pp. 47–51
16 PRO AIR 14/669
17 AHB *Narrative*, vol. II, Appendix E
18 Gibson, *op. cit.*, p. 68
19 PRO AIR 14/669
20 Sir Basil Embry, *Mission Completed*
(Methuen, 1956: Quality Book Club
edn), p. 147
21 H. P. Lloyd, unpublished diary in
archives of RAF Museum, Hendon

5: *Against the Flood: France*

1 Thetford, *op. cit.*, pp.252–5
2 PRO AIR 41/AHB Narrative,
*The Campaign in France and the Low
Countries*, p. 27/200 (Admin)
3 PRO AIR 14
4 Supreme War Council 8th meeting,
2nd session, PRO AIR 41/, p. 182
5 PRO AIR 41, *op. cit.*, p. 173
6 *Ibid.*, p. 204; AIR 27/164 (12
Sqdn ORB)
7 PRO AIR 41, *op. cit.*, pp. 206–7
8 PRO AIR 41, *op. cit.*, p. 222
9 Communication: Leonard Clarke
to author
10 PRO AIR 41, *op. cit.*, pp. 460, 475
11 Embry, *op. cit.*, pp. 148–9
12 PRO AIR 41, *op. cit.*, pp. 254–5;
AIR 27/681, 685 (82 Sqdn ORB)
13 M. J. F. Bowyer, *2 Group RAF*
(Faber and Faber, 1974), p. 85
14 *Ibid.*, p. 89
15 PRO AIR 41, *op. cit.*, pp. 234–5;
WM 119/120 Conclusions &
Secretary's Standard File
16 PRO AIR 41, *op. cit.*, 236–7
17 *Ibid.*, pp. 235–6
18 *Ibid.*, p. 478
19 *Ibid.*, Appendix M
20 Embry, *op. cit.*, pp. 154–85
21 PRO AIR 41, *op. cit.*, p. 478
22 *Ibid.*, p. 437
23 Communication: Ian Hawkins
(nephew of R. Hawkins) to author
24 PRO AIR 41, *op. cit.*, p. 478
25 *Ibid.*, p. 475

26 PRO AIR 41, *op. cit.*, pp. 107–8, 393
27 Leonard Cheshire VC, *Bomber Pilot* (Hutchinson, 1955), p. 44
28 *Ibid.*, p. 44
29 Donnelly, *op. cit.*, p. 134
30 Bomber Command Association Newsletter No. 8, p. 7
31 PRO AIR 41, *op. cit.*, p. 474
32 Communication: Alan Nicoll to author
33 PRO AIR 41, *op. cit.*, p. 474
34 *Ibid.*, p. 451
35 Gibson, *op. cit.*, p. 94

6: *The Flood Stemmed: Britain*

1 Alfred Gollin, *No Longer an Island* (Heinemann, 1984), p. 1
2 AHB *Narrative*, vol. II, p. 113
3 *Ibid.*, p. 124
4 Richards, *The Fight at Odds*, p. 163
5 AHB *Narrative*, vol. II, p. 124
6 *Ibid.*, Appendix U
7 *Ibid.*, p. 114
8 Gibson, *op. cit.*, p. 101
9 AHB *Narrative*, vol. II, p. 115
10 *Ibid.*, p. 116
11 Führer Conferences on Naval Affairs, 1940 (Admiralty, 1947), p. 80
12 AHB *Narrative*, vol. II, Appendix U
13 Chaz Bowyer, *For Valour: the Air VCs* (William Kimber, 1978); *London Gazette*, 20 August 1940
14 AHB *Narrative*, vol. II
15 Richard Hough and Denis Richards, *The Battle of Britain: the Jubilee History* (Hodder & Stoughton, 1989), p. 171
16 *Ibid.*, pp. 248–9
17 PRO AIR 14/1930
18 W. L. Shirer, *Berlin Diary*, quoted in Telford Taylor, *The Breaking Wave* (Weidenfeld & Nicolson, 1967), pp. 156–8
19 Hough and Richards, *op. cit.*, p. 244
20 Shirer, *op. cit.*, in Taylor, *op. cit.*, pp. 156–8
21 C. Bekker, *The Luftwaffe Diaries* (Macdonald, 1967), pp. 171–2
22 Hough and Richards, *op. cit.*, pp. 248–9; Richards, *The Fight at Odds*, pp. 190–2
23 Richards, *The Fight at Odds*, p. 183

24 AHB *Narrative*, vol. II, p. 126
25 Quoted in Richards, *The Fight at Odds*, p. 187
26 E. Wheeler DFC, *Just to Get a Bed* (Square One Publications, 1990), p. 36
27 Sawyer, *op. cit.*, p. 38
28 AHB *Narrative*, vol. II, p. 128
29 Führer Conferences, 1940, p. 101
30 *London Gazette*, 1 October 1940
31 PRO AIR 14/567
32 *Ibid.*
33 J. James, *The Paladins* (Futura, 1991), p. 258

7: *The Means of Victory?*

1 M. Gilbert, *The Finest Hour* (Heinemann, 1983), p. 769
2 Printed in Webster and Frankland, *op. cit.*, vol. IV, pp. 128–31
3 AHB *Narrative*, vol. II, Appendix C3
4 *Ibid.*, pp. 12–14. For OTUs, see PRO AIR 41 (AHB *Flying Training Narrative*)
5 J. Currie, *Lancaster Target* (Goodall Publications, 1981), pp. 7–8
6 T. Sweet, *Enemy Below* (Square One Publications, 1991), p. 52
7 Currie, *op. cit.*, p. 8
8 Sweet, *op. cit.*, p. 53
9 AHB *Narrative*, vol. II, Appendices D1 and D2
10 Winston Churchill, *The Second World War* (Cassell, 1949), vol. II, pp. 603–4
11 Sawyer, *op. cit.*, pp. 39–40
12 Printed in Webster and Frankland, *op. cit.*, vol. IV, pp. 133–4
13 Webster and Frankland, *op. cit.*, vol. I, p. 226
14 AHB *Narrative*, vol. II, pp. 171–90
15 COS (40) 390, WP (40) 168

8: *'Transportation and Morale'*

1 Printed in Webster and Frankland, *op. cit.*, vol. IV, pp. 135–40
2 *Ibid.*, p. 195
3 AHB *Narrative*, vol. II, pp. 13–18
4 *Ibid.*, pp. 21–2
5 *Ibid.*, pp. 24–6; AHB *Flying Training Narrative 1934–42*, pp. 165–91

6 AHB *Narrative*, vol. II, Appendix F
7 *Ibid.*, pp. 67–9
8 AHB VC file: Ward
9 Wheeler, *op. cit.*, pp. 61–2
10 AHB VC file: Edwards
11 *Ibid.*
12 AHB *Narrative*, p. 17
13 *Ibid.* p. 169
14 *Ibid.*
15 *Ibid.*
16 Roskill, *op. cit.*, vol. I, p. 487
17 AHB *Narrative*, Vol. II, p. 150
18 *Ibid.*
19 Webster and Frankland, *op. cit.*, vol. I, p. 250
20 Printed in Webster and Frankland, *op. cit.*, vol. IV, pp. 205–13
21 AHB *Narrative*, vol. II, p. 65
22 Quoted more fully in: Richards,
23 *Portal*, pp. 189–91; Portal papers at
24 Christ Church, Oxford, File 2; PRO AIR 8/440
25 AHB *Narrative*, vol. II, p. 95
26 *Ibid.*
27 Printed in Webster and Frankland, *op. cit.*, vol. IV, p. 142
28 Webster and Frankland, *op. cit.*, vol. I, p. 256

9: *Low Point: New Hopes: New Commander*

1 C. Carrington, *Soldier at Bomber Command* (Leo Cooper, 1987), p. 74
2 Führer Conferences, January 1942
3 *Ibid.*, 29 December 1941, pp. 135–6
4 Communication: John Partridge to author.
5 Roskill, *op. cit.*, vol. II, p. 354
6 Carrington, *op. cit.*, p. 75
7 G. Aders, *The German Night Fighter Force* (Jane's Publishing Co., 1979), pp. 224–5
8 *The Rise and Fall of the German Air Force* (Air Ministry, 1948), pp. 185–7
9 Aders, *op. cit.*, pp. 239, 242–3
10 Communication: Alan Nicoll to author
11 Sawyer, *op. cit.*, p. 83
12 AHB *Narrative*, vol. III, p. 162; vol. IV, pp. 131–2 (ID 4/376, 479)
13 Carrington, *op. cit.*, p. 75

14 For Harris's early career, see: Harris, *Bomber Offensive*; Dudley Saward, *Bomber Harris* (Cassell/Buchan and Enright, 1984); *Dictionary of National Biography* (1981–5)
15 Richards, *Portal*, p. 322
16 Carrington, *op. cit.*, p. 85
17 Harris, *Bomber Offensive*, pp. 51–2

10: *Spring Offensive, 1942*

1 The directive of 14 February 1942 is printed in Webster and Frankland, *op. cit.*, vol. IV, pp. 143–8
2 Dudley Saward, *The Bomber's Eye* (Cassell, 1959), pp. 52–61
3 AHB *Narrative*, vol. IV, Appendix 1
4 *Ibid.*, Appendix 5
5 H. Moyle, *The Hampden File* (Air Britain Publications
6 AHB *Narrative*, vol. IV, p. 36
7 *Ibid.*, p. 214; W M (42) 14 Conclusions 2 February 1942
8 AHB *Narrative*, vol. IV, pp. 216–18
9 Communication: Harold Yeoman to author
10 Quoted in M. Middlebrook and C. Everitt, *The Bomber Command War Diaries* (Penguin, 1990), p. 245
11 Harris, *op. cit.*, p. 105
12 *The Goebbels Diaries* (Hamish Hamilton, 1948), p. 113
13 Quoted in Jack Currie, *The Augsburg Raid* (Goodall Publications, 1987), pp. 6–7
14 *Ibid.*, p. 66
15 Communication: Eric Howell to author
16 'Pip' Beck *A WAAF in Bomber Command* (Goodall Publications, 1989), p. 53
17 *Goebbels Diaries*, pp. 138–9
18 Webster and Frankland, *op. cit.*, vol. I, p. 394
19 D. C. T. Bennett, *Pathfinder* (Goodall Publications, 1988), pp. 116–30

11: 'MILLENNIUM'

1 Ralph Barker, *The Thousand Plan* (Reprint Society, 1965)

2 PRO AIR 14/276
3 Saward, *The Bomber's Eye*, pp. 122–3
4 AHB *Narrative*, vol. IV, p. 167
5 Webster and Frankland, *op. cit.*, vol. I, p. 403
6 AHB *Narrative*, vol. IV, p. 169
7 Saward, *The Bomber's Eye*, pp. 125–6
8 Quoted in full in Saward, *The Bomber's Eye*, p. 129
9 Barker, *op. cit.*, p. 116
10 *Verse from the Turret*, ed. W. R. Rainford (Bomber Command Museum edn), p. 5
11 AHB *Narrative*, vol. IV, p. 171
12 VC citation, *London Gazette*, 23 October 1942
13 AHB *Narrative*, vol. IV, pp. 171–2
14 Marie Vassiltchikov, *The Berlin Diaries 1940–45* (Mandarin, 1985), p. 67
15 Albert Speer, *Inside the Third Reich* (Macmillan, 1970), p. 279
16 Harris, *op. cit.*, p. 113
17 Webster and Frankland, *op. cit.*, vol. I, p. 487
18 AHB *Narrative*, vol. IV, pp. 181–4
19 *Ibid.*, p. 95
20 *Ibid.*, p. 190
21 Harris, *Bomber Offensive*, p. 102

12: *Policy and the USAAF*

1 COS (41) 284; Churchill, *op. cit.*, vol. III, pp. 619–23
2 AHB *Narrative*, vol. IV, p. 1
3 W. F. Craven and J. L. Cate, *The Army Air Forces in World War II* (University of Chicago Press, 1948), vol. I, p. 652
4 AHB *Narrative*, vol. IV, p. 2
5 Harris, *Bomber Offensive*, p. 99
6 AHB *Narrative*, vol. IV, pp. 232–6
7 PRO AIR 8/989; Richards, pp. 204–5
8 Quoted in J. Parton, *Air Force Spoken Here* (Adler and Adler, 1986), pp. 139–40
9 Webster and Frankland, *op. cit.*, vol. I, p. 341
10 *Ibid.*, p. 342
11 *Ibid.*, p. 341
12 AHB *Narrative*, vol. IV, pp. 9, 12; PM Personal Minute M378/2
13 Churchill, *op. cit.*, vol. IV, p. 404

14 AHB *Narrative*, vol. IV, pp. 247–8; COS (42) 288 (o)
15 *Ibid.*, vol. IV, p. 250; COS (42) 345 (o)
16 *Ibid.*, vol. IV, p. 249; COS (42) 379 (o)
17 Webster and Frankland, *op. cit.*, vol. I, p. 378

13: *The Advent of the Pathfinders*

1 AHB *Narrative*, vol. IV, p. 48
2 *Ibid.*, pp. 63–4
3 *Ibid.*, p. 66
4 Webster and Frankland, *op. cit.*, vol. I, p. 432n
5 Bennett, *op. cit.*, pp. 13–132
6 *Ibid.*, p. 92
7 Details of this and other raids at this time are in the main taken from: Webster and Frankland, *op. cit.*, vol. I; AHB *Narrative*, vol. IV; Bomber Command HQ Operations Record Book and Operational Research Section Raid Reports; Middlebrook and Everitt, *op. cit.*
8 AHB *Narrative*, vol. IV, pp. 226–8
9 *Ibid.*, Appendix 21, p. 33
10 AHB VC file; *London Gazette*, 15 January 1943
11 AHB *Narrative*, vol. IV, pp. 300–2; BC/ORS Day Raid Report No. 135
12 Harris, *Bomber Offensive*, p. 143

14: *Towards the Main Offensive*

1 R. V. Jones, *Most Secret War* (Hamish Hamilton, 1978), pp. 276–7
2 OBOE details are mainly taken from AHB *Narrative*, vol. IV, pp. 75–8, and AHB Narrative, *Signals*, vol. III (*Aircraft Radio*), pp. 211–23
3 H2S details are mainly taken from AHB Narrative, *Signals*, above, pp. 21–51, and AHB *Narrative*, vol. IV, pp. 78–84
4 Jones, *op. cit.*, pp. 318–19
5 *Ibid.*, pp. 388–90
6 AHB *Narrative*, vol. IV, pp. 85–90
7 *Ibid.*, Appendices 1 and 3
8 *Ibid.*, p. 271 (AM file CM3 330, Part I, minute 50)

9 *Ibid.*, p. 272 (WP (43) 11)
10 Directive reproduced in Webster and Frankland, *op. cit.*, vol. IV, pp. 152–3
11 AHB *Narrative*, vol. IV, p. 275
12 Directive reproduced in Webster and Frankland, *op. cit.*, vol. IV, p. 155
13 AHB *Narrative*, vol. V, p. 23 (US Strategic Bombing Survey: German Submarine Industry Report, p. 19)
14 Harris, *Bomber Offensive*, p. 137
15 Webster and Frankland, *op. cit.*, vol. II, p. 98
16 Harris, *Bomber Offensive*, p. 137
17 Middlebrook and Everitt, *op. cit.*, pp. 344–6
18 AHB *Narrative*, vol. IV, p. 268
19 *Ibid.*, vol. V, p. 55
20 *Ibid.*, p. 54
21 *Ibid.*, pp. 57–8
22 *Ibid.*, p. 39
23 *Ibid.*, p. 28; Middlebrook and Everitt, *op. cit.*, p. 360
24 AHB *Narrative*, vol. V, p. 26

15: *'The Battle of the Ruhr'*

1 Description of raid based mainly on: Bomber Command HQ Form 540; D. Richards and H. St G. Saunders, *The Fight Avails* (HMSO, 1954), pp. 283–7; Webster and Frankland, *op. cit.*, vol. II, pp. 114–18; Harris, *Bomber Offensive*, pp. 114–16; and AHB *Narrative*, vol. V, pp. 37–8
2 Middlebrook and Everitt, *op. cit.*, pp. 366–7
3 *Ibid.*, p. 407
4 Details of raids based mainly on: Bomber Command HQ Form 540; Richards and Saunders, *op. cit.*, pp. 287–96; Webster and Frankland, *op. cit.*, vol. II, pp. 108–37; AHB *Narrative*, vol. V, pp. 35–44 and 53–8; and Sir Arthur Harris, *Despatch on War Operations* (1945), pp. 17–18
5 Webster and Frankland, *op. cit.*, vol. II, p. 168
6 Gibson, *op. cit.*, p. 292
7 John Sweetman, *The Dambusters Raid* (Arms and Armour, 1993), p. 116

8 Webster and Frankland, *op. cit.*, vol. II, p. 291
9 Details of the dams raid based mainly on: Webster and Frankland, *op. cit.*, vol. II, pp. 168–80; Gibson, *op. cit.*, pp. 236–302; Paul Brickhill, *The Dambusters* (Pan edn, 1972), chapters I–VIII; Sweetman, *op. cit.*, *passim*; and W. J. Lawrence, *No. 5 Bomber Group RAF* (Faber and Faber, 1958)

16: *Mining: 2 Group: 'POINTBLANK'*

1 AHB *Narrative*, vol. II, Appendix X2
2 *Ibid.*, vol. III, p. 180
3 *Ibid.*, vol. IV, pp. 325–6
4 *Ibid.*, vol. IV, pp. 324–5
5 Roskill, *op. cit.*, vol. II, pp. 167, 264
6 AHB *Narrative*, vol. V, p. 31; Middlebrook and Everitt, *op. cit.*, p. 382
7 Roskill, *op. cit.*, vol. II, p. 394; vol. III, p. 96
8 *Ibid.*, vol. II, p. 395
9 Richards and Saunders, *op. cit.*, p. 141
10 *London Gazette*, 1 March 1946
11 AHB *Narrative*, vol. V, p. 64
12 The Combined Bomber Offensive plan is printed in Webster and Frankland,
13 *op. cit.*, vol. IV, pp. 273–83
14 *Ibid.*, vol. IV, p. 159
15 The POINTBLANK directive is printed in *ibid.*, vol. IV, pp. 158–60
16 Lawrence, *op. cit.*, pp. 142–3
17 Middlebrook and Everitt, *op. cit.*, p. 407
18 AHB *Narrative*, vol. V, p. 85 (BC Op. Order No. 173)

17: *Hamburg: Italy: Peenemünde*

1 Martin Middlebrook, *The Battle of Hamburg* (Allen Lane, 1980), p. 84
2 Webster and Frankland, *op. cit.*, vol. II, pp. 141–5; AHB *Narrative*, vol. V, pp. 86–8
3 Middlebrook, *op. cit.*, p. 128
4 Craven and Cate, *op. cit.*, vol. II, pp. 677, 846; Middlebrook, *op. cit.*, p. 217

5 Craven and Cate, *op. cit.*, vol. II, pp. 677, 847; Middlebrook, *op. cit.*, p. 231

6 Middlebrook, *op. cit.*, p. 278

7 Extensive extracts are published in Webster and Frankland, *op. cit.*, vol. IV, pp. 310–15

8 Middlebrook, *op. cit.*, p. 244

9 Details of the damage and general results of the raids derive from: the US Strategic Bombing Survey No. 32 (Effects of Area Bombing on Hamburg); the British Bombing Survey Unit Report on German Towns; Bomber Command Operational Record Section Report No. 8240 (29 October 1945); and a Hamburg Police Report of 10 September 1943. They are summarised and discussed in Middlebrook, *op. cit.*, pp. 322–35; Webster and Frankland, *op. cit.*, vol. II, pp. 260–3; AHB *Narrative*, vol. V, pp. 89–91; and H. St G. Saunders, *The Fight is Won* (HMSO, 1954), pp. 10–11

10 Webster and Frankland, *op. cit.*, vol. II, p. 260

11 AHB *Narrative*, vol. V, p. 93

12 *Ibid.*, p. 93

13 *Ibid.*, pp. 95–6

14 Saunders, *op. cit.*, p. 325

15 Harris, *Despatch*, p. 22

16 Jones, *op. cit.*, pp. 69–70

17 *Ibid.*, p. 333

18 For the story of Hitler's V weapons and the Allied countermeasures see David Irving, *The Mare's Nest* (Corgi, 1966)

19 Jones, *op. cit.*, p. 340

20 AHB *Narrative*, vol. V, p. 99

21 See BC Op. Order No. 176, reproduced in Martin Middlebrook, *The Peenemünde Raid*, (Allen Lane, 1982), p. 375

22 Quoted in Middlebrook, *Peenemünde Raid* p. 79

23 The details of the raid which follow are mainly taken from: Middlebrook, AHB *Narrative* Vol V, Peenemünde Raid Bomber Command Final Night Raid Report.

18: 'The Battle of Berlin'

1 AHB *Narrative*, vol. V, p. 35 (BC file S/23746/4 Enc. 146A)

2 *London Gazette*, 14 December 1943

3 Main sources for raid details on pp. 203–8 are taken from: Bomber Command HQ Operations Record Book; AHB *Narrative*, vol. V, pp. 67–98, 109–20; Webster and Frankland, *op. cit.*, vol. II, pp. 157–67; M. Middlebrook, *The Berlin Raids* (Viking, 1988), pp. 21–97; Middlebrook and Everitt, *op. cit.*, pp. 417–45

4 AHB *Narrative*, vol. V, p. 121 (AM folder ID/4/23). Quoted in Webster and Frankland, *op. cit.*, vol. II, p. 48

5 AHB *Narrative*, vol. V, p. 122

6 *Ibid.*, p. 124; *Goebbels Diaries*, pp. 425–7

7 Speer, *op. cit.*, p. 288

8 AHB *Narrative*, vol. V, p. 124

9 Speer, *op. cit.*, p. 289

10 AHB *Narrative*, vol. V, p. 125; *Goebbels Diaries*, pp. 437–8

11 Quoted in full in Webster and Frankland, *op. cit.*, vol. II, pp. 54–7

12 *Goebbels Diaries*, p. 485

13 AHB *Narrative*, vol. V, p. 154

14 *Ibid.*, p. 135

15 *Ibid.*

16 Main sources for raid details on pp. 208–18: Bomber Command HQ Operations Record Book; AHB *Narrative*, vol. V, pp. 109–50; Webster and Frankland, *op. cit.*, vol. II, pp. 190–211; Middlebrook, *Berlin Raids*, pp. 98–305; Middlebrook and Everitt, *op. cit.*, pp. 446–88

19: Prelude to 'OVERLORD'

1 Final report of 'QUADRANT' Conference (CC 319/S) printed in Michael Howard, *Grand Strategy* (HMSO, 1972), vol. IV, p. 684

2 AHB *Narrative*, vol. VI, p. 5; Saward, *Bomber Harris*, pp. 246–8

3 PRO AIR 20/3223, Portal papers, Christ Church, Oxford, File 10, 1944. Quoted in Richards, *Portal*, p. 316

4 R. V. Jones, *op. cit.*, pp. 358–9
5 *Ibid.*, p. 461
6 Saunders, *op. cit.*, p. 152
7 AHB *Narrative*, vol. VI, p. 13
8 *Ibid.*, pp. 15–22
9 Harris, *Bomber Offensive*, p. 203
10 Middlebrook and Everitt, *op. cit.*, pp. 486, 492, 494
11 AHB Narrative, *The Planning and Preparation of the AEAF*, p. 476.
12 Harris, *Despatch*, p. 24
13 AHB Narrative, *The Planning and Preparation of the AEAF*, p. 542
14 AHB *Narrative*, vol. VI, p. 36
15 Middlebrook and Everitt, *op. cit.*, p. 490
16 *London Gazette*, 26 October 1945

20: *Normandy and the V-weapons*

1 Quoted in Saunders, *op. cit.*, vol. III, p. 105
2 Saunders, *op. cit.*, vol. III, p. 110; Harris, *Despatch*, p. 25, para. 123; AHB *Narrative*, vol. VI, Appendix 10
3 AHB *Narrative*, vol. VI, p. 84
4 Harris, *Bomber Offensive*, p. 208
5 *London Gazette*, 11 October 1946
6 AHB *Narrative*, vol. VI, p. 257
7 Webster and Frankland, *op. cit.*, vol. III, p. 160, vol. IV, p. 122; Middlebrook and Everitt, *op. cit.*, p. 327
8 Harris, *Bomber Offensive*, p. 210
9 AHB *Narrative*, vol. VI, p. 87
10 Quoted in Saunders, *op. cit.*, p. 130
11 AHB *Narrative*, vol. VI, p. 88
12 D. Irving, *op. cit.*, p. 231
13 Middlebrook and Everitt, *op. cit.*, p. 540
14 *London Gazette*, 17 August 1945
15 *Ibid.*, 8 September 1944

21: *The Last Autumn*

1 Saunders, *op. cit.*, vol. III, p. 191
2 Raid details in the above pages are mostly taken from: AHB *Narrative*, vol. VI, pp. 89–90 and Appendix II; Middlebrook and Everitt, *op. cit.*, Section 20
3 The *Tirpitz* account is derived

mainly from: Roskill, *op. cit.*, vol. III, Part 2, pp. 155–71; AHB *Narrative*, vol. VI, pp. 71–3, 103–4; P. Brickhill, *op. cit.*, pp. 225–46; A. Cooper, *Beyond the Dams to the Tirpitz* (Goodall Publications, 1980), pp. 82–97, 104–24
4 The directive is reproduced in Webster and Frankland, *op. cit.*, vol. IV, pp. 172–3
5 AHB *Narrative*, vol. VI, Annex
6 *Ibid.*, pp. 136–7; AHB *Signals History*, vol. III, pp. 253–88
7 Harris, *Bomber Offensive*, p. 239; Webster and Frankland, *op. cit.*, vol. III, p. 205
8 Reproduced in Webster and Frankland, *op. cit.*, vol. IV, pp. 321–36
9 *Ibid.*, vol. III, p. 94
10 AHB *Narrative*, vol. VI, Appendix 18
11 Reproduced in Webster and Frankland, *op. cit.*, vol. IV, pp. 178–9
12 *Ibid.*, p. 177
13 *Ibid.*, pp. 337–40

22: *The Ardennes : Oil : Dresden*

1 AHB *Narrative*, vol. VI, p. 186
2 *Ibid.*, Appendix 10
3 *Ibid.*, p. 186; B. H. Liddell Hart, *The History of the Second World War* (Pan Books, 1978), pp. 678, 690
4 *London Gazette*, 24 March 1945; Middlebrook and Everitt, *op. cit.*, p. 636
5 Substantial extracts from the Harris–Portal correspondence are in Webster and Frankland, *op. cit.*, vol. III, pp. 76–94, and in Richards, *Portal*, pp. 318–24. Most of the originals may be studied in Portal's papers at Christ Church, Oxford (File 10, 1944)
6 Webster and Frankland, *op. cit.*, vol. III, p. 77
7 *Ibid.*, p. 310
8 *Ibid.*, p. 77
9 Portal's papers at West Ashling House
10 AHB *Narrative*, Appendix 10
11 *Ibid.* Vol VI

12 *Ibid.*, p. 173
13 *Ibid.*, Appendix 10
14 AHB *Narrative*, vol. VI, pp. 188–9
15 *London Gazette*, 20 February 1945
16 Middlebrook and Everitt, *op. cit.*, pp. 660–1
17 Webster and Frankland, *op. cit.*, vol. III, p. 103
18 *Ibid.*, p. 101
19 *Ibid.*, p. 103
20 David Irving, *The Destruction of Dresden* (William Kimber, 1963), p. 113
21 Webster and Frankland, *op. cit.*, vol. III, p. 106
22 Irving, *Destruction of Dresden*, p. 96
23 *Ibid.*, p. 112
24 *Ibid.*, p. 153
25 *Ibid.*, p. 195
26 *Ibid.*, p. 238
27 David Irving in a letter to *The Times*, 7 July 1966
28 AHB *Narrative*, vol. VI, p. 204
29 *Ibid.*, p. 203
30 Webster and Frankland, *op. cit.*, vol. III, p. 112
31 *Ibid.*, p. 117

23: *Victory*

1 Middlebrook and Everitt, *op. cit.*, p. 672
2 *Ibid.*, p. 669; AHB *Narrative*, vol. VI., p. 225
3 *London Gazette*, 24 April 1945
4 AHB *Narrative*, vol. VI, pp. 255–6; Middlebrook and Everitt, *op. cit.*, pp. 678–9
5 Middlebrook and Everitt, *op. cit.*, p. 681
6 Webster and Frankland, *op. cit.*, vol. IV, p. 178
7 AHB *Narrative*, vol. VI, p. 213 and map
8 *Ibid.*, pp. 230–1; Middlebrook and Everitt, *op. cit.*, p. 668
9 AHB *Narrative*, vol. VI, p. 231; Middlebrook and Everitt, *op. cit.*, p. 680
10 AHB *Narrative*, vol. VI p. 231; Middlebrook and Everitt, *op. cit.*, p. 683
11 Middlebrook and Everitt, *op. cit.*, p. 685

12 *Ibid.*, p. 685; AHB *Narrative*, vol. VI, p. 232
13 Harris, *Bomber Offensive*, p. 255
14 Webster and Frankland, *op. cit.*, vol. III, p. 252
15 Middlebrook and Everitt, *op. cit.*, p. 661
16 *Ibid.*, p. 684
17 AHB *Narrative*, vol. VI, p. 211
18 Webster and Frankland, *op. cit.*, vol. IV, p. 516
19 *Ibid.*, pp. 382, 386
20 *Ibid.*, p. 379
21 AHB *Narrative*, Appendix 10
22 Harris, *Bomber Offensive*, p. 220
23 Roskill, *op. cit.*, vol. III/2, p. 290
24 *Ibid.*
25 AHB *Narrative*, vol VI, pp. 238–42; Roskill, *op. cit.*, vol. III/2, p. 457
26 AHB *Narrative*, vol. VI, p. 237
27 *Ibid.*, p. 238
28 *Ibid.*, p. 244
29 *Ibid.*

24: *Retrospect*

1 Webster and Frankland, *op. cit.*, vol. IV, p. 428
2 *Ibid.*,
3 *Ibid.*,
4 *Ibid.*, pp. 421, 428
5 *Ibid.*, p. 428
6 *Ibid.*, pp. 455–7; Harris, *Despatch*, p. 44
7 Harris, *Bomber Offensive*, p. 103
8 Middlebrook and Everitt, *op. cit.*, p. 707
9 Harris, *Bomber Offensive*, p. 101
10 *Ibid.*, p. 163
11 Middlebrook and Everitt, *op. cit.*, p. 760
12 AHB Commonwealth Statistics folder
13 Communication: Mackey to author
14 Webster and Frankland, *op. cit.*, vol. IV, pp. 524–5
15 Roskill, *op. cit.*, vol. III, part II, p. 457
16 Webster and Frankland, *op. cit.*, vol. IV, p. 44
17 *Ibid.*, p. 53
18 *Ibid.*, p. 49
19 AHB *Narrative*, Vol VI. p. 253

20 Webster and Frankland, *op.cit.*, Vol IV, p. 494

21 *Ibid.*

22 Speer: interrogation in Webster and Frankland, *op. cit.*, vol. IV, p. 394

23 *The RAF Medical Services*, ed. S. C. Rexford Welsh, vol. II: *Commands* (HMSO, 1955), pp. 123–4

24 Webster and Frankland, *op. cit.*, pp. 440–4; Middlebrook and Everitt, *op. cit.*, p. 708

25 Harris, *Bomber Offensive*, p. 267

Acknowledgements

The author and publishers wish to thank Her Majesty's Stationery Office for the use of documents in Crown copyright, and for the use of quotations from the following HMSO publications:

Sir Charles Webster and Noble Frankland, *The Strategic Air Offensive Against Germany* (4 vols)
Denis Richards, *Royal Air Force 1939–1945*, vol. I: *The Fight at Odds*
Hilary St G. Saunders, *Royal Air Force 1939–1945*, vol. III: *The Fight is Won*

The author and publishers also wish to thank for the use of quotations the copyright owners of the following works:

Pip Beck, *A WAAF in Bomber Command* (Goodall Publications)
D. C. T. Bennett, *Pathfinder* (Goodall Publications)
M. J. F. Bowyer, *2 Group RAF* (Faber and Faber)
C. C. Carrington, *Soldier at Bomber Command* (Leo Cooper)
Raymond Chance, *The Chance Papers*
Leonard Cheshire, *Bomber Pilot* (Goodall Publications)
George Cocker in *Verse from the Turret* (Bomber Command Museum)
Jack Currie, *Lancaster Target* and *The Augsburg Raid* (Goodall Publications)
Raymond Daniell in *The New York Times*
G. L. Donnelly, *The Whitley Boys* (Air Research Publications)
Sir Basil Embry, *Mission Completed* (Methuen)
Guy Gibson, *Enemy Coast Ahead* (Michael Joseph)
Sir Arthur Harris, *Bomber Offensive* (Greenhill Books/Presidio Press)
J. James, *The Paladins* (Futura)
R. V. Jones, *Most Secret War* (Hamish Hamilton)
D. Mourton in the Bomber Command Association Newsletter
Dudley Saward, *The Bomber's Eye* (Cassell)
Tom Sawyer, *Only Owls and Bloody Fools Fly at Night* (Goodall Publications)
W. L. Shirer, *Berlin Diary*
Ted Sweet, *Enemy Below* (Square One Publications)
Viscount Templewood, *Empire of the Air* (Collins)
Marie Vassiltchikov, *The Berlin Diaries 1940–45* (Mandarin)
Edwin Wheeler, *Just to Get a Bed* (Square One Publications)

The author expresses his warmest thanks to the following members of Bomber Command Association for their responses to his enquiries, and apologises for any omissions or inaccuracies in the list. The aircrew ranks given, except in one or two cases, are the *wartime* ones.

PILOTS
Flt Lt J. K. Badcock MBE, AE; Fg Off. A. J. Ball DFC; Grp Cpt K. S. Batchelor CBE, DFC, *Légion d'Honneur*; Flt Lt M. Beetham DFC (later MRAF Sir Michael); Fg Off. E. R. Bowden DFC; Flt Lt D. G. Bowker; Flt Lt R. M. Brookbanks DFC; Flt Lt R. Chandler AE; Flt Lt R. D. Cooling AE; Flt Lt R. C. Corley DFC; Flt Lt O. C. Cronshaw DFC; Flt Lt N. C. Croppi AFC; Plt Off. J. Curtiss (later AM Sir John); Flt Lt H. G. Davies CBE, AE; Flt Lt L. A. Davies DFC; Flt Lt M. E. S. Dickenson; Flt Lt P. A. Dorehill DSO, DFC; Flt Lt A. T. Dugdale DFC; Flt Lt T. W. B. Fanning; Flt Lt D. R. Field; Fg Off.

J. C. Gardner DFC; Flt Lt M. Garton DFC; Sqn Ldr J. W. Gee DFC and bar, AE; Flt Lt B. P. Giles DFC; Wt Off. E. L. G. Hall MBE; Flt Lt D. Hawker DFC; Fg Off. A. R. Hopkins; Sqn Ldr P. S. James DFC, AE; Flt Lt E. G. Jones DFC, AFC; Flt Lt F. D. Jones DFC; Flt Lt B. M. Kaplansky DFC; Flt Lt P. J. Legge; Sqn Ldr W. B. Mackley DFC and bar; Flt Lt G. Martin DFM; Flt Lt H. Matthews DFC; Fg Off. C. E. Mears DFC; Fg Off. H. L. Merrett DFC; Flt Lt C. A. Nicoll; Fg Off. W. D. Parlett; Wg Cdr J. E. Partridge DSO, DFC and bar; Wg Cdr R. M. Pinkham DFC; Sqn Ldr T. Prickett DSO, DFC (later ACM Sir Thomas); Sqn Ldr C. G. C. Rawlings DFC, OBE; Sqn Ldr R. A. Read DFC; Flt Lt W. J. Simpson DFC; Flt Lt G. T. South DSO, DFC; Wg Cdr W. Surtees DFC; Sqn Ldr N. H. Svendsen DFC; Flt Lt R. G. Thackeray DFM; Aircrew Cdt G. Thompson; Sqn Ldr R. G. Truman AE; Flt Lt J. L. Whiteley DFC; D. E. Wilburn; Sqn Ldr B. H. Williams DFC, AFC; Flt Lt F. A. Wood; Flt Lt H. Yeoman.

NAVIGATORS/OBSERVERS
Wt Off. S. E. Adams; Flt Lt M. S. Allen DFC and 2 bars; Flt Lt A. Arthurson DFC; Fg Off. S. W. Barrett DFM; Sqn Ldr H. N. Blundell DFC; Flt Lt. B. Bressloff DFC; Fg Off. W. W. Burke; Sqn Ldr J. D. Cazes DFC; Flt Sgt A. R. Clarke; Wt Off. V. Coleman; Wt Off. K. P. Collins AE; Plt Off. J. Condon; Flt Lt T. W. Copson DFM; Flt Lt R. Davey; Flt Lt J. M. Dyer; Flt Lt R. J. Fayers; Plt Off. F. F. Fish DFM; Flt Lt St John Foot; Flt Lt D. B. Francis DFC; Flt Lt (later AV-M) J. Furner CBE, DFC, AFC; Fg Off. D. A. Gage; Flt Lt A. R. Galbraith DFC; Sqn Ldr E. J. Gibson AE; Fg Off. L. G. Gillard; Sqn Ldr W. Grierson DFC, AFC; Flt Lt D. G. J. Griffiths DFC; Flt Lt F. P. Hall DFC; Fg Off. G. A. Hammond; Flt Lt F. W. Harding; Sqn Ldr G. Haworth DFC, DFM; Flt Lt R. A. Hine; Flt Lt J. R. Hood DFC; Flt Lt C. L. Hughes DFC; Wt Off. F. Johnson; Flt Lt H. F. Le Marchant; Flt Lt E. A. Mansfield DFC; Fg Off. K. W. Marshall; Flt Lt A. Martin DFC; Flt Lt J. Mason DFC; Flt Lt A. Matthews DFC; Flt Lt H. F. S. Mitchell DFC; Wt Off. H. R. Moyle; Flt Lt J. A. Neve DFC; Fg Off. R. T. Newberry; Wt Off. T. G. O'Shaughnessy; Flt Lt K. M. Pincott DFM; Wt Off. J. E. Regan DFM; Sgt K. F. Shepherd, *Croix de Guerre avec Palme*; Flt Lt D. T. N. Smith DFC and bar; Flt Lt F. G. Smith; Plt Off. K. C. Stewart; Flt Lt R. A. Strachan DFC and bar; Flt Lt J. Vnoucek, Czech War Cross and bar, Czech Medal for Gallantry; Flt Lt J. Waterhouse DFM; Wt Off. D. J. R. Wilson; Flt Lt E. H. Woods AE; Fg Off. M. C. Wright DFM; Plt Off. R. Wright DFC, US Air Medal and Oak Leaf Clusters, later Capt. USAAF.

WIRELESS OPERATORS (AND WOP/AGS)
Wt Off. E. Allison; Fg Off. R. Armstrong MBE; Plt Off. W. A. Atkins; Flt Lt A. D. Barker DFC; Mrs Bird (Wt Off. W. A. Bird); Flt Lt C. G. A. Brazier; Flt Sgt A. W. Brown; Flt Sgt L. R. Clarke; Plt Off. D. F. A. Cockbill; Flt Lt C. B. Cox; Fg Off. E. A. Davidson DFM; Flt Lt D. J. Drake DFC, DFM; Wt Off. K. Goodchild; Flt Sgt K. C. Haley; Sgt R. Hammersley DFM; Wt Off. C. E. Harrison; Wt Off. W. Hedges; Sgt W. Holway; Fg Off. I. B. Hoy; Flt Lt R. W. Jefcoate; Flt Sgt J. Kerr; Sqn Ldr G. Klein DFC; Flt Sgt D. Mourton; Flt Lt T. B. Nisbett DFC; Mrs Norfolk (Flt Lt R. J. Norfolk DFC); Fg Off. J. K. Penrose; Flt Lt J. P. E. Peters; Sqn Ldr B. C. Sandall DFC and Bar; Wt Off. J. J. F. Smeaton DFC; Wt Off. E. H. Sweet; Fg Off. A. J. Tod DFC; Wt Off. M. Tripp; Flt Lt E. A. Wheeler DFC; Flt Sgt W. H. Williams.

AIR-BOMBERS
Flt Sgt M. Bird; Fl Lt N. N. Brown DFC; Fg Off. E. A. Eyres; Flt Sgt R. T. Francis; Flt Sgt M. G. L. Harmes; Wt Off. A. R. Harris; Fg Off. A. G. Harrison DFC; Wt Off. A. F. Hulyer; Wt Off. N. St Clair l'Amie; Fg Off. J. P. Le Blanc; Wt Off. H. Lloyd Lyne, Polish Cross of Valour; Flt Lt J. Mace; Flt Lt R. T. Mayhill DFC; Sgt D. H. Meade; Flt Lt W. E. Milner; Wt Off. F. C. Parry; Flt Lt B. Power; Fg Off. J. C Richardson; Flt Lt W. G. Seymour DFC; Flt Lt C. E.

Smith; Flt Lt W. D. Spence; Wt Off. W. Taylor; Flt Lt T. M. Telford; Flt Lt E. J. Thomason; Wt Off. N. A. Tranter; Flt Lt L. R. Tyrrell; Flt Lt S. T. Wingham DFC; Flt Lt J. M. Woodrow DFC; Flt Lt J. H. Woodward.

FLIGHT ENGINEERS

Flt Lt E. Appleton DFC; Flt Lt E. Blanchard DFC; Flt Sgt S. Bridgman; Fg Off. G. Cairns OBE; Sgt C. H. Chandler; Fg Off. E. J. Clark DFM; Plt Off. E. G. W. Collyer; Fg Off. A. Cunningham; Fg Off. C. Dickenson AE; Wt Off W. R. Donaldson; Plt Off. R. J. Durran; Sgt S. Fletcher; Flt Sgt G. E. O. Haggard; Flt Sgt B. R. W. Holmes; Flt Sgt R. Hulland; Fg Off. K. W. Marshall DFC; Flt Lt B. W. Martin; Flt Sgt N. R. Mason DFM; Fg. Off H. R. Oldland DFC, MBE; Flt Sgt R. Palmer; Sgt D. Pope DFC; Sgt I. W. Porter; Mrs Potten (Sgt C. Potten); Flt Lt T. N. C. Prosser DFM; Sgt E. C. C. Stocker; Flt Lt E. E. Stocker DSO, DFC; Fg Off. M. W. Stoneman; Flt Sgt A. D. Tait; Wt Off. J. A. Thomas; Flt Sgt D. Thurman; Fg Off. D. C. Tritton; Wt Off. L. N. Watson; Wt Off. W. Wescomb.

AIR-GUNNERS

Fg Off. A. R. Baldwin; Flt Lt J. M. Catford DFC, AE; Flt Sgt R. Child; Wt Off A. W. Edgby; Flt Lt L. A. Davies DFC; Fg Off. F. Garrett DFM; Wt Off. R. H. J. Gorham; Fg Off. J. H. Griffith; Plt Off. R. I. Hudson; Mrs Hughes (Sgt P. Hughes); Wt Off. J. Hurst; Wt Off. E. S. Jarvis DFM; Wt Off. A. S. Johnson; Sqn Ldr D. G. Knight DFC; Wt Off. H. Lavey DFM; Fg Off. N. G. Loads; Sgt P. Lovatt; WO J. Major-Dunkley; Flt Sgt D. F. McElligott

MBE; Plt Off. L. J. S. O'Hanlon DFM; Flt Sgt G. L. Osborne; Wt Off. R. F. Pritchard; Flt Sgt K. T. Redshaw; Flt Lt L. R. Sidwell; Flt Lt P. J. Smith; Fg Off. A. K. N. de Souza; Wt Off. F. Spence; Flt Sgt C. E. Tinker; Sgt H. C. Towler; Wt Off. W. F. Trivett; Fg Off. P. A. S. Twinn DFC; Fg Off. R. Wakeham; Flt Sgt R. Ward; Flt Sgt P. W. Wattis; Wt Off. L. P. Wooldridge DFC.

GROUND STAFF/GROUND CREW

LAC D. F. Aris; Cpl Mary Giddings (Mrs Atkins); Sgt R. J. Ball; Sgt L. O. Baughey; LAC A. F. Chapman; Sgt J. R. J. Clark; LAC I. Curtis; LACW Selina Barton (Mrs Duanes); Sgt B. Edmond; Cpl R. W. Elliott; Sgt E. W. English; Sgt G. F. Everett; Sgt J. W. Grimstone; LACW Amy Birdson (Mrs Haley); Cpl F. A. Haynes; Sgt W. McLean Hirons; LAC E. Howell; LAC J. W. Huggins; Sgt T. M. Hughes; Sgt P. C. Knight; Sgt Nancy Older (Mrs Lowther); Sqn Ldr P. D. McNeil; Cpl C. Manning; Cpl K. Morton; LAC W. E. G. Nunn; Cpl G. Parfitt; Flt Sgt R. Powell; Sgt E. J. Read; LAC V. Redfern; Sgt C. F. Scandrett; LACW Dorothy Search; LAC R. A. Sewell; LAC J. C. Smith; Sgt R. A. Stamp; Sec. Off. Arlette Harris (Mrs Tedder); Cpl D. Terry; Sgt J. A. Thomas; Sgt W. E. Tidy; Flt Lt M. Tomlinson; AC2 A. Turner; Wt Off. B. Turner; LACW Cicely Taylor (Mrs Versey); Cpl F. L. Warner; Sgt W. Wescombe; LACW Margo Allcock (Mrs West); LAC P. West; Sgt W. E. Wilkinson; LAC E. D. Wilson; Cpl D. A. Wiltshire; Cpl R. H. Wratten.

Index

NOTE: Ranks and titles are generally the highest mentioned in the text. Subsequent rank, etc., attained by senior officers is indicated in brackets.

40; attacks German invasion
forces in Battle of Britain, 57,
62–8; Coastal Command borrows
from, 70, 106, 127, 138; increasing
strength, 70; Commonwealth
and Allied personnel, 74, 295–7;
shipping attacks, 82–3, 92–3, 102,
182, 299; allotted coastal area, 92;
navigational inadequacy, 94–7,
106, 113, 135, 158, 289; 1941
conservation directive, 101; attacks
ports and naval bases, 101; and
German warships' Channel dash,
104–6; Harris takes command of,
108–11; concentrated raids, 116–17;
strength and growth, 135–8, 141,
154, 161, 231, 291, 297–8; loss-rates,
160–1, 173, 231, 236, 291; in
Combined Bomber Offensive with
US 8th Air Force, 185; attacks
Peenemünde, 198–9; losses at
Berlin and Nuremberg, 218–19;
SHAEF in higher control of, 219,
226; pre-OVERLORD activities,
221–8, 233, 290, 299; supports
D-Day landings and Normandy
campaign, 233, 237–40, 245, 248,
299–300; escorted daylight raids,
237; attacks V-weapon sites, 240–2;
and Allied 1944 advance, 248–50;
in autumn 1944 offensive, 255–60;
and Ardennes offensive, 261–2; and
oil targets, 265–7, 281–3; and urban
targets, 275, 300; flies home released
POWs, 286; ground crews given
air tours at war's end, 288; bomb
tonnages dropped, 291–2; aircraft,
292–5, 356; achievements, 297–302;
aircrew numbers, 305; casualties,
305, 363
Bomber Command (RAF) Groups:
No. 1, 16, 51, 70, 87, 200, 271;
No. 2, 11, 44, 50, 87, 128, 154, 182,
184, 221n, 254; No. 3, 11, 13, 87,
134, 147, 199, 254–5, 257–8, 271;
No. 4, 11, 14, 44, 87, 110, 199, 303;
No. 5, 11, 14, 87, 110, 123, 152, 177,
180–1, 200, 228, 230, 256, 271, 273,
303; No. 6 (later 91), 67, 71, 115,
128, 133, 161, 200, 245, 258, 271,
296; No. 7, (later 92), 67; No. 8, 271,
285, 293, 303; No. 93, 138; No. 100
(Bomber Support), 211, 234, 271,
285, 293
Bomber Command (RAF) Squadrons:
No. 7, 146, 155; No. 9, 28, 75, 251,
280, 285–6; No. 10, 124; No. 12,

117; No. 15, 155; No. 21, 58; No. 35,
146; No. 37, 28, 70; No. 38, 27,
70; No. 44 (Rhodesian), 55, 121–2,
296; No. 49, 61; No. 50, 130, 213;
No. 51, 2, 23–4, 33; No. 57, 58; No.
58, 2, 297; No. 61, 206; No. 75 (New
Zealand), 89, 243, 296; No. 77, 25,
37, 236; No. 78, 90n; No. 82, 29,
58; No. 83, 22, 35, 56, 61, 66, 105,
196, 199, 234; No. 90, 92; No. 97,
121; No. 101, 95; No. 102, 34, 53–4;
No. 105, 91, 151, 184; No. 106,
149, 241, 322; No. 107, 20, 33, 91;
No. 109, 146, 168, 263; No. 110,
20–1; No. 115, 27; No. 139, 1, 20,
184, 199; No. 141 (formerly Fighter
Command), 211; No. 142, 150;
No. 144, 27; No. 149, 27–8; No. 150,
64; No. 156, 146; No. 169 (formerly
Fighter Command), 211; No. 192,
211; No. 218, 234; No. 239 (formerly
Fighter Command), 211; No. 300
(Polish), 74, 295; No. 301 (Polish),
74, 295; No. 304 (Polish), 74, 295;
No. 305 (Polish), 74, 295; No.
311 (Czech), 74, 90, 296; No. 346
(French), 296; No. 347 (French),
296; No. 405 (Canadian), 296;
No. 408 (Canadian), 296; No. 419
(Canadian), 235, 296; No. 420
(Canadian), 296; No. 434, 198;
No. 460 (Australian), 211, 296;
No. 463, 252; No. 466 (Australian),
296; No. 467 (Australian), 296;
No. 487 (New Zealand), 183;
No. 578, 219; No. 582, 263; No. 617,
175, 179, 207, 214, 228, 230, 234,
242, 249–51, 256, 280, 284n, 285–6;
No. 630, 241
bombs: armour-piercing, 40;
improvements and developments,
74, 358; incendiary (4-lb), 74, 128,
314; 4,000-lb ('blockbuster' or
'cookie'), 99, 151; target-indicator,
150–1, 164; designed against dams,
174–5; 12,000-lb High Capacity,
214; 12,000lb ('Tallboy'), 234, 249,
251, 256, 293; 22,000-lb ('Grand
Slam'), 280
bombsights and bomb aiming, 92,
359–60
Bonn, 258, 262, 271
BOOZER (radar countermeasure), 160
Bordeaux (France), 82
Bornholm (Danish island), 224
Boston (aircraft), 87, 104, 120, 153,
182, 356